NARROW GAUGE RAILWAYS

Patrick Stephens Limited, a member of the Haynes
Publishing Group, has published authoritative,
quality books for enthusiasts for more than twenty
years. During that time the company has established a
reputation as one of the world's leading publishers of
books on aviation, maritime, military, model-making,
motor cycling, motoring, motor racing, railway and railway
modelling subjects. Readers or authors with suggestions
for books they would like to see published are invited to
write to: The Editorial Director, Patrick Stephens Limited,
Sparkford, Nr Yeovil, Somerset, BA22 7JJ.

ENCYCLOPAEDIA
OF
NARROW GAUGE RAILWAYS

of Great Britain and Ireland

Thomas Middlemass

Foreword by David Woodhouse, MBE

GUILD PUBLISHING
LONDON · NEW YORK · SYDNEY · TORONTO ·

*For my wife Josephine — also born of
railway stock*

This edition published 1991 by
Guild Publishing
by arrangement with Patrick Stephens Ltd.

© Thomas Middlemass 1991

First published in 1991

CN 6812

Maps drawn by Claire Loakes

Printed in Great Britain

10 9 8 7 6 5 4 3 2 1

Contents

Foreword *by David Woodhouse MBE, Chairman, Joint Marketing Panel of the Welsh Narrow Gauge Railways*

The narrow gauge railways of Great Britain, the Isle of Man and Ireland have been the subject of many books, and excellent histories exist which have been written on an individual or geographical basis. However, never before has such a wealth of information been presented on a collective basis such as this.

The narrow gauge railways of the British Isles were all very different in character and many other respects, and the purposes for which they were built varied considerably. Slate immediately comes to mind when the Welsh lines are being considered, whereas service of agricultural communities was the main function of most of the Irish lines. The majority carried passengers and most served their local communities well for many years.

Although it is perhaps surprising that some lines lasted as long as they did, their passing was a matter of regret for many. Those of us who were fortunate enough to ride the Irish narrow gauge are richer for the experience. Fortunately, a number of lines survive and we should be grateful to the dedication of all concerned that so many examples survive for all to experience and enjoy.

The narrow gauge railway has contributed much to the railway world in general and it is perhaps fitting that the birthplace of railway preservation as we know it today took place on the narrow gauge in Wales.

Mr Middlemass and his publishers are to be congratulated on producing a fine encyclopaedia which I am sure will not only serve as a reminder of things past, but will also act as a reference book for the present and, hopefully, the future.

Preface

Although the term 'light railway' has never lent itself to exact definition, the fact that many light railways were built to narrow gauge proportions does not warrant assumption that all narrow gauge concerns were, *ipso facto*, light railways. One has only to consider the 3 ft 6 in main lines still being employed in Africa, New Zealand and elsewhere to appreciate this. Nevertheless, as railway construction blossomed throughout the second half of the nineteenth century, the positive epidemic of narrow gauge metals which spread all over the world held great significance, and undoubtedly owed its origin to two powerfully persuasive factors, cheapness of construction, and the comparative ease with which gradients could be surmounted. Certainly Great Britain had good cause to respect the medium during her Empire-building days, and, at home, narrow gauge construction in Wales saw railways built where standard gauge metals would not deign to tread. Whether Ireland gained comparable benefit from her miscellany of narrow gauge ventures is a rather more debatable proposition.

With tramways the story is only marginally different. Here, too, economy in construction

Cheapness and ease of construction. Permanent way standards varied considerably on British narrow gauge railways, but, despite the comparative tidiness of the scene, the basic elements are clearly visible in this view of the Welshpool & Llanfair station at Cyfronydd, 2¹/₄ miles east of Llanfair Caereinion. Typical features are the modest station shelter and short siding, the elementary level crossing, and the cattle grid. (Author's Collection)

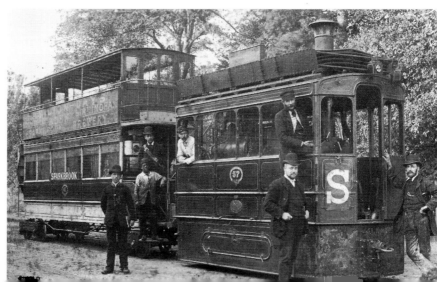

Between the years 1878 and 1901 Kitson & Co of Leeds built over 300 steam tram units for service all over the world. Complete with trailer car, this was one of many employed on the City of Birmingham's extensive 3 ft 6 in gauge street tramway system. Vertical boilers have by now given way to horizontal ones, and an elaborate condensing system functions at roof level. Track was buried flush with the road surface. (Author's Collection)

Merryweather & Sons of Greenwich were even earlier practitioners in the field of steam tram construction, and established their reputation by supplying Paris tramways with 46 engines in 1875-77. In this view, taken at Merryweather's works around 1880, a new tram engine under construction is seen before it acquired its bodywork and protective metal plating. (Author's Collection)

played a vital role, and the tramcar's ability to facilitate urban and rural inter-communication added a second attractive dimension. Again, no clear definition emerged. In France, a line which usurped part of a public highway for most of its course qualified unhesitatingly as a tramway; next door, in Belgium, such installations were regarded as light railways. Britain, *vide* her Tramways Act of 1870, favoured the employment of metals sunk to ground level. Certainly, laid thus they offered minimum impedance to other vehicular traffic. None the

Narrow gauge metals on the Isle of Man served a distinct 'main line' function. Here, in the mid-1950s, No 8 Fenella simmers at the head of a Peel train at Douglas station. The leading coach, F65, is a bogie rebuilt of two 1873-74 four-wheelers. Typical of the times, an overflow of holiday visitors, bound for Port Erin, patiently awaits the arrival of an extra coach or two. Fenella, as it happened, was the last of the small-boiled tanks to remain in service, and along with Nos 5 and 9 is now in the hands of the Isle of Man Railway Society. (Steamchest)

less, there, as elsewhere, a moving tram, or one pausing to load, never failed to command appropriate respect. Ireland, less generously endowed with electricity, sought refuge as often as not in narrow gauge steam tramways. These alienated part of the roadway, and often resembled conventional railways in appearance. There, however, the illusion ended — for Irish tramways did not hesitate to pluck passengers from the roadside. Lacking membership of the Irish Railway Clearing House, they could not, however, compete for freight traffic. In Wales, slate traffic was all important when narrow gauge tramways first appeared, and only in later days did goods and passenger traffic assume consequence.

First official mention of 'light railways' as far as the UK was concerned cropped up in the Regulation of Railways Act of 1868; and on that occasion the Board of Trade contented itself with imposing (a) a maximum weight limit of 8 tons on any one axle, and (b) an overall speed limit of 25 mph. Soon, of course, wider interpretations were being sought. Engineers joined in the debate, and possibly the most pertinent contribution came from Sir John Wolfe Barry in 1897, when, as President, he addressed the Institution of Civil Engineers.

'Light railways,' he opined, 'should be similar, but slightly superior, to the temporary, or service, lines made by contractors in constructing ordinary lines. Rails, sleepers and ballast should merely be adequate for a limited weight upon the wheels of a suitable locomotive, which need not be heavier for the wider gauge. Earth works may be light, as the gradient for normal loads may be steep. Bridges over and under roads will in most cases be unnecessary, and Board of Trade safety appliances should be greatly simplified. The gauge should be unbroken at the point of contact.'

The implications of that last sentence pinpointed straight away a grave defect in Ireland's already established network of passenger carrying light railways. Light railways can operate in any of three ways: (1) they may provide quite extensive main lines in their own right, (2) they may merely act as feeders to larger standard gauge ventures, or (3) they may function as short, but quite independent, local lines. Ireland, in treating herself to some of each, had the misfortune to fall neatly between three stools. In England and Scotland, on the other hand, standard gauge metals had such a grip from the birth of steam that narrow gauge construction was usually undertaken as a measure of sheer economy. Conversely, the Welsh slate industry, traditionally obliged for geographical reasons to rely on horse-drawn tramways, lifted the ultra narrow gauge concept to international heights in due course, thanks to the inspired beliefs of C. E. Spooner and his family. If only for that reason, Wales deserves to lead the four main sections which constitute this book.

PART 1

Welsh narrow gauge railways

All through United Kingdom history, England has enjoyed — nay, continues to enjoy — immense trading advantages. Her proximity to Europe, her shrewd exploitation of the Industrial Revolution, London's pre-eminence in financial matters; these are but some of the factors which determined England's ultimate capital wealth *vis-à-vis* the comparative hand-to-mouth existence of Scotland, Ireland and Wales.

Yet Wales had its own riches: coal and slate. A glance at an encyclopaedia, for instance, reminds us that for countless decades Wales cherished a world-wide reputation for quality slate; just as it reveals that up to 1900, before the USA took pride of place, Britain was the world's leading producer of coal, with South Wales possessing 25 per cent of the country's reserves. Handling Wales' two exports, however, required vastly different techniques where rail transport was concerned.

Even in 1905 it was estimated that 26 billion tons of coal lay unworked in South Wales and Monmouthshire at depths of up to 4,000 feet. But 'depths' is the operative word; for though stationary steam engines could play a part in raising the coal, once it reached the surface its nationwide value was such that Britain's network of standard gauge metals *had* to be used to ensure its swift disposal. In South Wales, therefore, pit sidings and internal rail workings would only have created rods for their own backs had they employed narrow gauge metals.

Further north, the disposal of Welsh slate, once it was mined or quarried, called for a vastly different solution. For centuries slate had been humped to the nearest port by an amalgam of man and pack pony. Roads were treacherous and few and far between, and the whole exercise was a studied torment of determination and sheer muscle power. Then came a breakthrough; for, even before men like Trevithick and George Stephenson were able to demonstrate the advantages of the Iron Way, miners in North Wales, and elsewhere, stumbled upon the merits of wooden tramroads. Horses, they found, could now haul superior loads over reasonable terrain. Subsequent use of gravity on balanced inclines helped even more to speed slate on its way down to sea level.

The proliferation of standard gauge steam railways which revolutionized English affairs throughout the first half of the nineteenth century spilled gradually into Welsh coastal regions, but had very little really to offer the slate industry in Wales. For one intractable problem remained: most of the slate was won from high mountainous regions. Sheer altitude, in many cases, made provision of 4 ft 8½ in metals an impractical engineering proposition; sheer lack of volume in many more would have made the institution of normal railway traffic an economic nonsense. What, then, was to be done?

The answer came as slate quarry owners abandoned wooden tramroads in favour of flat-plate tramways, primitive though the earliest were. Horses were retained as motive power, as was the traditional tramroad gauge of around 2 feet. Then, quite rapidly, iron-railed tramways superseded plateways, and by the early 1830s every great quarry in North Wales was so equipped. Penrhyn, Dinorwic, Ffestiniog, Portmadoc — their very names echo down the corridors of Welsh narrow gauge history! The ultimate transition, that from horse haulage to steam, took little longer. In 1848 the Padarn Railway started the process by introducing steam on its 4-foot gauge line which linked Dinorwic quarries with the coast. Fifteen years later the Ffestiniog Railway, *vide* the Spooner family, wrenched the potential of 2-foot gauge steam transport far beyond anyone else's wildest dreams, and, following close behind, the Talyllyn Railway ensured its own niche in railway history by employing steam traction from inception. But it was the Ffestiniog which finally persuaded Authority that passengers ran no abnormal risk by travelling on 2-foot gauge metals. None the less, up to 1900, when the slate industry's decline proved to be terminal, Welsh narrow gauge railways gave paramount importance to mineral traffic. By then, however, the natural beauty of Wales was attracting ever-ncreasing numbers of tourists; and railways were born which aimed to give pleasure as well as picking such extraneous freight traffic as was

Fitted with a tender cab, but still in 0–4–0ST form, the Festiniog Railway's Blanche *approaches Garnedd Tunnel with her Dduallt train on 24 September 1966, some six years before the loco was converted to a superheated 2–4–0ST and given new cylinders. In its original form,* Blanche *worked Penrhyn Quarry's last 'main line' trip on 27 July 1962.* (Steamchest)

available. For that reason the Welsh narrow gauge railways which appear in this section have been divided into two broad categories, corresponding to the following tables.

The slate era

| Railway | Traction | | Railway closed | Main mineral handled | Standard gauge railhead | Gauge (ft in) |
	Horse	Steam				
Penrhyn	1801	1876	1965	Slate	Port Penrhyn	2 0
Padarn	1824	1848	1969	Slate	Port Dinorwic	4 0 and 1 10¼
Nantlle	1828	–	1872	Slate	Caernarvon	3 6
Saundersfoot	1832	1874	1940	Coal	Saundersfoot	4 0³⁄₈
Festiniog	1836	1863	1946	Slate	Portmadoc	1 11½
Corris	1859	1879	1948	Slate	Derwenlas	2 3
Croesor	1863	–	1901	Slate	Portmadoc	1 11½
Gorseddau	1863	1875	1894	Slate	Portmadoc	2 0
Talyllyn	–	1865	1950	Slate	Towyn	2 3
Festiniog & Blaenau	1863	1875	1883	Slate	Blaenau	1 11½
Hendre-ddu	1867	–	1908	Slate	Aberangell	1 11
Glyn Valley	1873	1888	1935	Slate	Chirk	2 4¼
North Wales Narrow Gauge	–	1877	1922	Slate & passengers	Dinas	1 11½
Welsh Highland	–	1922	1937	Slate & passengers	Dinas	1 11½
Kerry Tramway	–	1888	1895	Estate produce	Kerry	2 3
Hafan & Talybont	–	1897	1900	Granite	Llanfihangel	2 3

Note Only the Saundersfoot, handling coal in Pembrokeshire, aspired to employ 4-foot metals. Padarn's 4-foot gauge 'main' line was a special circumstance, and Nantlle's insistence on 3 ft 6 in gauge was no doubt influenced by Robert Stephenson.

The passenger era

Railway	Opened	Closed	Standard gauge railhead	Gauge (ft in)
Snowdon Mountain	1896	Still extant	Llanberis	2 7½
Great Orme Tramway	1902	Still extant	Llandudno	3 6
Vale of Rheidol	1902	Still extant	Aberystwyth	1 11½
Welshpool & Llanfair	1903	1956 (part reopened 1963)	Welshpool	2 6
Fairbourne Railway	1916	1983	Fairbourne	1 3
Fairbourne & Barmouth Steam Railway	1986	Still extant	Fairbourne	1 0¼

The slate era

PENRHYN RAILWAY

Opened: 1801
Closed: 1965
Gauge: 2 ft 0 in

The slate quarries at Penrhyn, a few miles inland from Bangor, can boast of a history dating back at least to the sixteenth century. In their heyday they were to blossom as the largest quarries in the world; but, of course, large-scale quarrying did not become feasible until their proprietor, Lord Penrhyn, built a tramroad to the coast in 1801. Costs, it has been deposed, were £175,000. Prior to that important event, only moderate quantities of slate could be conveyed from quarry to port on the backs of horses. Now, on the 2-foot gauge Penrhyn Tramroad the same horses could haul much heavier loads. Significantly, the currently accepted medium of flat-plate tram rail, with all its drawbacks, was abandoned on this occasion in favour of oval-formed edge rail; wheel rims were necessarily concave. Latterly, though, it was found that this arrangement created energy-consuming friction, and flat-topped rails were substituted. Thus greater loads than ever became feasible, and horse traction continued to give every satisfaction until 1847. That was the year in which the decision was made to resite the line and introduce steam locomotion.

The new route, completed in 1876 and still retaining a 2-foot gauge along its 6½-mile length, was designed to maintain as easy gradients as possible. Between coast and quarry it rose 550 feet, and, allowing for a stretch of ¼ mile at 1 in 37 and 3 miles at 1.

Above *When Penrhyn Quarries ventured into steam traction in the 1870s, the Caerphilly firm of De Winton supplied ten vertical-boilered 0–4–0s.* Violet, *one of three built for Penrhyn 'main line' use in 1876, lasted until 1902, 20 years after the first conventional Hunslet-built 0–4–0STs arrived at Penrhyn. All De Winton locomotives were vertical-boilered, with two cylinders secured below by plates and brackets. Direct drive obtained on one axle, and total weight varied between 4 and 5 tons.* (Steamchest)

Below Blanche, *built by Hunslet in 1893 for Penrhyn 'main line' use, is proudly posed with a typical quarrymen's four-wheeled coach. 15-inch diameter wheels and a microscopic wheelbase must have guaranteed the latter's occupants a fairly rough ride! Built originally as an 0–4–0ST, Blanche was purchased by the Festiniog Railway in 1963, and now operates as a superheated 2–4–0ST with tender combined.* (Author's Collection)

Above Charles, *the first-built of Penrhyn's three Hunslet 'main line' 0–4–0STs, is seen here with Lord Penrhyn's special saloon which, apart from being furnished a little more comfortably, ran on 20-inch wheels. Both engine and coach can now be seen at the Penrhyn Castle Museum.* (Author's Collection)

Below Alan George *(Hunslet 1894/606), weighing only 6 tons, was one of four 'Small' class 0–4–0STs which were provided for work within the quarries. Seen here in its native environment, the little loco has since found a secure home on the Vale of Teifi Narrow Gauge Railway.* (Author's Collection)

in 40, the average gradient emerged as 1 in 91. Flat-bottomed rails were laid at first, but these were replaced in 1894 by the 50 lb bullhead variety. Meanwhile, orders were placed for ten locomotives. Seven were to be used at the quarries, three were to work the 'main line' to the coast, and all were vertical-boilered 0–4–0 tanks supplied by De Winton's Union Works at Caernarvon. This firm built some 60 narrow gauge vertical-boilered locos for quarries all over Wales ere it closed in 1902.

In 1882 Penrhyn switched to more conventional locomotion, and between then and 1909 a positive spate of tank locos flowed, new, from Hunslet Engine Co. All were 0–4–0 saddle tanks, with weight and power variations introduced to meet specific Penrhyn requirements. Three were designed to work the 'main line', three were employed shunting at Port Penrhyn. Four of the smallest were confined to quarry work, and these were supplemented a few years later when six larger tanks arrived. As it happened, the latter were the last *new* purchases by Penrhyn, for post-First World War years brought such economic instability that second-hand locos were not hard to find. Penrhyn bought 12 such from 1922 onwards. In 1923 three ex-ROD Baldwin 2–6–2Ts were also imported for 'main line' use, but, as happened elsewhere in Britain, they were never popular, and their working life was short.

Throughout the years rolling-stock at Penrhyn was, of necessity, primitive, but robust. Certainly it was profuse enough in quantity, for 600 wagons alone were employed on the 'main line'. Most were slate wagons of 2-ton capacity, but provision was made for other cargoes, notably coal, slate filler, and slate slabs. In the quarries themselves use was found for over 2,000 wagons and sleds of infinite variety. In addition four-wheeled carriages were provided to convey quarrymen to and from working sites. Using the same 15-inch wheels as the wagons, each carriage could accommodate 24 men. A special saloon reserved for

Linda, *the last of Penrhyn's celebrated 'main line' trio, was loaned to the Festiniog Railway during the summer of 1962. It and* Blanche *were purchased outright the following year, and* Linda *is seen here at Boston Lodge, still in original form (the chimney extension may be regarded as a temporary adornment!). A shade too lively at first on Festiniog metals, both locos were soon fitted with England tenders, and have been refined in several other ways since.* (Steamchest)

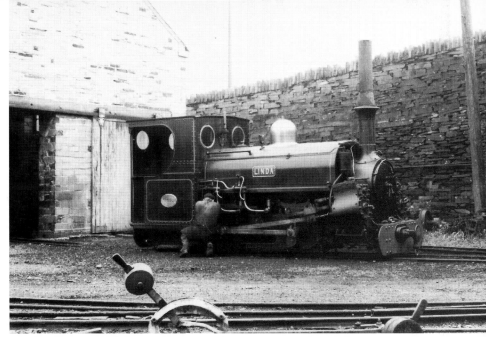

One of three 0–4–0STs supplied by Hunslet in 1883-85 for shunting duties at Port Penrhyn, Winifred *was still active at the age of 77 when she was photographed at the quarries on 21 August 1962. The loco now rests on its laurels at Terre Haute, Indiana, USA.* (Hamish Stevenson)

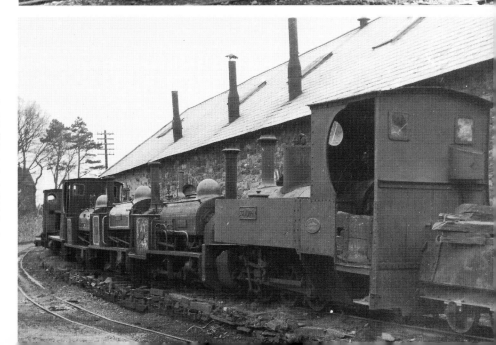

Penrhyn locos, laid up at Bethesda, make a sad sight in March 1959. Yet all escaped oblivion. From right to left: Sergeant Murphy *is now in Conwy Valley Railway Museum;* Lilian *works on the two-mile-long Launceston Steam Railway;* Gertrude *is now, alas, a sectioned exhibit at the Science Museum. Toronto; but* Edward Sholto *was fortunate enough to find a new home at Athens, Ontario.* (Hamish Stevenson)

Another of Penrhyn's many escapees, Bronllwyd *(Hudswell Clarke 0–6–0WT 1643/1930) serves today on Bressingham Gardens' two-mile-long 1 ft 11½ in gauge Nursery Railway. The figure in the foreground is, of course, Alan Bloom, Bressingham's well-known proprietor.* (Steamchest)

use by Lord Penrhyn and his staff was given 20-inch wheels and, not unnaturally, was furnished a little more luxuriously.

It took a Second World War in 1939 to bring its own difficulties to Penrhyn, but the quarries survived. Then in post-war years loomed the menace which was to affect all railways: road transport. Ever-increasing intrusion by the internal combustion engine proved lethal, and Penrhyn's 'main line' was closed in July 1962. The quarry rail complex hung on awhile; but three years later it, too, succumbed. The lorries had won.

The wholesale disposal of locos which followed must have been painful to all concerned. But, fortunately, few were lost. *Blanche* and *Linda* found both a new home and a fresh lease of life on the revitalized Festiniog Railway; and, between the years 1963 and 1966, four narrow gauge locos were rescued by Bressingham Steam Museum. One of them, *Bronllwyd*, was rebuilt in 1969 with a boiler from a fifth, *Stanhope*. The list of others which still survive, together with sundry coaches and wagons, is impressive.

LOCOMOTIVES
Details of the three phases of Penryn Railway locomotive history are given in the following tables.

Vertical-boilered locomotives

Name	Type	Date built	Maker	Maker's number	Remarks	Present location
Edward Sholto	VB 0–4–0T	1876	De Winton	—	For 'main line use'	Withdrawn 1907
Hilda	VB 0–4–0T	1876	De Winton	—		Withdrawn 1911
Violet	VB 0–4–0T	1876	De Winton	—		Withdrawn 1902
Georgina	VB 0–4–0T	1876	De Winton	—	Originally shunters at Penrhyn. Posted to quarries in 1883	Withdrawn 1904
Ina	VB 0–4–0T	1876	De Winton	—		Withdrawn 1911
Lord Penrhyn	VB 0–4–0T	1876	De Winton	—	All for quarry use	Withdrawn 1909
Lady Penrhyn	VB 0–4–0T	1876	De Winton	—		Withdrawn 1911
Alice	VB 0–4–0T	1876	De Winton	—		Withdrawn 1911
Kathleen	VB 0–4–0T	1877	De Winton	—		Withdrawn 1939
George Henry	VB 0–4–0T	1877	De Winton	—		Narrow Gauge Museum, Tywyn

Post-1882 Hunslet-built locomotive

Name	Type	Date built	Maker	Maker's Number	Remarks	Present location
Charles	0–4–0ST	1882	Hunslet	283	'Main line' locos, weight – 12¼ tons	Penrhyn Castle Museum
Blanche	,,	1893	,,	589		Now 2–4–0ST on
Linda	,,	1893	,,	590		Festiniog Railway
Gwynedd	0–4–0ST	1883	Hunslet	316	'Port' class. Built for shunting at Port Penrhyn. Weight – 7 tons 10 cwt	Bressingham Steam Museum
Lilian	,,	1883	,,	317		Launceston Steam Railway
Winifred	,,	1885	,,	364		Terre Haute, Indiana, USA
Margaret	0–4–0ST	1894	Hunslet	605	'Small' class for working at Quarries. Weight – 6 tons	Cadeby Light Railway, Leics
Alan George	,,	1894	,,	606		Vale of Teifi Narrow Gauge Railway
Nesta	,,	1899	,,	704		Mumfreesboro', Tennessee, USA
Elin	,,	1899	,,	705		Lincolnshire Coast Light Railway
Hugh Napier	0–4–0ST	1904	Hunslet	855	'Large' class, for quarry work. Similar to 'Port class, but boiler carried higher on frame. Weight – 7 tons 12 cwt	Penrhyn Castle Museum
Pamela	,,	1906	,,	920		Newbold Vernon, Leics
Sybil Mary	,,	1906	,,	921		Lynton & Barnstaple Rly Assoc
George Sholto	,,	1909	,,	994		Bressingham Steam Museum
Gertrude	,,	1909	,,	995		Science Museum, Toronto, Canada
Edward Sholto	,,	1909	,,	996		Athens, Ontario, Canada
Llandegai	2–6–2T	Ex-ROD	Baldwin	47143		Withdrawn 1927, Scrapped 1940
Felin Hen	,,	,,	,,	46828		,,　　1927,　,,　　,,
Tregarth	,,	,,	,,	46764		,,　　1928,　,,　　,,

Post-1922 second-hand locomotives

Name	Type	Date built	Maker	Maker's number	Remarks	Present location
Lilla	0–4–0ST	1891	Hunslet	554	Purchased from Cilgwyn Quarries, 1928	Knebworth House, Stevenage
Jubilee	,,	1897	Manning Wardle	1382		Narrow Gauge Museum, Tywyn
Sergeant Murphy	0–6–0T	1918	Kerr Stuart	3117	Purchased 1922	Conwy Valley Railway Museum
Sanford	0–4–0ST	1900	Bagnall	1571	Purchased from Maenofferen	–
Skinner	,,	1906	,,	1766	Quarry in 1929	–
Eigiau	0–4–0WT	1912	Orenstein & Koppel	5668	Purchased from Aluminium Corp, Dolgarrog, 1929	Bressingham Steam Museum
Bronllwyd	0–6–0WT	1930	Hudswell Clarke	1643	Purchased from Surrey County Council, 1934	Bressingham Steam Museum. 1969 with *Stanhope*'s boiler
Stanhope	0–4–2ST	1917	Kerr Stuart	2395	Purchased from Durham County Water Board, Wearhead, 1934	See *Bronllwyd* above
Ogwen	0–4–0ST	1933	Avonside	2066	,,　　　　1936	Terre Haute, Indiana, USA
Marchlyn	0–4–0T	1933	,,	2067	,,　　　　1936	Mumsfreesboro', Tennessee, USA
Cegin	0–4–0WT	1931	Barclay	1991	,,　　　　1936	,,　　　　　,,
Glyder	0–4–0WT	1931	,,	1994	,,　　　　1938	Terre Haute, Indiana, USA

Two small locos also served during Penrhyn's very early steam days:
Fronllwyd VB 0–4–0T Used to drive slate-sawing tables at Quarry. Scrapped in 1906.
George Sholto 0–4–0T Operated around Quarry *circa* 1876. Fate unknown.

Certain items of Penrhyn rolling stock have also been rescued from demolition. One quarrymen's coach, Lord Penrhyn's special saloon (1882), and four open wagons are all held by the National Trust at Penrhyn Castle Museum. Two quarrymen's coaches, 'F' and 'J', one slate wagon No 205, one Fullersite wagon No 46, and coal wagon No 2 are all now exhibited at Chalk Pits Museum, Amberley, W Sussex.

PADARN RAILWAY

Opened: 1824
Closed: 1969
Gauges: 4 ft and 1 ft 10¾ in

So rich was the County of Caernarvon in minerals that a second port grew up, only a few miles down the coast from Penrhyn, to meet an ever-increasing world demand for North Wales Slate. Named Port Dinorwic, it served as an outlet for the quarries at Llanberis, 7 miles inland. And here, in fact, history repeated itself; for the story of Dinorwic's development bears close resemblance to that of Penrhyn.

It all started in 1824, when a tramway was built from Llanberis to the coast by the quarry owner, Thomas Assheton-Smith, at a cost of £25,000. Stone sleeper blocks, cast-iron chairs and wrought-iron rails were duly employed. So, too, was the labour of horses. Yet even this archaic combination had such a stimulating effect on production that plans were soon being laid for a new, and more convenient, track alignment. £35,000 more was spent, and the Padarn Railway re-opened in 1848, with steam locomotives replacing horses.

So called because its new route ran alongside Lake Padarn, the Padarn, however, differed from the Penrhyn Railway in one important respect: it employed a gauge of 4 feet for its 'main line'. That apart, Padarn's whole fleet of 1 ft 10¾ in gauge wagons remained in use throughout the various working levels of the quarries. Still manhandled from workface to rope-worked incline, they were loaded, four at a time, on to

4-foot wagons which then conveyed them to Port Dinorwic. Not until 1870, however, were steam engines introduced within the quarry confines themselves

Two in number, the locomotives first employed on Padarn's 4-foot gauge 'main line' came from S. Horlock & Co of Northfleet Ironworks, Kent, and were quite remarkable in design. Outside-cylindered 0-4-0 tender engines were a scarce enough commodity in the world of steam; but these two, not content with incorporating Crampton's inordinately long wheelbase, also utilized screw reversing gear. Valve gear, driven off the front axle, was a feature later patented by Fletcher Jennings Ltd. Providentially, Padarn's No 1 *Fire Queen* is today in the safe keeping of the National Trust, at Penrhyn Castle Museum. Whatever, three Hunslet 0-6-0 tanks followed as replacements during the years 1881–95, and there Padarn's 4-foot gauge stock remained. Gradually the quarry company built extensive workshops at both Llanberis and Port Dinorwic, and it is no small tribute to this remarkably self-contained empire that in later years it could find time and resources to re-boiler several locomotives for the Snowdon Mountain Railway.

Dinorwic Quarries, 2,565 feet above sea level, were massive. They covered a total area of 700 acres, and were divided into two main sections. Each section was, in turn, subdivided into 20 or so galleries, and these were linked by a series of rope-worked inclines, some as steep as 1 in 3. Gallery tracks were traditionally 1 ft 10¾ in, and this gauge remained unchanged, even when steam locomotives were introduced in

Below Jenny Lind, *an early Crampton type, was one of two 4-foot gauge tender 0-4-0s built by A. Horlock & Co in 1848 for use on Padarn's 'main line'. Cylinders and boiler were lagged with wood, the only braking was located on the tender, and sanding was effected behind the rear coupled wheels. Note how the long wheelbase brought the trailing wheels behind the firebox in accordance with the Crampton principle.* (Steamchest)

Right *Both* Jenny Lind *and sister engine* Fire Queen *were withdrawn around 1886. Fortunately, the latter survived to find refuge at Penrhyn Castle Museum, now National Trust property.* (Steamchest)

1870 to work the gallery 'main' lines. Manipulating trucks to and from track to workfaces remained at all times a prerogative of human labour.

Between the years 1870 and 1932 Hunslet Engine Company supplied a total of 18 small 0–4–0Ts for gallery use. Only two which worked at lower level possessed the luxury of a cab. It follows that over the years Dinorwic Quarries continued to present an astonishing sight to visitors, as small engines swarmed like bees all over the mountainside. Trains assembled

Above *Originally named* Vaenol, *0–4–0ST* Jerry M *was one of 18 supplied by Hunslet during 1870–1904 to work the maze of 1 ft 10³/₄ in metals around Dinorwic Quarry and its galleries. Busy shunting empty slate wagons,* Jerry M *is seen here at Gilfach Dhu, Dinorwic, on 22 June 1909. Only two engines destined to work at lower quarry level enjoyed the luxury of a cab.* (LCGB, Ken Nunn Collection)

Below *Although the slate trade was in the throes of terminal decline,* Sybil *(Bagnall 1906/1760) and* George B *(Hunslet 1898/680) were still working at gallery level in August 1959. These are two of the many ex-Padarn locos which survive to this day.* (Hamish Stevenson)

This Hunslet 0–6–0T (Works No 410) was introduced as Pandora in 1886 for service on Padarn's 4-foot gauge 'main line'. Renamed Amalthaea in 1909, she was still serving at Llanberis in August 1959. Note the narrow gauge 'tubs' lined up on the bank beyond, which have just returned by 'piggy-back' from Port Dinorwic. (Steamchest)

at lower quarry level, for dispatch by 'piggy back' over two-foot gauge metals to Port Dinorwic, carried, on average, 130 tons of slate. Once they arrived at the port, the narrow gauge trucks were eased off the parent ones, and lowered down a short steep incline to the dock, whence the slate proceeded to its ultimate destination by main line rail, or by sea. The Quarry Company even owned steamers in its own right. Latterly, as quayside work increased, Hunslet supplied two more narrow gauge 0–4–0Ts (1922). One was replaced by a Ruston & Hornsby diesel in 1935.

Like the Penrhyn, the Padarn Railway was not authorized to carry passengers, as far as the general public was concerned. But a workmen's train ran mornings and evenings between port and quarries, and for this purpose 23 four-wheeled carriages, each seating 60 men, but unnumbered and bearing only alphabetical letters, were supplied by Gloucester Railway Carriage & Wagon Co. On the night trip

many were slipped at strategic points to afford shelter to men awaiting the train next morning. Thus, life proceeded systematically at Dinorwic, until the 1960s brought a severe decline in the slate trade. Inevitably, the increasing employment of lorries saw the 'main line' closed in October 1961. Sadly, the network of narrow gauge rails followed suit when the quarries themselves closed in 1969.

As in the case of Penrhyn, life was merciful to Padarn's little locos, for most were salvaged and are now preserved in various parts of Great Britain and Canada. Some went to the Llanberis Lake Railway, one of the present 'Great Little Railways of Wales', whose 1 ft 11½ in gauge passenger-carrying tracks even incorporate part of the former Padarn 4-foot right of way. Another four found a new life on the 4½-mile Bala Lake Railway. Thus, the spirit of the early Welsh slate industry still flourishes in the heart of the Principality.

LOCOMOTIVES

4-foot gauge locomotives

Name	Type	Date built	Maker	Maker's number	Remarks	Present location
Fire Queen	0–4–0	1848	Horlock		—	Penrhyn Castle Museum
Jenny Lind	0–4–0	1848	,,		—	Scrapped 1886
Dinorwic	0–6–0T	1882	Hunslet	302	—	—
Pandora	0–6–0T	1886	,,	410	Renamed *Amalthaea* in May 1909	—
Velinheli	0–6–0T	1895	,,	631	—	Launceston Steam Railway
Also a four-cylinder petrol locomotive by Hardy Motors Ltd, 1925. Weighed 12 tons						

The Hunslet tanks could be uncoupled automatically from their trains by manipulating a lever on the foot-plate. Usually one engine was in steam at a time, with one spare and another undergoing overhaul.

1 ft 10¾ gauge locomotives

Name	Type	Date Built	Maker	Maker's Number	Remarks	Present location
Charlie	0–4–0ST	1870	Hunslet	51		Withdrawn in 1916
George	,,	1877	,,	184		,,
Velinheli	,,	1886	,,	409		Inny Valley Rly, Cornwall
Alice	,,	1889	,,	492	Renamed *King of the Scarlets*	Langstaff, Ontario, Canada
Enid	,,	1889	,,	493	Renamed *Red Damsel*	Llanberis Lake Railway renamed *Elidir*)
Rough Pup	,,	1891	,,	541		Narrow Gauge Railway Museum, Tywyn
Cloister	,,	1891	,,	542		Hants Narrow Gauge Railway Society
Wellington	,,	1898	,,	678	Renamed *Bernstein*	Ran on Lythan Creek Rly to 1979. Now on Bala Lake Rly as *Jonathan*
Covert Coat	,,	1898	,,	679		Launceston Steam Railway
George B	,,	1898	,,	680		Cotswold Narrow Gauge Railway
Holy War	,,	1902	,,	779		Bala Lake Railway
Alice	,,	1902	,,	780		,,
Maid Marian	,,	1903	,,	822		,,
Irish Mail	,,	1903	,,	823		West Lancs Light Railway
Wild Aster	,,	1904	,,	849		Llanberis Lake Railway
Michael	,,	1932	,,	1709		Langstaff, Ontario, Canada
Sybil	,,	1906	Bagnall	1760		Inny Valley Railway, Cornwall
Vaenol	,,	1895	Hunslet	638	Renamed *Jerry M*	Hollycombe House, Liphook
Port Dinorwic	,,	1898	,,	671	Renamed *Cackler*	Thursford Museum, Norfolk

The following two locomotives were used for shunting on narrow gauge lines at Dinorwic:

Name	Type	Date Built	Maker	Maker's Number	Remarks	Present location
No 1	0–4–0ST	1922	Hunslet	1429		Knebworth House, Stevenage. Renamed *Lady Joan*
No 2 *Dolbardan*	,,	1922	,,	1430	Sent to quarry in 1935, and replaced on quayside by Ruston & Hornsby diesel loco	Llanberis Lake Railway

NANTLLE RAILWAY

Opened: 1828
Closed: 25 July 1867
Gauge: 3 ft 6 in

Three Acts of Parliament were required before the Nantlle Railway, 9¼ miles long, finally opened in 1828. Again, slate traffic was the target, and on this occasion Gloddfarlon Quarries, near Nantlle Pool, were linked to the quayside at Caernarvon. Capital of £20,000 envisaged in the first Act of 20 May 1825 was soon found insufficient. It was doubled in a second Act, dated 21 March 1827; but a third Act still had to be obtained in May 1828 to extend the time of completion. Intriguingly, both Robert Stephenson the elder and his brother, George, were directly involved in laying the track. Robert advocated a wider gauge, but his suggestion was not adopted; so Nantlle metals rested, as was customary, on stone sleeper blocks, to the original specification of 3 ft 6 in. Mineral traffic was horse-drawn from beginning to end. It seems, too, that despite lack of Parliamentary sanction, a modicum of passenger traffic also evolved.

Progress continued unspectacularly enough, until main line railways began to penetrate North Wales. Both Ports Penrhyn and Dinorwic were breached in a subsequent flurry of standard gauge building; and latterly a second potentially famous name emerged when one C. E. Spooner was appointed Engineer to the newly-created Caernarvonshire Railway Company. Sanctioned by Act of 29 July 1862, the latter's aim was to build a 27¾-mile standard gauge line between Portmadoc and the LNWR's Bangor & Caernarvon branch. As it happened, the course of the Nantlle Railway lay geographically within the proposed Scheme.

Inevitably, the Caernarvon concern obtained control of the Nantlle Railway; and, under new proprietorship, and with the blessing of an 1867 Act, the section of the Nantlle between Caernarvon and Penygroes was duly widened to 4 ft 8½ in.

Inconvenience caused by the break of gauge which now obtained at Penygroes was tolerated awhile. When, however, the LNWR finally assumed ownership of the Caernarvonshire Railway in 1870, Board of Trade co-operation was soon enlisted; and in 1872 the remaining 1½-mile section to Nantlle (Talysarn station) was also re-gauged to standard dimensions. For the next 60 years properly authorized passenger trains passed along this section — until they were ultimately withdrawn by the LMS in August 1932.

SAUNDERSFOOT RAILWAY

Opened: 1829
Closed: 1940
Gauge: 4 ft 0⅜ in

The first railway in Pembrokeshire, the Saundersfoot was built to carry coal; for, around the beginning of the nineteenth century, the area it was about to serve was producing some of the finest anthracite in the world, albeit in a primitive and amateurish way. Typical of the times, transport to the coast presented problems, and in 1828, in an attempt to improve the economics of the situation, a proposal was advanced to construct a harbour at Saundersfoot, and add a rail link to local collieries.

Thus, a Saundersfoot Railway & Harbour Company Bill successfully negotiated Parliament on 1 June 1829. It contained authority to build a main line of 4¾ miles, and two branches totalling a further 1¾ miles. Powers expired before the latter were tackled, but the main line, single track throughout, with passing loops, was duly completed to a most unusual gauge of 4 ft 0⅜ in. It opened for horse-hauled mineral traffic in 1832. Four-wheeled iron coal drams

During its 50-year existence, the Stoke-on-Trent firm of Kerr Stuart & Co Ltd built some 1,500 locomotives. Most, standard and narrow gauge alike, were designed for industrial use at home and abroad, and many 'Standard' types appeared in their catalogue. One distinctly non-standard product, however, was Bull Dog, an 0-4-0ST built specially in 1915 to meet Saundersfoot Railway requirements. The tank weighed 12½ tons, but its overall height had to be confined to 6 feet for tunnel clearance reasons. This Works photograph illustrates the remarkably neat engine Kerr Stuart produced. (Steamchest)

were the only rolling stock the Company ever used; and three of these, when loaded, required the combined exertions of two horses. A prominent feature of the tramroad was a self-acting incline of 1 in 5, 300 yards long, situated ½ mile inland from the harbour.

Nevertheless, the improvement such elementary equipment brought about in coal traffic soon prompted construction of the two modest branch lines. Parliamentary permission was obtained in 1842. Thus, still horse-served, further local collieries were brought within Saundersfoot's orbit. Traffic in iron ore also developed, and in 1849, when a new iron-works opened at Stepaside, opportunity was taken to extend Saundersfoot's services. For the next 60 years the Saundersfoot Railway was never to look back, and in 1874 the entire line was relaid with heavier flat-bottomed rails, duly spiked to transverse wooden sleepers. The Age of Steam was about to arrive.

It arrived modestly, in the shape of a Manning Wardle 0–4–0 saddle tank. Restricted by tunnel clearances, the working weight of the locomotive was only 9½ tons. Named variously *Bonville* and *Rosalind*, then latterly nameless, it served Company fortunes faithfully as they waxed and waned during the years which led to the First World War. In 1914, all against the evidence of general industrial decline, the Saundersfoot Railway opted to expand by 1½ miles when a new pit was sunk at Reynalton. A new locomotive was specially built to handle this section. Named *Bull Dog*, again it was a 0–4–0ST, this time from Kerr Stuart. Although it weighed 12½ tons in working order, its height was confined to 6 feet — for one tunnel it was required to work through offered a clearance of only 6½ feet! Alas, Renalton Colliery's life was short, for it closed in 1921, and *Bull Dog* was sold to a pit nearer Saundersfoot. Nine years later *that* pit closed, and prospects suddenly began to look bleak for the Saundersfoot Railway. Within less than a decade a substantial part of the line fell near-derelict.

A local colliery revival in 1933 had every appearance of bringing fresh life to the little railway. Once again the two saddle tanks found full employment. Then the outbreak of war in 1939 saw the boom collapse; and the Saundersfoot Railway closed again — this time for good. Wartime conditions ensured that rolling-stock and the Manning Wardle tank were immediately gobbled up for scrap. Only *Bull Dog* escaped, and, sold to Llanelly Steelworks, it served its new masters well until 1951.

Today one can walk round the Saundersfoot area; but little remains to remind posterity that the Saundersfoot Railway ever existed.

LOCOMOTIVES

Name	Type	Date built	Maker	Maker's number
Bonville	0–4–0ST	1874	Manning Wardle	476
Bull Dog	,,	1915	Kerr Stuart	2401

FESTINIOG RAILWAY

Opened: 20 April 1836
Closed: 1 August 1946; re-opened 1955
Gauge: 1 ft 11½ in

Even where modern road traffic is concerned, Portmadoc and its twin town, Tremadoc, still form the gateway to the Lleyn Peninsula, one of the earliest inhabited parts of Wales. Yet, prior to the nineteenth century neither town existed, though schemes to recover the sands at the mouth of the Traeth Mawr had been entertained as far back as 1625. Reality came in 1807, when a gentleman called W. A. Madocks built a mile-long embankment across the river mouth, and laid a railway along it. Madocks, who was, incidentally, MP for Boston (Lincs), was authorized to levy a toll of 3d a ton on slate traffic conveyed thus. As a financial scheme it met with little success.

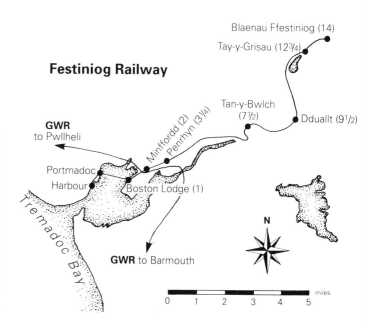

Festiniog Railway

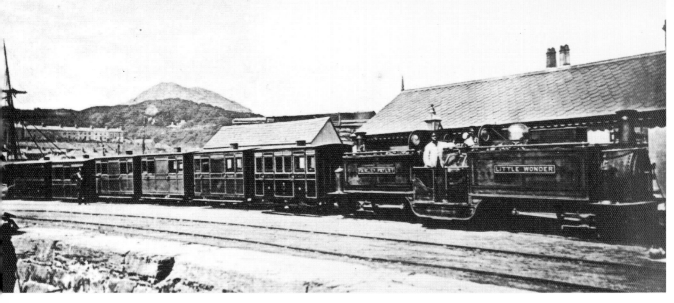

Proudly posed at Portmadoc Harbour with its train of four-wheeled coaches, Little Wonder, *the Festiniog's pioneer double-Fairlie, wrote its way into narrow gauge history in September 1869 when it hauled a 111¾-ton test train all the way to Blaenau Festiniog without faltering. Its success paved the way for the Festiniog's subsequent reliance on the type, though the loco itself was broken up in 1882.* (Steamchest)

Nevertheless, through the perseverance of one man in particular the little railway survived to become the embryo of Wales' most celebrated narrow gauge railway — the Festiniog.

The catalyst was James Spooner. Holidaying locally at a time when the embankment was being surveyed,

An interesting view at Boston Lodge circa 1905. Locos (left to right) are Taliesin, *the solitary Fairlie single introduced in 1876,* James Spooner, *a double-Fairlie built by Avonside Engine Co in 1872, and No 2* Prince, *one of four 8-ton 0–4–0 tender/tanks delivered by George England & Co in 1863-64. The latter engine still plays a major part in Festiniog activities, and was rebuilt as recently as 1980.* (Steamchest)

he was immediately attracted to the profession of engineering. He returned to the area, and there he settled down. Madocks secured the Acts of Parliament, but Spooner it was who built the mile-long railway — and dreamed of ultimately serving the slate quarries at Blaenau Ffestiniog, some 14 miles inland. The fact that the quarries were 700 feet above sea level did not deter his dream. Gathering about him a vigorous local committee, he pressed on determinedly; and, on 23 May 1832, Parliament sanctioned the creation of the Festiniog Railway Company.

Engineering work was immense, and it took three years to complete. In some places the single 1 ft 11½ in track threaded its way high on valley hillsides. In others it employed narrow stone embankments to find its way across deep ravines. Many cuttings were made through solid rock, and, deep in the heart of the slate-producing area, a tunnel was pierced, 60 yards long. To avoid a second tunnel a cable incline was incorporated in another mountainous section. Six years later, this solution was abandoned in

Prince's sister engine Princess acquired the melancholy distinction of hauling the old Festiniog's last train on 1 August 1946; but, completely run down and beyond economic repair by the time the railway was revived in 1954, she has had to be content latterly with a place of honour in the Railway Museum at Portmadoc Harbour Station. (Author's Collection)

favour of a 730-yard tunnel. In all, by cunning employment of curves which only narrow gauge trains could negotiate, the average climb over Festiniog's 14-mile length was confined to 1 in 92; surely a remarkable engineering achievement. In keeping with specification, stone sleepers were employed, while the wrought-iron rails and chairs used weighed 40 lbs to the yard — 'the same as on the Caernarvon and Nantlle railroads'.

The Festiniog was opened with appropriate ceremony on 20 April 1836. As was the custom, horses provided the muscle power, hauling strings of empty trucks up to Blaenau, whence they enjoyed a free ride in dandy cars at the end of loaded slate trains as they dropped back by gravity to Portmadoc. A brakesman controlled each descending train by friction. By the early 1850s James Spooner was already advocating the use of steam haulage, but he died in 1856 without unearthing a practical source of locomotive manufacture. His son, Charles Easton, a stalwart assistant to his father since he was a young lad of 14, had steam locomotion very much in mind when, that same year,

he was appointed Manager and Engineer of the Festiniog Railway. It is believed that at this time the Festiniog was also handling a modicum of tourist traffic.

By 1863, 'young' Spooner, now 43 years of age, convinced his Directors that increasing traffic cried out for the use of steam locomotives. The problem of who would build such specialist machines resolved itself when George England & Co of Old Kent Road, London, undertook to produce two very special 0-4-0 tanks at a cost of £900 each. At $7\frac{1}{2}$ tons working weight they were smaller than anything ever seen before. None the less, both Princess and her companion succeeded in lifting 30 tons up the line at

No 8 James Spooner carried two Works Nos (1872/929 and 930), as did all double engines shopped by Avonside Engine Co. It is seen here at Minffordd on 14 August 1913, waiting to proceed on the 9.30 am Duffws-Portmadoc train. By now, iron-framed bogie coaches form the backbone of Festiniog passenger stock – but a clutch of four-wheelers still rattle along at the rear! (LCGB, Ken Nunn Collection)

13 mph when put on trial and were adjudged such a success that two more locos were placed on order. Next, official permission was sought to institute a passenger service. Parliament gave its blessing, and a series of five trains, up and down, commenced operations between Portmadoc and Dinas on 6 January 1865. Later that year alternate trains advanced as far as Duffws. Later still, in 1870, all trains ran right through. Passenger traffic, in fact, so blossomed that a brace of more powerful 0–4–0Ts were commissioned from George England in 1867.

By now, however, other railways were exploring the area. Festiniog Directors accordingly felt compelled to increase their railway's capacity. An Act of 1869 authorized doubling of the line, and, by sanctioning construction of a short line at Minffordd, it also made possible exchange siding facilities with the standard gauge Cambrian Railways. Again the problem arose of providing more powerful locomotives; and this time Spooner made railway history by pinning his faith in Robert Fairlie's invention, the double-bogie articulated engine. Once more George England & Co rose nobly to the occasion, and No 7 *Little Wonder* was made ready for trials in September 1869.

Results were sensational. Matched against *Little Giant*, the new articulated loco doubled conventional haulage at a stroke by handling a test train consisting of 111 slate wagons, 6 passenger coaches, and 12 goods wagons — a total of 111¾ tons, excluding

engine weight — with consummate ease. At a cost of £2,000 the Fairlie engine was a complete triumph; and subsequent varied tests, try as they might, could not shake that conviction. In 1872 a second Fairlie locomotive, designed by Spooner's son, George Percival, and appropriately named after his grandfather, was ordered from Avonside Engine Co. A single-type Fairlie, again designed by G. P. Spooner, also made its début in 1876. This 0–4–4T coped well enough with Festiniog conditions, but the Company reverted to 'double-enders' for its last two engines. Typical of Festiniog enterprise, both were built in its home works at Boston Lodge.

Festiniog enterprise was not, however, confined to locomotives. C. E. Spooner did more than any other man to convince the world that narrow gauge operation need not suffer the limitations which were too often attributed to it. By 1869 he began eliminating 30 lb rail, and, employing an ingenious type of fish-plate invented by himself, he relied totally on 48½ lb rails, laid with as much care as on any standard gauge concern. Ballast, drainage, super-elevation, all were treated with the respect which still hallmarks the present-day enthusiast-run Festiniog Railway.

Original Festiniog carriages were, as might be expected, rather primitive four-wheelers; but, by 1878, Europe's first iron-framed narrow gauge passenger bogie coaches were introduced. By then the Festiniog's success was attracting worldwide attention, and an Imperial Commission from Russia had already paid a visit of instruction in 1870. The Festiniog's healthy dividends were also fomenting the convictions of narrow gauge and Fairlie locomotive enthusiasts — so much so, that some were advocating a similar conversion for the London & North Western Railway! Meanwhile, in view of the little Welsh railway's undoubted success Robert Fairlie conferred upon the Festiniog permission to use his patent free of royalties.

Exactly half-way through the Festiniog's ultimate

Welsh Pony, a George England product of slightly later vintage, was at Boston Lodge when this photograph was taken on 4 April 1926. An enlarged (10-ton) version of the earlier England locos, Welsh Pony *and* Little Giant *took over much of the main line work from their smaller brethren. Each could handle 70 empty wagons per trip.* Little Giant *perished in 1932, and* Welsh Pony *was withdrawn for overhaul a few years later. Stored for many years at Boston Lodge, the latter, painted red, now stands on a plinth outside Portmadoc Harbour station.* (LCGB, Ken Nunn Collection)

career came two sobering blows; the death of Charles Spooner and a gradual decline in slate traffic. Spooner died on 18 November 1889, and by that time both the GWR and LNWR had built standard gauge lines direct to Blaenau Ffestiniog. Thus, slate traffic was being tapped at source, and coastal shipping at Portmadoc gradually strangled. In any case, roof tiles were becoming cheaper to produce, and were rapidly ousting slate in the house-building market. A reasonably healthy tourist trade kept the Festiniog on an even keel for a few more years, but, gradually, signs emerged which were all too significant. A last dividend on Festiniog ordinary shares was paid in 1912. Preference shares followed suit in 1921, and by 1923, in an effort to reduce working expenses, the Festiniog applied, successfully, for a Light Railway Order.

That year, inspired possibly by the words 'light railway', Festiniog management saw fit to appoint the redoubtable Colonel H. F. Stephens, of Tonbridge, Kent, as their new Civil Engineer and Locomotive Superintendent. Meanwhile, under the Order, the

Taliesin (the second) prepares to leave Portmadoc in April 1959. Built at Boston Lodge in 1886, the Fairlie ran initially as No 11 Livingstone Thompson. *Rebuilt in 1905, and renumbered 3, the loco was given the name* Taliesin *in 1932, when the Fairlie single of that name was withdrawn. Reconditioned at Boston Lodge, the loco returned to Harbour Station on 2 September 1956 and, three days later, handled the first train to be hauled by a double engine under the new Festiniog regime. Renamed* Earl of Merioneth/Iarll Meirionydd *in April 1961, the loco re-entered Boston Lodge Works a decade later; and the upshot was that a new* Earl of Merioneth, *embodying important original components of the original engine, entered traffic in 1979. The superstructure of the old Earl was, however, carefully put aside for future use, and has recently been incorporated in a cosmetically restored* Livingstone Thompson. (Steamchest)

Festiniog was also authorized to build a short section of line at Portmadoc, to form a link between Festiniog metals and those of the newly formed Welsh Highland Railway. Col Stephens' aegis was duly extended to embrace both railways, and the two managements evinced every desire to work hand in hand. Two years later Stephens was promoted to the posts of Chairman

At Minffordd, 2¹/₄ miles from Portmadoc Harbour, exchange facilities with standard gauge track were still being used in August 1961. Note the coal shute leading down to the Festiniog wagons. The sidings were constructed in 1872 to permit interchange of mineral traffic between the Festiniog and the Cambrian Railways' new coast line. (F. C. Le Manquais)

Above *The first two Garratts that Beyer Peacock built were four-cylinder compound 2-foot gauge 0–4–0–0–4–0s for Tasmanian service, in 1908. Each engine weighed 33½ tons. Then, when the North East Dundas Tramway closed in 1929, at least one, No K1, remained in Tasmanian Government service until it was withdrawn in 1947. Beyer repurchased the loco for exhibition at Gorton Works, and when the latter closed in 1965 ownership of the Garratt passed to the Festiniog Railway. Delivered to Portmadoc on 24 March 1966, its potential conversion for use on Festiniog metals has provoked lively discussion since! Seen above at Portmadoc during those abortive years, the Garratt was eventually loaned to the National Railway Museum in June 1976.* (Steamchest)

Below *Also in the mid-1960s,* Prince, *by now a centenarian, was caught by the camera as it left Portmadoc Harbour Station on a comparatively light train of two bogie coaches. Taken out of service in 1968,* Prince *returned to traffic in 1980 as an oil-burner.* (Steamchest)

and Managing Director of the combined exercise; but, despite the undoubted energy he contributed, the experiment was not a success. Trouble was, Stephens insisted on controlling his, by now extensive, light railway empire from an office in Tonbridge; and local Welsh railwaymen did not take kindly to the welter of military-like memos and instructions which flowed unceasingly their way!

By November 1933 Welsh Highland financial affairs were in a parlous plight. Two main line companies, when asked to take over the line, declined; and after prolonged local negotiations the Welsh Highland was leased to the Festiniog, as from 1 July 1934, at a nominal rent of £1 for the first six months, and a proportion of traffic receipts thereafter. Give Stephens his due — strenuous efforts were made to restore Welsh Highland fortunes, and nothing was spared in an effort to attract tourist traffic. Bright new paint was lavished everywhere, locomotives were spruced up, and hundreds of new sleepers were laid.

There was no through running, however, and Fairlie locomotives never set wheel on Welsh Highland track. Four and, later, six trains ran daily between Portmadoc and Bedgellert. Significantly, at the latter station a reduced service took passengers 'beyond the frontier' to Dinas. In late 1935 passenger services were abandoned for the winter; and, though reinstated for summer months, they finally ceased on 19 September 1936. Festiniog management had found it all too difficult. Goods and mineral traffic staggered on, to terminate on 1 June 1937; and, surely enough, the outbreak of war in September 1939 was enough to clinch complete closure of the Welsh Highland Railway.

While all this was happening, the Festiniog Railway's domestic fortunes were faring little better.

All through the 1920s buses competed to snatch local passenger traffic, leaving only tourists and quarrymen to support the little narrow gauge railway. There was little the Festiniog could do to combat such pressure. From 1930 onwards, full passenger services were confined to summer months only. Even then only four trains ran each way daily. The winter passenger service consisted solely of a morning and evening train for the quarrymen's benefit. Finally, on 16 September 1939, shortly after war was declared, a sombre decision was taken — and passenger traffic on the Festiniog was totally suspended. Slate trains continued to run, as required, between Blaenau and Minffordd some two or three days a week. The drastically reduced revenue this situation produced made it,

Above *The first Fairlie double built at Boston Lodge, No 10 Merddin Emrys was not far short of its hundredth year of service when it was photographed, with open cab, leaving Portmadoc on a typical mixed train. The year is 1971, but, patently, Festiniog's elderly four-wheeled 'bug' boxes still afford great delight to younger enthusiasts!* (Steamchest)

Below *Shortly after being purchased in 1962,* Linda *was given an increased boiler pressure of 160 psi, and when boiler repairs became necessary in 1969 the loco was superheated. A pony truck was also added to steady the front end before* Linda *returned to traffic in 1969. Then, in accordance with new Festiniog practice, the loco made her first run as an oil-burner in November 1970. This photograph was taken at Portmadoc on 30 March 1972.* (Steamchest)

of course, impossible for Festiniog management to even contemplate rehabilitating the line once hostilities ceased. The sad alternative was accepted, and the Festiniog Railway closed down on 1 August 1946.

Strange years followed. The Festiniog track soon began to deteriorate. Yet it could not, legally, be abandoned. The Ministry of Transport, when approached, vouchsafed that only an Act of Parliament could produce the required Warrant. Meanwhile, only a short section at Blaenau remained active, and that was worked by a slate quarry's own internal combustion locomotives. This operation continued, in fact, until 1962.

Many were the schemes proposed to restore Festiniog Railway fortunes; but closer investigation by interested parties invariably saw them back off. Latterly, a 17-year-old schoolboy provided the touchstone, when he called a public meeting at Bristol in September 1951. This saw the formation of a Festiniog Railway Society. Public appeals for funds were launched — and proved ineffective — until a well-known businessman and railway enthusiast, Alan F. Pegler, stepped in, with others, to save the day. The rest is modern railway history. Eventually the Festiniog was set up, a tremendous amount of voluntary labour was harnessed, and on 23 July 1955 a Festiniog Railway passenger train again traversed one mile of track between Portmadoc and Boston Lodge.

Encouragingly, the Preservation Society's avowed aim of seeing Festiniog metals extend 13 miles from Portmadoc right through to Blaenau Ffestiniog has been accomplished; and a brand new interchange station with British Rail at Blaenau, opened in May 1982, must enhance future prospects. But the cost of this was enormous, both in money and labour; for, thanks to the intervention of the British Electricity Authority in 1956 in taking compulsory possession of FR track above Dduallt, and a subsequent lengthy legal battle, the Festiniog's progress was subjected to a 16½-year hiccup. The token service between Portmadoc and Boston Lodge that had been accomplished by 1955 was extended to Penrhyndeudraeth, reached by 1956, and Tan-y-Bwlch by 1958. Then came a pause for consolidation before Dduallt Station was opened in 1968. Subsequent legal battle with the electricity authorities exacted compensation of £106,700 in lieu of lost profits. Though this sum was insufficient to meet the full costs of a deviation line from Dduallt (9½ miles) to Blaenau Ffestiniog, work commenced, never the less, in 1965. After much fund-raising, Tanygrisiau (12¼ miles) was reached in 1978; and the through service to Blaenau followed triumphantly in 1982. The 2½-mile deviation line cost over £600,000, and it says much for various public-spirited bodies in Wales, plus the Manpower Services Commission and Festiniog Railway's bank, that the little railway has recaptured its rightful place as the doyen of Welsh narrow gauge activity.

LOCOMOTIVES

Locomotives built by and for the Festiniog Railway

No	Name	Type	Date built	Maker	Remarks
1	(The) Princess	0-4-0	1863	George England	Rebuilt 1895 at Boston Lodge
2	(The) Prince	,,	1863	,,	Rebuilt 1892 at Boston Lodge
3	Mountaineer	,,	1864	,,	Damaged beyond repair 1879
4	Palmerston	,,	1864	,,	Sold 1974 after sundry rebuilds
5	Welsh Pony	,,	1867	,,	Static exhibit, Harbour station
6	Little Giant	,,	1867	,,	Withdrawn 1932
7	Little Wonder	0-4-4-0	1869	,,	Withdrawn 1882
8	James Spooner	,,	1872	Avonside	Withdrawn 1933
9	Taliesin	0-4-4	1876	Vulcan	Renumbered 7. W/D 1932
10	Merddin Emrys	0-4-4-0	1879	Boston Lodge	Rebuilt 1896, 1921 and 1970
11	Livingston Thompson/Taliesin Earl of Merioneth	,,	1886	,,	Withdrawn 1971, and cosmetically restored as *Livingston Thompson* by 1988 for presentation to National Railway Museum, York.
—	Earl of Merioneth	,,	1979	,,	New 'Super Fairlie' built incorporating a few earlier components

How easily the course of narrow gauge railway history might have been altered! Shortly after C. E. Spooner was appointed Manager and Engineer of the Festiniog Railway no less an authority than Robert Stephenson expressed an opinion that the use of steam locomotives on such a minute gauge as 2 feet was quite impractical. Fortunately, Spooner put this discouraging intelligence behind him — and went on to sire a whole pedigree of 'impossibilities'! The very first offsprings, built in 1863, were products of remarkable collaboration between dreamer and locomotive builder.

Both locos were 0–4–0 side tanks, yet with a separate tender for coal and toolbox. Wheels were a mere 2 feet in diameter, and in working order each engine weighed 7½ tons. Two similar locos joined the ranks in 1864, and later, by converting all four to saddle-tanks, water capacity was increased by nearly 50 per cent to 334 gallons. Ever-increasing traffic soon pinpointed their weakness — lack of adhesion; and when Nos 5 and 6 arrived in 1867, water capacity, wheel diameter and working weight were seen to have been enlarged to 418 gallons, 2 ft 8 in and 10 tons respectively. Yet the Festiniog's fast-growing traffic *still* contrived to outpace locomotive performance!

It was at this juncture that differences in judgment as to how the traffic problem should be tackled produced yet another critical development in Festiniog locomotive affairs. Management felt that doubling the line was the answer. Indeed, Parliament sanctioned such a course on 26 July 1869. Then Spooner, clinging tenaciously to his view that such an enormously expensive procedure could be avoided, produced his trump card — a locomotive which could handle double-length trains. His collusion with Robert Fairlie proved to be a master stroke.

The triumphant début of *Little Wonder* has already been described. The 'double-ender' weighed 19½

tons, bore side tanks on each boiler, and on tests against *Little Giant* even produced a fuel saving of 25 per cent. Within a short time the success of Fairlie's engine was being acclaimed all over the world; and by 1870 Avonside Engine Co was building locomotives to Fairlie's Patent. The Festiniog's second 'double-ender' came, in fact, from that source. Differences in detail from No 7, part practical, part cosmetic in character, set a standard by which the Festiniog's last two Fairlie 'doubles' were built. It says much for the railway's complete confidence that they were constructed in Festiniog's own Boston Lodge workshops.

Today, over a century later, five original Festiniog engines still survive, as does much of the little railway's basic character. No 2 *Prince* still works for a living, after re-boilering in 1955 and a re-build in 1980. No 10 *Merddin Emrys*, too, has completed its century. No 1 *Princess* is now a museum exhibit at Porthmadog, and No 5 *Welsh Pony* graces a plinth outside the Harbour Station. *Taliesin*, renamed *Earl of Merioneth* in 1961, and withdrawn ten years later, contributed power bogie frames towards a new *Earl of Merioneth*, and a new boiler supplied by Hunslet Engine Co saw the very special 'Super Fairlie' launched in 1979. By now oil-burning was standard practice on the Festiniog. Meanwhile, No 3's superstructure had been carefully stored, and in October 1988 a cosmetically restored *Livingston Thompson* was handed over to the National Railway Museum, York.

Steam locomotives subsequently acquired by the Preservation Society are an engaging 'mix', as can be seen from the accompanying table, and a dozen four-wheeled diesel units complete the railway's very healthy locomotive stock. Purchase dates range from 1923 to 1971.

Festiniog carriage stock in 1955 was a venerable, but sadly dilapidated, collection of four-wheelers and

Locomotives acquired by the Preservation Group

Name	Type	Maker	Arrival date	Obtained from	Remarks
Volunteer	0–6–0ST	Peckett (2050/1944)	1957	Harrogate Gas Works	Presently in store
Blanche	0–4–0ST	Hunslet (589/1893)	1962	Penrhyn Quarry	Tender added. Now a superheated 2–4–0
Linda	0–4–0ST	Hunslet (590/1893)	1962	,,	,,
No K1	0–4–0 –0–4–0	Beyer Peacock (5792/1909)	1965	Ex-Tasmanian Railways	On loan to National Railway Museum, York
Mountaineer	2–6–2PT	Alco, USA (57156/1916)	1967	Ex-Tramway de Pithiviers à Toury, France	Former War Department tramway engine during First World War
Britomart	0–4–0ST	Hunslet (707/1899)	1965	Penyrorsedd Quarry	Privately owned

bogie coaches. Most were eventually repaired, and were soon joined by a few more of Welsh Highland and Lynton & Barnstaple origin. Since then, the years 1964–81 have witnessed a steady annual increment of Festiniog-built bogie coaches; and no fewer than 15 modern vehicles now assist the railway in handling anything up to half a million passengers a year.

A recently announced project to build a reproduction of the single Fairlie *Taliesin* confirms the Festiniog's intention to remain in the fore. 'Taliesin 2000', the title of the project, acknowledges its long-term nature, and a donation appeal requesting pledges of monthly increments remains at the moment the major hope on which ultimate completion rests. Costs are estimated, formidably, at £¼ million.

CORRIS RAILWAY

Opened: 30 April 1859
Closed: 20 August 1948
Gauge: 2 ft 3 in

In the mid-nineteenth century, Machynlleth, a name which was to feature prominently in light railway history, was but a small country town tucked in the north-west corner of Montgomeryshire. Not far away lay an area which produced slates of worldwide

renown. Yet, when a Mr T. S. Nicholls decided to emulate the Festiniog Railway's success, and set about surveying a possible route for a tramroad, he was scoffed at. Fortunately he persisted despite local indifference; and, on 12 July 1858, the Corris, Machynlleth and River Dovey Tramroad received powers to provide quarries at Aberllefeni and Corris with a rail outlet on the quayside at Derwenlas. Traffic, mineral only, on the 2 ft 3 in tramroad was handled by horses. A further Act of 25 July 1864, acknowledging subsequent penetration by standard gauge metals into the locality, sanctioned a cutback of the tramline west of Machynlleth, altered the company's name to the Corris Railway Company, and granted permission to use locomotives. In the event, 14 years elapsed before steel rails replaced the rudimentary track, and three 0-4-0 saddle tanks were imported from the Falcon Engine Works of Loughborough. It was then, too, that the system passed under the control of Imperial Tramways Co Ltd, Bristol.

The latter development was to prove significant; for when the Corris tried to obtain Parliamentary permission to run passenger trains every possible obstacle was placed in its way by the quarry owners, who feared consequent deterioration of their own freight services. Corris, conveniently aided by its new masters, adopted the ploy of instituting a passenger road service in August 1879. Encouraged on this occasion by public approval, it even succeeded, on 18 June 1883, in obtaining the necessary Act to carry passengers by rail. Within less than a month, passenger trains were plying between Machynlleth and Corris, albeit a mandatory speed limit of 15 mph obtained. Four years later services were extended to Aberllefeni.

In its day the Corris Railway was nothing if not enterprising. Road coach services into the Talyllyn area worked hand in hand with the railway to attract visitors by the thousand. Posters, timetables and guides, many of them treasured relics to this day, were produced in profusion. Yet, curiously, eight carriages sufficed to meet the railway company's needs during its lifetime. No doubt this was a logical product of its close collaboration with road transport interests. Anyhow, slate traffic flourished, and by 1902 the Corris was handling 16,000 tons a year. As so often happened in Wales, the quarries supplied most of the wagons required; so, again, the railway escaped considerable expense on rolling-stock. Very likely it was this economy in overheads which made feasible a rebuild of Machynlleth station in 1905, construction of a new steel bridge over the River Dovey in 1906 and erection of a carriage shed at Machynlleth in the following year. An attempt, however, to initiate Sunday passenger services fell on deaf ears locally, and, rather than offend Welsh religious susceptibilities, the proposition was quietly dropped.

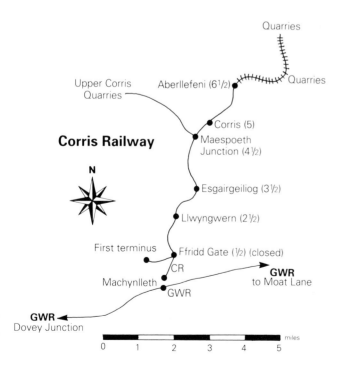

Corris Railway

N

Quarries

Upper Corris
Quarries

Aberllefeni (6½)

Quarries

Corris (5)

Maespoeth
Junction (4½)

Esgairgeiliog (3½)

Llwyngwern (2½)

First terminus

Ffridd Gate (½) (closed)

CR

GWR
to Moat Lane

Machynlleth

GWR

GWR
Dovey Junction

0   1   2   3   4   5   miles

This view of Corris station, looking towards Aberllefeni, was taken on 29 June 1909, some nine years after Corris four-wheeled coaches were paired on bogie underframes. Although an Act of Parliament sanctioned the use of locomotives from 1864, 14 years elapsed ere the Corris Railway acquired its first steam engines. These were employed on freight traffic only, and horse-drawn passenger trains continued to frequent Corris Station until 1883. Aberllefeni saw its first steam-hauled passenger train four years later. (LCGB, Ken Nunn Collection)

Everything is spick and span at Corris station as one of the Falcon 0–4–0STs poses proudly with its train of bogied coaches. Despite its 2 ft 3 in gauge, Corris Railway track was much too tortuous to tolerate other than four-coupled tanks. The introduction of ex-WD 4–6–0Ts would have been disastrous. But the Corris's ambitious efforts to attract tourists and visitors are self-evident from the immaculate nature of this scene. The only element missing is the passengers! (Lens of Sutton)

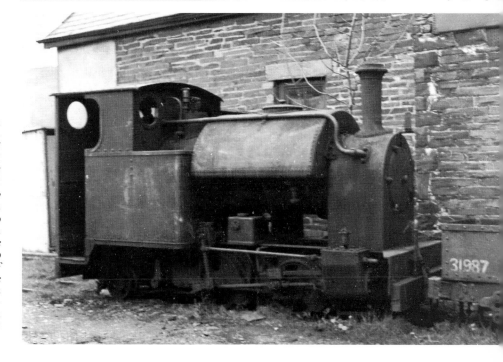

Only two Corris locos remained in existence by the time the little railway was closed, under British Rail auspices, in August 1948; placed on the GWR's Sales List, Nos 3 and 4 lay stored behind Machynlleth station until they were sold in 1951 to the Talyllyn Railway Preservation Society. No 4 (Kerr Stuart 4047/1921) is seen here during its lonely vigil. The purchase price of £50 for the two locomotives, with a quantity of Corris slate wagons and a brake van thrown in, proved to be a great bargain, and the end products can be seen today at Tywyn in the form of Sir Hadyn and Edward Thomas. (Steamchest)

A subsequent attempt to advance the Company's welfare by seeking a Light Railway Order to extend Corris metals west to Talyllyn and Abergynolwyn was, mercifully perhaps, never implemented. Meanwhile, attention was gradually being focused on the desirability of replacing the Corris's horse-drawn tourist coaches by motor omnibuses. The General Manager, J. J. O'Sullivan, was cautiously realistic in his approach, for the Talyllyn route contained some fearsome hills. Eventually, however, one bus sailed forth, in May 1908, under Corris colours. By 1911, the company was running three.

During the First World War some loss in tourist traffic was inevitably experienced; but the Corris kept on going. The reopening of several local quarries in post-war years brought an initial flurry of timber traffic; and, to supplement ageing locos, a fourth engine, *Tattoo*, was bought from Kerr Stuart. But slate traffic never regained pre-war heights, and throughout the 1920s, the Corris management was obliged to concentrate rather feverishly on bus services. Here they were on distinctly shaky ground, for the GWR by now was stalking motor services in the Machynlleth vicinity. Events could only lead in one direction, and on 4 August 1930 the Corris Railway was purchased by the Great Western Railway. The bus services were promptly merged within the parent concern, and, on 1 January 1931, the Corris Railway line was closed to passenger traffic. Such mineral and freight traffic as remained was handled by one daily train in each direction. During the Second World War even this meagre service was deemed excessive, and thrice-weekly working was instituted.

Nemesis finally came when the GWR was redesignated British Railways (Western Region) on 1 January 1948. Flooding in the Dovey Valley had already caused concern, the Corris route was at constant risk, and with rail traffic at its present low ebb the case for closure could not be combated. So, on 20 August 1948, a last train ran over one-time Corris metals. Demolition was swift, and within less than a year little remained to remind one of the little railway's 89-year existence. The surviving locos, Nos 3 and 4, were placed on the GWR's Sales List, and were sold in March 1951 to a newly-risen Talyllyn Railway Company. There they serve today, in conjunction with a quantity of other Corris equipment; yielding pleasure, as of yore, to a constant flow of visitors to the Dovey valley.

LOCOMOTIVES

No	Type	Date built	Maker	Maker's number	Remarks
1	0-4-0ST	1878	Hughes & Co, Falcon Works	324	Rebuilt as 0-4-2ST 1895. Withdrawn 1930.
2	,,	1878	,,	322	Rebuilt as 0-4-2ST 1898. Withdrawn 1930.
3	,,	1878	,,	323	Rebuilt as 0-4-2ST 1900.
4	0-4-2ST	1921	Kerr Stuart	4047	Now *Edward Thomas* on the Talyllyn Railway

The three 0-4-0 saddle tanks first supplied were typical light railway products from Falcon Works, Loughborough. The footplate was dropped at the rear to provide headroom for the driver, and his 'cab' consisted merely of a roof mounted on four pillars. The wheelbase proved to be much too short for the Corris's sharply curved route, hence the subsequent provision of a pony truck. Even then, flange wear of the pony trucks warranted tyre renewal every 1½ years or so.

Nos 1 and 2 failed to survive GWR inspection in 1930, and were cut up at Machynlleth. Nos 3 and 4 were stored, sheeted up, behind Machynlleth station from August 1948 until the Talyllyn Railway Preservation Society removed them to Towyn in March 1951. There they flourish today, still running under their old Corris Railway numbers, but with new names, *Sir Hadyn* and *Edward Thomas*.

CROESOR TRAMWAY

Opened: 1863
Closed: 1922
Gauge: 1 ft 11½ in

The fame of this privately constructed tramroad rests less on its brief dedication to the slate industry than on the fact that it ultimately became an integral part of the Welsh Highland Railway. Constructed without Parliamentary powers during the year 1863 by a landowner, H. B. Roberts, the tramroad was 7 miles in length, and employed the same gauge as the Festiniog. The latter factor no doubt influenced its future. It ran from Portmadoc deep into the Croesor Valley; and inland, beyond Croesor, several double-tracked, gravity-worked inclines assisted the climb into the Moelwyn Mountains. Within a year impending descent on the area by the Cambrian Railways obliged the proprietor to think in terms of opening his tramroad to the public.

Latterly, only part of the tramroad was chosen to be converted thus, that between Carrig Hylldrem and Portmadoc, and it is of interest to note that the expense estimate for the proposed works was drawn up by none other than C. E. Spooner, Engineer to the Festiniog Railway. Authorized capital was duly pitched at £25,000, and the new Croesor & Portmadoc Railway Company received Parliament's blessing on 5 July 1865. Gauge was stipulated at 2 feet, though a section of the Act contained latitude to expand to 4 ft 8½ in if necessary. By 1870, however, neither passenger traffic nor locomotive traction had materialized.

In the meantime, formation of the North Wales Narrow Gauge Railways Company in 1872 rather altered the rules of play, for, with prominent local businessmen and Festiniog Railway office holders at its helm, the NWNGR assumed a General Undertaking which postulated construction of a 23-mile 2-foot gauge line. Designed to serve both slate and passenger traffic, and starting from a junction with the C&PR, this new project aimed to reach Bettws-y-Coed via Beddgelert. Difficulties, however, ensued, and the Undertaking was shelved in 1876 with no work done. Next, by Act of 21 July 1879, the C&PR changed its name to the Portmadoc, Croesor & Beddgelert Tram Railway Company. Despite receiving additional sanction to construct a branch, 4 miles long, between Llanfrothen and Beddgelert, nothing happened — except for the melancholy appointment of a Receiver three years later.

With the Receiver still in charge of Croesor affairs, the turn of the century saw a new flourish of proposals.One group proposed to buy the near-derelict tramroad, electrify it, and build a branch to Beddgelert. The PC&B's main mortgage holder agreed, subject to compensation being paid; and on 17 August 1901 the old Croesor title finally disappeared. The new project, the Portmadoc, Beddgelert & South Snowdon Railway Company, was incorporated in due course with an authorized capital of £270,000. The main mortgagor had been bought off, but original shareholders in the Croesor Tramway lost everything.

In the event much legal manoeuvring followed, and the North Wales Narrow Gauge Railways reached an ambitious agreement with the PB&SSR. Despite that, the section between Portmadoc and Croesor Junction remained a horse-drawn goods line until the Welsh Highland Railway came on the scene in 1922. The rest of the one-time Croesor Tramway, including the three double-tracked gravity inclines, remained as private property — and was even offered for auction

in October 1936. The track was not lifted until the 1950s.

GORSEDDAU TRAMWAY

Opened: 1875
Closed: 1894
Gauge: 1 ft 11½ in

Exactly like the Croesor, the Gorseddau Tramway was built without Parliamentary powers around 1863 to carry mineral traffic to Portmadoc. Originally 8 miles long, it was constructed by the slate company which owned Gorseddau Quarry, and it reached the coast by wayleave arrangement with sundry landowners. In 1872 application was made to construct a 5-mile extension further inland to Blaen-y-Pennant; and by dint of an Act dated 25 July 1872, the Tramway's somewhat precarious position was regularized under a new title, the Gorseddau Junction & Portmadoc Railway. Under this Act the erstwhile horse-drawn Tramway also found itself authorized to employ locomotives — *and* offer a public passenger and goods service. Only two of these three options were ever taken up, in that goods traffic commenced on 2 September 1875, and 'locomotion' appeared in the form of a vertical boiler, mounted on four coupled wheels — a product, needless to say, of de Winton & Co, of Union Works, Caernarvon. Only part of the proposed 5-mile extension was ever built, and the GJ&PR's total length remained at 11 miles until its dying day.

Despite other provisions in the Act, authorizing intimate and useful interchange with the Croesor Tramway at strategic points, the Gorseddau undertaking appears to have cut very little financial ice during its lifetime. Returns for 1878 claimed ownership of 15 wagons. Privately-owned quarry wagons and, no doubt, some Festiniog Railway vehicles would also be employed. Whatever, this figure was reduced to seven wagons by 1893, and by 1894 the line had ceased working altogether. Thus, incidentally, vanished one of several narrow gauge level crossings over the Cambrian Railways in and around Portmadoc.

TALYLLYN RAILWAY

Opened: 1 December 1866
Closed: 6 October 1950; re-opened 1951
Gauge: 2 ft 3 in

Still flourishing today as venerable and friendly rivals, the Talyllyn and Festiniog Railways would appear at

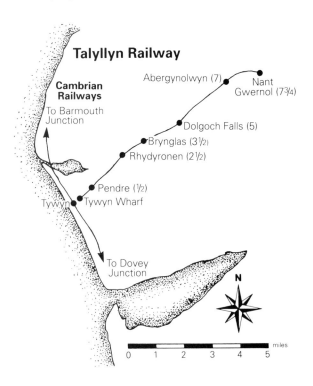

Talyllyn Railway

Cambrian Railways

To Barmouth Junction

Tywyn

Tywyn Wharf

Pendre (½)

Rhydyronen (2½)

Brynglas (3½)

Dolgoch Falls (5)

Abergynolwyn (7)

Nant Gwernol (7¾)

To Dovey Junction

N

miles
0 1 2 3 4 5

Thus, it retains its happy distinction of being the first British narrow gauge railway to operate steam locomotives from its *inception*.

Certainly the successful introduction of locomotive traction on the Festiniog in 1863 helped to fire the creation of the Talyllyn. About that time the Aberdovey Slate Company, owners of highly productive quarries at Bryn Eglwys, 8½ miles inland and 900 feet above sea level, were seriously seeking a better alternative for their quarry products than transport by pack pony down to the Dovey estuary. What better course, they deduced, than follow the Festiniog's example!

So, the Talyllyn Railway was formed, with a capital of £15,000. An Act of Incorporation was obtained on 5 July 1865, J. S. Spooner, elder brother of C. E. Spooner of Festiniog fame, was appointed Engineer in charge of construction, and work rapidly got under way. Problems were not severe. Apart from the provision of two stations, at Towyn and Abergynolwyn, the only engineering feature of consequence was a three-arch brick-built viaduct at Dolgoch. This cost £3,000. Overall costs emerged at £2,150 per mile, about one-fifth of those of the Festiniog. The curious fact that the Talyllyn's Act insisted on no gauge of *less* than 2 ft 3 in being employed suggests that future liaison with the Corris Railway was being held firmly in mind.

The slate company's original intention was to build a railway line down the Afon Fathew Valley to the sea, then proceed along the coast to Aberdovey. But, as it happened, the Aberystwyth & Welsh Coast Railway was also being promoted at the time. Freed, therefore, from the need to construct a coastal section, the Talyllyn's promoters settled for a single line, 6½ miles long, between Abergynolwyn and Towyn.

It follows that provision of transhipment facilities to

first sight to be 'two of a kind'. In fact, the only idiosyncrasy they ever shared was the odd characteristic that both railways terminated some 3 miles short of the destinations their titles purported to serve. That said, the two companies' operating practices were, traditionally, poles apart. The Talyllyn was as sparing in its provision of locomotives and maintenance of track, etc, as the Festiniog was prestigious in almost everything it touched. Yet, unlike the apparently more worthy Festiniog, the Talyllyn Railway never closed.

The Whitehaven firm of Fletcher Jennings was very proud of Tal-y-llyn when it built the 0–4–0ST over 125 years ago. Three years later trailing wheels were added, and by the time this photograph was taken at Towyn Wharf around 1900 a somewhat tight-fitting cab had been added. Despite her faults the little loco was very dear to Talyllyn men's hearts. (Author's Collection)

standard gauge metals at Towyn was vital, if the Talyllyn's slate traffic was to flourish. Certainly direct access to the Cambrian Railways station at Towyn would enhance passenger traffic prospects. Quite logically, therefore, such powers were carefully embodied in the Talyllyn's Act of 1865. Alas, through a variety of circumstances, this aim was never achieved. Instead, TR management had to content itself with a terminus at Towyn Wharf. Here facilities were, to put it mildly, rudimentary; for incoming slate wagons had to be moved by hand on to one of four small turntables ere they could be positioned on a single track which ran parallel with the Cambrian Railways sidings. Needless to say, all loading and unloading was accomplished by hand.

Construction of the Talyllyn's 'main line' hardly constituted a major engineering feat, yet many of its features were of great interest. The steepest gradient faced was 1 in 60, and the sharpest curve 6 chains in radius. Each of the seven bridges built over the line, however, was so narrow in span, and offered such limited side clearance, that Talyllyn management professed itself obliged to operate public service with one side of its passenger coaches permanently locked and barred. The Board of Trade was none too keen on this unusual proposal; but latterly, in view of the Talyllyn's mandatory speed limit of 15 mph, they conceded the point. So evolved the extraordinary tradition whereby passengers on the Talyllyn Railway entered and alighted from coaches on the north side only. In another

Once Dolgoch, *a second, albeit remarkably different, Fletcher Jennings product joined the ranks in 1866, the two locomotives shared all Talyllyn traffic for the next 80 years. Left in 1945 to cope single-handedly,* Dolgoch, *seen here on duty at Abergynolwyn station, still managed to serve the Talyllyn Railway Preservation Society until 1956, when it had to be withdrawn for eventual reboilering.* (Talyllyn Railway)

A closer look at the Talyllyn Railway's initial three Brown Marshall coaches, however, reveals the low esteem with with the Talyllyn management regarded passenger traffic. With no light, heat or brakes available, maximum complements of 24 seated passengers in each of the two leading coaches must have placed great credence on 'safety in numbers'! (Author's Collection)

economy, worthy of the Glasgow subway, company lettering was also confined to that side of the coach!

The nature of three coaches and one guard's van, all four-wheeled, which were ordered from Brown Marshall of Birmingham in time for the opening in December 1866 bespoke the comparatively low priority placed by the Talyllyn on passenger traffic.

Below *This is how Abergynolwyn village looked when viewed from the top of the Talyllyn Railway's fearsome 150-feet high incline. Wagons containing coal and other supplies arrived in the village either by counterbalanced descent or by cable. Note the turntables below, where various offshoot tracks enabled goods to be delivered practically to the door!* (Author's Collection)

Bottom *A look, many years later, inside the drumhouse at the top of Abergynolwyn village incline. In this view, taken in August 1961, the Talyllyn's mineral extension to Bryneglwys Quarries can be seen passing through from left to right. The incline itself was completely overgrown by then.* (F. C. Le Manquais)

Thoroughly spartan in design, and devoid of light, heat, or continuous brake, each coach contained three compartments wherein 24 passengers made the best of it. At least, the saving graces of being timber-built and well-sprung enabled the coaches, if not the passengers, to survive the ravages of time extremely well! Again, from the outset, in the interests of economy and to avoid the need to staff stopping places as they developed, Talyllyn guards were given the supernumerary task of issuing tickets. Years later, in about 1902, the van was ingeniously rebuilt to function as a mobile Booking Office. Meanwhile, a fourth coach, all-third, was secured from the Lancaster Wagon Co in 1870, and there Talyllyn passenger traffic ambitions rested.

Slate traffic was, of course, a different proposition. Up to the turn of the century some 200 four-wheeled wagons found full employment. On occasion up to 20 of these could be seen trailing at the end of a mixed train. Often, in the midst of heavy summer traffic, a number of wagons were shamelessly re-jigged to carry passengers. Use was also found for ordinary goods wagons and vans, mainly to carry coal and provisions to the village of Abergynolwyn. An occasional gunpowder wagon could also be seen in transit.

The Talyllyn's original track was no more inspired. Flat-bottomed, and weighing 44 lbs to the yard, rails were spiked and chaired to wooden sleepers spaced about a yard apart. Fishplates were not introduced until a later date, and maintenance never approached that of the Festiniog in quality or consistency. No form of semaphore signalling appears to have existed. Telephones and telegraph played no part in Talyllyn affairs, and, in keeping with such frugal ambitions, the 'one engine in steam' principle was adopted. Two Fletcher Jenning locomotives sufficed to meet the line's traction requirements for its first 80 years, and whichever of these two stalwarts handled a train, 40 minutes were allowed for the 6½-mile journey.

Gradually over the years a number of intermediate stations and halts evolved along the length of the Talyllyn. Less than half a mile from Wharf, a passing loop funnelled into Towyn Pendre station. The latter had double significance for the Talyllyn, for passengers were encouraged to entrain or alight here, rather than attempt to make use of Wharf terminus. Pendre also served as the Talyllyn's mechanical headquarters. Here a stone building housed both engine shed and workshops, and, nearby, a 'carriage shed' offered minimal protection from wind and rain. Typically, Pendre's single platform lay on the north side, as did that at Cynfal, the only halt of four which could boast a platform; the other three were simply occupational crossings.

Five miles out from Wharf came Dolgoch, 200 feet above sea level. Then, after traversing 1½ miles of even wilder country, such passengers as remained

debouched at Abergynolwyn station. This, as far as they were concerned, was the end of the road, even though the village they sought still lay a quarter of a mile away. Visitors were no luckier; for with two up trains only performing on weekdays, and each train pausing only 20 minutes at Abergynolwyn before setting out again for Towyn, there was little time for sightseeing. Even though one additional train ran on Saturdays, and extra trains were laid on in summer, the highly desirable objective of viewing Dolgoch Falls remained a problem for tourists right through the years to 1952!

Freight traffic on the Talyllyn was rather more complicated, for, after reaching Abergynolwyn, a 2-mile mineral extension, embracing four fearsome inclines,

Above *No 6 Douglas, heading the 10.25am ex-Towyn Wharf, halts at Dolgoch's rather primitive water column on 8 August 1961. The train is an engaging 'mix': the leading vehicles are ex-Corris Railway 3rd class coach No 17, now riding on a new underframe and painted in Corris livery, and ex-Corris brake van No 6; next come two original Talyllyn Railway four-wheeled coaches, Nos 4 and 3, built in 1870 by the Lancaster Wagon Co and 1866 by Marshall & Co; while No 9, a Talyllyn bogie product of 1954, brings up the rear. Note, too, the sand which has been liberally applied on the rails to ensure a firm restart.* (F. C. Le Manquais)

Below *Abergynolwyn, 8 August 1961. The 11.50 am is ready to return to Towyn, and invites a close look at the Talyllyn Railway's unique guard's van cum booking office. Still bearing No 5, the van, supplied by Brown Marshall in 1866, was converted to its present form at the turn of the century.* (F. C. Le Manquais)

lay ahead. Standard practice for mixed trains was for the engine to detach coaches at Abergynolwyn station, using the run-round loop provided. Then, coming behind the wagons which remained, it would propel them along half a mile of precarious single line to the head of an incline whose summit towered 150 feet above Abergynolwyn village.

Two options now presented themselves, depending on whether the wagons were destined for the quarries, or were carrying provisions to the village. If the latter was the intention the wagons were branched off from the mineral extension, and were nudged, one by one, on to a small turntable within a drumhouse which dominated the incline head. From now on gravity would take over, and the locomotive retreated. The incline itself was double-tracked, which convenience permitted counter-balancing by ascending wagons whenever this was feasible. Alternatively, a hand brake on the winding drum took sole care of descending wagons. At the foot of the incline the line reverted to single status, and as it passed through the village pro-

vision of further turntables enabled selective delivery to be made. Abergynolwyn village possessed both a saw mill and a goods shed. In the circumstances, delivery of coal to a villager's backyard never presented much of a problem either!

Empty wagons bound for the quarries faced an even more perilous prospect. Proceeding straight along the mineral section, and ignoring a second small turntable which offered last-minute access to the village, they were taken to the first of three quarry inclines, Alltwyllt, whence a winding drum perched high above attended to their ascent. Horses then took over at the summit, and pulled the wagons half a mile to the next incline, Cantrybedd, which in turn lifted the rails to an altitude of nearly 700 feet. From there the track divided. One section climbed Beudynewydd Incline to reach outpost slate workings, while the other, climbing higher still, forked off to terminate at Bryn Eglwys Quarries themselves. Truly, the amount of money and ingenuity expended in reaching these objectives reflected the supreme importance the

Talyllyn Railway placed on slate traffic. Nowadays, sadly, the whole upland area is a wasteland.

The Talyllyn's intended link with the Corris Railway never, of course, materialized, though an engaging activity called the 'Grand Tour' assisted Talyllyn passenger traffic for many years. A typical Edwardian delight, the 'Grand Tour' involved intricate use of three railways. First, passengers travelled to Machynlleth by Cambrian train. There they switched to the Corris Railway, and, having travelled as far as Corris, they switched to Corris horse coach. The spectacular journey which followed took them through some of Wales' finest country, including Tal-y-llyn itself, before terminating at Abergynolwyn station. The Talyllyn Railway then returned them to Towyn, whence the thoroughly sated tourists found their way home via Cambrian Railways. Immensely popular, and highly publicized, the Grand Tour, alas, came to an untimely end when the Corris Railway lost its independence.

Meanwhile, the Talyllyn's 'bread and butter', slate traffic, functioned well enough up to the turn of the century. Precious few years, though, showed a clear working profit. Yet, despite a slight improvement during First World War years, there was worse to come, for post-war years witnessed a sad decline in the slate industry. Fortunately, Sir Henry Hadyn Jones MP, a prominent landowner who had purchased both quarry and railway, decided that for the sake of his tenants the little railway should continue to operate — during his own lifetime at least. So, at some financial cost to Sir Hadyn, the Talyllyn Railway soldiered on.

Still functioning with two locomotives, five carriages, and track dating back to the 1860s, the Talyllyn did well to lurch into the 1940s. By now all passenger accommodation had been made third class, and running time for the 6½ miles had been increased to 45 minutes. Then came major misfortune, in 1945, when *Tal-y-llyn*, completely worn out, had to be laid aside. *Dolgoch* was, thus, left single-handed to cope with such traffic as remained. Troubles, of course, never come singly, and what might have been a death blow to the Talyllyn followed quite soon, when Bryn Eglwys Quarries closed down in 1947. Grossly overworked in years gone by, they had deteriorated dangerously; even if capital had been available to restore safety levels, it is extremely unlikely that skilled labour, after its experiences in the Second World War, could have been coaxed back to such a remote area. Whatever, deprived thus of slate traffic, its major reason for existence, the Talyllyn Railway seemed doomed.

Fortunately for all, Sir Hadyn stuck to his original pledge, and with his financial assistance a passenger service was kept going, in summer months at least.

The next crisis to hit the Talyllyn came on 3 June 1950, when Sir Hadyn Jones departed from this world. As a mark of respect Talyllyn management struggled to maintain the railway service that summer. Alas, by 6 October even *it* had to admit defeat. With little option left, Lady Hadyn Jones and her daughter, the sole surviving shareholders, were advised to seek an Abandonment Order, and thereafter sell off the Talyllyn Railway's meagre possessions for scrap. Thus, but for a miracle, the Talyllyn Railway story might have ended.

The miracle, which came from totally unexpected sources, is now, of course, part of railway preservation history. A group of enthusiasts, desperately unhappy at watching the death throes of yet another Welsh narrow gauge railway, sponsored a public meeting in Birmingham on 11 October 1950. As a result of their deliberations, the Talyllyn Railway Preservation Society was formed. Be not misled however, by the title; the aim of the Society was to see the railway carry on, *not* preserve it. Happily, Sir Hadyn Jones' executors, when approached, were most helpful, and Lady Jones went on to demonstrate her sympathy in even more practical fashion by transferring all her Talyllyn Railway shares to a new holding company. The railway, incidentally, was valued at £1,350, and it was agreed as a matter of honour that such a sum should be returned to Lady Jones should the new venture fail.

The subsequent story is a classic of railway preservation courage and enterprise. Suffice it to say that the Talyllyn Railway gradually emerged from decades of obscurity and near disaster to become a living legend amongst railway enthusiasts and general public alike. During the 30 years which have elapsed enormous improvements have been effected in the way of locomotives, carriages, track and stations. All, too, with voluntary labour. But, true to the Society's Charter, the original character of the old Talyllyn has never been surrendered. Steam still dominates, and the gauge remains at 2 ft 3 in. Long may it continue to do so!

The Talyllyn's passenger route has even been extended ³/₄ mile, along the old mineral extension to Nant Gwernol. Naturally, the Society's first preoccupation lay with restoring the passenger service between Tywyn and Abergynolwyn. Once this was accomplished, however, energies focused on extension, and on 22 May 1976 the TR's additional section to Nant Gwernol was opened for public use. A new station at Abergynolwyn was completed in 1969.

Today, the Talyllyn Railway carries some 170,000 passengers annually, as opposed to 15,628 in 1951, and occupies a high place in the hierarchy of Welsh narrow gauge concerns. This in itself is a fitting tribute to the enthusiasm and energies of Preservation Society members. Trains operate from Easter to the end of October, daily except October, and Christmas holidays are fully exploited. At Tywyn Wharf, the

An interesting peep inside Towyn Museum in August 1961. Dot, Beyer-built in 1887 for Horwich Works' 18-inch gauge circuit, dominates the foreground. On the right can be seen ex-Guinness Brewery 1 ft 10 in gauge 0–4–0T No 13. George Henry, the last-built of Penrhyn Railway's De Winton vertical-boilered 0–4–0Ts (1877), also appears on the left of the photograph. (F. C. Le Manquais)

time-honoured starting point for would-be Talyllyn passengers, a Narrow Gauge Railway Museum, established in 1956, still displays its unique, and beguiling, collection.

LOCOMOTIVES

Lowca Engine Works at Whitehaven, a venerable institution founded in 1763, began to manufacture locomotives in 1840, under the aegis of Tulk & Ley. In 1857 Fletcher Jennings took over, and concentration was placed entirely on the production of four- and six-coupled industrial tanks. *Tal-y-llyn* was, in fact, the firm's first venture into North Wales, and their first narrow gauge engine built with plate frames. Proud of their achievement, Lowca Works featured an engraving of *Tal-y-llyn* in its catalogue for many years to come. It was supported by a somewhat euphemistic caption — 'As supplied to many Welsh quarry railways'!

Typical of her times, *Tal-y-llyn*, it must be admitted, was less then sophisticated in design. Her saddle tanks held 275 gallons of water, but the coke bunkers which flanked the firebox could only accommodate 3 cwt of fuel. Above the firebox, meanwhile, sat a large dome, carrying Salter safety valves, which, when they blew, played freely on the enginemen. The footplate was completely exposed, and offered only a handrail as its sole safety measure. The working weight of 8½ tons was acceptable enough, even on the Tallylyn's rough track. But the engine's short wheelbase produced a rolling effect which could not be tolerated, and once *Dolgoch* appeared on the scene in January 1867 *Tal-y-llyn* was sent back to Whitehaven to have a pair of trailing wheels fitted. Ironically, *Dolgoch*'s wheelbase, half as long again at 6 ft 6 in, rode none too comfortably either, and was capable at times of playing havoc in its own peculiar way with the Talyllyn's lightly laid track.

Apart from being a well tank, which fact immediately reduced total water capacity to a mere 150 gallons, *Dolgoch* differed in many other respects from her sister engine. H. A. Fletcher had by now patented a design for 0–4–0 industrial tanks wherein all four wheels were driven; the aim was to provide maximum adhesion. Fletcher's Patent gear, with eccentrics fixed to the front axle, and eccentric rods facing backwards to drive Allan linkage, also tended to produce a longish wheelbase, and there can be little doubt that, had *Dolgoch* been employed on superior track, she would have been a smoothly riding engine. As it was, Talyllyn men traditionally preferred *Tal-y-llyn*, despite her faults. Rather ironically, though she herself was in dire mechanical straits, *Tal-y-llyn*'s last duty in 1945 was to sustain all traffic single-handedly while *Dolgoch* went off to Shrewsbury for complete overhaul.

Talyllyn locomotives never bore numbers until the railway was taken over by the Preservation Society, whence *Tal-y-llyn* and *Dolgoch* became Nos 1 and 2 respectively. No 2 carried on as before under the new regime, but had to be taken out of service in 1956; a further six years elapsed ere funds could be raised to

provide her with a new boiler. No 1, laid up at Pendre since 1946, was quite unfit for active service, and did not reappear on the scene until 1958. Meanwhile, by a fortuitous stroke of fortune, British Rail's Western Region had not yet disposed of the Corris Railway remains. Committee members promptly swung into action, and in March 1951 several precious items of salvage arrived at Towyn Wharf: two Corris locomotives, all remaining Corris wagons, and one brake van.

Thus, locos Nos 3 and 4 came early into new Talyllyn ownership, and were fittingly named *Sir Hadyn* and *Edward Thomas* after the little railway's former owner and Traffic Manager. A fifth loco, *Douglas,* an industrial 0–4–0T (Barclay 1431/1918) presented to the Society in 1953, was rather confusingly numbered 6 — for a Ruston & Hornsby four-wheeled diesel unit of 1940 vintage was already occupying No 5 as *Midlander.* The present No 7, dubbed *Irish Pete,* is another Barclay (0–4–2T 2263/1949), currently undergoing rebuild and transformation from 3-foot gauge. No 8 *Merseysider* is a Ruston & Hornsby diesel (476108/1964), and No 9 *Alf,* another diesel, hailed from Hunslet in 1950.

On the coaching side, Nos 1–5 are now rightly

Motive power at the reconstructed Towyn Wharf station. Dolgoch simmers quietly on the left, while 0–4–2ST No 4 Edward Thomas girds its loins on an adjacent Abergynolwyn train. Fitted with a Giesl ejector in the late 1950s, No 4 is hardly recognizable now as an ex-Corris Railway No 4, much less a Kerr Stuart product. (Steamchest)

occupied by Talyllyn's original four-wheeled stock of 1866–70. The Corris brake van occupies No 6, and a Penrhyn Railway-type van, built in 1963, No 7. Initial attempts to employ open 'toast-rack' coaches from the Penrhyn quarry railway proved unsuccessful; but their design was not forgotten when the TR introduced three four-wheelers (Nos 11–13) in the 1950s. Other TR types occupy Nos 8–10, 16, and 18–23. One ex-Corris third class bogie coach, built in 1898, now bears No 17, after laborious reconstruction from garden shed condition; and, somewhat similarly, two ex-Glyn Valley Tramway four-wheeled first class coaches were restored to active service as Nos 14 and 15. The TR's more modern stock, bogie coaches Nos 18–23, although built from 1965 onwards, contrive very subtly to supplement the authentic Welsh narrow gauge atmosphere which persists at Tywyn (modern Welsh spelling!) to this very day.

Name	Type	Date built	Maker	Maker's number	Remarks
Tal-y-llyn	0–4–0ST Later rebuilt as 0–4–2ST	1864	Fletcher Jennings	42	Taken out of service in 1945
Dolgoch	0–4–0WT	1866	,,	63	Sometimes known as *Pretoria*

FESTINIOG & BLAENAU RAILWAY

Opened: 30 May 1868
Closed: 13 April 1883
Gauge: 1 ft 11½ in

Despite its illustrious name, the Festiniog Railway of 1836 did not serve its namesake, for, of course, it terminated at Duffws, 3½ miles short of the village of Festiniog. This explains why a separate company, known as the Festiniog & Blaenau Railway, was formed in August 1862. It duly attained its objective on 30 May 1868, when a 3½-mile narrow gauge line opened for traffic between Blaenau-Ffestiniog and Manod Quarries. Purpose was twofold: to get slate down from the quarries, and, more importantly, to provide a passenger service for quarrymen and others travelling to and from work.

Four stations were provided: at Ffestiniog, Tyddyngwyn, Tany-Manod, and Duffws. The FR and F&BR stations at the last-named were a short distance from each other, but physical connection was established to allow slate trains to run through for transhipment at Minffordd, or shipment by sea from Portmadoc. It follows that, to all intents and purposes, the F&BR was a branch of the larger railway concern. Certainly the same gauge was chosen from the outset.

By 1878 the F&BR's passenger traffic had settled down to a regular pattern. Six trains ran each way on weekdays, and eight on Saturdays; no Sunday service, of course. The 3½-mile journey took 20 minutes.

Four carriages were devoted to three classes of passenger, and quarrymen, who provided the bulk of the traffic, were catered for by 19 open, and somewhat more plebian, vehicles. From the outset, the company owned two locomotives. Surprisingly, both they and F&BR rolling-stock deviated markedly from standard Festiniog Railway practice.

Only too soon, however, the Festiniog area began to attract standard gauge metals. The LNWR, already implicated since 1867, even contemplated joining the Festiniog Railway at Dinas by a 2-foot gauge extension. Then, thinking better of it, the 'Premier Line' compromised by opening a 4 ft 8½ in line into Blaenau itself on 22 July 1879. This brought more exchange sidings into use.

Another company, the Bala & Festiniog Railway, exploring the area under the GWR aegis, had a tougher physical route to carve. Nevertheless, in November 1882 it succeeded in justifying its title by opening a standard gauge line between Bala and Llan Ffestiniog. Tempting communication from there to Blaenau already existed in the form of Festiniog & Blaenau's narrow gauge track, and within a year the inevitable occurred — the F&BR was vested jointly in the GWR and the Bala & Festiniog as from 13 April 1883. A break of gauge was obviously highly undesirable, so track was swiftly torn up, and on 1 September 1883 the F&BR's erstwhile narrow gauge line re-opened as part of a standard gauge complex. Later, when the Bala & Festiniog was absorbed by the GWR, on 1 July 1910, everything passed into main line ownership.

LOCOMOTIVES

No	Type	Date built	Maker	Maker's number	Remarks
1	0–4–2ST	1868	Manning Wardle	259	Both locos sold. Never entered GWR stock.
2	,,	1868	,,	260	

High-chimneyed, and with a prominent dome surmounting a raised-top firebox, these little locos were quite different from anything that ever appeared on the Festiniog Railway. Front and rear weatherboards bent towards each other, and were joined by two horizontal bars over which a tarpaulin could be hung in rough weather. The engines were outside-cylindered, and coupled wheels were 2 feet in diameter. Standard coaches were four-wheeled, with back-to-back seating inside. The whole coach was lit by a single oil lamp in the roof, and both coaches and locomotives had central spring buffers, with coupling hook and chain below.

HENDRE-DDU TRAMWAY

Opened: 1868
Closed: 1940
Gauge: 1 ft 11 in

On railways, as elsewhere, big fish attract little fish. It only required the Cambrian Railways to open up communications in the Dovey Valley for a local magnate, Sir Edmund Buckley, to sponsor, and indeed finance, yet another standard gauge railway, the Mawddwy. It used as a starting point a junction with the Cambrian at Cemmes Road, near Aberangell village. From there it ran 7 miles north to Dinas Mawddwy, hoping to serve slate and mineral enterprises in this rich part of Wales. It figures that, once the Mawddwy Railway commenced operations on 1 October 1867, local quarry owners, seizing an opportunity to feed off a new arrival, combined forces to build a private tramway, 5 miles long, linking various slate quarries in the Afon Angell Valley with the Mawddwy Railway's station at Aberangell. The tramway, nominally gauged at 1 ft 11 in, was a rough and ready affair. Its gamble on relying on the Mawddwy Railway for an existence was equally unfortunate, for in later years the parent fish proved to be a financial disaster.

Primitively laid, with lightish rails spiked to slab wooden sleepers at yard intervals, the Hendre-ddu Tramway opened, it is known, hot on the heels of the Mawddwy; history fails to record the exact date. At Aberangell a wharf, wagon turntable and small yard sufficed to enable transhipment to be effected. The quarries served were 750-800 feet above sea level, so loaded wagons travelled to Aberangell by gravity, and empties were returned up the valley by horse-power. Whatever its demerits, life on the tramway proceeded uneventfully enough — until financial problems hit the Mawddwy Railway at the turn of the century. Mawddwy passenger services were consequently suspended from 17 April 1901, and remained so until 8 April 1908. By then, however, affairs had worsened, and all public services were abandoned.

During these long 7 years, local quarries had to pay extra heavy rates of carriage to sustain the working of one daily Mawddwy goods train through Aberangell. This, as can be imagined, had a lethal effect on output. One major quarry, failing to last the pace, closed, and its relevant Hendre-ddu branch metals were lifted during the First World War. By then, even the re-opening of the Mawddwy Railway under Cambrian auspices in 1911 could not stem the process of gradual deterioration in the slate industry. Production pottered on in post-war years, with an ex-War Department road tractor replacing horses as Hendre-ddu empty wagons were returned from Aberangell. Later still a Simplex petrol locomotive was purchased to perform the same function. By the Second World War, however, Hendre-ddu Quarry was deemed to be more useful as a storage dump for ammunition. The tramway was duly closed, and the rough road which soon replaced it testified to yet another victory for road transport.

The Mawddwy branch of British Railways, original source of the tramway's inspiration, fared little better; by April 1952 it, too, was dismantled.

GLYN VALLEY TRAMWAY

Opened: April 1873
Closed: 6 July 1935
Gauge: 2 ft 4¼ in

Far from witnessing the birth of the Principality's only roadside tramway, the Ceiriog Valley, an area rich in slate and granite, might conceivably have been breached initially by standard gauge metals; for passage of the Railway Construction Facilities Act in 1864 prompted the Ceriog Slate Quarries Company and other interested parties to seek Parliamentary approval for the construction of a roadside line, 13 miles long, down the valley from Glyn. Obviously, standard gauge metals were clearly in mind, as were working arrangements with both the GWR and Cambrian Railways. Accordingly, the Ellesmere & Glyn Valley Railway was incorporated in 1866, and five years were allowed for completion. Raising the authorized capital of £120,000, however, proved a major deterrent, and no progress was made over the next two years. By then, the Regulation of Railways Act had appeared on the Statute Book, and this legislation, with its first mention of 'light railways', offered opportunity for reflection. The Ellesmere Port project, ambitions duly trimmed, and now seeking only £25,000 in capital, was duly refreshed by a second Act in 1869. Within 12 months, however, the rules of the game were completely altered, when Westminster, anxious to encourage embryo experiments in street tramways, launched its Tramways Act of 1870.

Confronted now with the prospect of using public highways, as opposed to seeking and renting turnpike road facilities, Ellesmere's promoters acted with understandable opportunism. A Glyn Valley Tramway

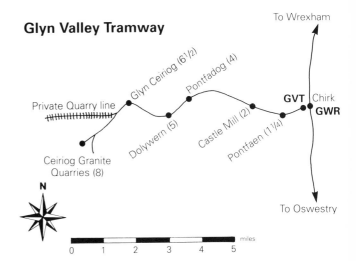

Glyn Valley Tramway

Act was successfully negotiated on 10 August 1870, the Ellesmere project was finally abandoned, and a newly incorporated Company, the Glyn Valley Tramway, took over such assets as remained. Its sponsors still aimed to build a tramway 8 miles long, linking the quarries with the Shropshire Union Canal. Parliament offered a wide choice of gauge between 2 feet and 4 ft 8½ in, and it was agreed that capital should not exceed £25,000. The only snag was that the GVT, though authorized to carry passengers, was forbidden to use other than horse-power in course of its operations.

But for major financial assistance from the Canal Company, behind whom lurked the LNWR, anxious to compete with the GWR and the Cambrian, it is highly likely that the GVT, too, would have fallen by the wayside. Capital, it found, was extremely difficult to raise; and even when, as a measure of desperation, estimated construction costs of £15,000 were pared back to £10,000, an ultimate capital subscription of £5,000 from the Canal Company was still required to get things moving. Still, once construction started in June 1872, work went well and the tramway was completed in well under a year.

So, in April 1873, goods and passenger services commenced between the village of Glyn Ceiriog and a canal wharf south of Chirk. Flat-bottomed 21 lb rail, spiked direct to sleepers, was used throughout, and, in accordance with Parliamentary tramway requirements, rail tops were kept flush with the road surface. Under the Act certain tolls were allowed to be charged. These ranged from a maximum permissible 3d-6d a mile per ton on various freight traffics to 2d a mile for passengers. Any individual carefree enough to rent a horse and car on the tramway could also do so for up to 1s 3d per mile!

Slate, of course, formed the bulk of the Glyn's traffic, and, for much of that, journeys terminated at Pontfaen, a mile short of the canal wharf. There it was unloaded on to carts and humped steeply uphill to Chirk for further dispatch by GWR. In traditional Welsh tramroad fashion, wagons descended from Glyn to Pontfaen by gravity; and, reminiscent of early days on the Festiniog, horses coasted down by dandy car at the rear of each train, ready to disembark and pull empties back to Glyn. East of Pontfaen fresh horses stood by to tackle the heavily graded mile-long section which led to Canal Wharf.

It all sounds rather industrious. In truth, the GVT only ever employed a handful of horses, and the tramway's entire passenger stock consisted of two four-wheeled carriages — one glazed, the other open-sided. Few details of GVT wagon stock, probably some 100 assorted vehicles, are known. But they, too, must have been primitive in the extreme. Perhaps the most curious factor of all was the GVT's choice of 2 ft 4¼ in gauge. Apart from being a neat division of standard gauge, its origin remains steeped in mystery.

Yet, for all its limitations, the arrival of the tramway was warmly greeted by local residents. After all, in Wales, as in Ireland, any railway development which offered hard-pressed areas even a glimpse of prosperity was thrice welcome. Alas, hopes were soon dashed, for within a year or two it became patently obvious that, despite appearances, the GVT was not paying its way. Even during its first full year, a net loss of £466 was sustained. Nor were reasons far to seek. Clumsiness apart, transhipment arrangements at Pontfaen were prohibitively expensive; and clearly only direct rail communication with the GWR at Chirk station could ever break this deadlock. Secondly, the Festiniog Railway's spectacular success with narrow gauge steam locomotion had demolished once and for all the viability of horse-drawn tramways. A classic Welsh epoch was coming to an end.

Annual losses continued to mount, and the Canal Company held on grimly to its part-interest in the tramway, hoping, no doubt, for better days. Indeed, a flicker of optimism seemed justified in 1875, when a separate company opened up a new granite quarry at Hendre, much higher up the valley. A traffic in granite setts did, in fact, develop. This granite, however, had to be carted 3 miles to meet the tramway at Glyn Ceirog, and, even with the assistance of gravity as far as Pontfaen, transport thereafter up that formidable gradient to Canal Wharf posed enormous problems. Ironically, too, just as granite traffic chose to expand on the GVT, so the slate industry lurched into decline. Almost in desperation, the GVT initiated another Bill in 1878, requesting, amongst other things, power to work the tramway with steam locomotives.

Westminster, in its wisdom, permitted the bulk of the second Glyn Valley Tramway Act to proceed, but declined to sanction its most important provision — that of introducing steam traction. Looking back now, one cannot really fault Parliament, for contemporary steam locomotives could never have handled that gradient at Pontfaen.

Then, a year later, came a national Act authorizing the use of mechanical traction on street tramways. This looked interesting, and the Canal Company, though tired of annual losses and almost continuous

The year is 1901, and Ceiriog Granite Co's 0–4–0T, a Lilleshall product of 1880, shunts a few wagons of granite on the Glyn Valley's two-mile-long mineral extension. Once mineral traffic declined in post-First World War years, the little tank lay idle for 20 years before being broken up in 1946. (Author's Collection)

acrimony, considered matters afresh. Nothing happened, however, until the GVT, taking the bit in its teeth, offered to buy the Canal Company's tramway shares outright for £2,000. Ruefully swallowing initial construction investment of £4,630 and subsequent running losses of £7,000, the Canal Company agreed. Transfer of management took place on 31 August 1881. The £2,000 paid by the GVT came, in fact, from the Glyn Ceirog Granite Co Ltd, owners of the quarry at Hendre, and it was at this stage that the name of Henry Dennis, a Director of the granite company, began to loom large in GVT fortunes.

During that first year of GVT management, the tramway appeared to prosper. It even showed a small profit. The slate quarries had closed, but carriage of 10,000 tons of granite more than compensated. Then, by 1882, the basic inefficiences of the horse-drawn tramway ensured once more the loss of much of this profitable traffic. Tentative overtures that the Canal Company might care to resume responsibility were firmly rebuffed, and in early 1885, their hands forced by events, the GVT Directorate prepared a Bill which sought conversion to steam traction.

The Bill, which saw Parliamentary light of day later that year, emerged under an already familiar title: the Glyn Valley Tramway Act. Nevertheless, it cleared the way for radical reconstruction. A 2-mile extension, designed to make direct contact with Hendre and Pandy granite quarries, was authorized at the Glyn end of the tramway. More important still, and much to the relief of all concerned, that vexatious gradient east of Pontfaen was finally abandoned in favour of a new route which led past the GWR's Chirk station before ending 3/4 mile further along, at Blackpark Canal Basin. With the use of steam now also sanctioned, a totally confident GVT Board got to work producing estimates. The final verdict was that rebuilding the tramway, complete with Chirk and Hendre extensions, plus the purchase of two loco-

motives and new rolling-stock, would cost £18,000. Total authorized capital was correspondingly hoisted to £38,000, and, such was local optimism, the additional funds were found by May 1886.

Work started at Pontfaen early the following year. Henry Dennis, by now a GVT Director, happened also to serve on the Board of the Snailbeach District Railway; and some measure of the latter concern's current inactivity can be gauged from his volunteered information that both Snailbeach locomotives were, in fact, available for hire. Thus, one morning early in spring, those on duty at Pontfaen witnessed an encouraging sight when two small saddle tanks, *Belmont* and *Fernhill*, arrived by road from Chirk station. Their advent was to have interesting consequences, for, though both locos were of 2 ft 4 in gauge, their eventual employment on the GVT's sharp curves so spread the metals that the GVT's 'unofficial' gauge widened to 2 ft 4½ in! Still, work proceeded apace, and the new GVT line, now 9 miles long, was completed in time to take steam-hauled mineral traffic by July 1888. Presumably either, or both, of the Snailbeach locos performed the honours, for *Sir Theodore*, the GVT's first locomotive, was not delivered until 17 October of that year. A product of Beyer Peacock's Manchester works, it was joined by sister engine *Dennis* in April 1889. Hence, one presumes, the Snailbeach locos returned to base.

The GVT's enterprise was rewarded by a substantial increase in granite tonnage over the next three years; it even induced the introduction of slate mining in the area for the first time, in 1890. Back in the gloomy days the GVT had abandoned the passenger service between Pontfaen and Glyn. Now, public demand was such that restoration became inevitable. Two terminal stations, at Chirk and Glyn Ceiriog, and two intermediate stations, were therefore built, and passenger traffic recommenced on 15 March 1891. At Chirk, apart from constructing a 60-yard platform, with

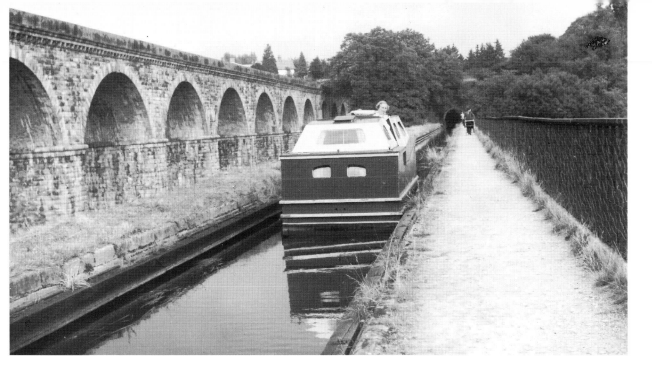

appropriate buildings, adjacent to that of the GWR, the tramway allowed itself the luxury of carriage shed, workshops, sidings, turntable and, most important of all, an inclined ramp to facilitate granite transhipment.

It follows that the opening day of the new steam-hauled passenger service was one of great rejoicing in the Ceiriog Valley. What had once been a derisory daily service of three cars each way now blossomed into a public utility of four trains a day in each direction, excluding, of course, Sundays. An extra down train ran on Wednesdays and Saturdays to meet local market demands. The 6-mile journey usually took 40 minutes. Next, additional trains were introduced in summer to encourage tourist traffic, and one round excursion developed to such an extent as to almost rival the Corris and Talyllyn Railways' 'Grand Tour' in popularity. Participants in this pleasant exercise travelled from Llangollen by horse-drawn barge down the Shropshire Union Canal, and, disembarking at Pontcysyllte aqueduct, walked less than 100 yards to Chirk station. There the GVT transported them as steam-hauled passengers up the valley to Glyn Ceiriog, after which the day-trippers found their own way back to Llangollen by road, or cross-country.

Parties of ten or more were given special terms.

Typical of Welsh narrow gauge practice, most GVT trains were 'mixed', and usually consisted of two or four coaches hitched next to the engine, with a tail load of wagons and brakes trailing behind. As GVT locos had cabs at the leading end only, the obligatory principle of working cab-first was observed by turning the engines at Chirk or Glyn at the conclusion of each journey. Increased traffic demands soon warranted provision of additional motive power, and a third locomotive, *Glyn*, joined the ranks in May 1892, again from Beyer Peacock.

In 1879, when Parliament first allowed mechanical traction to be used on street tramways, it imposed a 10 mph speed limit on all such locos. Glyn's Act of 1885, couched in even more pessimistic terms, specified an even lower speed limit of 8 mph. Despite that handicap, however, the GVT's three tram locos contrived to handle all traffic competently enough for nearly half a century. Only one service interruption occurred — during the General Strike of 1926. Figures for the new GVT's first five full working years alone reveal the advantages which accrued from steam working:

	1889	1890	1891	1892	1893
Paid-up capital	£31,663	£43,524	£53,970	£61,472	£63,972
Traffic returns					
Passengers	–	–	13,020	15,623	20,907
Minerals & goods (tons)	–	20,327	28,039	49,022	45,132
Train miles	10,134	20,325	18,149	24,988	27,439
Stock					
Locomotives	2	2	2	3	3
Coaches	3	3	4	7	12
Wagons	135	158	203	213	231
Gross profit (loss)	£230	(£616)	£1,338	£1,940	£1,544

Despite its habit of working 'two engines in steam', the GVT, taking advantage of its status as a street tramway, never employed signals or train staff control. Fortunately, no serious accident occurred to cast retrospective doubts on this potentially dangerous procedure, and life amongst GVT staff moved on its gentle way. The tramway was to reach its peak during the two decades which led up to the First World War, by which time it had acquired its maximum holding of 14 coaches and 258 other vehicles. Granite accounted for 90 per cent of an average annual freight tonnage of about 52,000 tons. Passenger traffic, though much more amenable to fluctuation, moved steadily towards 40,000.

Post-war years, however, brought a decline in mineral traffic, and losses were consistently recorded during the years 1919 to 1926, all of which made more difficult the second-hand purchase of a fourth locomotive in 1921. The latter, an ex-WD Baldwin-built 4–6–0T, reconditioned at Manchester, was only obtained by recourse to a temporary loan of £2,000 by Beyer Peacock. Over the next ten years the GVT made sufficient profit to repay Beyer. Then, by 1932, annual losses recurred, and granite traffic plummeted to 21,000 tons. Traffic in road chippings from Hendre Quarry, once GVT's sole prerogative, had already been sorely eroded when motor lorries gained access to the quarry, and the felony was compounded in 1932, when a motor bus service began to ply the Ceiriog Valley.

Reaction to bus competition came in inevitable form, when GVT passenger services were abandoned from 1 April 1933. Such minor economies as this achieved were hopefully garnered in an attempt to combat the greater menace of lorries. But, of course, the latter's greater flexibility offered no hope to the sadly harassed steam tramway. Losses were again registered in the years 1933-34, and the GVT Directors, facing no other option, assumed the melancholy task of closing the tramway to all traffic on 6 July 1935.

In October of that year, the GVT's once-thriving business was wound up; and within 12 months rails were lifted, locomotives were broken up *in situ* at Chirk, and the metal content of coaches and wagons went for scrap. A quantity of GVT rail went to Gresford Colliery, Wrexham, of 1935 disaster fame, to be laid in new underground workings; and, almost miraculously, two coach bodies survived long enough alongside Chirk vicarage's lawn to be rescued by Talyllyn Railway enthusiasts. Lovingly restored, they resumed public service in 1958 as Talyllyn first class coaches, with their old GVT monogram proudly displayed on their sides.

LOCOMOTIVES

No	Name	Type	Date built	Maker	Maker's number	Remarks
(1)	*Dennis*	0–4–2ST	1888	Beyer Peacock	2970	Despite Tramway Act
(2)	*Sir Theodore*	,,	1888	,,	2969	regulations, Nos 1, 2 and 4
3	*Glyn*	,,	1892	,,	3500	did not carry numbers
(4)		4–6–0T	1917	Baldwin	45221	

Although the design specification for GVT locomotives was clearly spelled out in the Glyn Valley Tramway Act of 1885, its tenor emerged unmistakably from the Use of Mechanical Power on Tramways Act 1879. This legislation required all street tramway locos to observe a speed limit of 10 mph, function as noiselessly as possible, emit neither fire, steam nor smoke, and ensure public protection from all moving parts. It was a tall order. Yet quite a number of enterprising British locomotive manufacturers set to with a will, and by 1896 some 560 steam tramway locos were functioning throughout the British Isles. Ironically, electric tramways took over in urban areas five years later, and the era of the steam tram came rapidly to an end.

Beyer Peacock, early practitioners in the field, had already built nearly 100 steam trams by the time the GVT Directors approached them in 1888. The two Beyer promptly supplied at a cost of £1,200 each turned out to be a highly intriguing amalgam of street tram and railway locomotive. Nominally 0–4–2 side tanks, and weighing 14½ tons, they were destined to operate as 2–4–0Ts for the rest of their lives, for regulations demanding a clear view for the driver required them to work cab-first. Initially they were coke-fired, and fitted with condensing apparatus; coal was substituted in later years, and the use of condensers was also abandoned on nuisance grounds. In the interests of public safety the locos were fitted with both whistle and bell. Governors, meanwhile, connected to a rather crude form of speedometer ensured that steam was shut off should a driver be reckless enough to exceed the GVT's mandatory 8 mph speed limit. Fortunately, accidents on the GVT were few in number, and rarely emanated from human error.

None the less, despite all these inhibitions, the

general appearance of GVT locos was less boxlike than that of many other steam trams, for, from the frame upwards, they strove hard to resemble conventional railway engines. Long, uncompromising side tanks certainly concealed the boiler, but a slim Beyer-type chimney which soared above, and a flat-topped steam dome surmounted by Ramsbottom safety valves, regulator, injector and whistle, offered an observer every assurance that he was travelling on a *railway*. Below the waist-line, wheels and motion were completely cased in by metal skirting, wherein three hinged plates provided necessary access for oiling and inspection. Two more doors could be found on the tank side, positioned at smokebox and cab level, and although coal was kept in a bunker at the rear of the cab, this offered no impediment to two rear windows which guaranteed the driver his vital clear view. On the first two Beyers the chimney side of the cab was cut away, but the arrangement proved inadequate in inclement weather, and portable screens were soon fitted. With this lesson learnt, *Glyn*, the GVT's third loco, was turned out with a totally enclosed cab. Its frame was also lengthened by one foot to afford enginemen more room.

In the early days both locos and carriages, reflecting company pride, were beautifully turned out in green livery, and the initials 'GVT' were prominently supported by red and gold leaf lining. Then, latterly, locos reverted to a more sober black, and flamboyant crests on the coach sides vanished in favour of simple lettering. When summer passenger traffic reached its peak, wagons, fitted with wooden forms, were often pressed into employment. No one, least of all any younger fry present, seemed to mind! One crossing loop at Pontfadog, where drivers waited as required, seemed to take reasonably good care of the hazards which attended 'two engines in steam' working.

All in all, apart from the year 1901, when healthily developing traffic warranted an order for four new coaches and 20 mineral wagons, the GVT contented itself with stock in hand. By 1921, however, the three tram locos were showing signs of wear, and to permit a modicum of withdrawal for overhaul purposes even the GVT's prudent management was obliged to think of purchasing a fourth locomotive. The answer came in totally unexpected form, as it did to other light railways in the UK, when the Ministry of Munitions exposed a number of ex-WD Baldwin-built side tanks on the second-hand market. Originally 60cm in gauge, the 4–6–0T which the GVT elected to buy was thoroughly overhauled and re-gauged by Beyer Peacock, and, at a cost of £3,000 for purchase and conversion, it became nominally No 4 in GVT stock. It never, in fact, bore either name or number, and was usually referred to at Chirk as the 'Baldwin'.

During reconstruction, Beyer had softened the Baldwin's rather harsh utilitarian American appearance by capping the stove-pipe chimney, and removing two large acetylene lamps. Then, with the open cab also closed at the rear, it was painted black, with the legend 'GVT' writ large on its side tanks. None too popular with GVT men, for, like her sisters elsewhere, she rode roughly and steamed unreliably, the Baldwin was rarely entrusted with passenger traffic. She also worked facing Glyn Ceiriog, for her 12 ft 4 in wheelbase could not be accommodated on GVT turntables. That said, the little loco contrived to put in 15 years' hard work ere she and the others met their end. At least the Baldwin's presence enabled the GVT to pursue its 'two engines in steam' policy while one engine was being washed out, and the other repaired.

When the tramway closed finally, and without ceremony, on 6 July 1935, all four locomotives found refuge at Chirk shed, and there they stayed, for all demolition was carried out by road lorries. Once the rails were lifted, the Wrexham firm responsible turned its attention to the locos, and in August 1936 the first victim, *Glyn*, submitted to the breakers' torch. Little time elapsed ere the other three followed. So, after nearly 60 eventful years, ended Wales' initial venture into the world of passenger steam tramways. Little remains today to remind us that such a bold concept ever existed.

NORTH WALES NARROW GAUGE RAILWAYS COMPANY

Opened: 21 May 1877
Acquired by Welsh Highland Railway: 1 Jan 1922
Gauge: 1 ft 11½ in

The precedents which anticipated incorporation of the above company by an Act dated 6 August 1872 have already been described in the section on the Croesor Tramway. At that time the NWNGR's Board included such prominent railwaymen as Livingston Thompson, and C. E. Spooner, both of Festiniog fame; yet the General Undertaking they proposed, of building 23 miles of narrow gauge track north from the Croesor Tramway to Bettws-y-Coed via Beddgelert, had to be abandoned by subsequent Act of 13 July 1876. A secondary proposal, called the Moel Tryfan Undertaking, was completed, however, in 1881. This Undertaking involved 12¾ miles of track which ran east from Dinas. The first 5½ miles took the railway to Tryfan Junction; then it moved off towards Bryngwyn, where a series of branches fanned out towards important slate quarries. The remaining 7¼ miles reached east and south from Tryfan Junction to terminate at Rhyd-ddu (later renamed

South Snowdon) in the parish of Beddgelert.

Although the authorized capital of the Moel Tryfan Undertaking was set at £66,000 — a much more modest target than the General Undertaking's £150,000 — financial difficulties still inhibited speedy completion, and the project was not implemented until May 1881. The stages tell their own story. The Bryngwyn branch and the section from Tryfan Junction to Quellyn were opened for goods and mineral traffic on 21 May 1877; passenger traffic followed on 15 August. A further ¾-mile extension to Snowdon Ranger came into service on 1 June 1878. But nearly three years elapsed before the last 2 miles to Rhyddu were operational. In the meantime, such was the depressive state of the slate industry, and so ominous were NWNGR's operating losses, that the High Court had already seen fit to appoint a Receiver on 13 December 1878. Rather belatedly, under an Act dated 31 July 1885, the NWNGR obtained authority to extend its line from Dinas to Caernarvon Harbour. Work on this scheme, however, was never tackled, and the powers were allowed to lapse. At this stage the NWNGR owned three locomotives, but little else.

The next significant turn in NWNGR affairs occurred when the Portmadoc, Beddgelert & South Snowdon Railway Company was formed on 17 August 1901. The very words 'Portmadoc' and 'Beddgelert' rekindled memories of former General Undertaking aspirations, and, hardly surprisingly, the two companies found themselves working in collusion within a year or two. Various plans, hatched jointly, were, however, foiled by legal complications. Meanwhile, the PB&SSR's link between Portmadoc and Croesor Junction continued as a horse-drawn goods line and, but for the fact that passenger traffic on the Bryngwyn branch ceased at the end of 1913, life on the NWNGR continued as before. Three trains ran daily in each direction between Dinas and Rhyddu, until ultimately withdrawn in October 1916. Any plans to link the companies and provide a through route between Portmadoc and Dinas were thwarted by the outbreak of war in 1914.

War or no war, the concept of through running had, never the less, captured the imagination of several local authorities, and once the conclusion of hostilities permitted the resumption of rational thinking the matter was promptly revived. A public inquiry held by the Light Railway Commissioners at Caernarvon on 18 October 1921 established that a joint committee, formed in 1914 under the title 'Portmadoc, Beddgelert & Caernarvon Light Railway Committee', still yearned to see through running established. The outcome was that the Committee applied afresh, in November 1921, for an Order to exercise sundry powers, both old and new. So, on 30 March 1922, under the auspices of the Light Railways Acts of 1896 and 1912, a new company, the Welsh Highland (Light Railway) Company, was born. By nature of its constitution, the Welsh Highland acquired, as from 1 January 1922, all property and powers which formerly belonged to both the NWNGR and the PB&SSR.

Such was Festiniog Railway influence in the 1870s that the NWNGR's first two locomotives were Fairlie singles. Moel Tryfan, *named after a local mountain, is seen here at Dinas at the turn of the century. A Westinghouse brake has subsequently been fitted, hence the air reservoir cylinder under the cab.* (Steamchest)

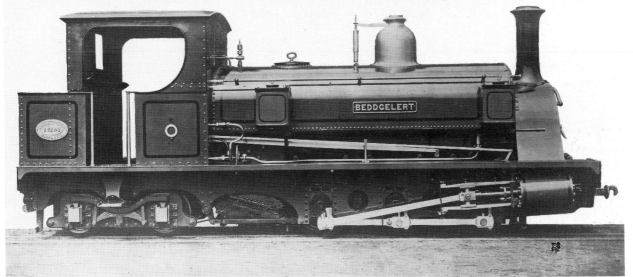

Above Beddgelert, *the 0–6–4ST Hunslet built in 1878 for service on the heavily graded Bryngwyn mineral branch, looks husky enough in this Works photograph. In the event it only lasted until 1906, when the even tougher Prairie tank, Russell, took its place.* (Steamchest)

Right Russell, *seen here at Dinas Junction circa 1910, was still outside-framed, though the provision of Walschaerts valve gear, longer sidetanks and increased coal capacity made the 20-ton locomotive look a much more modern proposition. Gowrie, the loco behind, was, despite appearances, even heavier. A 1908 reversion to the Fairlie single boiler type, and probably the last of the species to be built, it was sold into Government service two years after NWNGR services ceased in October 1916.* (Author's Collection)

LOCOMOTIVES

Name	Type	Date built	Makers	Maker's number	Remarks
Snowdon Ranger	0–6–4T	1875	Vulcan	739	Withdrawn in 1917
Moel Tryfan	,,	1875	,,	738	
Beddgelert	0–6–4ST	1878	Hunslet	206	Scrapped in 1906
Russell	2–6–2T	1906	,,	901	
Gowrie	0–6–4T	1908	,,	979	Sold in 1915

The NWNGR's first two locomotives, supplied to work the main line when it opened in 1877, offered clear indication of C. E. Spooner and Festiniog Railway influence. Fairlie engines, with single boilers and motor bogies, they bore a striking resemblance to a four-coupled design introduced by G. P. Spooner on the Festiniog a year later. At 14½ tons, though, they weighed 5½ tons less. After a quarter of a century of hard main line work, both NWNGR locos were over-hauled by Davies & Metcalf of Stockport. It was possibly at this stage that Westinghouse brakes were fitted. Six years later, in 1908, *Snowdon Ranger* was back at Hunslet Engine Co for repair, and by 1917 both locos were adjudged to be in a badly run down condition. The NWNGR management's response was both frugal and practical. *Snowdon Ranger's* frames, the sounder of the two, were removed and fitted under *Moel Tryfan*. The resultant hybrid engine worked on under the latter name, and such material as remained was scrapped.

Beddgelert (ambitious name!), built for work on the Bryngwyn branch, was an altogether tougher proposition. Outside framed, rugged in appearance, and weighing all of 17 tons in working order, the 0–6–4ST boasted a neatly flared chimney, as opposed to previous stove-pipes. In recognition, too, of the continuous gradients she would have to face, her boiler was slightly inclined, to maintain water level. One can only presume that the resultant wear and tear of mineral branch working was the cause of her rather premature withdrawal in 1906. A brand new 2–6–2 tank, again from Hunslet, took her place.

Russell introduced startling new elements into NWNGR locomotive practice. Gone was the Fairlie concept, gone was the old-fashioned saddle tank of *Beddgelert*; and in their place came a modern powerful-looking 2–6–2T, still outside framed, but with Walschaerts valve gear, long side tanks, and an overall weight of 20 tons. *Russell*, in fact, was to prove the toughest of the lot, and lived to be auctioned off in June 1942.

The NWNGR's last acquisition came two years later, when the cannibalization of *Snowdon Ranger* reduced motive power to an unacceptably low level. No doubt the fact that *Gowrie* was destined to work the main line induced a reversion to the Fairlie single-boiler type; though, in this instance, the new locomotive, built by Hunslet, differed considerably in appearance from her earlier Vulcan Foundry sisters. The boiler was longer and larger, water capacity was increased to 440 gallons, and coal capacity was more than doubled at 1 ton 2 cwt. Consequently, *Gowrie* outweighed her predecessors by 4 tons. It follows too that when NWNGR passenger services closed down in October 1916 *Gowrie* was still in good enough condition to be sold to the British Government a year or so later. Thus, only two NWNGR locos, *Moel Tryfan* and *Russell*, survived to enter Welsh Highland Railway ownership when the latter company was formed in 1922.

WELSH HIGHLAND (LIGHT RAILWAY) COMPANY

Opened: 1 June 1923
Closed: 1 June 1937
Gauge: 1 ft 11½ in

As from 1 January 1922, when it assumed responsibility for the combined affairs of the PB&SSR and the NWNGR, the Welsh Highland Railway management appeared to act in a brisk and businesslike manner.

Authorized capital was fixed at £120,000, but only £90,000 of that was issued, taking the form of fully paid shares which were handed out in lieu of purchase money. The NWNGR received £40,000, and the PB&SSR £50,000. The only snag was that as the years progressed neither party ever received a penny in dividends! The Ministry of Transport, meanwhile, subscribed £35,774 in Debenture Stock, and various local authorities advanced £29,000 in similar fashion. Again, the WHR's total Debenture Stock of £84,774 proved to be a bad investment, for interest payments lapsed after 31 December 1923.

This uneasy financial behaviour was to prove a fair reflection of the parlous railway career which lay ahead. Even then, initial action appeared convincing when, in March 1922, work began on the task of reconditioning NWNGR metals. The section from Dinas to South Snowdon was re-opened to passenger traffic on 31 July 1923, but the Bryngwyn branch, though also restored, continued to carry mineral traffic only. A new 8¾-mile section of track was also forged between South Snowdon and Croesor Junction, and, once reconditioning of the former PB&SSR line was completed, through passenger trains between Dinas and Portmadoc became feasible from 1 June 1923. The WHR's method of establishing a firm presence in Portmadoc was interesting. It built a station, called Portmadoc (New), immediately south of the GWR's Cambrian main line, and gained access thereto by breaching the GWR line by a cast manganese steel crossing. Then, from New station the WHR line carried on to Portmadoc Harbour. The Festiniog Railway collaborated nobly by building a new line through Portmadoc streets, so that the two railways might be linked. Thereafter, nearly all Festiniog trains ran to and from New station.

Another problem was that of motive power. *Russell* and *Moel Tryfan*, the only two locos inherited from the NWNGR, were too high to traverse tunnels on the Festiniog, so both had to attend Boston Lodge works to have their chimneys cut down. *Moel*'s cab also required lowering. During their temporary absence, Festiniog locos were left to maintain WHR services. *Moel Tryfan*, when she returned from surgery, presented quite an elegant Festiniog appearance; but *Russell*'s original symmetry had gone for ever. Meanwhile, work on the Bryngwyn branch demanded an additional locomotive, and an ex-Government Baldwin 4–6–0 tank was obtained. Never considered reliable enough to handle passenger trains with any great consistency, the Baldwin, No 590, remained a carrier of goods for most of its life. A similar shortage of rolling-stock was met by the purchase of six Government surplus open cars, and, fitted with improvized roofs, these, plus a few loaned vehicles from the Festiniog, saw the Welsh Highland on its unsteady way.

From inception, however, expenditure on the WHR persisted in exceeding income. Steady encroachment by road transport as the 1900s progressed also ensured that, where tourist traffic was concerned, the WHR was fighting a losing battle. It was, in fact, in the midst of this particular trauma that the ubiquitous Lt Col H. F. Stephens arrived on the scene, having been appointed Receiver to the WHR in March 1927. Already Chairman and Locomotive Superintendent of the Festiniog Railway, Stephens had every reason to exert his time-honoured flair for railway economies, and promptly set to work. One of his first actions was to install a small halt at Portmadoc immediately *north* of the GWR crossing. Passengers from Dinas and Beddgelert were then obliged to alight at the halt, and cross the GWR line by foot to reach Portmadoc (New) station, where the Festiniog provided a shuttle service to and from Portmadoc Harbour. This tactic spared the WHR from making payments towards maintaining and manning the GWR crossing!

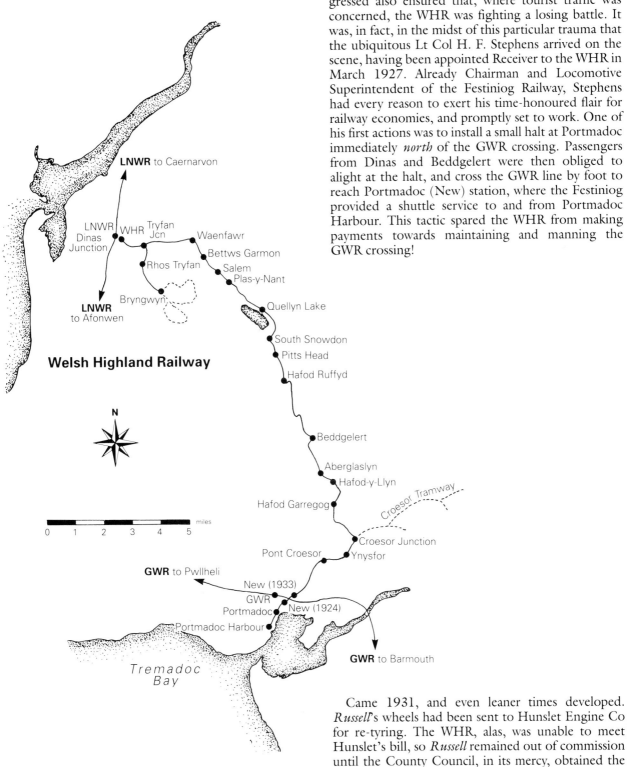

Welsh Highland Railway

Came 1931, and even leaner times developed. *Russell*'s wheels had been sent to Hunslet Engine Co for re-tyring. The WHR, alas, was unable to meet Hunslet's bill, so *Russell* remained out of commission until the County Council, in its mercy, obtained the locomotive's release. That year *Moel Tryfan* worked

The Welsh Highland's Baldwin 4–6–0T No 590 was rarely entrusted with passenger traffic, but it was caught on one such occasion on 11 August 1934. The scene is the WHR's second Portmadoc (New) Station, a mile from Portmadoc Harbour. This extremely elementary halt was created by Colonel Stephens around 1930 as an alternative to sharing costs of maintaining the GWR/ WHR crossover in the left background. (F. C. Le Manquais)

Russell, with boiler mountings cut down to accommodate passage through Festiniog Railway tunnels, rests at Beddgelert on 11 August 1934 after bringing in a train from Dinas, 13 miles distant. At this 'frontier' post, Baldwin 4–6–0T No 590 waits at the head of an adjacent train, ready to carry 'transfer' passengers on to Portmadoc (New) Station. Note (left) the breezy coach livery introduced by Colonel Stephens. In these days a passenger with two hours to spare could travel the 21¼ miles between Dinas Junction and Portmadoc for an excursion fare of 2 shillings (10p). Observation car seats cost 6d extra. (F. C. Le Manquais)

Another dream ends. Shortly after all West Highland Light Railway traffic came to a close on 1 June 1937, 2–6–2T Russell (Hunslet 901/1906) ventured up the line to Beddgelert to collect salvageable material. Thereafter, it and Baldwin No 590 mouldered in increasingly desolate circumstances inside a shed at Dinas. The two locomotives are seen here, quite derelict with sundry wagon stock, shortly before the Ministry of Supply requisitioned the lot for £1,280 in 1941. Fortunately, Russell, auctioned at Dinas the following year, escaped extinction, and moved on to new industrial pastures. Later employed in Dorset from 1948, the loco was preserved by Birmingham Locomotive Club in 1955, and has since been restored to use on the new Welsh Highland Light Railway's 60cm gauge metals. (Photomatic Ltd)

alone, handling a skeleton thrice-weekly passenger service. On other weekdays goods trains were run, with Baldwin No 590 at their head. Resources could not have been stretched more tightly.

By November 1933 the local authorities, saddled with worthless WHR Debentures, had had enough. They urged closure of the line. Portmadoc UDC, however, clinging to hopes that some of the local quarries might work again, demurred. In the event this point of view won the day; but subsequent invitations to both the LMS and GWR to take over the Welsh Highland were politely, but firmly, declined. During this period of profound uncertainty the WHR soldiered on, with goods and mineral traffic working the year round, and passenger traffic closing between October and June. Local fears grew that passenger services might not resume in June 1934, and, as pressure mounted, long and rather desperate negotiations began with Festiniog Railway management. Ultimately came the result: the WHR was leased to the Festiniog, as from 1 July 1934, at a nominal rent of £1 for the first six months and a proportion of traffic receipts thereafter.

Subsequent events have already been referred to in the section on the Festiniog Railway. Formerly, with the sole exception of No 590, WHR locomotives had retained the NWNGR's Midland red livery. Now, under Festiniog management, *Russell* was repainted light green, and the Baldwin exchanged funereal black for Midland red. The dark green of the WHR coaches vanished too, in exchange for a positive rainbow selection of colours. Stations were given a facelift; that at Nantmor was renamed Aberglaslyn, and the refreshment room at Dinas was re-opened, albeit under Snowdon Mountain Tramroad management.

Yet, for all the gallant efforts of Colonel Stephens and others, WHR affairs could not, and would not, prosper. Ominously, passenger traffic in 1935 did not resume until 8 July, and although it survived to re-open in the summer of 1936, it finally lumbered to a stop on 19 September of that year. The Festiniog management, acknowledging the futility of its task, was ready to negotiate surrender of its lease. Next, goods and mineral traffic ceased on 1 June 1937. Three weeks later, *Russell* was given the melancholy chore of running between Beddgelert and Portmadoc to collect the Baldwin tank and such wagons as lay *en route*.

So, for the next few years *Russell*, No 590, eight passenger coaches and 104 wagons mouldered uselessly at Dinas. The die was finally cast when, in 1941, the Ministry of Supply requisitioned the lot as salvage to help the war effort. The sum of £1,280 was paid in compensation, and rolling-stock and permanent way were purchased by George Cohen & Sons Co Ltd. Track on the Dinas–Tryfan Junction–Bryngwyn sections was lifted by May 1942. Thence, carriages were auctioned at Dinas, and Baldwin No 590 was cut up on the spot. Only *Russell* and *Moel Tryfan* escaped. One final indignity came, when a compulsory winding-up Order was made on 7 February 1944.

LOCOMOTIVES

No 590, the Baldwin 4–6–0 tank, was the only locomotive bought by Welsh Highland management; and, bearing Maker's No 45172, its performance had the same limitations as those purchased by other British light railways. Mention might be made, however, of an 0–6–0 diesel loco which ran experimentally on WHR metals during 1928. Built by Kerr Stuart, this 60 hp machine (Maker's No 4415) was a first design by Mr K. W. Willars, and it employed a McLaren Benz engine. Little is known of its activities on the WHR, and by 1929 it had passed to a firm of Lancashire contractors. Later still, it was regauged to 3 feet, and passed into Irish ownership via the Castlederg & Victoria Bridge Tramway. Thence it was repurchased by the makers and sold for service in Mauritius.

Russell's fate was rather less traumatic. Auctioned at Dinas in 1942, it put in useful work at the Hook Norton ironstone mines of the Brymbo Steel Company, and subsequently moved to Pike Bros/Fayle & Co's mineral line near Corfe Castle, Dorset. In 1954, however, *Russell*'s end seemed nigh, when a boiler certificate was refused. Mercifully, enthusiasts belonging to the Birmingham Locomotive Club stepped in to purchase the locomotive, and it became an exhibit at the Narrow Gauge Museum, Towyn. Even more encouragingly, a series of subsequent, and heartening, events culminated in the formation of a Welsh Highland Light Railway (1964) Ltd.

Various setbacks to date have prevented the new Company from negotiating purchase of the old WHR trackbed. But in 1973 occupation was allowed of a siding at Portmadoc, where slate used to be trans-shipped from narrow gauge to standard gauge wagons. Passenger operations on the line commenced on 2 August 1980, and official opening followed on 18 July 1981. Plans are presently well in hand to extend another 1½ miles to Pont Croesor.

The names *Snowdon Ranger* and *Moel Tryfan* flourish again, on two comparatively recently built Bagnall 0–4–2 tanks. Sundry other 60 cm gauge locos, steam and diesel, have arrived from various other parts of the world. So, too, have two Hudson/WHR bogie coaches; and, with work progressing on the rehabilitation of *Russell*, the day may not be too far distant when a once-familiar sight and sound may again awaken Welsh Highland territory. The original *Moel Tryfan* was broken up in the early 1950s after lying derelict at Portmadoc shed for a number of years.

Possession of 55 miscellaneous freight wagons, plus one from the former Snailbeach Railway, and a four-wheeled passenger brake van from the Vale of Rheidol

Welsh Highland Light Railway (1964) Ltd locomotives

Name	Type	Date built	Makers	Maker's number	Remarks
2-foot gauge *Moel Tryfan*	0–4–2T	1953	Bagnall	3023	Ex-Rustenberg Platinum Mines, South Africa
Snowdon Ranger	0–4–2T	1953	,,	3050	,,
Karen	0–4–2T	1942	Peckett	2024	Ex-Selukwe Peak Light Railway, S. Rhodesia
1 ft 11½ in gauge *Russell*	2–6–2T	1906	Hunslet	901	Ex-Brymbo Steel Co, Wrexham
60 cm gauge *Nantmor*	0–6–0WT	1921	Orenstein & Koppel	9239	Ex-Pejao Coal Mines, Pedorido, Portugal
Pedemoora	0–6–0WT	1924	,,	10808	,,
Plus sundry diesel units					

Railway, should, together with the Welsh Highland's engaging miscellany of steam and diesel locos, ensure a bright future for yet another Welsh narrow gauge enterprise.

KERRY TRAMWAY

Opened: March 1888
Closed: April 1895
Gauge: 2 ft 0 in

This privately-owned tramway also took advantage of a standard gauge railway's local presence, by bridging a 3-mile gap which existed between the Cambrian Railways' station at Kerry, in mid-Wales, and an Estate called Bryn-Llywarch. The intention of the estate owner, Mr C. J. Naylor, was to facilitate movement of timber, granite slabs and general merchandise to and from his property. Rails came, most opportunely, from the Glyn Valley Tramway which was being rebuilt at the time. Branches within the tramway served a slab quarry, saw mills and various woodlands, as well as the main house, and traffic appears to have commenced in March 1888, when Bagnall supplied *Excelsior,* an appropriately diminutive 0–4–2 tank. Flat-bottomed 20 lb rails, on wooden sleepers, were employed, and one can only presume that things functioned satisfactorily — until April 1895, when Mr Naylor left the district. At any rate, traffic ceased that month, and the rolling-stock was sold to a firm of Manchester contractors. *Excelsior* was later employed in the construction of the Lynton & Barnstaple Railway.

The tramway route, except for a branch or two, was

re-used in 1917, when the Forestry Commission laid a timber-haulage tramway, once more to 2-foot gauge. A petrol tractor, horses, and a Kerr Stuart 0–4–0T were variously brought into use, and German prisoners of war provided the labour force. Once the war ended, and the prisoners were repatriated, the timber working was taken over by an Epsom firm. They introduced a second Kerr Stuart engine, a larger six-coupled tank obtained from the War Store Disposal Board. By the early 1920s, however, timber work came to an end, and most of the track was lifted. The two tank engines were sold, and functioning under new names, *Diana* and *Kashmir,* they lived on to serve slate and granite quarries elsewhere.

HAFAN & TALYBONT TRAMWAY
(Plynlimmon & Hafan Railway Company)

Opened: 12 May 1897
Closed: 1914
Gauge: 2 ft 3 in

Lead, granite and other valuable mineral deposits were all to be found in that wild Welsh area south of the Dovey valley, and towards the end of the nineteenth century, a local speculator decided to build a tramway from the Cambrian Railways station at Llanfihangel some 8 miles up and into the mineral reaches. Work commenced on 11 January 1897, and on 12 May that year a first run by Hafan's solitary engine ended in locomotive failure after 300 yards. Next day 'the full run was made'.

Traffic arrangements were typical of Welsh tramroad practice, as were the steep climbs required to reach the mines. Such wagons as were owned were used mainly for granite, and little is known of them beyond 15 which passed into Vale of Rheidol Railway ownership. The track, however, was remarkably substantial, and consisted of 30 lb rail, well spiked, earth ballast and sleepers at 1 yard intervals. Its very nature suggests that the tramway sponsors nursed healthy ambitions. A certain recklessness emerges, though, in the fact that passengers were carried without authority. Two separate fatalities occurred in 1897, when a man and a child were thrown from open wagons.

Despite that discouragement, modest passenger services persisted and platforms were erected at Llanfihangel and Talybont the following year. A bogie coach capable of holding 60 passengers was introduced, as was a 3d fare. Meanwhile, mineral traffic descending from the heights was transhipped on to standard gauge metals at Llanfihangel station. Alas, as it had to be unloaded again at Aberystwyth for final shipment, Hafan's transport costs were high; and offered no hope of stimulating heavy traffic. It is unlikely, therefore, that Hafan's locomotive, a vertical-boilered 0–4–0, found full employment, even at the receiving end of the tramway. Certainly the use of horses and gravity at the other was quite commonplace.

A second engine was obtained from Bagnalls of Stafford in 1897. But little use could have been made of it either, for the inexorable burden of high transport costs, plus a decline in the granite trade, obliged the tramway to close down in 1900. The track was dismantled, and subsequent sundry efforts made to resuscitate the line finally came to naught when war erupted in 1914.

LOCOMOTIVES

Name	Type	Date built	Makers
Victoria	0–4–0VB	1897	Slee & Co
Talybont	2–4–0T	1897	Bagnall

Victoria, a completely enclosed four-cylinder vertical-boilered engine, was the only locomotive ever accredited to Slee & Co, of Earlestown. This rather suggests that the firm were agents rather than locomotive builders. *Talybont*, built by Bagnall for overseas service, was to bear the name *Treze de Maio*; but, never delivered thus, she was regauged from 2 ft 5½ in and sold to Hafan. When the tramway closed the loco was passed on to Pethick Bros, contractors for the Vale of Rheidol Railway. Rebuilt by Bagnall in 1901, and regauged, this time to 1 ft 11½ in, *Talybont* duly worked on construction trains. Light and short wheelbased, it proved so useful and popular that eventually it entered official Vale of Rheidol stock as No 3 *Rheidol*. So, too, did various Hafan wagons, and six of them linger at Aberystwyth to this day.

The passenger era

SNOWDON MOUNTAIN RAILWAY LIMITED

Opened: 6 April 1896
Closed: Still extant
Gauge: 2 ft 7½ in

The Snowdon Mountain Railway might well have been conceived 25 years earlier. For when the Bangor & Caernarvon Railway extended its single standard gauge line, in July 1869, by opening a branch to Llanberis, engineering ambitions to tackle Snowdon itself were promptly inflamed. Experiments in rack railways had been taking place in both Europe and America, and, undoubtedly, the contemporary, and much lauded, success of Riggenbach's Rigi rack railway in Switzerland inspired a group of influential North Wales businessmen to put up a Snowdon Railway Bill for consideration by Parliament in its 1872 session.

The proposed line, just over 4 miles long, was to commence opposite Llanberis station, and proceed by

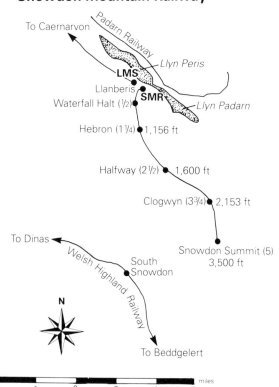

Snowdon Mountain Railway

To Caernarvon
Padarn Railway
Llyn Peris
LMS
Llanberis
Waterfall Halt (½)
SMR
Llyn Padarn
Hebron (1¼) 1,156 ft
Halfway (2½) 1,600 ft
Clogwyn (3¾) 2,153 ft
To Dinas
Welsh Highland Railway
South Snowdon
Snowdon Summit (5) 3,500 ft
To Beddgelert
N
miles
0 1 2 3 4 5

sundry hazardous gradients to a terminus at Crib-y-ddysal, some 500 feet below the mountain summit. Building costs were postulated at £20,000, and the line, though described as 'a railway or tramway', was obviously intended to be single-rack in nature. The Bill, in fact, never passed beyond the committee stage at Westminster, and its failure can be attributed to the fact that a prominent local landowner, G. W. D. Assheton-Smith, refused to lend his support.

Assheton-Smith's position in the matter was interesting. The vast estate he owned included Snowdon mountain. Therefore he, of all men, could veto such development as he chose. Yet he was no Luddite; for across the water, on the other side of Lake Padarn, the huge Dinorwic Quarries also came within his kingdom, and were already operating an extensive narrow gauge steam railway system. As a direct consequence the slate boom of the 1860s had brought considerable prosperity to the locality. The arrival of standard gauge metals in 1869, with their ability to deposit visitors within 5 miles of Snowdon itself, offered Llanberis an additional tourist popularity the village folk were not slow to accept. Llanberis, in other words, was doing nicely; and in that context Assheton-Smith saw no advantage whatever to the community or himself in allowing the proposed mountain railway to disturb the quiet beauty of his Welsh mountainside. Later, around 1880, C. E. Spooner and another Festiniog Railway official hatched a ploy to conquer Snowdon by running a rack railway to the summit, then descending on the *other* side of the mountain to Rhyd-ddu, where anticipated contact with the North Wales Narrow Gauge Railway would be made. This quite remarkable proposition was again defeated by landowner opposition.

Yet, ironically, it was the NWNGR's arrival in Rhyd-ddu in 1881 which triggered off a change of mind in Snowdon affairs. Rhyd-ddu, as it happened, was 1¾ miles nearer the summit than Llanberis, and a little later the NWNGR management, in a flash of inspiration, decided to capitalize on this fact by renaming their station 'Snowdon'. The effect of this tactical manoeuvre was traumatic. NWNGR passenger traffic burgeoned, and the tourist trade at Llanberis slumped accordingly as the village's former monopolistic reliance on Mount Snowdon vanished. Meanwhile, a severe depression in the slate industry throughout the 1880 served to add a final touch to Llanberis' distress, and by the early 1890s pressures towards the reconsideration of a rack railway from Llanberis to the summit began to mount. Give Assheton-Smith his due — he not only recognized the village was in dire peril, but wholeheartedly withdrew his former opposition to the railway scheme, and sanctioned sale of such land as was necessary.

From that very practical step things moved swiftly, and on 16 November 1894 the Snowdon Mountain

The success of Riggenbach's Rigi rack railway in Switzerland inspired the idea of conquering Snowdon in similar fashion, and the North Wales Narrow Gauge Railway's subsequent cool enterprise in renaming its Rhyd-ddu station 'Snowdon' stung Llanberis villagers into action. Exactly as seen in this view of the Rigi Railway's Summit station, the rack rail system pioneered by Dr Abt, a disciple of Riggenbach, was adopted when construction of the Snowdon Mountain Railway commenced in December 1894. (Steamchest)

Tramroad & Hotels Co Ltd was formally registered. Nominal capital was fixed at £70,000. The railway's rather complicated title is explained by the fact that the new Company took a lease over the Royal Victoria Hotel at Llanberis, and expressed an intention to build a second new hotel near the mountain summit. With a survey already completed, a Liverpool firm undertook construction of the rack railway by 1 July 1895. The fee of £64,000 would be paid in SMT&H Co shares. The immensely difficult proposition of climbing 4¾ miles to an altitude of 3,493 feet above sea level prompted the engineers to look towards Swiss experience; almost inevitably, the rack system pioneered by Dr Roman Abt, a disciple of Riggenbach, was chosen. So, too, was Abt's recommended gauge of 2 ft 7½ in (800mm).

Momentum was such that the first sod of the new rack railway was turned on 15 December 1894.

Llanberis rejoiced accordingly, and one notes with interest that in course of inevitable speeches open reference was made to the possibility of employing electric traction, should sufficient water power be found, as well as steam. Meanwhile, two steam locomotives had been ordered, at a cost of £1,400 each, from the Swiss Locomotive & Machine Co of Winterthur, and five carriages of Swiss rack railway design were under construction by the Lancaster Carriage & Wagon Co Ltd. Track-laying was taken

Loco No 4 Snowdon was almost new when this photograph was taken at the turn of the century. The semi-open Swiss-type carriage was one of five supplied by the Lancaster Carriage & Wagon Co Ltd, and the board along its roof bears the Company's full title – 'Snowdon Mountain Tramroad & Hotels Company Limited'. Snowdon was taken out of service in 1939, but was able to resume operations in 1963 after overhaul at Leeds. (Steamchest)

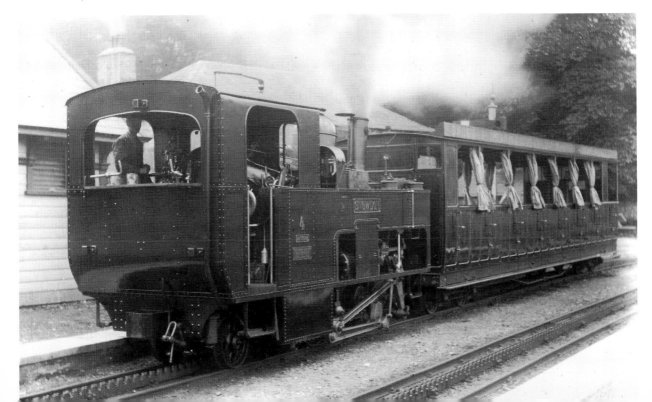

very seriously from the start, and some measure of the Company's integrity in that field can be gauged from the fact that the original track lasted well into the 1960s before major replacement was required. Apart from secure provision of two running rails, the Abt system required the addition of two rack blades, bolted with equal impregnability to the centre of the track. These blades were milled, with rack teeth, from solid steel bars, and in action their teeth were engaged by two cogged wheels, pinion racked, on each locomotive. Entering into the spirit of things, a British firm, Richard Cammell & Co, undertook the skilled task of milling the bars.

In the event three Swiss locos travelled across Europe to reach Llanberis by 1895. All were six-wheeled tanks, with boilers inclined at 9 degrees to preserve safe water levels during ascent and descent. One might have described them as 0–4–2 tanks, but for the fact that, although the driving *pinions* were coupled, the track wheels themselves rode loose. Hence, rather like the quaint contraptions which functioned on Ireland's Listowel & Ballybunion mono-railway, the Snowdon locos tended to defy conventional Whyte classification. Two more Winterthur locos arrived in 1896 and 1897, and this sufficed to meet Snowdon requirements until the years 1922-23, when three more were added.

Meanwhile, the smooth nature of Snowdon Railway loco and carriage provision was by no means matched by construction of the railway itself. Laying Abt system track was a very precise operation which could only be accomplished by starting at one end and working uninterruptedly to the other. It follows that any delay in completing earthworks etc presented serious hindrance towards ultimate completion, and just such a problem arose as the higher of two necessary viaducts was being built. Time thus lost was only recovered by housing the men in huts on the mountainside during Mondays to Fridays, and letting them walk down to Llanberis for leisure purposes at weekends.

No 7 Aylwin *(left) and* No 3 *Wyddfa, demonstrating the Snowdon Railway's two types, rest quietly at Llanberis shed, where a single rack blade suffices to permit movement on level terrain. No 7, with extra-deep well tanks, can accomplish a round trip to Snowdon Summit and back without water refill.* (Steamchest)

By April 1895 more than 200 workers were being employed in a desperate bid to meet the completion date of 1 July. Despite rapid progress, however, and a subsequent track-laying performance of 4¼ miles in 72 working days, the summit was not reached until 6 January 1896. Three days later, laden with sundry officials, a first two-coach train left Llanberis, and arrived at the upper terminus 1 hour and 12 minutes later. Pausing for 20 minutes, and expressing every satisfaction with what they saw, the official party then embarked on a safe descent to Llanberis. Disappointingly, the Snaefell Mountain Railway, in the Isle of Man, had, in the interim, succeeded in snatching the honour of operating Britain's first mountain railway by placing its cars at the public's disposal on 21 August 1895.

Despite continuing protests from various parties who viewed the construction of a mountain railway as a despoilation of Snowdonia, the Snowdon Mountain Railway opened for public service on Easter Monday, 6 April 1896. Final construction costs had emerged at a very creditable £76,152, three engines and five coaches were standing by for use, and, looking ahead, an order had already been placed for two more locomotives. Both hotels were also ready for the great day; an atmosphere of positive excitement pervaded Llanberis station that morning as an initial one-coach public train steamed off towards the summit.

Such was the overflow of would-be passengers that a second train of two coaches was pressed into service, and shortly afterwards it left, with loco No 1 *Ladas* at its head. Both trains reached the summit safely. But, almost ominously, heavy mist began to drift as *Ladas* led the downward trek. Fifteen minutes later, just short of Glogwyn station, disaster struck. The train lurched violently, speed increased at an alarming pace,

and in the ensuing panic two passengers jumped for their lives. Fortunately, Snowdon's General Manager had the presence of mind to apply the carriage brake, and the short train came safely to a stop.

The first discovery to greet passengers as they hastily alighted was truly astonishing. *Ladas* had disappeared! As can be imagined, speculation which followed was almost hysterical in nature, and the mystery was only resolved when her driver and fireman limped on to the scene. *Ladas* had, in fact, left the rails, and had toppled down the mountainside. Here was a testimony, if ever there was one, to Snowdon's wise precaution of leaving engine and coaches uncoupled. Both train crew members had managed to leap clear, but of the two passengers who had taken the same course, one, it was found, had sustained fatal injuries.

Meanwhile, the driver of *Enid*, waiting at the summit for the 'all clear', decided after 45 minutes to venture down with great caution. Even then, *Enid* ploughed into the two stationary coaches as she reached the fog-bound scene of the accident. Fortuitously, both carriages were empty; but it was a sad end to Llanberis' day of celebration. No further trains were run that day, and all public services were suspended pending investigation. At a subsequent inquest on the deceased passenger, the ruling was that he met his end by his own involuntary action.

As for the cause of the accident, little evidence could be produced to show why *Ladas* was derailed. Thorough inspection of the line was made by various experts, and a general conclusion was reached that a minor subsidence in the trackbed was the likeliest source. To prevent a recurrence, guard rails were later installed on each side of the track, which made contact with 'grippers' fitted beneath locos and coaches; it is interesting to note that a number of Swiss rack railways, alarmed at Snowdon's accident, were quick to adopt the same fail-safe procedure. Snowdon's precautions, meanwhile, were hampered by a spell of wintry weather, but re-opening of the line as far as Clogwyn was planned for Easter Monday 1897.

Early on the morning of 19 April, a pilot train made a precautionary round trip ere public services resumed at 10.45 am. All went well, and five trains ran that day. Public celebrations seemed a trifle muted, but this could probably be attributed to the fact that the inhabitants of Llanberis were well used by now to the sight of Snowdon locomotives in their midst. Modifying the line and rolling-stock had cost the company £2,292, and, in addition, *Ladas*, an asset worth £1,500, had been written off. Her mangled remains were found scattered all down the mountainside. The boiler was intact, but the rest proved unworthy of salvage.

Successfully re-opened, the Snowdon Railway settled down to a long period of smooth, trouble-free working. The convenient ascent of Snowdon it offered appealed greatly to rapidly increasing numbers of tourists, and even during First World War years it was found possible to offer uninterrupted, though slightly restricted, public service. Post-war years brought a positive boom in tourism, and the company cheerfully braced itself to meet new demands. Three

new locomotives were ordered from Winterthur, at a significantly increased cost of £3,649 each, and four more carriages were also obtained. Then, in 1928, came a resolution to increase company capital to £100,000. On 15 May of that year, too, a successful application to the Board of Trade saw SMT&H Co's rather unwieldy title altered to Snowdon Mountain Railway Ltd. The mantle of what had once been a serious challenge, in the shape of the NWNGR, had fallen upon the Welsh Highland Railway by now. In effect, the current misfortunes of the latter concern posed little threat to the Snowdon Railway's welfare.

Even the calamitous outbreak of a second world war in 1939 took time to affect Snowdon affairs to any noticeable extent. Fairly normal summer services operated through to 1941, though during the year which followed the installation of Ministry of Supply experimental work at the summit imposed reduction to twice-daily trains on a weekday basis only. By 1944 the Snowdon Railway drew a complete blank, for security reasons; but public services were duly restored on 4 May 1945. Curiously, it was then, despite receipt of Government compensation and a brisk resumption of tourist traffic, that SMR finances began to lag. To be sure, renovations and repairs were crying out to be done. But finding money *and* materials in post-war Britain was no easy task. Loco No 4, for instance, already withdrawn in 1939, had to wait in Llanberis yard until 1961 ere its complete overhaul could be undertaken. Priority, meanwhile, was being given to the conversion of carriages from semi-open status to modern closed vehicles. This job was tackled, one coach per year, and in 1957, once all seven had been modernized, the SMR's sole remaining specimen of 1895 vintage was scrapped.

Work also commenced in 1952 on improving hotel facilities at the summit; and the year was made doubly memorable when, on 11 August, an RAF Anson aircraft crashed just above Clogwyn station. Apart from the lamentable loss of three air crew, passengers in a

With his rear cab windows thrust wide open, the driver of No 2 Enid relaxes for a moment to enjoy the view at the Summit before embarking on his five-mile descent to Llanberis. By now all seven Snowdon Railway coaches have been rebuilt as modern closed vehicles. (Steamchest)

Snowdon train already in the act of descending were stranded for the night high on a bitterly cold Welsh mountainside. On 31 December 1951 the SMR also disengaged itself from the hotel lease at Llanberis. Management then addressed itself to the problem of financing repairs and renovations. *Snowdon*'s long-awaited overhaul was still not feasible; but at least *Enid*, Snowdon's oldest engine, was given the benefit of Hunslet Engine Co's meticulous attention in 1958.

Modernization of ground-level facilities at Llanberis in 1960 assisted matters considerably, and within the next few years 4,320 yards of track were replaced. Snowdon's four oldest locos also attended Hunslet Engine Co's Leeds workshops in turn. Thus, *Snowdon* steamed proudly back in action in 1963.

Since then, however, all locomotive work has been carried out at Llanberis. It follows that the SMR, pausing only to join the celebrated marketing consortium known at the 'Great Little Trains of Wales', entered the 1970s in good heart.

Financial requirements in the early 1980s were partly resolved by selling the freehold of the Summit site to Gwynedd County Council, who undertook requisite expenditure and development — the while SMR obtained a 999-year lease. A spectacular share issue which followed in 1985 brought the enormous sum of £685,000 to the little railway's coffers, all of which made possible the purchase, at a cost of over £200,000 each, of two four-wheel 320 hp diesel hydraulic locomotives from Hunslet Engine Co in 1986. A new carriage was also obtained in 1988.

The new diesels introduced previously unheard of standards in both fuel economy and flexibility, and, naturally, these virtues have been exploited to the full. But perhaps the greatest tribute to SMR proficiency lies in the Company's Swiss steam locomotives, which, apart from reboilering at intervals of some 30 years, still function in largely original form. With that kind of record behind them there seems no reason why they should not complete their century.

LOCOMOTIVES

No	Name	Date built	Makers	Maker's number	Remarks
1	*Ladas*	1895	Swiss Loco & Machine Co	923	Name taken from initials of Mrs Assheton-Smith. Loco scrapped after accident on opening day, 6 April 1896
2	*Enid*	1895	,,	924	Named after daughter of G. W. D. Assheton-Smith
3	*Wyddfa/ Yr Wyddfa*	1895	,,	925	Named after highest peak in Snowdonia
4	*Snowdon*	1896	,,	988	Out of service between 1939 and 1963
5	*Moel Siabod*	1896	,,	989	Named after mountain 6 miles east of Snowdon
6	*Sir Harmood/ Padarn*	1922	,,	2838	Named after SMR's first Chairman, Sir Harmood Banner. Rechristened in 1928 after a 16th-century Celtic saint who lived in the area
7	*Eryri/Aylwin/ Ralph Sadler/ Ralph*	1923	,,	2869	Named *Eryri* for a very brief period only. Named *Ralph Sadler* in 1978, after late Consultant Civil Engineer. Later renamed *Ralph*
8	*Eryri*	1923	,,	2870	Named after Snowdon range — 'Abode of eagles'
9	*Ninian*	1986	Hunslet	2949	Named after SMR Chairman, Ninian Davies
10	*Yeti*	1986	,,	2950	Name chosen from children's competition on BBC TV

The SMR's steam locomotives, all of the familiar Continental 'kneeling cow' variety, came, it will be noted, in two instalments, and today Nos 2-8, still serving, form two distinct locomotive categories. Nos 2 to 5 use saturated steam and slide valves, and their side tanks extend right to the front buffer beam. Each tank has two compartments; the smaller one, in front, holds water for compression-cooling purposes, while that at the rear, supplemented by well tanks, contains the main boiler supply. Engines Nos 6 to 8, on the other hand, are superheated, have piston valves, and their (shorter) tanks are reserved for boiler feed only. Water for compression-cooling is drawn from the boiler. Engines Nos 7 and 8, with deepest well tanks of all, can handle a round trip without refill. All others require one water refill *en route*. Where brake power is concerned, all SMR locos follow conventional rack railway practice, by being able to fall back on three separate systems, operated by hand, steam and air. Snowdon locos were originally liveried in dark red, but over a period of time this graduated through unlined black to its present pleasant apple-green.

Operating procedure is, perforce, unusual. In all ascents one locomotive pushes one coach, but the two are *never* coupled. Passenger accommodation is limited to 60, and a speed restriction of 5 mph is strictly observed. When delivered, all engines were guaranteed by Swiss Locomotive Co to be capable of lifting 18 tons up a 1 in 5½ gradient at a speed of 4.2 mph. In practice, the climb for the first 3½ miles out of Llanberis is formidable enough. But, once Clogwyn, 2,541 feet above sea level, is reached, certainly gradients of 1 in 5½ are required to lift the train one more mile to Snowdon Summit. The latter, at 3,493 feet above sea level, is the highest station in the land. Even the station platforms are set on a concluding gradient of 1 in 20! When descent is made, the locomotive, now being *pushed* by its train, counters the effect of gravity by employing its counter-pressure air brake. In viewing a photograph taken on the mountainside one can always detect a Llanberis-bound train by the fact that the engine's flat cap has been swivelled across to close the chimney aperture. This procedure minimizes draught, thereby keeping the firebox in good fettle for the next ascent.

Constructed as a single line, with passing loops at Henton, Halfway and Clogwyn, the SMR had little need for elaborate signalling arrangements. Indeed, in 1930 a few lower quadrant semaphores, initially installed in 1896, were removed without consequent prejudice to safety. It will be appreciated, too, that the precise laying of Abt system rack blades makes the provision of points a difficult procedure. Fortunately, only 11 points in all are required to render the whole 4½ miles functional. At ground level, Llanberis enjoys one slight bonus, in that a single rack blade between the running track is sufficient to generate locomotive movement. But, even that blade has to be bridged across inspection pits.

The SMR's first five carriages were plainly, but sturdily, built at Lancaster to current Swiss design, as were four small goods wagons which accompanied them. Freight traffic failed to develop, however, and the wagons were allowed to wither away. In 1923 four more new coaches were imported from Switzerland, again to original design. Semi-open coaches invariably found favour on mountain railways, as a compromise between passenger comfort and gale-force currents which play havoc with a narrow gauge train. Snowdon is no exception; for, once beyond the shelter of Clogwyn cutting, a train can be subjected to tornado-like winds. Considerable improvements in passenger comfort have, however, been made over the years, as the company's present stock of seven saloon bogie coaches testifies. It also owns a bogie works car and a four-wheeled open wagon.

But even today, thanks to the forces of Nature, possession of a ticket to the Summit is still no guarantee that the train will venture that far. Even the recent acquisition of the two Hunslet-built diesel units will do little towards ameliorating that situation.

GREAT ORME TRAMWAY
Opened: 31 July 1902
Closed: Still extant
Gauge: 3 ft 6 in

Largest of all the Welsh coastal resorts, the town of Llandudno, in keeping with the times, aspired around the turn of the century to capitalize on its quite considerable natural attractions. The most spectacular of these were two headlands which dominated the town — Great Orme and Little Orme. Thus, in 1898, was sanctioned the creation of a 3 ft 6 in gauge tramway which would transport visitors almost to the 679-foot-high summit of Great Orme's Head. Built in two sections, with passengers changing cars half-way, the project was completed when the upper section, 827 yards long, was opened on 8 July 1903. The maximum gradient thereon was 1 in 10.3. The lower section, which took passengers out through the back streets of Llandudno, had already been open for nearly a year; 800 yards long, it incorporated a climb of 1 in 4.4.

Cable traction was employed from inception, and any overhead wires to be seen were used only for signalling purposes. Cable and pulleys were contained in a central paved conduit in the lower, town, section, but once the upper section was reached they appeared above ground, mounted on conventional sleepers. Both sections were single-tracked, although the lower had, for convenience reasons, a short stretch of double line, with a common middle rail. Up to the 1950s the tramway cable was steam driven; since then the winding and control gear, located at half-way house, has been operated by powerful electric conduction motors.

On 1 January 1949 the tramway was taken over from the Great Orme Railway Company by Llandudno Urban District Council, and, still starting, as of yore, from a point not far from Llandudno Station, it has never failed to remain a popular feature of Llandudno summer life. Quite remarkably, the original 1902-03 stock of four 6½-ton tramcars, each accommodating 48 passengers, in carrying out their basic 20-minute summer service, with extra trips as custom demands, still continue to serve a delighted public.

VALE OF RHEIDOL LIGHT RAILWAY

Opened: 22 December 1902
Closed by BR: 5 November 1988; under new ownership
Gauge: 1 ft 11½ in

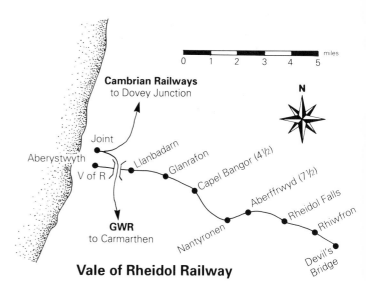

Vale of Rheidol Railway

Travelling on present-day Vale of Rheidol metals, one would have difficulty in realizing that this narrow gauge line was born primarily to encourge mineral traffic. Yet such was the case, for around the 1850s lead mines inland from Aberystwyth were experiencing traditional problems in transporting their ore by pack horse for eventual shipment by sea. In 1861 the Manchester & Milford Railway proposed to relieve the situation by constructing a line between Aberystwyth and the mines at Devil's Bridge. Alas, typical of that unfortunate concern, no work was ever undertaken.

Decades passed. Then, much later in the century, Aberystwyth began to acquire prestige as a seaside resort. Soon, arguments for an inland railway were being advanced by three distinct parties: those interested in developing tourism, mine-owners still seeking easier egress for their ore, and local foundry-masters yearning for more facile communication with the mines. Pressures grew, and as far as the general welfare of Aberystwyth was concerned the case became unanswerable. A Board of Trade inquiry held in the Town Hall in March 1897 was followed by a meeting of the Light Railway Commissioners in April; and, taking advantage of the Light Railways Act of 1896, creation of the Vale of Rheidol Light Railway was authorized by an Act of 6 August 1897. Two separate projects

were envisaged: an 11¾-mile main line linking Aberystwyth and Devil's Bridge, and a short Harbour branch within Aberystwyth itself. The Bill postulated a 'nominal gauge' of 2 feet, contained authority to widen to standard gauge if necessary, allowed five years for completion, and fixed the authorized capital at £68,000.

Despite these tidy arrangements, local enthusiasm proved strangely reluctant to express itself in terms of cash, and, so slowly did capital accumulate, that 1901 arrived ere a start could be made on construction work. Even then, it was only made possible by the contractors Pethick Bros, accepting payment in company shares in lieu of cash. Pethick, meanwhile, had seized an opportunity of acquiring 2–4–0T *Talybont*

2–4–0T No 3 Rheidol, *the Vale of Rheidol's oldest locomotive, specialized in handling traffic on the Harbour branch. Seen here, nameless and in Cambrian Railways livery, at Aberystwyth on 3 June 1920, it was scrapped three years later by the GWR. (LCGB, Ken Nunn Collection)*

With coal stacked on top of the fire-box in traditional fashion, VofR's pioneer locomotive No 1 *Edward VII* awaits departure from Aberystwyth on 28 June 1909. Note the ornamental station seat in the right background. A complete absence of platforms at all Vale of Rheidol stations required the provision of low footboards on all carriages. (LCGB, Ken Nunn Collection)

and 15 wagons from the then defunct Hafan & Talybont Tramway.

Initial progress on building the Rheidol line was painfully slow. But once a suitable influx of labour came to hand, work speeded up, and in the late summer of 1902 the completed line was declared ready for inspection. A Board of Trade inspector duly descended; but, so unsatisfactory was his train's progress that permission to operate passenger traffic was deferred for a month or two, pending necessary alterations. In the meantime, two specially built 2–6–2 tanks had been delivered by Davies & Metcalf, and, on 5 November 1902, a special train, hauled by No 1 *Edward VII*, offered officials and local celebrities a sample trip to Devil's Bridge and back. In a further formal ceremony the line was opened to the public on 22 December.

In keeping with standards laid down by Charles Spooner, of Festiniog fame, the VofR adopted a 1 ft 11½ in gauge, and matched that famous railway in its meticulous attention to permanent way, The line, built single, with passing loops at Capel Bangor and Aberffrwd, was worked by electric staff, and a twin wire telephone system running the length of the track

afforded an extra safety factor. Hardly surprisingly, the Harbour branch was worked in less sophisticated fashion.

Viewed from old photographs, the VofR's original terminus at Aberystwyth still looks a model of elegance and prosperity. True, the station buildings were modest, and passengers mounted from ground level; but rows of beautiful cast-iron lamp-posts contrived to echo a sense of tidiness which was encouraged all along the line. Staff kept immaculate gardens, and strove annually to compete in this respect. In 1902 the VofR provided four stations between Aberystwyth and Devil's Bridge, but by 1904 the excellence of tourist traffic justified provision of three more halts. Not far from the VofR's Aberystwyth terminus lay the all-important link with the Cambrian Railways main line station. Thus, interchange was not too tiresome an affair where visitors were concerned. Quite justifiably, VofR management viewed summer seasons with every satisfaction during the halcyon years which led to the First World War.

Another interesting aspect of Vale of Rheidol life was the manner in which its main line divided itself

When the line was constructed in 1901-2, passing loops were provided at Capel Bangor (4½ miles) and Aberffrwd (7½ miles). The tidy appearance of Capel Bangor station in this vintage view was, and still is, typical of Vale of Rheidol practice; and the signal post in the foreground remains substantial by any standards. (Author's Collection)

8

Not long after being taken over by the Cambrian Railways in 1913, cabs on the Rheidol's two 'Prairie' tanks were widened to provide coal bunkers on either side. Then, when the locos passed under GWR jurisdiction, No 1, nameless by now and numbered 1212, entered Swindon Works in November 1922. There it was overhauled, and given GWR standard fittings, before being returned to Aberystwyth. Withdrawn ten years later, No 1212, placed on GWR's Sales List, stood in the open for some months before being cut up. The loco's original Stephenson motion shows clearly in this photograph, taken at Swindon on 28 May 1933. (Steamchest)

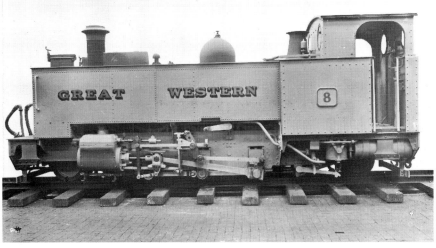

To augment the Vale of Rheidol's stock two additional 2–6–2Ts were built at Swindon in July 1923. Though equipped with Walschaerts valve gear, and some 2,000 lb greater in tractive effort, Nos 7 and 8 were essentially the same design as the VofR originals. In June 1956, in accordance with British Rail policy, No 8 was given the name Llywelyn. (Author's Collection)

into two strangely disparate sections. Starting from Aberystwyth, the narrow gauge metals headed south, past a small loco shed, and on to Harbour Branch Junction on the north bank of the river estuary. From here they struck inland, studiously following the river's course, never rising more than a few feet above water level for all of 4½ miles. But once Capel Bangor was reached, things changed dramatically, and 7 miles of severe curvature, with gradients of 1 in 50, had to be faced as trains struggled on to reach Devil's Bridge. Here, at the end of it all, fully 680 feet above sea level, tidy gardens and a profusion of lamp-posts calmly welcomed travellers and weary train crews as they stepped out into a scenic wonderland.

Yet it was this stirringly beautiful second section which drew tourists, and, despite the mineral-orientation of its origin, the VofR did its utmost from inception to stimulate passenger traffic.

Twelve bogie coaches were ordered from the Midland Carriage & Wagon Co in good time for opening day, and the same firm also supplied 14 wagons between the years 1902 and 1906. During the heavy summer traffic months, the VofR pressed a number of these wagons into use as passenger observation vehicles. Seated behind wire fencing, passengers paid an extra 3d for the privilege of riding thus in state. The wagons, devoid of vacuum brake, were marshalled at

the rear of the train. Meanwhile, the ex-Hafan loco, *Talybont*, and sundry wagons also passed into VofR ownership once construction work was completed. Rechristened *Rheidol*, the little tank was, in the light of its 10-ton weight and short wheelbase, given complete monopoly on work on the Harbour branch. Goods items usually travelled in wagons at the rear of passenger trains, though special mineral and timber trains were quite frequently run. Most of the latter ran direct, via the Harbour branch, to Rotfawr Wharf, whence *Rheidol* attended to wagon distribution along the quayside.

This, then, was the background which attended the VofR's first prosperous decade of life. Something of a hiatus, though, did occur in 1909, when the Board found itself obliged to divide on a contentious issue — that of constructing a new line between Devil's Bridge and Aberayron. Ironically, powers to do this had already been granted in 1898, but these had lapsed. Whatever, the issue was eventually dismissed, a few Directors saw fit to resign on principle, and a newly constituted VofR Board turned its attention to what appeared to be more cogent matters. One such was the receipt of a proposition in 1912 that the water power of the River Rheidol should be harnessed to convert the VofR into an electric tramway. Quite startlingly, the electric element of this ambitious plan

In 1925 the Vale of Rheidol's narrow gauge metals were extended by 150 yards to reach a more convenient starting point alongside the GWR's main line station at Aberystwyth. In this view, taken on 21 June 1937, the VofR's other pioneer 2–6–2T, GWR No 1213, formerly No 2 Prince of Wales, is all set to leave on the 2 pm to Devil's Bridge. (F. M. Gates)

turned into a veritable bolt of lightning when, in the midst of obtaining estimates of cost, the VofR management discovered that large blocks of Rheidol shares had been bought by nominees of the Cambrian Railways. As so often happens in financial affairs, the end product was both swift and brutal; the Cambrian Railways took over, and the Vale of Rheidol Company ceased to exist as from 1 July 1913.

As if absorption by 'big brother' were not enough, the eruption of war in 1914 made doubly sure that the VofR's golden years came truly to an end. As recently as 1910 the company had opened an extra halt, called Lovesgrove, to serve a busy Territorial Camp which lay nearby. Now, with the outbreak of war this lucrative traffic ceased, and the halt was closed in 1914. The next blow was the shutdown of Rheidol Mine, with consequent heavy loss of mineral traffic. Meanwhile, as the UK tightened its belt in a long bitter war struggle, normal passenger services on the Cambrian's VofR metals gradually withered away. Nor did the restoration of peace in 1919 bring much in the way of joy. In early post-war years local lead mines slid into permanent depression, and, despite intensive VofR efforts to reinvigorate tourist traffic, the deadly enemy, motor competition, began to make its presence felt. Clear indication that railways all over

the country were suffering similarly was given when Grouping was resorted to in 1922. Under that ordinance the Cambrian Railways and five other Welsh companies had already moved into amalgamation with the GWR as from 1 January 1922. Thus, once again, the Vale of Rheidol found itself serving new masters.

Changes were, of course, inevitable, and the first casualty was the Harbour branch, no longer a viable proposition thanks to the decline in mineral traffic; it was closed in 1924, though tracks were not lifted until 1930. Next, hopeful of supporting VofR's valiant efforts to stimulate passenger traffic, the GWR completely rebuilt the old Cambrian Railways station at Aberystwyth, and managed to present a brave new face to the travelling public in time for the summer of 1925. VofR narrow gauge metals were at the same time extended by seven chains to reach a more convenient terminal point alongside the main line station. The old VofR terminus was abandoned, though the small loco shed remained. From there on, normal VofR passenger servives settled down at two trains daily each way. During summer months extra trains were run on Mondays to Fridays as circumstances required. Curiously, passenger traffic on Saturdays warranted only the meagrest of service. Soon, how-

Though the Vale of Rheidol's old terminus at Aberystwyth was abandoned in 1925, the narrow gauge engine shed remained in use until 1967, when BR's shed, no longer required for standard gauge steam locos, was translated into narrow gauge use. In this early morning study, taken in July 1965, No 8 Llywelyn is being prepared for duty outside the old narrow gauge shed. (Steamchest)

Aberffrwd Station, a traditional passing point and source of water on the Vale of Rheidol, presents an animated scene as No 8 partakes of liquid refreshment on 17 July 1955. (Steamchest)

ever, the gloom of the late 1920s descended all over Britain, and the deep depression which followed saw VofR winter services completely withdrawn as from New Year's Day 1931. This sad state of affairs persisted right up to 1939, when the outbreak of the Second World War steamrollered *all* VofR activity to a stop.

All through the war, the VofR's locos — now four in number, for the GWR scrapped *Rheidol* in 1923, and added two more Prairie tanks — were stored, out of action. Such rolling-stock as could be accommodated in the carriage shed at Capel Bangor was also protected from the worst of the elements. The reminder lay, silent and sheeted, in the open. The VofR track, relaid by the GWR in 1925, received a modicum of attention over the years. This at least facilitated rehabilitation when peace came, and a weekdays-only public service was resumed on 23 July 1945.

As befitted the lean post-war years, however, the VofR service confined itself to two trains each way on weekdays, with no service on Sundays. Freight traffic had long since terminated. A journey either way took 1 hour of a passengers's time, and, though the little railway's original speed limit of 17 mph had been gradually stepped up to 20 mph, a 10 mph restriction still obtained on the more acutely curved sections.

With two engines only in use, and one spare, the few passing loops which existed hardly mattered any longer.

Truth was that the desultory nature of VofR affairs at this time reflected only too accurately the agonies which all British railway companies were facing. During the Second World War the internal combustion engine had gained a grip which was never to be loosened. Lorries were flourishing, and local bus services, plus private transport, were eating cancer-like into railway branch services. Patently, something had to be done — and the outcome of Government thinking on the subject emerged as legislation in the form of the Transport Act 1947. Under its aegis all railway properties passed into the ownership of a newly created British Transport Commission. Thus, from 1 January 1948, most of what had been previously GWR domain acquired a new title: British Railways (Western Region). Included in the package, of course, were the VofR's narrow gauge metals.

Looking back now, one can understand, if not condone, BR's initial shabby treatment of the little Welsh railway. After all, BR's steam stock was in a sad state. A major programme of dieselization was also in the offing, and thus soon the implications of the Beeching axe were clearly to be seen. It follows that

In the late 1960s, British Rail offered Vale of Rheidol trains a much more convenient terminus inside Aberystwyth station, by converting the former Carmarthen bay into narrow gauge use. No 9 Prince of Wales, *formerly VofR No 2, looks quite at home as it sets out for Devil's Bridge in the summer of 1970.* (Steamchest)

while summer service on the VofR was maintained, almost as a duty, the provision of winter trains in such a remote spot hardly merited high priority in BR's catalogue of woes. None the less, the growing vitality throughout the 1950s of the Welsh railway preservation movement, plus the eventual creation of a Wales Joint Marketing Panel, seemed to offer much-needed stimulus, for in 1956 BR started to publicize the Vale of Rheidol — and supplemented its appeal by naming all three VofR locomotives. Sunday trains were also re-introduced. Sadly, this marked improvement soon receded when, in the mid-1960s, the VofR was transferred to the London Midland Region of British Rail. By 1967 everything was shoddy. Locomotives which had previously sparkled now looked down at heel. Even their nameplates had been removed as an anti-theft precaution.

Renaissance came when a group of very practical railway enthusiasts offered to buy the line. BR first agreed, then retracted. But at least it redeemed itself by paying much more attention to the line. Room in a former Carmarthen bay at Aberystwyth station was found to offer the VofR's narrow gauge tracks a much more felicitous terminus; and protection for VofR locos and coaches was ensured by converting the

former standard gauge locomotive shed into a capacious narrow gauge shelter. The old VofR shed was closed. In a final touch of imagination, locomotive nameplates were restored, and both locos and coaches were repainted in BR blue livery. Formation of a Vale of Rheidol Railway Supporters Association came in 1970, since when its members have collaborated nobly with BR in sponsoring and protecting the welfare of what is, after all, a unique national property. Reward came in 1975, when the VofR carried 179,000 passengers, an all-time record for the line. Five years later, a decision by BR to revive the line's earlier character saw loco No 8 *Llywelyn* restored to full GWR livery. Three wagons were also restored to 1902 VofR livery, and a named train, 'The Welsh Dragon', was inaugurated. In 1982 the VofR's oldest locomotive, No 9 *Prince of Wales*, carried public appeal a stage further by appearing in original yellow ochre livery, fully lined and crested.

No doubt a very rare, and injury-free, derailment south of Nantyronen on 26 May 1986 gave BR food for thought. But it came as a shock when, on 5 November 1988, BR, relinquishing future ownership, ran four last trains to Devil's Bridge. Firework displays along the line, celebrating the 'end of steam on BR', did little to minimize the sombreness of the occasion. Fortunately, new owners, in the shape of the Brecon Mountain Railway, took over formally a few months later. They plan to emulate BR's previous timetable, commencing in Easter 1989, and countless railway enthusiasts will wish the new venture every success.

No 7 Owen Glyndwr, *one of the Swindon-built tanks, makes a brave showing as it approaches Nantyronen station, almost halfway between Aberystwyth and Devil's Bridge, on a heavy summer train. BR's latest symbol shines bravely on the loco's blue-painted tank sides.* (Steamchest)

LOCOMOTIVES

VofR No	GWR No	BR No	Name	Type	Date built	Makers	Withdrawn	Remarks
1	1212	—	*Edward VII*	2–6–2T	1902	Davies & Metcalfe	1932	Scrapped in 1938
2	1213	9	*Prince of Wales*	,,	1902	,,		
3	1198	—	*Rheidol*	2–4–0T	1896	Bagnall	1923	Ex-Hafan & Talybont Tramway
—	7	7	*Owain Glyndwr*	2–6–2T	1923	GWR Swindon		Named in June 1956
—	8	8	*Llywelyn*	,,	1923	,,		Named in June 1956

It was rather remarkable that the VofR's first two locomotives were built by Davies & Metcalfe, of Romiley, Manchester, for that well-known, and highly esteemed, firm specialized in the provision of injectors and boiler fittings, etc, and was never known to venture again into the field of locomotive manufacture. Possibly local connections at Aberystwyth were responsible for the VofR's order being placed. Whatever the circumstances, the Manchester firm did a splendid job, and the brace of 2–6–2 tanks they turned out must have looked magnificent in VofR livery, light green with elaborate white lining. Lynton & Barnstaple Railway drawings must also have been closely studied, for the Rheidol engines bore a marked similarity to those built by Manning Wardle in 1897 for the English narrow gauge concern. In the case of the VofR enginess, however, long side tanks stretched the whole length of the boiler, and coal was carried in a bunker on top of the firebox. Weight in working order was 22 tons and, despite the presence of outside frames, Stephenson link motion was neatly deployed. In 1923, in the course of overhaul at Swindon Works, No 2 was fitted with Walschaerts valve gear.

First World War years saw the end of the gay VofR livery, for, in 1915, the Cambrian Railways removed the names and insignia from the 2–6–2Ts. For a while the locos functioned in unlined black, then latterly the word 'Cambrian' was added in yellow block letters. Came 1923, and the tanks were reclothed in GWR green. *Rheidol*, the vintage ex-Hafan 2–4–0T, was withdrawn that year, and two new Prairie tanks joined the fold. Beautifully built at Swindon from original drawings, and slightly more powerful than their predecessors, they were given numbers 7 and 8. Of the two original VofR tanks, No 1213 (formerly VofR No 2) was brought up to full GWR standards in 1924. The other, No 1212, ex-VofR No 1, received only minor alterations — and once Rheidol winter services ceased on 1 January 1931, it was made redundant. Withdrawn in December 1932, it was placed on the GWR's Sales List, and lingered for many years at Swindon Works before it was finally dismembered in 1938.

Post-war survival seemed to lie in the lap of the gods. Then, in March 1949, came a faint stirring, when No 1213 was renumbered 9 as a modest measure of BR rationalization. A much more heartening event took place in June 1956, when all three VofR locos were given names. No 9 resumed its original title as *Prince of Wales*. The names, carried on large brass plates fixed to the tank sides, still remain, and one cannot doubt that they play a large part in public appeal. Meanwhile, the VofR's present stock of three steam locomotives, 16 bogie coaches, a VofR brake van and wagons, plus sundry wagons salvaged from Hafan & Talybont days, ensures that the old Vale of Rheidol atmosphere will continue to exercise its charm.

WELSHPOOL & LLANFAIR LIGHT RAILWAY

Opened: 4 April 1903
Closed: 3 November 1956; re-opened 6 April 1963
Gauge: 2 ft 6 in

When, on 10 June 1861, the Oswestry & Newtown Railway's first passenger train headed south through Montgomeryshire, and paused briefly at Welshpool, many of that market town's 60,000 inhabitants saw in the event an omen that their own surrounding countryside might be opened up with equal facility by 'railway magic'. Thus, in July 1862, the Earl of Powis, a local landowner of critical importance, received, but rejected, a first tentative railway proposal. Growing enthusiasm, however, was not to be deterred, and two more schemes were floated that year. Both postulated routes which led from Llanfair, and even though those, and several others, fell consistently by the wayside, the villagers of Llanfair clearly began to sense the role they were to play in future developments.

Welshpool & Llanfair Light Railway

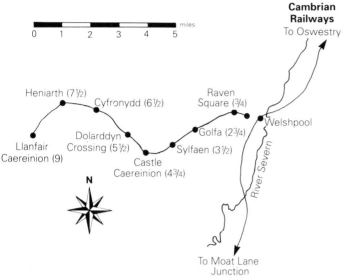

Decades slipped past; so, too, did many other railway aspirations. As late as 1887 propositions were still falling like ninepins; though one promoting group actually contrived to garner £4,000 in capital subscriptions before bowing the knee. Then, as a result of a series of Parish Council meetings held at Llanfair during the years 1895-96, the whole problem of providing Llanfair and district with railway facilities crystallized into a clear choice between two routes. One, supported by 11 local parishes out of 12, proposed to link Llanfair to Ardleen by standard gauge metals which would run along the Meifod Valley. The trouble was that the Cambrian Railways would have to be persuaded to build the line. The other, backed only by Castle Caereinion parish, visualized narrow gauge tracks laid along a much more difficult route, but running direct from Llanfair to Welshpool. The problem here was that estimated construction costs hovered around £25,000. Where was the money to come from?

The verbal battle which ensued between the rival

Welshpool & Llanfair men have every reason to feel proud as they pose alongside No 1 The Earl *and two beautiful coaches at Llanfair Caereinion Station, not long after the nine-mile line was opened in 1903. Low footsteps from quite elaborate verandahs assisted passengers to reach ground level. (Author's Collection)*

Renumbered 822 in GWR stock, but still bearing the name The Earl *and still hauling the Welshpool & Llanfair's two bogie coaches, the little 0-6-0T none the less presents a considerably different appearance as it departs from Welshpool in the early 1930s. A new boiler, standard GWR chimney and top feed were all products of a rebuild at Swindon Works in 1930. The W&L's narrow gauge engine shed, with its distinctive smoke vents, appears above the second coach, and Welshpool's transhipment shed lies on the extreme right. (Author's Collection)*

Although the GWR terminated W&LR passenger services on 9 February 1931, one return freight train between Welshpool and Llanfair was allowed to run daily, with occasional augmentation, for the next 25 years. Coal and farm produce provided most of the traffic, and here, in the summer of 1952, we see No 823, formerly The Countess *but now nameless, arriving at Welshpool with a short train of empty wagons. Some, no doubt, will be loaded at the transhipment shed, a little further on. But rail connections between BR and the W&LR were eventually severed in July 1963. (Steamchest)*

camps was given greater edge late in 1896, when the Government passed the Light Railways Act, with all its tantalizing implications that remote agricultural areas might receive grants to assist railway development. Welshpool townsfolk promptly urged their own Corporation to seek such assistance. Locals who supported the Meifod Valley project retaliated by redoubling their appeals to the Cambrian Railways; only in August 1897 was the impasse finally resolved, when the Light Railway Commissioners met at Llanfair to hear evidence from both sides. One month later came the Commissioners' verdict: the merits of Welshpool-Llanfair had won the day. Church bells rang, the coast was now clear, and the promoters of the direct line swung briskly into action.

Their efforts saw a Welshpool & Llanfair Light Railway Order obtained on 8 September 1899. It authorized construction of a single line, 9½ miles long, which would commence from an unfenced site adjoining Cambrian Railways station at Welshpool. Two unusual factors also emerged: a gauge of 2 ft 6 in was specified, and a prime condition of the Order insisted that an existing railway company should operate the narrow gauge concern.

Accordingly, a 99-year Agreement was entered into with the Cambrian Railways on 6 March 1900, whereby the parent company undertook to work the W&L in return for 60 per cent of its gross receipts. In the all-important matter of finance, the Treasury conceded a Free Grant of £17,500. Local inhabitants raised £20,000 in capital subscriptions, and four local Councils saw fit to advance a total sum of £14,000 in 50-year loans. Even then, thanks to the passage of time, ultimate costs of permanent way alone rose to

meet the *total* construction costs as previously estimated. Fortunately, much of the required land was donated free by local landowners, which included the Earl of Powis' successor! First sods were cut with appropriate ceremony at Welshpool on 30 May 1901, and the serious task of construction got under way.

On the face of it, rail communication between Welshpool, 210 feet above sea level, and Llanfair, 450 feet above sea level, would, spread over a distance of 9½ miles, appear to present few problems. In practice, the W&L's narrow gauge line faced three immediate hazards at the Welshpool end. These were a complex exit from the Cambrian Railways main line premises; an immediate climb at 1 in 33 to surmount the Shropshire Union Canal; and a speed restriction of 5 mph while trains wove a difficult passage through Welshpool town, almost brushing the sides of dwelling houses in the process. After that came the W&L's first halt, Seven Stars, at the junction of Hall Street and Union Street. From here a further quarter-mile climb at 1 in 36 had to be surmounted ere Welshpool's town environment began to peter out at Raven Square. But, not until the main Welshpool-Llanfair road was breached, a few yards further on, was the 5 mph speed limit relaxed. Thus far, one mile had been traversed — and 100 feet gained in altitude.

Although the line now chose to follow the main road to Llanfair as it wound through delightfully rural countryside, Golfa Incline still lay ahead; for the next 1¾ miles, gradients ranged from 1 in 29 to 1 in 320 as trains were painfully lifted by a series of reverse curves. Even after Golfa a short deceptive stretch of line led towards a final ¾-mile climb at 1 in 63 ere the W&L's second, and final, summit, some 3¼ miles out, was reached. From there on, W&L metals enjoyed a much easier, though still undulating, course as they ambled on through Sylfaen, Castle Caereinion, and Cyfronydd. Two substantial viaducts had to be built to reach Heniarth; then a final climb of just under 2 miles took the W&L into Llanfair itself. The terminus here could at least boast of a corrugated-iron booking office, waiting room and raised platform. No such amenities graced the Welshpool end of the W&L.

Despite financial strains and stresses, completion of the line was achieved by January 1903. Flat-bottomed rail, weighing, at 42 lbs per yard, 8 lbs lighter than that used by the Vale of Rheidol a year earlier, was employed throughout. Spiked to pine sleepers at sufficient intervals to tolerate maximum axle loads of 8 tons, it proved in the event to be perfectly adequate for all traffic needs. Intention was to work the line with one engine in steam, or divided into two sections — depending on traffic conditions. One passing loop was provided at Castle Caereinion. Signalling, therefore, was minimal, and communication was established by single wire telephone.

Management's original ambition was to acquire three locomotives. Shortage of funds, however, forbade such luxury, and early in 1903 two identical 0–6–0 tanks arrived from Beyer Peacock at a combined cost of £3,000. R. Y. Pickering & Co of Wishaw had already supplied three fine bogie passenger coaches, 32 open wagons, and four goods vans. After two

inspections, the Board of Trade granted the necessary certificate, and goods traffic on the W&L commenced on 4 March 1903. One month later, on 4 April, a highly decorated 0–6–0T, *The Countess*, was given the honour of leaving Welshpool at 11.15 am at the head of a special train packed with Directors, special guests and local luminaries. Suitable stops were made *en route* and, despite extremely inclement weather, the villagers of Llanfair turned out to a man to welcome their first passenger train. Once the train returned to Welshpool the inevitable celebratory luncheon was enjoyed by all. Even a medal was struck.

The W&L's first timetable, restoring a sense of proportion, was content to advertise three trains daily each way. One extra train was provided, twice monthly, on Welshpool Fair Days. But, typical of Welsh railways, not a wheel turned on Sundays. Initial passenger traffic was no more than reasonable in character; but the operation of separate coal, goods and timber 'specials' sustained hopes that prosperity lay round the corner. A local stone quarry, too, offered a modest, but welcome, modicum of mineral traffic.

Within five years, however, portents were brutally clear, and, financially embarrassed, the W&L Directors pleaded for temporary release from further capital repayments to local authorities who had lent so generously in 1900. During the First World War a rather desperate situation was eased by considerable improvement in timber traffic. By 1920, just the same, lock authorities again had to be importuned, and capital loan repayments were suspended for a further seven years. The next major event occurred on 1 Janury 1922, when the Cambrian Railways vanished into GWR ownership. The Cambrian's obligations towards the W&L being operational, *not* proprietorial, the narrow gauge line's identity remained intact until January 1923, when a special arrangement saw it, too, absorbed into the Great Western fold.

As happened with Irish narrow gauge railways, new

One good reason why Welshpool Borough Council denied W&LR trains access to and from Welshpool town itself after August 1963. This 1961 view underlines the acute problems the original narrow gauge railway faced as it struggled for a mile to clear the immediate town environment. Modern civic conditions could not possibly tolerate steam trains brushing past dwelling house windows! Ergo, the Welshpool & Llanfair Preservation Society had to content itself with purchase of the railway from Raven Square eastwards. (F. C. Le Manquais)

Exciting times for W&L Preservation Society members in August 1961. Ex-Admiralty 'toast-rack' coaches Nos 199 and 196, freshly obtained from the Lodge Hill & Upnor Railway, are carefully stored at Golfa, 557 feet above sea level and just under 2 miles from Raven Square, in anticipation of a grand re-opening in the foreseeable future. Latterly found to be unsuitable for vacuum brake conversion, these coaches, and two others, were, perforce, transferred to the Sittingbourne & Kemsley Railway in 1978. (F. C. Le Manquais)

Two miles further west, The Earl, closely sheeted against the elements, waits patiently, also in August 1961, with sundry vehicles on the loop line at Castle Caereinion. The signal box on the right was closed by the GWR in 1931, but will soon experience a new lease of life. (F. C. Le Manquais)

Two years later came the Great Day itself, 6 April 1963, when the new Welshpool & Llanfair Light Railway re-opened for public service. The loop line at Castle Caereinion presents a vastly different scene as a highly polished The Earl prepares to forge 4½ miles on to Llanfair. Although the Chairman's special train had conducted the Earl of Powis and guests earlier that day from Welshpool's narrow gauge yard to Llanfair, where the opening ceremony was performed, the W&LR's future programme of three trains each way on Saturdays, Sundays and Bank Holidays would, of necessity, confine itself to the Llanfair and Castle Caereinion section. Eighteen more years would elapse ere public trains ran all the way from Llanfair to Raven Square. (Steamchest)

The new W&LR busily laid the foundations of its uniquely varied locomotive stock. 0–8–0T No 10 Sir Drefaldwyn, seen here in steam at Castle Caereinion on 1 April 1972, came from Austria in December 1969. Built as an 0–8–0 tender loco by Société Franco-Belge (Works No 2855) in 1944 for German Military Railways service, and later captured by American Occupation Forces, the engine subsequently served on two Austrian narrow gauge railways. In addition to acquiring the number 699-01, it was also rebuilt in 0–8–0T form in 1957. Its nominal tractive effort of 13,535 lb certainly made it a powerful, and useful, acquisition where the W&LR was concerned. No 10 was officially named and presented with a cast of the Montgomeryshire crest on 5 September 1971. (Steamchest)

and powerful ownership did little to halt the W&L's decline. 1925 was a particularly crucial year, for it was then that the GWR's increasing absorption in local bus services induced the parent company to introduce road competition on the Welshpool-Llanfair circuit. Results were totally predictable. Whilst a meagre enough figure of 20,712 passengers had used Welshpool's narrow gauge railway during 1925, the first quarter of 1926 yielded a return of fewer than 1,000. Perhaps in expiation, the GWR continued to maintain full passenger services right through the 1920s. By 31 January 1931, however, Swindon decided to call it a day, and public notice was given that W&LR passenger services would cease in one week's time.

As might be expected, the announcement triggered off a barrage of local protest. Despite representations at high level, however, the GWR held fast to its intention — and the W&L's last passenger train ran on 9 February 1931. Ironically, it was poorly patronized by the very people who had protested. That year the W&L's three lovely coaches went to Swindon for scrapping, and the signal box at Castle Caereinion,

now considered redundant, was closed.

Living now in a strange state of limbo, the little Welsh line struggled on, despatching one return freight train daily, and gratefully adding extra trains as circumstances demanded. Miraculously, it survived the rigours of the Second World War. But the post-war economics of paying a small army of staff to maintain a derisory freight service between two small towns in the heart of Montgomeryshire must have weighed heavily on British Railways' mind when it assumed command in 1948. Somehow, the W&L steamed on, to become Britain's last (non-preserved) public freight-carrying narrow gauge railway. There came a time, though, when even that accolade could not be justified on grounds of expense. Thus, in November 1956, all rail services were withdrawn.

It was fortunate that the concept of narrow gauge railway preservation had already gained credence throughout Wales, for it was the very success and vitality of the Festiniog and Talyllyn Railway movements which inspired a group of enthusiasts to form a Welshpool & Llanfair Preservation Society almost from the moment that British Railways gave up. The road was not an easy one, however, as a few pioneers entered into determined, but painfully protracted, negotiations with both BR and the Ministry of Transport. Gradually, however, progress was made, and 1960 saw the formation of the present-day Welshpool & Llanfair Light Railway Preservation Co Ltd. Two years later, a lease of the line from Raven Square to Llanfair was conceded, and since then direct purchase has been achieved. It came as no real surprise that hopes of working trains straight into the heart of Welshpool town, as of yore, had to be abandoned; Llanfair was therefore accepted as the railway's new

base. Commencing in 1963, when the 4¼ miles to Castle Caereinion were reopened for public use, the revitalized W&LR has gradually forged east towards a brand-new terminus at Raven Square, Welshpool. The first public train ran, double-headed, from Raven Square to Llanfair on 18 July 1981.

Even a 2 ft 6 in gauge railway can produce a study of dignity and impudence! Seen at Llanfair Caereinion on 1 April 1972, W&LR 0–4–0T No 8, built by A. Barclay Sons & Co (2207/1946) for Glasgow Corporation's Provan Gas Works, measures itself for size against No 12 Joan. *The latter, a Kerr Stuart 0–6–0T (4404/1927) and a veteran of Antigua Sugar Factory employment, had only been at Llanfair a matter of months, and will require considerable attention before it can undertake gainful employment on W&LR metals. Christened* Dougal, *the little Scottish tank was first steamed in December 1975, and, painted Midland red,* Joan *entered regular service on 10 April 1977.* (Steamchest)

LOCOMOTIVES

W&L No	GWR No	Name	Type	Date built	Makers	Maker's number
1	822	*The Earl*	0–6–0T	1902	Beyer Peacock	3496
2	823	*The Countess/ Countess The Countess*	,,	1902	,,	3497

The W&L's 'identical twins' arrived from Manchester in time for opening day, and No 2 was given prime honours. Their works numbers, incidentally, are out of context for the year 1902, and were, in fact, two vacant numbers taken from a previously cancelled contract of 1892. That aside, there was nothing old-fashioned about their design, which, for instance, involved the first narrow gauge use, contractors' locos excepted, of Walschaerts valve gear. Outside frames, short wide firebox, stove-pipe chimney, Ramsbottom safety valves, warning bell on cab roof — all contributed to produce a brace of distinguished-looking little tanks. Despite its working weight of only 19½ tons, each loco packed a tractive effort of 8,175 lbs. This power was to be put to good use, particularly

when the engines tacked Golfa Incline, with its half-mile stretch at in 1 in 29 — the steepest gradient ever worked by Cambrian Railways passenger trains.

As Welshpool possessed the W&L's only loco shed, all traffic was regulated from that end of the line; and, in the complete absence of turntables, locos always worked with smokebox facing Llanfair. The W&L's lovely 9-ton coaches, on the other hand, were turned periodically on a triangular layout in Welshpool yard. The object here was to equalize wear on wheel flanges. Flights of steps on each coach assisted passengers to mount from ground level at the Welshpool 'terminus'. The latter had no connection with the Cambrian's main line station, and was really just a single siding; of course, a transhipment shed and mixed gauge cattle dock lay alongside.

From the outset, the W&L's two locos were very smart in appearance. They sported Cambrian Railways livery, black with red and grey-white lining, but the brass nameplates, with vermilion backgrounds, more than compensated as they gleamed from the tank sides. Oval number plates on the cab sheets contrived to include the little railway's name in full. Even when the GWR took over in 1923, such changes as were effected were largely cosmetic in nature. GWR number plates appeared, Ramsbottom valves were replaced by standard GWR safety valves and covers, and the locos were painted GWR green. As the letters 'GW' now flanked the number plates, the nameplates were remounted high on the cabside. Owing to lack of space, No 2's name had to be truncated to *Countess*. Major alterations came in November 1929 and July 1930, when first *The Earl*, then *Countess*, entered Swindon Works for heavy repairs. Opportunity was taken to fit new boilers and fireboxes, specially built to previous dimensions; but the addition of Swindon-type smokebox and boiler fittings altered the locos' appearance considerably. During the Second World War, standards of maintenance lapsed, as elsewhere, and the black livery reappeared for a while. The greatest ignominy of all came in March 1951, when locomotive nameplates were removed as an anti-vandal precaution!

Once live traffic ceased at Welshpool in November 1956, both locos were stored at Oswestry; and there they lay until they were sold to the W&L Preservation Society — No 1 in August 1961, No 2 in July 1962. Finding coaching stock for the W&L's 2 ft 6 in metals presented the Society with quite a problem. Fortunately, the Admiralty had abandoned its Lodge Hill and Upnor narrow gauge railway in 1961; thus five useful bogie coaches found their way from Kent to Wales. In 1968 the W&L augmented its preserved stock by obtaining four four-wheeled coaches from the Zillertalbahn, a 760cm gauge Austrian railway. *Monarch*, an articulated 0–4–4–0 tank from Bowaters Paper Mills in Kent, also entered revenue-earning service in 1973. An ex-Styrian Provincial Railways 0–8–0T had arrived at Llanfair, and, rechristened No 10 *Sir Drefaldwyn*, was already handling passenger trains. No 12 *Joan*, a Kerr Stuart 0–6–2T from Antigua, and No 14, a Hunslet 2–6–2T formerly owned by the Sierra Leone Railway, plus four modern English-built bogie coaches from the same source, have since accentuated the cosmopolitan flavour of present-day W&LR activities. Nevertheless, a sufficient quantity of vintage Welsh wagons and vans can be seen around Llanfair to remind us of days gone by. Meanwhile, the revived Welshpool & Llanfair Railway competes very vigorously in what is now a keenly contested battle of Preservation Societies.

LOCOMOTIVES

Locomotives of the Welshpool & Llanfair Preservation Society

No	Name	Type	Date built	Maker	Maker's number	Remarks
1	*The Earl*	0–6–0T	1902	Beyer Peacock	3496	Ex-BR
2	*The Countess*	0–6–0T	1902	,,	3497	Ex-BR
3	*Raven*	0–4–0DM	1934	Ruston & Hornsby	170374	Sold 1974
4	*Upnor Castle*	0–4–0DM	1954	Hibberd 'Planet'	3687	Sold to Festiniog Railway, 1968
5	*Nutty*	0–4–0VB	1929	Sentinel	7701	To Narrow Gauge Railway Museum, Towyn, 1971
6	*Monarch*	0–4–4–0T	1953	Bagnall	3024	Acquired 1966
7	*Chattenden*	0–6–0DM	1949	E. E. Baguley	2263	Acquired 1968
8	*Dougal*	0–4–0T	1946	Barclay	2207	Acquired 1969
9	*Wynnstay*	0–6–0DM	1951	John Fowler	4160005	Sold to Whipsnade, 18 March 1972
10	*Sir Drefaldwyn*	0–8–0T	1944	Franco-Belge	2855	Ex-Steiermarkische Landesbahnen, 1969
11	*Ferret*	0–4–0DM	1940	Hunslet	2251	Ex-Admiralty, 1971
12	*Joan*	0–6–2T	1927	Kerr Stuart	4404	Ex-Antigua Sugar Co, 1971
14	SLR 85	2–6–2T	1954	Hunslet	3815	Ex-Sierra Leone Rly, 1975
15	(JR No 5)	2–6–2T	1948	Tubize	2369	Ex-Jokoisten Rly, Finland, 1983

FAIRBOURNE RAILWAY

Opened: 1890
Closed: 30 October 1983; re-opened as
12¼ in gauge 28 March 1986
Gauge: 1 ft 3 in

True to Welsh traditions, even this miniature railway owed its origin to horse-drawn tramway days. In this instance, however, slate was *not* the magnet.

It all started when the Cambrian Railways, thrusting north, reached Barmouth Junction in July 1865. Barmouth Bridge, the longest in Wales, was opened two years later, and, as much of its stone came from nearby quarries, the contractors made use of the time-honoured and convenient medium of horse-drawn trams. One Cardiff firm, Solomon Andrews & Son, was already well known for its ownership of the Pwllheli & Llanbedrog Tramway, and once land on the south side of the Barmouth estuary fell ripe for house-building development various contractors decided to emulate Solomon Andrews' methods.

One such was Mr McDougall, later of self-raising flour fame. He began in 1890 by setting up a modest brickworks north-west of what was to become Fairbourne station. From there he ran a 2-foot gauge horse-drawn mineral tramway as far as the beach. Thence the tramroad, turning north, followed the seashore right past Penrhyn Point, to terminate near the Barmouth ferry. Rails, flat-bottomed and weighing only 16 lbs to the yard, were spiked direct to wooden sleepers.

The tramroad's purpose, of course, was to convey bricks and building materials to the various sites as a colony of private houses was created all along the promontory. Once the housing programme was completed, however, a new business departure, that of catering for summer visitors, presented itself; and Mr McDougall, alert to all possibilities, promptly switched his industrial tramroad to passenger use.

Two passenger cars, probably conversions from earlier wagons, were introduced, and with one horse allocated to each car, a 2d fare was instituted. The line offered visitors a pleasant 1-mile ride, weather permitting, from the Cambrian Railways Fairbourne station, opened in 1912, to Barmouth Ferry. Meanwhile, ownership of the Fairbourne Estate passed, in 1911, from Mr McDougall to a Mr Peacock. Thus it remained until 1916, when unexpected developments took place.

The concept that miniature gauge steam railways might expand beyond garden toy status into public service first gained credence in 1904, when a Northampton firm, Bassett-Lowke Ltd, supplied the necessary equipment for such a venture at Blackpool. So successful was the experiment that other seaside resorts followed suit. Most were run by Narrow Gauge Railways Ltd, in close liaison with Bassett-Lowke; and almost inevitably, the same partnership took over at Fairbourne in 1916. Bassett-Lowke supplied one of its 'Improved Little Giant' 'Atlantic' locomotives, *Prince Edward of Wales*, plus four four-wheeled passenger cars. Built to a scale of 3 inches to 1 foot, the 2-ton miniature loco was quite capable of handling loads of up to 60 passengers. Typical of its type, it burned coke.

Although the course of the new miniature railway still followed that of the former tramway, many changes were effected by a much more sophisticated management. The section between the brickworks and Fairbourne station, for instance, was abandoned, and what seemed at the time to be an appropriate miniature terminus was built adjoining the Cambrian Railways level crossing. Apart from a station building,

Count Louis, *Fairbourne's long serving Basset-Lowke 'Atlantic',*
poses elegantly in a passing loop approximately halfway along the
two-mile line. Summer traffic was at its height then, in August
1961. (F. C. Le Manquais)

Trouble at Fairbourne terminus on 6 August 1961. Prince Charles, *a temporary import from Dudley Zoo, has just failed on the 2.30 pm train for Barmouth Ferry, and is being removed to make way for* Count Louis. Dingo, *a petrol-driven loco, stands by (left) in case of ultimate need, but holiday visitors, naturally, prefer to ride behind steam! The trouble, however, could not have been too serious, for, just over one hour later,* Prince Charles *and* Count Louis *combined to doublehead a heavily laden 3.30 pm ex-Fairbourne.* (F. C. Le Manquais)

A little further along the line Dingo *retrieves two empty cars, to help relieve the holiday pressures at Fairbourne station. The locomotive at the rear is No 15* Rachel, *a 1959 product of G&S Light Engineering Co.* Dingo *was built in 1951.* (F. C. Le Manquais)

it contained a signal box, a small loco shed and a passing loop. Halts were also established at Bathing Beach, Golf Links, Sand Dunes, Penrhyn Point, and Barmouth Ferry. The titles tell their own story. Fairbourne's solitary locomotive was treated to a dark green livery with maroon lining. Red oxide paint and black ironwork, however, sufficed for the coaches, and in a revised scale of charges the previous fare of 2d per trip was gently increased to 3d.

Post-First World War years brought several changes of fortune. In 1921 the railway was hired to a co-operative of ex-servicemen, who traded under the name of Barmouth Motor Boat & Ferry Co. Within two years, however, bad summers combined to put this commendable enterprise out of business, and in 1924 proprietorship of the miniature railway passed to Fairbourne Estate & Development Co Ltd. In the meantime, one major event that had already occurred in locomotive affairs, when *Prince Edward of Wales* left Fairbourne in exchange for *Katie,* a Heywood 0–4–0T which had previously been performing on the Llewellyn Miniature Railway at Southport, and the Ravenglass & Eskdale Railway.

The exchange proved disastrous, for *Katie,* built freelance, as it were, at Duffield Bank in 1896, was crude, both in appearance and performance, com-

pared to Bassett-Lowke's accurately scaled models. Her intermittent ability to maintain a head of steam proved latterly such an embarrassment that her new owners were soon obliged to lay her aside. Replacement? Came Easter 1925, and another splendid Bassett-Lowke 'Atlantic', *Count Louis*, arrived on the scene. The name bespoke its source, the estate of Count Louis Zbrowski, the celebrated motor racing driver who met his death on the race-track. Yet, splendid purchase though the 'Atlantic' was, one awkward fact of life still remained: any time that *Count Louis* was taken out of action for repair, *all* traffic ceased on the Fairbourne Railway.

The solution which management adopted to offset this vexing problem was even more remarkable than the acquisition of *Katie* — and certainly as impractical — for late in 1926 Fairbourne Estate purchased a 1 ft 6 in gauge Stirling 'Single'. Built by Bagnalls in 1893, she was clearly an elegant creation, and could 'fly' with a light load. But a single pair of driving wheels was hardly germane to the kind of loads a busy miniature railway could germinate. Apparently unworried, however, by technical considerations, Fairbourne management proceeded to lay an extra rail to accommodate its new giant, and got as far as Penrhyn Point by 1930. Within five years sheer disillusionment saw the extra rail lifted, and in 1936 the Stirling 'Single' moved on to pastures new. By now a Lister petrol-engined rail-truck had been imported to share duties with *Count Louis*. It was just as well, for the steam loco fractured a connecting rod in 1939, and the Lister ended the season on its own. As if that calamity were not enough, the outbreak of war that year saw

the bulk of Fairbourne's staff called up for military service. National war disciplines soon pre-empted any likelihood of sustained public support, and, accepting the inevitable, the little railway closed down completely in 1940.

The Second World War was notoriously hard on British coastal railways, and the Fairbourne was not spared in any way. Winter storms of 1943 battered the track almost beyond recognition, and subsequent use of amphibious vehicles in preparation for D-Day completed the destruction. The miracle was that, once the war was fought and won, a group of three West Midlands industrialists who visited the scene of carnage in 1946 summoned vision and courage enough to buy the line. Their aim was rehabilitation. Away went *Count Louis* and the Lister for much-needed attention; back came the Lister, with two contractors' wagons in tow, and track-laying commenced in September 1946. This time heavier rail was laid. Despite adverse weather conditions, work continued with such impetus that a modified public railway service was reintroduced in time for Easter 1947. As before, the Lister soldiered on alone until July, when *Count Louis* made a most welcome return. By the end of 1947 only one last short section of track to Ferry remained to be completed; and, almost in celebration, a second Lister unit was purchased. Second-hand, it was converted from 2-foot gauge to meet Fairbourne requirements.

1948 was a good year. A new bridge was constructed near Ferry, where an earlier bridge and embankment had collapsed, and everything was completed in time for a grand gala opening that summer. Mercifully, the public responded so well that five more coaches had to be ordered from Northampton. Heartened thus by public support, management then embarked on further improvements. A new and more spacious terminus was built at Fairbourne, and, alongside, a combined loco shed and workshop offered vastly improved facilities. A beautifully fitted bogie coach, fresh from service on the Hardwicke Manor Railway, near Tewkesbury, arrived to enhance the Fairbourne's rolling-stock in June 1950. No doubt its presence inspired the complete replacement of original carriage stock in 1951, when articulated stock took over.

From that point the Fairbourne never looked back, and refinement after refinement was added over the years, so much so that the company saw fit to drop the word 'miniature' from its title in 1958. Further steam locomotives were added to share *Count Louis*' load, as were a succession of internal combustion locos; and, partly linked administratively with the Talyllyn Railway, the 2-mile long Fairbourne Railway lived on to add lustre to an already fascinating Welsh narrow gauge railway scene.

Unfortunately for the Fairbourne, Welsh narrow gauge railway competition stiffened enormously during the 1970s, and that, plus something of an economic recession, saw a last Fairbourne Railway 15 in gauge train run on 30 October 1983. Some months later the concern was acquired by a newly formed company, the North Wales Narrow Gauge Railway Limited. Its Managing Director, Mr J. W. Ellerton, already had considerable experience of 12¼ in gauge railway activity in France, and it was decided to test his conviction that small gauge locos modelled faithfully on 2-foot gauge examples with closest cosmetic care would reattract the public. Thus, the new Fairbourne & Barmouth Steam Railway ran its first public 12¼ in gauge train on 28 March 1986. The Fairbourne terminus was reconstructed, and named Gorsaf Newydd (New Station), a ten-road carriage shed was added, and the whole of the former 2-mile 1 ft 3 in gauge line was reconstructed in 12¼ in gauge form. Porth Penrhyn, the station at the other end of the line, was also remodelled, and water towers and signal boxes were constructed at both ends. Some 28 carriages and 17 wagons of various types have since been added, and it is heartening to note that a complement of 34,183 passenger bookings in 1984 swelled under the new auspices to 54,000 by 1987.

LOCOMOTIVES

15-inch gauge locomotives

No	Name	Type	Date built	Makers	Makers number	Remarks
–	*Prince Edward of Wales*	4–4–2	1914	Bassett-Lowke	22	Sold *circa 1922*
4/3	*Count Louis*	4–4–2	1924	,,	32	Now at Birmingham Railway Museum
1	—	4–2–2	1898	Regent St Polytechnic/ Bagnall		18 in gauge. Now at Sandy Bay Countryside Museum, Exmouth
–	*Katie*	0–4–0T	1896	A. P. Heywood, Duffield Bank Wks	4	Dismantled 1926. Frames now with Ravenglass & Eskdale Railway
–	*Prince Charles*	4–6–0	1946	G&S Light Eng & Maintenance Co		Loaned to Fairbourne 1953-62. Now operating at Carnforth as a 4–6–2
–	*Ernest W. Twining*	4–6–2	1949	,,		Loaned to Fairbourne from 1961. Shipped to Japan in 1987.
14	*Katie/Shon*	2–4–2	1954	,,		Purchased 1965. To Haigh Railway, Wigan, 1984
18	*Sian/Sydney*	2–4–2	1963	,,		Sold 1985 to Littlecote House, Hungerford
–	*Tracey-Jo*	2–6–2	1964	,,		Petrol-hydraulic. Returned to makers, 1986
5	*Whippit Quick*	0–4–4	1935	Lister		Sold 1975. Originally 0–4–0 petrol mechanical, latterly diesel
6	*Gwril*	0–4–0 petrol	Bought 1947	,,		Originally 2-foot gauge. Sold 1985
–	*Dingo*	4w+4w	1951	,,		Scrapped 1975
15	*Rachel*	0–6–0	1959	G&S Light Eng		Petrol-hydraulic. Sold 1985 to Haigh Railway, Wigan
14A	*Sylvia*	4w+4w	1961	,,		Petrol, rebuilt in 1985 as diesel-hydraulic. Regauged as *Lilian Walter*, to 12¼ in gauge, 1986

Fairbourne & Barmouth Steam Railway locomotives (12¼ in gauge)

No	Name	Type	Date built	Makers	Remarks
1	*Yeo*	2–6–2T	1978	D Curwen	Based on Lynton & Barnstaple locos
2	*Bedgellert*	0–6–4ST	1979	,,	Based on North Wales Narrow Gauge loco
3	—	4w+4w petrol railcar	1978	,,	
4	*Sherpa*	0–4–0ST	1978	Milner Eng	Based on Darjeeling-Himalaya type
5	*Russell*	2–6–4T	1985	Fairbourne Loco works	Extensive rebuild of *Elaine*, built by Milner Engineering in 1979
6	*Lilian Walter*	4w+4w diesel-hydraulic	1985	,,	Rebuild of 15-inch gauge *Sylvia*
7	*Gwril*	4w battery-electric	1987	,,	
8	*Sandy River*	2–6–2	1989	,,	Based on Sandy River & Rangeley Lakes loco No 24

PART 2

Irish narrow gauge railways

An empty cattle special bound for Dingle pauses while locos 1T and 2T take well-needed water in July 1950 (see page 109).
(Steamchest)

Though they relied largely on Government legislation for their ultimate development, it cannot be argued that Ireland's light railways suffered the derisory treatment which befell her earlier standard gauge enterprises. True, funds were never easily prised from England's purse, either public or private, and Government lead was rarely inspired; but at least a Tramways Act passed by Westminster as far back as 1860 recognized Ireland's desperate need for rail transport in remote, but congested, areas where standard gauge metals had so far failed to penetrate. Ireland's plight, in fact, was plain for all to see. Her fishing ports were operating at a grave disadvantage compared to English and Scottish counterparts, agriculture throughout the country was in an acute state of depression, and, most ominous of all, successive famines and their aftermath, death and emigration, had played havoc with the Island's population.

The Act of 1860 meant well, but it fell lamentably short of target. At first only animal power was sanctioned for tramway use, and that absurdity remained law until 1871, when an amendment was passed authorizing employment of mechanical devices. Even then, speed restrictions of 6 mph along roads, and 3 mph through towns and villages, hardly fired the imagination. The Act's most grievous deficiency, however, lay in the all-important field of finance. Earlier decades had witnessed the growth of that peculiarly Southern Irish institution, the Baronial Guarantee system, whereby local authorities, by underwriting payment of annual interest on such railway capital as was subscribed, carried on their own backs the consequences of failure, or part-success. Such a practice, with its inbuilt implication of taxation without representation, would have had Westminster hopping long ago had it applied to English affairs. As it was, railways in Ireland were left, under the Act, to soldier on in time-honoured fashion. A Relief of Distress Amendment Act, dated 1880, made some belated effort to introduce a blend of local and State support. But its benefits applied only to certain scheduled lines, and the effect was slight.

By the early 1880s a mere 80 miles of narrow gauge railway had been constructed in Ireland, and every inch of these favoured Northern Counties. So grave now was the plight of southern and western Ireland that even

Westminster had to admit that more generous provision of State aid was crucial if further railway extension was to be envisaged. The result was the enactment of the Tramways and Public Companies (Ireland) Act of 1883. Under its provisions the Treasury undertook to relieve Baronies of half the amount paid by them under Guarantee, provided that:

(1) the new line was maintained in working order, and carried traffic,

(2) no more than 2 per cent of the capital of any one railway was so paid,

(3) *total* state liability in respect of Baronial Guarantees did not exceed £40,000 per annum.

Another section of the Act ordained that railways which persisted in yielding deficits over a period of two years should be handed over to the appropriate Grand Jury, ie County Council, to become, like it or not, their property and responsibility. In the event this provision was enforced on four occasions, and two of the railways affected, the Schull & Skibbereen and Tralee & Dingle, were narrow gauge concerns. But some relaxation was permitted in existing tramway regulations. Where, for instance, a tramway operated more than 30 feet from the centre of a road, speed restrictions no longer applied. The most unwitting time bomb of all, however, lay buried deep in an Order issued by the Lord Lieutenant when the terms of the 1883 Act were promulgated in Ireland. Relief in respect of normal gauge schemes, it warned, would only be allowed 'if no Guarantee is asked for on as much of the expenditure as is rendered necessary by departure from 3 ft gauge'.

Here, if you please, was a certain recipe for proliferation of small independent companies, each with its own management and staff — and heavy overheads. Thus the Act, though genuinely purporting to ease access to Treasury funds, really misfired in conception. So cumbersome, too, were the legal preambles it imposed on would-be promoters, and so little lighter were the financial burdens it left on local authorities, that its total effect on the welfare of Irish railways was sadly muted. Nevertheless, 16 new light railways and tramways took advantage of its provisions, as may be seen from the table overleaf.

Light railways and tramways constructed under the Tramways Act 1883

Project No	Railway	Mileage 5 ft 3 in gauge	Mileage 3 foot gauge	Capital	Interest at 5% guaranteed by Baronies	Less maximum Treasury relief ie 2% of capital	Line opened
1-7	Various	75½	–	£365,585	£18,280	£7,312	1887-90
8	West Donegal	1	4	17,000	850	340	1889
9	Schull & Skibbereen	—	14½	57,000	2,850	1,140	1886
10	Clogher Valley Tramway	—	37	123,310	6,165	2,466	1887
11	West Clare	—	27	163,500	8,175	3,270	1887
12	South Clare	—	26	120,000	6,000	2,400	1892
13-14	Cork & Muskerry	—	26½	105,000	5,250	2,100	1888
15	Cavan & Leitrim	—	48½	190,585	9,530	3,811	1887
16	Tralee & Dingle	—	37½	120,000	6,000	2,400	1891
	Totals	76½	221	£1,261,980	£63,100	£25,239	

One glance at these figures betrays the gross imbalance which still persisted between State and local liabilities; for, of course, the Baronies stumped up even more if railway working losses were incurred. In 1886 the Allport Commission, when invited to assess the growing complexities of Irish Railways, seized on precisely that point, and went on to criticize the 1883 Act in no uncertain terms. Ultimately, its Report, issued in 1886, thrust three new rules firmly before the Government.

1. State Guarantee should be made directly available to those who supplied capital.
2. Local contributions should be limited in amount, and should bear some proportion to the resources of the Districts concerned.
3. Strict Governmental scrutiny should be exercised over the engineering and general merits of any scheme proposed. (This proposal was a reflection of the scandalous state of contractual neglect found raging, unchecked, on many Irish railways).

Give Westminster its due. The Report was by no means accepted in its entirety, but within a year the Light Railways (Ireland) Act 1889 became law. Under its terms State finance became much more readily available, in the form of Free Grants. They were subject, of course, to a not unreasonable precaution. Equally importantly, matters relating to siting, constructing and operating new railway schemes now passed firmly under the joint aegis of the Lord Lieutenant, the Treasury, and the Board of Works. In short, the contractors' heyday was over. At first existing railway companies fought shy of promoting new schemes, but gradually, as further improved legislation was introduced, 13 new railways ventured construction, as detailed in the table below, and more new territory was opened up.

Westminster's next legislation took shrewd

Light railways constructed under the Light Railways Act 1889

Project No	Worked by	Mileage 5 ft 3 in gauge	Mileage 3 foot gauge	Free Grant by State	Capital	Interest at 5% guaranteed by Baronies	*Less* maximum Treasury relief ie 2% of capital	Line opened
1-11	Various	195	—	£895,224	£250,000	£12,500	£5,000	1893-95
12-13	County Donegal	—	43½	£245,322	£2,000	£100	£40	1893-95
	Totals	195	43½	£1,140,546	£252,000	£12,600	£5,040	

cognisance of the fact that not all Irish railways were flourishing as they might. With some railways, in fact, annual dividend deficiencies which the Treasury were obliged to make good were beginning to assume a permanent character. To discourage this tendency the Tramways Act (Ireland) was passed in 1895. Often called the 'Commutation Act', it gave the Treasury the option of shedding liabilities of this nature by paying a Grand Jury concerned a once-and-for-all sum of up to 33⅓ times the annual deficit. This right, hardly abused by the Treasury, was exercised on three occasions, when liabilities towards the West Donegal, Tralee & Dingle, and Mitchelstown & Fermoy Railways were sloughed off.

The following year, in rather more optimistic vein, the Government introduced its Railways (Ireland) Act of 1896. Though suffering somewhat from haste in preparation, it represented, none the less, an earnest intention to stimulate further extension of railways, piers, jetties, even steamboat and coach services, in Ireland. Under its aegis the Treasury was endowed with powers to override an adverse decision of the Lord Lieutenant, should it think fit — *and* throw in a Free Grant. Conversely, the Board of Works was authorized to institute an official inquiry should the working or maintenance of any Irish railway arouse public concern. Three out of four investigations ultimately carried out warranted no action. However, as can be seen from the table below, only two new lines were added under the 1896 Act.

From there on little legislation was passed which affected Ireland's railways, light or otherwise. One Act of 1900 made a further attempt to alleviate ratepayers' burdens by confining liability under Baronial Guarantees largely to a period *after* a line was opened. Then, in 1906, a Viceregal Commission was appointed to enquire closely into the working of all Irish railways. A Majority Report in 1910 recommended unification. The Minority, whilst agreeing on all matters financial, differed as to how control should be effected. Westminster, deeply preoccupied at the time with Empire and political affairs, took no action. Britain went to war in 1914, and, as we shall see, this act, plus subsequent political developments, had devastating consequences for every light railway and tramway in Ireland.

In conclusion, while there can be no doubt that the Acts of 1860–1896 made possible the construction of lines which would not have been undertaken by the larger railway companies, the emphasis placed for economic reasons on narrow gauge construction by the Lord Lieutenant in his Order of 1883 did Ireland, in the long run, a poor service. For here it was that the 'break of gauge' heresy took firm root. And heresy it was, for to a railwayman non-interchangeability of rolling-stock means waste. When evidence was given before the Allport Commission in 1886, one GWR manager testified that Paddington's habit in dealing with break of gauge was to add 20 miles' rates to cover the cost of transhipment. The same Commission estimated that Ireland's narrow gauge railways might conceivably have been built to standard gauge dimensions at an additional cost of only £500 per mile. Consequent inter-availability of rolling-stock would easily have absorbed this extra expense.

Costs and lack of capital. These were the perennial banes of Ireland's narrow gauge system. Too much capital was absorbed too soon by construction costs, yet hardly a

Light railways constructed under the Railways (Ireland) Act 1896

Route	Mileage 3-foot gauge	Free Grant by State	Total cost to build	Deficiency made up by Baronies 4% Stock	Maximum Treasury Relief	Line opened
Buncrana-Cardonagh	18½	£98,527	£103,824	£5,000	Nil	1901
Letterkenny-Burtonport	49½	£313,648	£315,450	£5,000	Nil	1903
Totals	68	£412,175	£419,274	£10,000	Nil	

Both lines were worked by the Londonderry & Lough Swilly Railway.

Railway	Building costs per mile	Annual averages for 5 years to 1916	
		Receipts	Expenditure
Clogher Valley Tramway	£3,286	£8,967	£9,891
Cork & Muskerry	£4,167	£11,260	£8,106
Schull & Skibbereen	£3,800	£3,412	£4,885
Cavan & Leitrim	£3,889	£13,986	£13,808

railway was built along the economic principles which Belgium, for one, so ably pioneered. In Belgium, light railways cost £3,000 a mile to construct. Ireland averaged £5,700, and even her *most cheaply* built lines proved expensive luxuries, as the figures above show.

Nor was Southern Ireland alone in her profligacy. Further north the Ballymena & Larne, the Ballycastle Railway and the Castlederg & Victoria Bridge Tramway cost £3,400, £5,723, and £3,300 respectively per mile to build. In too many instances permanent way and stations were oversubstantial for the amount of traffic they could possibly hope to generate. Add over-staffing here, under-employment there, and the weakness of the Irish narrow gauge is clear to see.

Another serious defect was the almost complete absence of professional supervision over contractors in the early days. Later inspection often revealed atrocious defects, yet, having satisfied the letter of the law by providing a line capable of being *opened*, the guilty men escaped retribution. Local communities footed the bill. Even the working of many a line was suspect from financial or safety aspects; sometimes both. Yet, not until the 1896 Act was passed was inspectorial light thrown on any form of serious mismanagement. Unfortunately,

powers vested in the Board of Works were so draconian in nature that their full severity was seldom inflicted.

Lastly, there was one running sore which affected the welfare of all Irish railways alike, and that long before motor transport dealt the final blow. That was the constant shift of population within the UK itself. Ireland was once a populous, and potentially self-supporting country. But in her case the introduction of the Railway Age failed, alas, to inspire either industrial or agricultural prosperity. The cost of this, plus famine, speaks only too clearly from the table below.

* * *

Eighteen in number, Ireland's narrow gauge railways would appear to present a very complicated package. In truth, understanding can be considerably simplified if two considerations are borne in mind:

1. The geographical factor. Most were built in an attempt to develop areas in Ireland's south-western and northern Counties which were left untouched by standard gauge metals. The Dublin and Belfast localities were already well served.

UK Population (in millions)

	1831	1841	1861	1891	1921	1971
England & Wales	14	15	20	29	37¾	51½
Scotland	2¼	2½	3	4	4¾	5
Ireland	7¾	8	5½	4¾	4¼	NI – 1½ Eire – 3
Ireland as percentage of total population	32	30	20	12	9	7

2. The political factor. The ultimate fate of all Irish railways hinged on the 1921 Partition. Narrow gauge lines totally contained within the Irish Free State, and still extant in 1924, passed into the ownership of the Great Southern Railways. Those operating exclusively on Northern Irish soil, and still existing by the time Stormont formed the Ulster Transport Authority, 1 October 1948, were gathered into the UTA

fold. Railways unfortunate enough to have one foot in each camp, as it were, became victims of political deadlock. Thus, Ireland's two largest narrow gauge concerns were left to pursue independent existences right to the bitter end.

When these two principles are jointly applied, four distinct groups emerge, corresponding to the following tables.

Southern Irish narrow gauge railways at the 1921 Partition

Railway	Date opened	Counties served	Mileage		Remarks
			Eire	N Ireland	
Cork, Blackrock & Passage	1850	Cork	16½	—	Note how the first five
Schull & Skibbereen	1886	Cork	15	—	served three of Southern
Cork & Muskerry	1887	Cork	18	—	Ireland's most south-westerly
Tralee & Dingle	1891	Kerry	37½	—	counties. All six railways were
West Clare & South Clare	1887	Clare	27	—	absorbed by the Great Southern
	1892	Clare	26	—	Railways on 1 January 1925
Cavan & Leitrim	1887	Cavan & Leitrim	48½	—	
		Total mileage	188½		

Northern Irish narrow gauge railways at the 1921 Partition

Railway	Date opened	Counties served	Mileage		Remarks
			Eire	N Ireland	
Ballymena Cushendall	1876	Antrim	—	16½	Absorbed by BNCR in 1884
Ballymena & Larne	1877	Antrim	—	30	Absorbed by BNCR in 1889
Portstewart Tramway	1882	Antrim	—	1¾	Absorbed by BNCR in 1897
Ballycastle Railway	1880	Antrim	—	16¼	Absorbed by NCC (LMS) in 1924
		Total mileage	—	64½	

Victims of Partition

Railway	Date opened	Counties served	Mileage		Remarks
			Eire	N Ireland	
Londonderry & Lough Swilly	1883	Londonderry and Donegal	96¾	2¼	Though each company possessed only a few miles of track in Northern Ireland, this was enough to debar them from Grouping under the GSR. Each was left to find its own salvation. By 1960 both had closed.
Co Donegal RJC (owned by MR)	1863	Tyrone and Donegal	106¼	3½	
			—	14½	
		Total mileage	203	20¼	

Lost causes

Railway	Date opened	Counties served	Mileage		Remarks
			Eire	N Ireland	
Dublin & Lucan Tramway	1883	Dublin	7	—	Closed 1925 (bus competition)
Listowel & Ballybunion	1888	Kerry	9¼	—	GSR declined amalgamation
Giant's Causeway Tramway	1883	Antrim	—	8	UTA declined assistance. Closed 1949
Bessbrook & Newry Tramway	1885	Armagh	—	3	Closed 10 January 1948
Castlederg & Victoria Bridge	1884	Tyrone	—	7¼	Closed 1933, after Railway Strike
Clogher Valley Tramway	1887	Tyrone and Fermanagh	—	37	Closed 1941
		Total mileage	16¼	55¼	

Note With the exception of the Listowel & Ballybunion and, latterly, the Dublin & Lucan Tramway, all conformed to Irish narrow gauge of 3 feet.

Southern Ireland

CORK, BLACKROCK & PASSAGE RAILWAY

Incorporated: 16 July 1846
Opened: 8 June 1850
Absorbed by GSR: 1 January 1925

Fully a decade before GS&WR standard gauge metals probed west to reach the outskirts of Cork, that venerable city had already anticipated the Railway Age, for a first proposal to link Cork with its immediate environment was mooted as early as 1836. Though nothing came of it, and the promoters' powers withered away, various elements fought on to obtain their revival, and nine years later no fewer than three companies found themselves jostling for Parliamentary approval. The importance of Passage, a dockyard and steamship town, found expression in the title of all three: the Cork, Passage & Kinsale, the Cork Passage, and the Cork, Blackrock, Passage & Monkstown Railways. The last-named won the day and, pausing only to tidy up loose ends, it set up in business as the Cork, Blackrock & Passage Railway.

At that time Westminster's parsimony towards Irish railways was quite flagrant. The Cork, Blackrock soon made its acquaintance, when a State loan of £15,000 was granted — at 5 per cent. Lord George Bentinck had already protested in the House that Government was raising such funds in the Money Market at little over 3 per cent; and later, probably in the interests of decency, the rate was dropped to 4 per cent. Meanwhile, with Irish standard gauge fixed at 5 ft

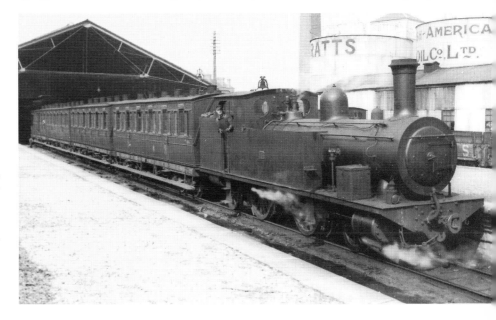

Cork, Blackrock & Passage Railway

3 in, the CB&PR duly complied when 6½ miles of single track were laid between Cork and Passage. Sufficient land was taken at the time to allow for future doubling, and total costs consequently emerged at something around £21,000 per mile. Local steamship companies maintained their monopoly over freight, but passenger traffic on the Cork, Blackrock flourished from the outset, and for the next half-century three small locos imported from Sharp Brothers of Manchester were kept fully employed. Workshops at Passage handled locomotive repairs, and later, as a measure of continued prosperi-

Cork, Blackrock's spacious terminus at Albert Street, Cork, was still functioning, under GSR auspices, when this photograph was taken of 2–4–2T No 7P with its train of bogie compartment coaches. The sands of time, however, were ebbing fast, and the whole of the Cork, Blackrock's 16 route miles were closed in 1932. No 7P, duly renovated at Inchicore, was transferred as 13L to the GSR's Cavan & Leitrim section, and lasted until 1954. (Steamchest)

Alice, the County Donegal Railway's No 1, was built by Sharp Stewart as far back as 1881. When sent to Cork on loan during 1918-21, and entrusted with, amongst other things, Admiralty Specials, the Cork, Blackrock, was so pleased with her performance that they offered the CDRJC £400 for the little locomotive. Alas, Henry Forbes declined the 'bargain', and Alice *perished in CDRJC harness in 1926.* (Author's Collection)

ty, a fine new CB&PR terminus was built at Albert Street, Cork. It opened in 1873.

Up to 1866 the Cork, Blackrock's cheerful supremacy in local passenger traffic blossomed unchallenged. Then the GS&WR bought out the Cork & Youghal Railway, and with it came valuable access to Cobh Harbour. Gradually, increasing competitive pressures were exerted by the larger company, and latterly the CB&PR was forced in self-defence to think of expansion. Funds were raised, and matters reached practical conclusion on 7 August 1896, when Parliament approved the Cork, Blackrock's plans for the construction of a 9½-mile extension to Crosshaven, on the southern end of Cork Harbour. Keenly conscious of earlier costs, the CB&PR

Directors opted on this occasion to build to 3-foot gauge. Even so, the capital subscribed proved woefully inadequate, and only a loan of £65,000 from the Board of Works enabled the extension to be completed by June 1904. During the waiting period, the CB&PR tackled the second enemy, local shipping, by acquiring maritime interests of its own. Now, with typical enterprise, its timetables displayed both rail and ship details.

Reaction to the problem of mixed gauges was no less positive. As early as 1900 the CB&PR's 6½-mile track from Cork was regauged to 3 foot; the original trio of 2–2–2 tanks were sold, and four new narrow gauge engines took their place. Equally audacious was a decision made to double the heavily used metals between Cork and Blackrock. This move, though unique in narrow gauge history, proved inspired; for as the whole line opened up, weekend traffic continued to multiply, particularly during the summer months. Even as the First World War dragged itself towards a weary conclusion, CB&PR traffic was able to resume in such prosperous vein that, under orders from the Irish Railways Executive Committee, five

All four Cork, Blackrock 2–4–2Ts were renumbered by the GSR in 1932 before being sent to its Cavan & Leitrim section. No 12L, formerly No 6P, seen here at Dromod in 1950, was overhauled at Glanmire Road Workshops, Cork, before being sent north. It was one of two which soldiered on until the line was closed in March 1959. (Steamchest)

third class carriages were borrowed from the Lough Swilly Railway in June 1918, as was *Alice*, a 2–4–0 tank owned by the County Donegal RJC. All were retained until 1921. The Cork, Blackrock took a liking to *Alice*, and offered to buy her for £400. The Donegal railway, however, declined.

Then, by the early 1920s, the picture began to change; by now the lengthening shadow of post-war road competition was beginning to fall on all Irish railways. Even the Cork, Blackrock's prosperity could not withstand this kind of assault, and there can be little doubt that Government legislation which forced the CB&PR into the national GSR fold must have come as a relief to an increasingly harassed management. Amalgamation itself, of course, could not resolve road pressures, and the GSR were still obliged to take a pragmatic view of the Irish Free State's new rail complex. In one bid to reduce overheads, the Cork, Blackrock's double section was again restored to single track in 1927. Alas, losses continued to multiply, and in 1932 the final solution was adopted. The Monkstown-Crosshaven section was closed on 31 May of that year and, the moment the summer season was over, the rest of the line followed suit on 10 September.

LOCOMOTIVES

Gauge	No	Type	Date built	Makers	Maker's number	GSR number 1925	GSR number 1932	Withdrawn	Remarks
5 ft 3 in	1	2–2–2T	1850	Sharp Bros	655	–	–	1900	Sold when CB&PR adopted 3-foot gauge
	2	2–2–2T	1850	,,	656	–	–	1900	
	3	2–2–2T	1850	,,	662	–	–	1900	
3 feet	4	2–4–2T	1899	Neilson, Reid	5561	4P	10L	1959	Renumbered into Cavan & Leitrim stock when CB&PR line closed in September 1932
	5	2–4–2T	1899	,,	5562	5P	11L	1939	
	6	2–4–2T	1899	,,	5563	6P	12L	1959	
	7	2–4–2T	1899	,,	5564	7P	13L	1954	

Perhaps the most outstanding feature of the CB&PR's standard gauge locomotives was the sturdy and uncomplaining manner in which they tackled all traffic until 1900. No 2 received a saddle tank at one stage; otherwise life went on as before. The long-serving Neilson tanks were distinctive on more cogent grounds. The only 2–4–2 tanks built throughout Ireland's narrow gauge history, their clumsy external appearance belied an ability to move like hares; and, with 4 ft 6 in diameter wheels spinning on the Cork, Blackrock's level and beautifully maintained track, speeds of over 50 mph were often recorded. Small wonder the railway was popular!

A new chapter opened up for the Neilson tanks in 1934; for, after repair at Cork (three) and Inchicore (one), all four were renumbered, and re-entered service on the GSR's Cavan & Leitrim section. Shortly after their arrival it was established that their employment on Cavan's tramway was not practicable. Even on the main line between Belturbet and Dromod they could not render truly satisfactory service, for their very propensity for speed and acceleration, once so valuable in a Cork urban context, meant little when a heavy coal train had to be lugged up Lauderdale Bank. None the less, apart from No 11L, which was retired at an early stage, the Blackrock engines served the Cavan & Leitrim well, and two soldiered on until the line was closed on 31 March 1959.

None has been preserved. But their memory will not likely be forgotten — even amongst strictly Cavan & Leitrim devotees.

SCHULL & SKIBBEREEN TRAMWAYS & LIGHT RAILWAY

Incorporated: 7 December 1883
Opened: 6 September 1886
Absorbed by GSR: 1 January 1925

Practically every light railway in Ireland had occasion at some time or other to complain about contractors' handiwork. Schull was no exception; and when the Vice-regal Commission of 1906 sat to hear evidence, that given by the Board of Trade's Inspecting Officer told an all too familiar tale:

'The engines supplied by the contractors were incapable of hauling a load of 30 tons up the steepest gradient, as provided in the specification; while the fireboxes leaked so badly as to extinguish the fires. The permanent way was laid defec-

Schull & Skibbereen Tramways & Light Railway

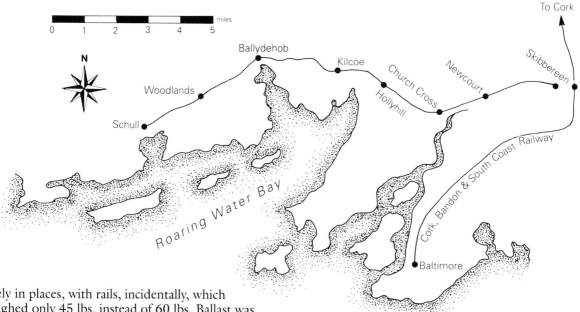

tively in places, with rails, incidentally, which weighed only 45 lbs, instead of 60 lbs. Ballast was insufficient, and turntables provided failed to function correctly. Because curves were excessively sharp, speed limits of 4 mph had to be observed at these points, and "stops" were also imposed at nine other places where level crossings intruded. Three days after opening, the line had to close again because of defective rolling-stock, and £1,600 was borrowed to restore it to working condition. The process took nine months.'

Put these grave defects aside, and one still marvels at the cupidity of two Irish Baronies in backing with a £57,000 guarantee a concept that profitable rail traffic could be generated in such a remote corner of Southern Ireland. Around 1875 the villages of Schull and Skibbereen would have been hard put to raise 3,500 inhabitants between them. Nevertheless, local ambitions were inflamed by the triumphant arrival of the Cork Bandon Railway at Skibbereen in 1877, and by 1883 enactment of the Tramways Act was enough to see discretion cast to the winds. A railway there must be! So, decision was taken to build a steam tramway round the northern shores of Roaring Water Bay.

Cannily accepting a starting point offered by the Cork Bandon's station at Skibbereen, the 3-foot gauge tramway wandered off to Schull, 15½ miles distant. Public highways offered an easy route for most of the way. But steepish gradients had occasionally to be surmounted and at Ballydehob coastline complications even demanded construction of a 12-arched viaduct. Capital costs soared accordingly.

Considering, too, that only small communities,

engaged in mining on the Mizen Peninsula and fishing at Schull, could possibly have benefited from the project, one marvels afresh that the West Carbery Tramway & Light Railway (Schull & Skibbereen) Branch really meant what its title implied — that this was only part of a much more comprehensive scheme! Providentially, both funds and ambition exhausted themselves by 1892, and a simpler title was adopted.

From the outset everything about the Schull & Skibbereen was modest to a degree. A service of two trains sufficed to meet weekday demands, and only on Fair Days and special occasions was this stretched to three. Sundays warranted one train only. Whatever the circumstances, rolling-stock which purported to differentiate between first and third class travel consisted in the main of four-wheeled boxes. Meanwhile, as all trains were mixed in composition, inevitable shunting manoeuvres *en route* took good care of the hour and 20 minutes allotted to each trip of 15½ miles. Back at Skibbereen a small workshop was set up. But only the lightest of repairs could be handled there, and any loco requiring more serious attention had to be transhipped to Cork.

From the beginning the implications were clear; and, if proof were needed, revenue, or lack of same, made the point. Between the years 1886 and 1916, for instance, working expenses contrived to exceed receipts by £39,912. Supporting Baronies not only paid their statutory penalty during these years, but had additional cause to feel aggrieved when, under the terms of the 1883 Act, Treasury relief was abruptly terminated, and the Tramway handed over, lock,

At Skibbereen, trains on the narrow gauge Schull & Skibbereen Tramway operated from a terminal bay which lay adjacent to the Cork, Bandon's broad gauge station, but had to reverse into a siding before leaving again for Schull. In this view, taken on 13 June 1934, 4–4–0T No 1S Gabriel has just arrived with its typically mixed train. The 1906 Peckett veteran kept its name right up to the moment of withdrawal in 1936. (F. C. Le Manquais)

Fifteen miles away, at the other end of the line, Schull station eked out a rather less sophisticated existence. Nevertheless, it had all the requisite facilities – station building, carriage and engine shed, and turntable. The long line of vans in this June 1935 study suggests, too, that fish traffic still played a prominent role in the little railway's activities. 4–4–0T No 4S, formerly Erin, again running chimney first, is ready to leave on its 1 hour 20 minute return journey to Skibbereen. (F. C. Le Manquais)

A perfectly preserved ex-Schull & Skibbereen 1st class coach, No 1S, still lay with sundry wagons in a siding at Ballydehob on 26 June 1935. Unfortunately, they contrived to elude Éire's rather fragmentary preservation movement. (F. C. Le Manquais)

stock, and barrel, to the Grand Jury's personal care. Tramway wheels had, indeed, turned with a vengeance!

A grave setback came Schull & Skibbereen's ailing way in 1914, when the First World War applied its stranglehold on Ireland's imports of coal. Alas, and only too symptomatic of Ireland's tortured history, even more disastrous events were imminent from within the country itself; for at the height of the Troubles of 1921 armed assaults on railway installations grew so in intensity that the military closed the Schull line, and three others in the vicinity, for a period of months. By 1922 evolution of an Irish Free State, albeit with Dominion status, brought some desperately needed semblance of civil order. A year or two later ratepayers in County Cork's most southernly enclave breathed more freely still when, as promised by the Railways (Directorate) Act of 1924, responsibility for Schull & Skibbereen affairs passed safely to the Great Southern Railways.

At least the new Irish Government held clearer views on the social value of railways than did its Ulster counterpart. Accordingly, the GSR were encouraged to keep the Schull line functioning, if only in traditionally modest fashion. But when the Second World War arrived, even Eire's declaration of neutrality could not spare her some of its consequences. Again coal shortage intervened. Once more attempts to run locomotives on peat proved inadequate, and latterly Schull services had to be suspended. Locos lay idle between April 1944 and December 1945.

Services had hardly been resumed 12 months when fuel problems struck again. This time the scale was even greater. In any case, in Ireland, as elsewhere, national railway portents were hardening, and on 27 January 1947 the Schull & Skibbereen ran its last train. Long before CIE managed to obtain an official order of abandonment in 1952, buses were plying between Cork and Schull. To the fishing folk of the Mizen Peninsula, steam had become a rapidly receding memory.

LOCOMOTIVES

No	Type	Name	Makers	Date built	GSR number	Withdrawn	Derivation of locomotive name
1	0–4–0T	*Marion*	Dick, Kerr	1886	–	1906	Mountain
2	,,	*Ida*	,,	1886	2S	1926	Mountain
3	,,	*Ilen*	,,	1886	–	1914	River
4	4–4–0T	*Erin*	Nasmyth Wilson	1888	4S	1954	Gaelic name for Ireland
1	,,	*Gabriel*	Peckett	1906	1S	1936	Mountain
3	,,	*Kent*	,,	1914	3S	1954	Thomas Kent, an Irish 'patriot', executed in Cork Barracks after the 1916 Rising

Schull's first three locos were of the steam tram variety, with boiler and mechanism encased, as statutorily required. As the Inspecting Officer later revealed, their contribution was highly unsatisfactory, and in 1905 they were extensively rebuilt, with tractive effort increased to 5,370 lbs. Once the tramway was reclassified as a light railway, a 4–4–0T was introduced. *Erin*, with a tractive effort of 7,720 lbs, in fact carried the first Belpaire firebox in Ireland. Two more, introduced in 1906 and 1914, were more powerful still, at 9,650 lbs, and differed additionally in having outside bearings to the coupled wheels.

Nominally, *Ida* passed into GSR stock, but within a year Schull locos were reduced to three in number. *Gabriel's* withdrawal in 1936 was rather belatedly offset two years later, when the Cork & Muskerry 0–4–0T No 6, formerly *The Muskerry*, was brought in. Renumbered 6S, she was, at first, found unsuitable for Schull purposes; but once Inchicore resolved the height of her couplings (!) she served the Schull & Skibbereen to the bitter end — on which sad occasion all three locos were conveyed to Inchicore. Strangely enough, their official withdrawal was deferred until April 1954.

CORK & MUSKERRY LIGHT RAILWAY

Incorporated: 12 December 1883
Opened: 8 August 1887
Absorbed by GSR: 1 January 1925

As the year 1900 heralded what was to be a tempestu-

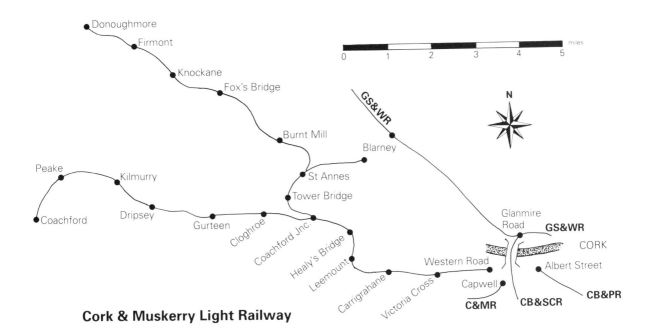

Cork & Muskerry Light Railway

ous new century for Ireland, the City of Cork's 80,000 inhabitants at least found themselves well served by rail; no fewer than *five* railway companies competed there, cheek by jowl, though no physical contact existed between any two! Cork's most recent acquisition, the Cork & Muskerry, seeing in the 1883 Act a golden opportunity to introduce tramways into the city itself, had laid 8¾ miles of narrow gauge metals from its Western Road terminus to the pleasant village of Blarney. By March 1888, 9¼ more miles of branch line were constructed; whence the blandishments of Coachford were added to the lure. The fact that the total journey by rail was 3 miles longer than by road mattered none in those days. Profitable development of tourist traffic was sufficient incentive to persuade local Baronies to support the C&M's capital of £75,000 by way of appropriate Guarantees.

Muskerry's 'main line' to Blarney was again tapped in 1893, when 8½ miles of branch line were added by the Donoughmore Extension Railway. The latter was a separate company, with its own capital of £30,000, again suitably guaranteed. The Cork & Muskerry, however, worked its trains from the outset, and,

An early Muskerry acquisition, No 4 Blarney, *seen here as built by Kitson & Co in 1888, possible carried condensing gear when it was introduced by the C&M's tramway-like metals. Whatever, it proved in the event to be too lacking in power for traffic requirements, and the little loco was sold in 1911. (Author's Collection)*

indeed, purchased two special locomotives for the purpose. Within a few years, continued annual deficits saw the Donoughmore concern pass into the none too eager hands of a Cork County Council Committee of Management. Unabashed, the C&M continued to work the branch right up to 1925. Interestingly, details of the Donoughmore venture were advanced in later years as evidence of the weakness of early Irish railway legislation. According to a deposition made by an Inspector:

'Layout and construction were imperfectly supervised, and a series of sharp reverse curves might have been avoided. Ballast, as originally supplied, was of poor quality.'

Trouble was, of course, that, under the 1883 Tramways Act, a Board of Trade Inspector's duty confined itself to ascertaining that the line was safe to carry passengers. He had no mandate to query the existence of a contractor's guarantee as to the future maintenance of that line.

Meanwhile, in Cork itself the art of 'no communication with the firm next door' was carried to extraordinary lengths when, in December 1898, a new rival, Cork City Tramways, chose to commence operations. Muskerry's initial 3½ miles had already taken a convenient course by following a public highway out of Cork. Now the new City electric tramway decided to follow suit by running alongside Muskerry metals for the best part of a mile. Where else but in Ireland could one have found steam and electric tramways running side by side!

Still, at least the City electric trams fulfilled one useful function, in linking Western Road, the C&M's terminus, with Glanmire and other railway termini. There was even talk of C&M traffic being run through to the Cork, Blackrock terminus, now the latter concern was switching to narrow gauge. In anticipation, in fact, of handling just such traffic, Cork Electric Tramways took unto themselves a very

No 8 Dripsey *was a somewhat lighter version of the same design as* Peake. *This vintage study clearly reveals inside bearings on the coupled 4-foot diameter wheels, and outside ones on the leading bogie, plus, of course, the Cork & Muskerry's handsome livery. Although* Dripsey *was one of those which were dismantled at Inchicore in 1935, the locomotive was never resuscitated.* (Author's Collection)

unusual gauge of 2 ft 11½ in; this to allow for the tapered flanges of railway rolling-stock wheels. Unfortunately, after all Cork Tramways' effort, the proposed through running never materialized.

The Cork & Muskerry's permanent way consisted of flat-bottomed rails, 50 lbs a yard, spiked to sleepers. The single line ran on its own right of way for 1 mile from Western Road, then switched to the left-hand side of a public road. The electric tramways later occupied the centre of the road! At Leemount, three stations on, Muskerry metals left the public highway and ventured off cross-country. 6¼ miles from Cork came Coachford Junction, and here the line divided, with the main portion of most trains working on to Blarney, while the rear coaches were held back to be taken to Coachford by branch line locomotive. At St Annes, 1 mile along the Blarney line, the Donoughmore branch separated, and looked after its own light share of passenger traffic. Gradients overall presented little problem, though the same could not be said for the Donoughmore branch's sharp curves. Prior to the outbreak of the First World War, six trains a day ran from Cork to Blarney, taking on average 37 minutes for the 8¾ miles. Five trains ran to Coachford, 15½ miles in 62 minutes, and three to Donoughmore, 15¾ miles in 67 minutes. These timings produce an average speed of 15 mph, with stops, of course. Sunday trains were run, and during summer months Blarney was served by eight trains a day. Most trains were mixed in composition, though freight trains ran as required. The C&M's lines were worked on a staff and ticket basis, and full signalling obtained at crossing points.

Despite the flurrying activity of tourist traffic, the C&M, however, was never a prosperous concern, and, only too typically, it leaned heavily on its Baronial Guarantees. Eventual absorption by the GSR as from 1 January 1925 at least relieved the Baronies of embarrassing liabilities; and the Government, recognizing

the C&M's need, continued to fill the gap by making special yearly payments. Light is thrown on the GSR's own continuing difficulties by the fact that when Government subsidy stopped on 31 December 1934 so, too, did all rail traffic on the Cork & Muskerry section. In any case road transport had filched most traffic by then. Up to that melancholy date, six C&M locos were at work. After closure they found their way to Inchicore Works, where they were dismantled, though all parts were carefully stored. Two were later re-assembled, the intention being to use them on the Tralee & Dingle and Schull & Skibbereen — but, probably because of differences in loading gauges, the scheme partly misfired. Thus, with coaches scrapped as they stood, and much of the trackbed restored to public use by Cork County Council, one would need sharp eyes today, and inspired knowledge, to detect any trace of the little railway which helped keep Blarney on the map.

LOCOMOTIVES

In view of the Cork & Muskerry's tramway-like début, the first three locos they obtained from Falcon Engineering Works in 1887 were fitted with condensing gear, and wheels and motion were covered in. Once regulations were relaxed both protection and condensing gear were removed, and a four-wheel bogie took the place of the leading axle. No 3 went in 1924, but the other two lived to enter GSR stock, and worked the C&M line until closure in 1934. No 4, another variation on the four-coupled tank theme, probably also bore condensing gear when built. It was found, however, to be too light for traffic requirements, and was sold in 1911. The next two arrivals were built in Leeds for the Donoughmore Extension, and although they weighed the same as Falcon's 0–4–2 tanks, 25 tons in working order, they were much more powerful, with a tractive effort of

No	Name	Type	Date built	Makers	Maker's number	GSR number (1925)	GSR Class	Withdrawn	Remarks
1	*City of Cork*	2–4–0T	1887	H. Hughes, Falcon Works	137	1K	DN6	1938	Later rebuilt as
2	*Coachford*	2–4–0T	1887	,,	136	2K	DN6	1938	4-4-0 tanks
3	*St Annes*	2–4–0T	1887	,,	138	–	–	1924	
4	*Blarney*	0–4–2WT	1888	Kitson	235	–	–	1911	Sold
5	*Donoughmore*	0–4–4T	1892	T. Green	180	5K	EN1	1938	Built for Donoughmore
6	*The Muskerry*	0–4–4T	1893	,,	200	6K	EN1	1944	Extension
7	*Peake*	4–4–0T	1897	H. Hughes, Falcon Works	274	7K	DN1	1935	C&M's largest locomotive
8	*Dripsey*	4–4–0T	1904	Brush	307	8K	DN7	1935	
4	*Blarney*	4–4–0T	1919	Hunslet	1200	4K	DN3	1927	Inside bearings throughout

11,100 lbs, as opposed to Falcon's 6,720 lbs. These were the two locos which were re-assembled at Inchicore Works from stored parts.

No 7 *Peake* arrived in 1897 from Falcon's successors, Brush Electrical Engineering Co, of Loughborough. A 4–4–0 tank, it had inside bearings to the coupled wheels and outside to the bogie wheels. No 8, from the same stable, was a slightly lighter version of the same design. Curiously, the C&M went to Hunslet for their last locomotive, in 1919. Opportunity was taken to restore the name *Blarney* and, with coupled wheels reduced to 3 ft 6 in, as opposed to the other 4–4–0T's 4 feet, the loco produced the greatest tractive effort of all, at 10,900 lbs. Despite that, its life was short.

Thus, of nine locomotives purchased, the C&M brought seven to the GSR fold, plus 27 coaches and 50 wagons. Most C&M passenger vehicles were bogied, and entrance was obtained, tram-fashion, by end platforms. There were only two classes, first and third, and, as might be expected, upholstery was confined to the former. Third class passengers had to put up with hard slatted wooden seats, arranged longitudinally in bogie cars and transversely in the C&M's few four-wheeled cars. The latter embodied a kind of Irish apologia by combining bare wooden seats with a modestly upholstered back. Rather sadly, no Cork & Muskerry passenger stock survived the Grouping. The last locomotive survivor, No 6, resuscitated at Inchicore in 1938, and renumbered 6S, was despatched to the GSR's Schull & Skibbereen section, where it worked, with varying fortunes, until fuel shortage suspended operations in April 1944. The loco itself was not withdrawn until April 1954.

TRALEE & DINGLE LIGHT RAILWAY

Incorporated: 17 September 1888
Opened: 31 March 1891
Absorbed by GSR: 1 January 1925

Inured as they were to humping the fruits of their labour by sea, or overland by pack mule, to the comparatively prosperous county town of Tralee, it is hardly surprising that the fishing and farming folk of Dingle, a remote spot in Co Derry, entertained thoughts of new and more rapidly accessible markets when the Tramways Act was put on the Statute Book in 1883. Accordingly, much satisfaction greeted a Privy Council decision in 1884 that a light railway might be built, linking Tralee and Dingle. Alas, no contractor could be found to undertake the difficult task, and four years elapsed ere matters finally got under way. Raising considerable funds proved to be a second major obstacle, and, local resources being what they were, it is highly doubtful if the requisite £150,000 capital would ever have been found, had not Baronial Guarantees marched alongside. When a contractor was finally unearthed he advocated a gauge of 5 ft 3 in, and if this had been adopted the T&D might well have shared the GS&WR's terminus at Tralee. As it was, no satisfactory agreement was ever reached. So the new line was built to the 3-foot gauge. The T&DR constructed its own modest terminus, and the two stations, only a few hundred yards apart, contented themselves with exchanging goods traffic by a short connecting spur.

Europe's most westerly railway, and certainly Ireland's most wayward railway venture, the T&DR took nearly three years to build — and spent all its money in the process. Ultimate costs of £2,700 per mile were, nevertheless, cheap, considering the wild terrain that had to be crossed.

Tralee & Dingle Light Railway

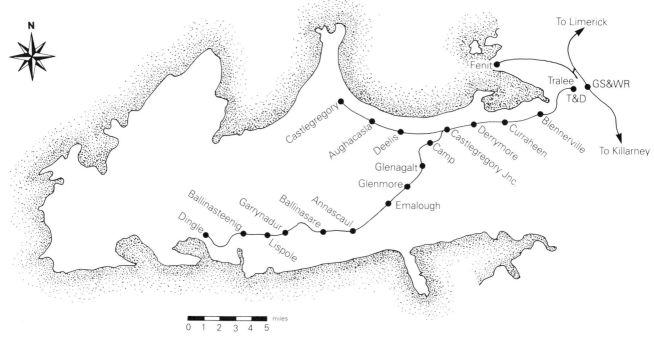

From Tralee the single line ambled off by the road-side for 10 miles and wandered from side to side as circumstances required. Then, at Castlegregory Junction a 6-mile branch looped off on a fairly easy course for Castlegregory itself, in the event the T&DR's largest station. Things were different on the main line, which now faced some of the wildest and toughest country in Ireland. Straight away the sever-est incline ever postulated by any passenger-carrying Irish railway, a 4-mile stretch of more than 1 in 30, had to be assaulted ere Glenagalt, 680 feet above sea level, could be reached. The subsequent descent to Annascaul, 3 miles distant, offered splendid views of Dingle Bay, but the price to be paid was a drop of 1¾ miles at 1 in 29. Then followed a second 5-mile climb to Garrynadur, and another hair-raising drop of 2 miles at 1 in 29, before 5 miles of easier running by

the roadside terminated at Dingle station. The latter was set back from the shore, and a steeply-graded half-mile extension led down to Dingle harbour. Add the fact that two awkward viaducts and a horse-shoe curve were also embodied in the T&DR's main line, and one begins to understand why a 31½-mile trip from Tralee to Dingle, with leisurely intermediate stops, took over 2¼ hours.

Whatever, despite trials and tribulations, the line

2–6–0T No 2 was one of three built by the Hunslet Engine Co in 1889 for Tralee & Dingle main line use. The influence of the Tramways Act of 1883 is readily apparent in the warning bell and condensing gear the locomotive carries. Rather unkindly, it and sister engine No 1T were scrapped at Inchicore after heading the Tralee & Dingle's last through train in June 1953. (Author's Collection)

was completed by 1890. A Board of Trade inspector faulted it on several counts. Alterations were duly effected and amidst great local rejoicing the Tralee & Dingle opened for business on 31 March 1891. Its total stock consisted of four locomotives and 47 vehicles of widely assorted nature. Coaches were built by Bristol Wagon Works. Alas, the local residents' euphoria soon faded, for, only too rapidly, conditions and working practices on the T&DR revealed themselves as being primitive in the extreme. Staff were overworked and underpaid, and drunkenness amongst train crews became an uncomfortable everyday occurrence. Stations, meanwhile, lacked telephonic communication, and livestock rash enough to stray through the T&DR's poor fencing often paid the supreme penalty. Soon, too, evidence began to emerge that the local gentry who had been appointed to the T&DR's Board knew nothing of railway affairs. Thus, from the outset the Tralee & Dingle's earnings failed to cover working expenses.

Incensed by the realization that they were subsidising what looked like being a permanent albatross, ratepayers revolted, and forced an Inquiry. This was held in March 1893. Local complaints, bitterly expressed, were duly noted; but in the absence of funds in T&DR coffers, little could be done. Two months later, loco No 1, driven on this occasion by an inexperienced Locomotive Superintendent, lost control of a train of livestock when descending Glenagalt Bank and finished up in the river below. The fact that three footplatemen were killed, and 13 passengers injured, was bad enough; but when a T&DR cheque given to an attending doctor was dishonoured by the Bank, the community was outraged beyond recall.

From there, almost incredibly, things went from bad to worse. In 1896, having failed over four years to yield a penny of profit, the T&DR, under terms of its own Act of Incorporation, was bound over to become the property of a none too happy Grand Jury. The latter's almost spontaneous reaction was a despairing, but unsuccessful, appeal for Government relief. Two years later the Treasury, recognizing that its own maximum liability of £2,400 a year was likely to be invoked in perpetuity, obtained release from the fracas by paying out, in terms of the 1895 'Commutation Act', a once-and-for-all settlement of £80,000.

Left thus in splendid isolation, T&DR affairs pursued their chaotic course. On 24 November 1898 a train was derailed by strong winds at Balinogue. Came Dingle Fair Day in November 1901, and a humiliating series of locomotive failures so haunted the Committee of Management that even they commissioned an independent report. This service was rendered by Mr Cusack, Engineer to the MGWR. Shocked at the neglect he found, he urged that staff and train services be severely pruned in a desperate bid for economy. On 1 March 1907 loco No 6 left the track at a sharp curve on Lispole Viaduct, killing one engineman; and events reached inevitable climax in 1910, when a Ratepayers Association was formed,

Right *Dingle station, second only to Valencia as Ireland's most westerly station. Its single platform at least had the luxury of an overall roof, and behind that, in this 1935 view, lay a water column and small engine shed. The single track carried on another half mile to Dingle Harbour.* (F. C. Le Manquais)

Below *No description of the Tralee & Dingle would be complete without a picture of one of its latterday cattle specials. Here, at Annascaul, 20 miles from Tralee, an empty special bound for Dingle pauses while locos 1T and 2T take well-needed water in July 1950, before tackling the 1 in 30 climb to Lispole. The same two locos were scrapped at Inchicore after handling the last of these memorable specials in June 1953.* (Steamchest)

clamouring for improvement. That same year Tralee station was almost destroyed by fire, and subsequent investigations revealed such serious discrepancies in T&DR books that the General Manager was suspended. Shortly afterwards he was dismissed.

By 1912 things gave some indication of being on the mend. But it was too late, for even more sombre events were looming on the horizon. First, the outbreak of war in 1914 imposed immediate and chronic coal shortage, while Government-imposed wage increases sent T&DR costs sky-high. Then post-war years brought the 'Troubles', and Tralee staff loyalties, mostly Republican in sympathy, were ruthlessly exploited by Sinn Fein. Civil war followed, the line was one of those temporarily closed by military instruction in 1921, and similar interruptions were again considered necessary in 1922-23. No one can doubt that absorption by the GSR in the 1925 Grouping came as other than a merciful release to the T&DR's sadly perplexed Committee of Management.

The Great Southern Railways strove hard to reduce costs, and from 1925 such heavy repairs as were required by Tralee locomotives were carried out at Limerick or Inchicore. But road competition was hardening all the time, and coach services received a real fillip early in 1939 when the road to Dingle was properly resurfaced. Faced with the reciprocal obligation of relaying narrow gauge metals, the GSR elected instead to close the Castlegregory branch in its entirety and to suspend all other T&DR passenger services from 17 April 1939. Bus services took over and railway activity narrowed to one goods train per day. Even that meagre contribution was brought to a halt by a national fuel shortage in 1947. Experiments in the use of peat failed, and such rail service as was eventually reinstated consisted solely of a cattle train once a month between Dingle and Tralee. Famous as far as railway enthusiasts were concerned, and spectacular to the end, the last of these ran in June 1953. One month later, on 22 July 1953, a light engine ventured as far as Dingle to recover some empty wagons — and the Tralee & Dingle's trauma was over.

LOCOMOTIVES

No	Type	Date built	Maker	Maker's number	GSR No (1925)	Withdrawn	Remarks
1	2–6–0T	1889	Hunslet	477	1T	1953	Scrapped at Inchicore after last train between Tralee and Dingle
2	2–6–0T	1889	,,	478	2T	1953	
3	2–6–0T	1889	,,	479	3T	1959	Transferred to Cavan & Leitrim section of GSR in 1941
4	0–4–2T	1890	Hunslet	514	—	1908	Sold to scrap merchant
5	2–6–2T	1892	Hunslet	555	5T	Preserved in Tralee	Transferred to Cavan & Leitrim section in 1950
6	2–6–0T	1898	,,	677	6T	1960	Transferred to West Clare in 1953, and Cavan & Leitrim in 1957
7	2–6–0T	1902	Kerr Stuart	800	7T	1928	Badly run down
8(4)	2–6–0T	1903	,,	836	4T	1959	Renumbered 4 in 1908. Transferred to Cavan & Leitrim section in 1941
8	2–6–0T	1910	Hunslet	1051	8T	1955	Transferred to West Clare section, and scrapped after dieselization

The Tralee & Dingle's predilection for 2–6–0 tanks was unusual in the UK, as was their employment of Walschaerts valve gear. The first three locos were built for main line use, whilst No 4, destined for the Castlegregory branch, was shopped with driver's cab and controls at both ends, in keeping with roadside tramway regulations. By 1892, however, the financial rot had already set in at Tralee, and only recourse to financial instalments spread over three years enabled Nos 5 (Tralee's sole 2–6–2 tank) and 6 to be bought. The T&DR later switched to Kerr Stuart for locos Nos 7 and 8. Yet, although the latter were more powerful than the Hunslet engines the Tralee railway found them oddly unsuitable in use; and when No 4

was sold for scrap, the T&DR reverted to Hunslet for its ninth, and final, locomotive. Unfortunately, by this time complete disorder in T&DR locomotive supervision had become a matter for public derision. The crowning humiliation came in 1914, when a New York resident, Eugene Egan by name, was appointed Locomotive Superintendent — and never took up the job.

At least shelter within the GSR restored some semblance of order. In all eight locomotives, 21 coaches and 78 wagons were handed over to the parent concern in 1924. From 1925, as locos attended Inchicore Works, their Hunslet chimney caps were replaced by those of standard design, and the letter 'T' was added to their running numbers. But once Tralee passenger services were abandoned in 1939, two Tralee locos were scrapped, and spare engine transfers began to be made. Nos 3, 4 and 5 found a new home on the Cavan & Leitrim section of the GSR. They coped well enough there, though the high ash content of Arigna's soft coal posed problems. In 1953 Nos 6 and 8 faced an even greater challenge when in the aftermath of heavy West Clare locomotive withdrawals they were despatched to Ennis. They could never have hoped, of course, to match their West Clare 4–6–0T predecessors in either power or popularity, but they soldiered on bravely enough until 1955, when the West Clare section was completely dieselized. Even then No 6T was reprieved and, completely overhauled

at Inchicore, it ended its days amongst old friends on the Cavan & Leitrim.

Odd man out, only No 5T survives today. Shipped to the USA in July 1959, it was subsequently exhibited at Pleasure Island, Wakefield, together with a Tralee & Dingle coach and *Lady Edith*, a 4–4–0 tank of Cavan & Leitrim fame. From there they moved to Steamtown, Vermont, then to the Pine Creek Railroad, where, no doubt, they continued to excite many an expatriate Irishman's dreams of stirring times on the Tralee & Dingle. These dreams have since been revived in Ireland; for in July 1986 No 5T was shipped home from Steamtown, Vermont, and is back again at Tralee, in the safe hands of the Great Southern Railways Preservation Society.

WEST CLARE RAILWAY

Incorporated: 15 December 1883
Opened: 2 July 1887

SOUTH CLARE RAILWAYS

Incorporated: 6 July 1884
Opened: 3 August 1892
Both absorbed by GSR: 1 January 1925

South of Galway Bay on the west coast of Ireland the windswept ocean-lashed County of Clare knew little of early Irish railway development. From 1869 a standard gauge line running north and south, the Waterford, Limerick & Western Railway, had penetrated Ennis, its county town; but so far Clare's extensive fishing activities had gained nothing from the Railway Age. An 1860 proposal to link Kilrush and Kilkee, fishing ports both, by 8¼ miles of standard gauge metals met with financial difficulties, and the scheme was abandoned. Then came the Tramways Act of 1883 and, with steamer services between Limerick and Kilrush still providing South and West Clare's sole link with the outside world, thoughts turned realistically towards a railway alternative.

The outcome was not immodest, for it only

involved 27 miles of narrow gauge line between Ennis and Miltown Malbay, a seaside resort on the west coast. The West Clare Railway Company was duly registered under the Act of 15 December 1883, and an Order in Council, dated 26 May 1884, authorized construction. Capital was £163,000 of which local authorities subscribed £16,500 in Ordinary shares. Sundry Baronies in Co Clare also took the time-honoured risk of guaranteeing interest payments. Opportunity was taken to share the Waterford, Limerick's station facilities at Ennis, and West Clare trains utilized a bay platform on the west side. Head office, works and running shed were all located in the immediate vicinity.

To reach Lahinch, a well-known watering place on the west coast, West Clare metals had to face a stiff climb for 2½ miles, and another 2-mile gradient of 1 in 52 intervened ere Miltown Malbay was reached. Hence, as WCR management discovered rather too late, powerful locomotives would be required. The four 0–6–0 tanks they provided initially served for five years, but their inadequacies were a frequent source of vexation. Meanwhile, the West Clare, running all the way on its own ground, opened for public service on 2 July 1897.

With Clare appetites thus whetted, a second railway company was set up in June 1884; and within a

The introduction of No 10 Lahinch *(Kerr Stuart 818/1903), the West Clare's most powerful loco, was probably inspired by the success of the 4–6–0T type further north in Co Donegal. Renumbered 10C by the GSR in 1925, the loco was accorded a class designation of its own, BN1, before bowing the knee in 1953, on which occasion three other West Clare 4–6–0Ts also perished at Inchicore.* (Steamchest)

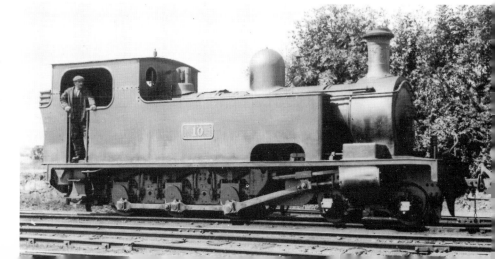

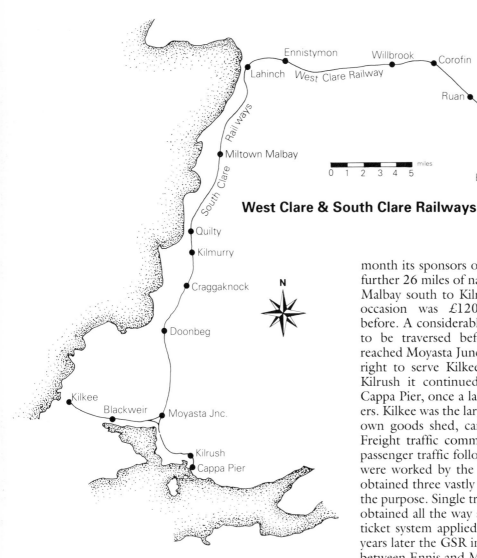

West Clare & South Clare Railways

month its sponsors obtained authority to construct a further 26 miles of narrow gauge track from Miltown Malbay south to Kilrush and Kilkee. Capital on this occasion was £120,000. Baronially supported as before. A considerable amount of bleak bogland had to be traversed before the South Clare Railways reached Moyasta Junction. From there the line forked right to serve Kilkee, and left to reach Kilrush. At Kilrush it continued for one mile more down to Cappa Pier, once a landing point for Limerick steamers. Kilkee was the larger installation, and possessed its own goods shed, carriage sidings and engine shed. Freight traffic commenced on 3 August 1892, and passenger traffic followed on 23 December. All trains were worked by the West Clare, which by now had obtained three vastly more successful 0–6–2 tanks for the purpose. Single track with a speed limit of 25 mph obtained all the way south from Ennis. The staff and ticket system applied from the outset, though many years later the GSR installed electric staff instruments between Ennis and Miltown Malbay.

No 2C, a West Clare 2–6–2T which once bore the name Ennis, *pauses at Ennistymon, nearly halfway between Ennis and Kilkee. The track and station buildings look very spruce indeed, even in July 1938. The loco itself lasted until all West Clare steam was eliminated in 1955.* (F. C. Le Manquais)

Ready for the road at Kilrush on 6 July 1938. No 3C, formerly named Ennistymon, *was one of the last two engines built for Irish narrow gauge use, and was supplied by the Hunslet Engine Co in 1922. Painted plain grey when the GSR took over, No 3C continued in local service until 1953.* (F. C. Le Manquais)

Typical of West Clare coaching stock, six-wheelers Nos 11C and 2C, one composite, the other 3rd class only, stand by for further use at Kilrush in July 1938. Although they remained gas lit to the end, the maroon-liveried coaches still look quite smart, and the GSR coat of arms wears well on their sides. (F. C. Le Manquais)

Prior to 1892 Limerick steamers calling at Cappa Pier provided the good folk of Kilrush with their only reliable link with the outside world. Then, when the South Clare Railway arrived on the scene, narrow gauge metals entering Kilrush were extended one mile down to the pier. Thus, using an avoiding loop at Moyasta Junction, it became feasible to run boat trains direct from Kilrush to Kilkee. This view of Cappa Pier metals was obtained in 1938. (F. C. Le Manquais)

Three 0–6–2Ts provided by Dübs & Co in 1892 were unusual in that driving and trailing wheels shared a common diameter of 4 feet. Ten years later the coupled wheels were reduced to 3 ft 6 in, and a useful boost in tractive effort resulted. No 5, once named Slieve Callan, was withdrawn in 1959, then was restored to original form at Inchicore two years later, before being placed on permanent exhibition at Ennis station. Quite well protected from the elements, it was still there in April 1962. (Steamchest)

Although the Clare railways were serving a sparsely populated area, initial services were quite generous. In winter three trains ran each way daily between Ennis and Kilkee, with connections to Kilrush, and there was one Sunday service. In summer months services were stepped up accordingly. The 48-mile journey took about 3 hours, which timing remained steady until dieselization reduced it to 2 hr 20 min in the 1950s. At Moyasta Junction an avoiding loop completed a triangle of South Clare metals, thus enabling boat trains to run direct from Cappa Pier to Kilkee. Passenger stock of varying vintages, all six-wheeled, offered first and third class travel only, and a few of West Clare's 35 coaches, built as 'tourist coaches', boasted clerestory roofs and saloon accommodation. High winds along the Atlantic seaboard, however, caused severe operational problems at times, and careful disciplines had to be introduced to prevent derailments. At Quilty, south of Miltown Malbay, an anemometer was installed, and once this indicated winds of 60 mph velocity all station masters were instructed to ensure that all trains, passenger and freight alike, took heavy concrete slabs on board. As or when wind velocity reached 80 mph all traffic was stopped. Gale conditions, in fact, with their attendant risk to telephone wires, could produce situations of sheer drama. If a stationmaster phoned on to find if a train might proceed, and received no answer, danger was automatically assumed. Poor West Clare, small wonder its trains were often hours late!

Subjected only too often to public ridicule, and sniped at by farmers whose animals strayed, fatally, on the line, the West Clare soldiered on into the twentieth century. As usual, Baronial Guarantees cushioned

lack of profitability, and the onset of severe road competition in post-First World War years made absorption by the GSR in 1925 an unmitigated blessing. Winter service was promptly reduced to two trains each way, and Sunday service vanished. In 1928 the GSR experimented with the use of two Drewry petrol-driven cars between Kilrush and Kilkee, but despite attractive running costs of only 9d a mile the cars were withdrawn after a year or two. Then in 1936 the possibility of through running between Limerick and Kilrush prompted a suggestion that Clare metals should be widened to 5 ft 3 in. This proposal, however, ignored the stark fact that Kilrush lay 71 miles by rail from Limerick, and only 51 miles by road. In any case, it was rejected on grounds of cost.

But for the Second World War, with its attendant petrol shortages, the West Clare would probably have gone under. As it was, its locomotive stock emerged badly run down, and in 1953, when four of West Clare's five powerful 4–6–0 tanks had to be withdrawn, the GSR reflected contemporary freight traffic requirements by transferring two Tralee & Dingle 2–6–0Ts. One was scrapped in 1955; the other moved on to Cavan & Leitrim pastures two years later. All West Clare passenger traffic had already been dieselized when four Walker Bros railcars were imported in 1951. One last stage came in 1955, when a decision was made to dispense with steam altogether, and three more Walker diesels arrived. For a while the diesel's increased efficiency appeared to enhance long-term prospects of survival. Alas, in 1961 came the grave decision — and the last of Ireland's historic narrow gauge lines closed down.

LOCOMOTIVES

No	Name	Type	Date built	Makers	Maker's number	Withdrawn	GSR number (1925)	GSR Class (1925)
1	—	0–6–0T	1887	Bagnall	730	1912	—	—
2	—	,,	1887	,,	738	1900	—	—
3	Clifden	,,	1887	,,	793	1922	—	—
4	Besborough	,,	1887	,,	794	1901	—	—
5	Slieve Callan	0–6–2T	1892	Dübs & Co	2890	1952	5C	LN1
6	Saint Senan	,,	1892	,,	2891	1956	6C	LN1
7	Lady Inchiquin	,,	1892	,,	2892	1922	—	—
8	Lisdoonvarna	2–6–2T	1894	,,	3169	1925	8C	PN1
9	Fergus	,,	1900	T. Green	229	1925	9C	PN1
2	Ennis	,,	1900	,,	234	1955	2C	PN1
4	Liscannor	,,	1901	,,	236	1928	4C	PN1
10	Lahinch	4–6–0T	1903	Kerr Stuart	818	1953	10C	BN1
11	Kilkee	,,	1909	Bagnall	1881	1953	11C	BN2
1	Kilrush	,,	1912	Hunslet	1018	1953	1C	BN4
3	Ennistymon	,,	1922	,,	1432	1953	3C	BN3
7	Malbay	,,	1922	,,	1433	1955	7C	BN3

The West Clare, it will be observed, never employed anything but six-coupled tanks. The first four, supplied in 1887, were W. G. Bagnall's first venture into passenger locomotive construction. Though they worked all traffic for five years, their lack of power was soon exposed. Accordingly, when the South Clare section was opened in 1892 three more powerful Dübs 0–6–2Ts were standing by. As their withdrawal dates indicate, they served the Clare railways well. No 5, restored to green livery in 1962, now stands proudly on public exhibition at Ennis station.

An intriguing feature of the 0–6–2Ts rested in the fact that their trailing wheels and driving wheels shared a common diameter of 4 feet. Original tractive effort emerged as 11,950 lbs, but ten years later, when the coupled wheels were reduced to 3 ft 6 in, this was boosted to a very useful 13,660 lbs. Meanwhile, West Clare's Loco Superintendent had already anticipated this logic by ordering a 2–6–2T from Dübs, very similar to the 0–6–2Ts, but with 3 ft 6 in coupled wheels. No 9, from T. Green of Leeds, held to this design, except that long side tanks were extended to the smokebox and coal capacity was stepped up to 2 tons. It and sister engines, Nos 2 and 4, were, incidentally, the heaviest locomotives ever built by T. Green. Well provided now with more powerful tanks, West Clare was content to withdraw two of its 0–6–0Ts.

West Clare's next loco development was probably inspired by the success achieved by Donegal Railways and the Letterkenny & Burtonport Railway in employing 4–6–0Ts on their respectively difficult lines. Whatever, No 10 emerged from Kerr Stuart's Stoke works in 1903. The most powerful engine West Clare ever possessed, *Lahinch* had 3-foot coupled wheels, weighed 36 tons in working order, and produced a tractive effort of 17,800 lbs. Later imports from Bagnall and Hunslet all reverted to 3 ft 9 in driving wheels. Hunslet's pair were, in fact, the last engines built for Irish narrow gauge use.

On 1 January 1925, when it passed into GSR ownership, the West Clare handed over 53 route miles of track and 11 of its original 16 locos. The GSR promptly removed all locomotive names and added the suffix 'C' to running numbers. No 8 was scrapped straight away, and No 4 followed in 1928. Nine survivors, painted plain grey, served on into the 1950s. The first major withdrawals came in 1953, when five 4–6–0Ts visited Inchicore Works for the last time. Two Tralee & Dingle tanks sent in lieu to handle diminishing freight traffic did not last long; and speedy encroachment by railcars and diesel locomotives subsequently put an end to steam on the West Clare.

CAVAN & LEITRIM RAILWAY

Incorporated: 3 December 1883
Opened: 24 October 1887
Absorbed by GSR: 1 January 1925

In Cromwell's day no Irish Count suffered more from the 'planting' of English landlords than Cavan and Leitrim. Peasants were dispossessed, evictions for non-payment of rent were commonplace, and from the resultant legacy of hatred and resentment the expressions 'boycott' and 'moonlighting' passed into the English language. Industry, of course, was never allowed to gain a foothold. Canals made some

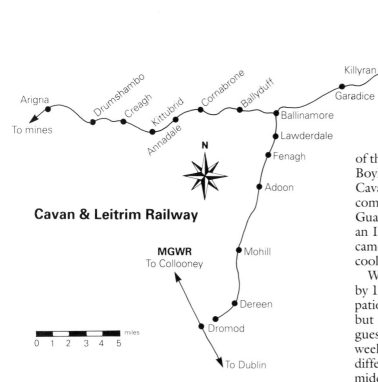

Cavan & Leitrim Railway

of the tramway project, and Arigna was substituted for Boyle as its proposed western terminus. Fortunately, Cavan and Leitrim Councils stood by their £190,585 commitment, and plans went ahead. In the event the Guarantee turned out to be the largest ever put up for an Irish railway. A somewhat less enviable distinction came later, when C&L building costs emerged at a cool £4,500 per mile.

Work began in earnest in the autumn of 1885, and by 17 October 1887 the main line was ready for occupation. Ostensibly it opened for goods traffic only, but on the first day quite a number of distinguished guests contrived also to share the experience. One week later the public were admitted, and savoured a different kind of excitement when a loco hauling the midday train broke down in open country, stranding 12 passengers. The GNR(I), meanwhile, kindly disposed towards the new concern, offered the C&L a home at its Belturbet station. At the Dromod end, however, a less charitable MGWR insisted that the C&L build its own terminal, and refused to countenance the idea of transfer facilities between the two stations. Official opening of the 14¾-mile tramway to Arigna followed on 2 May 1888.

Ambitious though the C&L promoters were, the brisk traffic which promptly developed, particularly in livestock, took them completely by surprise, and orders had to be hurriedly placed for additional rolling-stock. And, strangely, as the years passed this peculiar pattern of improvidence so persisted that the true potential of the railway was never realized. Plans were constantly being made, and thwarted, to extend

attempt to open up communications, and periodically the MGWR was 'tapped' to expand, but not until 1883 did any determined railway proposal emerge. Financially it could only come from landowners themselves; ambitions were duly laid before the public when the Cavan, Leitrim & Roscommon Light Railway & Tramway Co Ltd was registered under the newly passed Tramways Act. The aim was to construct a 33¾-mile light railway from Belturbet, Co Cavan, to Dromod, Co Leitrim, and add a tramway which would branch off at Ballinmore to join the MGWR at Boyle, Co Roscommon.

Hopes that all three Baronies would join in a £251,000 guarantee were foiled when Co Roscommon chose to defect. This, in turn, defeated part

The Cavan and Leitrim's 33¾-mile main line between Belturbet and Dromod, opened in 1887, was sufficiently easily graded to permit employment of light 4-4-0Ts. One of eight supplied that year by R. Stephenson & Co, No 2 Kathleen, stands by the nerve-centre of C&L activity, the workshops and locomotive shed at Ballinamore. Withdrawn in 1959, the loco is now resident in Belfast Transport Museum. (C. R. G. Stuart)

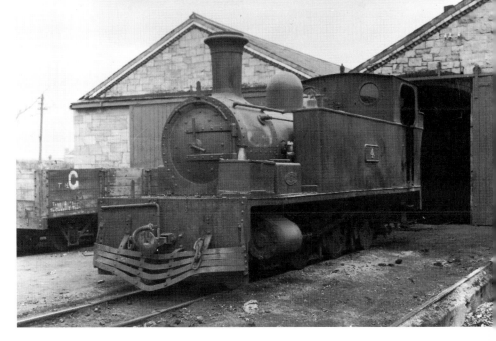

in many directions; yet few realistic steps were taken to tap the potentially lucrative mineral traffic which lay so close to hand, albeit just beyond tramway reach. Cavan management had a fatal fondness for committees, and, somehow, delicate negotiations with iron and coal mining interests in the Arigna valley were not their forte. In 1905 the C&L was still nibbling at the problem when the Government stepped in boldly to offer a Free Grant of £24,000 towards construction of the required tramway extension. The railway might well have agreed, but Leitrim Council, deeming itself already deeply enough committed in the way of C&L

dividend deficits, refused to support another Guarantee. The matter was dropped.

Two years later the GNR(I) intervened, and offered a modest £500 guarantee in perpetuity if the C&L was prepared to venture construction. Not surprisingly, the proposition was declined. Next, the coal owners themselves tried to push through an Arigna Valley Railway Bill, but, thanks largely to C&L opposition, the measure was defeated in Parliament. In the end the wartime shortage of coal in Ireland forced the Government to build the extension, and its 3½ miles were completed in June 1920 — at a cost of £60,000.

As far back as 1932, four of the Cork, Blackrock's classic 2–4–2Ts had already been absorbed, and renumbered, into Cavan & Leitrim section stock. Though hardly designed to handle heavy coal trains on the Arigna Extension, they made themselves useful enough in general service. Here, for instance, No 10L starts out from Ballinamore in August 1958 on the 7.00 pm mixed train to Dromod. (M. Swift)

Another marked defect in C&L operations was lack of quality in staff; though it might be added that their Locomotive Superintendents were an honourable exception to this rule. But, for exactly the same reasons as obtained on the Tralee & Dingle, the rates of pay the C&L was obliged to offer were derisory — and practically guaranteed poor service throughout the company's history. Conversely, neither local management nor C&L Directors, oddly ensconced in Dublin, possessed sufficient expertise to extract consistent profit from a railway which laboured under so many handicaps. No working surplus appeared until 1893, and although operating losses were avoided from then on, remorseless payment of dividends remained a cross which ratepayers and Treasury had to bear. In 1895 a change of name to the Cavan & Leitrim Railway was effected. Average receipts per mile still hovered around £3.10s, as opposed to the promoters' sanguine prognostications of £6. C&L activities, in fact, were drily summed up when evidence was given before the Viceregal Commission of 1906 — 94 per cent of C&L receipts, it was deposed, were swallowed up in working expenses, and between 1884 and 1905 ratepayers were saddled with total losses of £75,450.

Came 31 December 1916. Wartime control descended on Irish railways, and soon the country itself was in a political ferment. One clear indication of C&L staff loyalties was given in December 1918, when an engine travelled all the way from Belturbet to Dromod bearing an Irish National flag on its smokebox. Soon Leitrim Council, too, had misgivings, and in 1920, anticipating the creation of an Irish Free State, it held back half-payment of its railway dividend subsidy — on the grounds that ultimate recovery from a 'foreign' Treasury might pose problems!

On raged the Civil War. During 1921 several narrow gauge lines in the South were closed for a matter of months by military instruction. The C&L escaped this indignity, though it did receive its fair share of vis-its from armed raiders. Mercifully, the C&L's days as an independent concern were already numbered, and passage of the 1924 Railway Act placed it securely under GSR jurisdiction.

The impact of GSR disciplines did not come kindly to Cavan men, but fortunately old loyalties took most of the strain. Soon the GSR earned further opprobrium, when strict economies were applied. Within a year or so the C&L workshops at Ballinmore were stripped of their best machinery, and subsequent removal of the carriage sheds set in train the rapid deterioration of Cavan rolling-stock. Then, in 1934 the mines around Derreenavoggy were reorganized. Traffic picked up, and four Blackrock 2–4–2Ts were imported to lend a hand. Despite this influx of traffic the GSR persisted in tabling in 1939 a proposal to close the entire C&L section.

The outbreak of the Second World War radically altered the complexion of things. Suddenly, Arigna's reserves of rather inferior coal became a national asset. Traffic flourished afresh, and in 1941 two Tralee & Dingle engines were brought in to assist in handling heavy coal trains. With inside frames they were a better proposition than the West Clare and Schull & Skibbereen locos the GSR contemplated sending in at one time. Two more followed from Tralee in 1950 and 1957. The last, No 6T, despite its comparatively brief sojourn at Ballinmore, put in a remarkable mileage on coal trains. Unlike the Cork, Blackrock immigrants, the Tralee conscripts were never renumbered.

When, in January 1945, the GSR's mantle was taken over by CIE, Cavan & Leitrim affairs remained comparatively unchanged. C&L coaches were increasingly being written off because of decay, and odd derailments and accidents continued to occur. Traditionally, Cavan men took the latter in their stride. Local courts, however, appeared increasingly unamused.

Ominously, traffic began to dwindle again by 1955,

but thoughts of closure were put aside when a new coal boom arose to add a few more years of life. By 1959, however, an annual loss of £40,000, increasing road competition, and general acceptance that the C&L section lacked modern handling facilities combined to force CIE's hand. The narrow gauge line's days were deemed to be over, and on 31 March 1959 one long last train panted into Ballinmore station,

there to debouch its human load. Soon both tramway and main lines were demolished, and local residents learned to resign themselves to the tender mercies of one-man buses. Lorries, once despised by Cavan & Leitrim men, assumed the handling of all freight — and one more epoch in Ireland's narrow gauge railway history was over.

LOCOMOTIVES

No	Name	Type	Date built	Makers	Maker's number	GSR No (1925)	Withdrawn	Remarks
1	*Isabel*	4–4–0T	1887	R. Stephenson	2612	1L	1949	Nos 1–8 rebuilt with larger boilers, 1902-06
2	*Kathleen*	,,	1887	,,	2613	2L	1959	Now preserved in Belfast Transport Museum with C&L clerestory bogie saloon coach No 6 of 1887
3	*Lady Edith*	,,	1887	,,	2614	3L	1959	Preserved in USA
4	*Violet*	,,	1887	,,	2615	4L	1959	Cut up at Dromod, 1960
5	*Gertrude*	,,	1887	,,	2616	5L	1925	Scrapped by GSR
6	*May*	,,	1887	,,	2617	6L	1927	,,
7	*Olive*	,,	1887	,,	2618	7L	1945	Idle at Inchicore from 1939
8	*Queen Victoria*	,,	1887	,,	2619	8L	1959	Cut up at Ballinmore
9	*King Edward*	0–6–4T	1904	,,	3136	9L	1934	Cut up at Inchicore

The C&L, it will be observed, acquired only one more locomotive after its initial flush of eight arrived in 1887. The intention was to name the octet after Directors' daughters, and it is said that only dissension by one Director permitted the inclusion of the reigning monarch. Whatever the truth of the matter, *Queen Victoria* lost her nameplates under 'patriotic' circumstances in 1923. When the plates were found the company insisted on restoring them. Within a few days they disappeared again, this time for good.

Locos Nos 5–8 were supplied complete with tramway gear, ie skirting over wheels, cowcatcher, bell, and headlamp at the back end. As an afterthought, condensing gear was added, and this raised the contract price to £1,138 per locomotive. Most unusually, duplicate driving controls were provided in each cab. This at least possessed the merit that drivers could keep their eyes on the road at all times. All eight were reboiled in due course, whence their working weight increased from 25 to 27 tons. Then when the lively traffic of the early 1900s begged further provision of motive power Stephensons supplied a more radically designed 0-6-4 tank. Weighing nearer 37 tons, it had a much larger grate, and employed Walschaerts valve gear. Though proudly hailed by C&L men, it soon proved a complete white elephant,

for its long wheelbase had an incurable habit of spreading track. Even run bogie-first, the loco still created havoc. In 1923, after many years of low mileage, it was put up for sale. There were no bidders.

Once the GSR took over in 1925, Nos 5 and 6 were scrapped as being unworthy of repair. *King Edward* followed in 1934. Meanwhile, the fireboxes of the remainder were fitted with brick arches, to take Welsh coal; Arigna's soft product had never really given satisfactory results. One recalls that Mr Maunsell of the GS&WR and Mr Glover of the GNR(I) were invited by C&L management in 1908 and 1914 respectively to adjudicate on this problem. Both advocated use of other coals.

From 1932 onwards Ballinmore suffered further reduction in status. Now all locos seeking heavy repair had to attend Inchicore for the purpose. Two years later, four Cork, Blackrock tanks arrived on the scene. They were hardly ideally equipped to handle coal trains, though their contribution was welcome none the less. Then, in 1941, came two Tralee & Dingle locos. Two more followed during the 1950s, and all engines and four C&L residents, adding a somewhat bizarre element to the end of yet another Irish narrow gauge railway.

Northern Ireland

BALLYMENA, CUSHENDALL & RED BAY RAILWAY

Incorporated: 18 July 1872
Opened: 8 October 1876
Absorbed by B&NCR: 14 October 1884

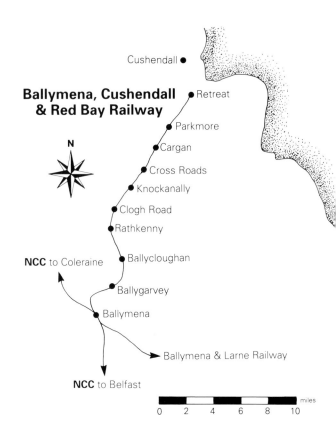

Ireland never did have much luck with mineral deposits. In the north-eastern tip of Antrim, for instance, considerable fields of iron ore were identified in the first half of the nineteenth century; but although mining commenced in 1868, the total absence of local coal supplies made smelting *in situ* impossible. So, railways had to be built to get the ore to a seaport.

The area, in fact, attracted Ireland's first 3-foot gauge railway. Built in 1873 to facilitate export of ore from new mines to Cloughor, the Glenariff Railway, just over 4 miles long, gave direct access to a pier at Carrivemurphy. Alas, mining petered out within three years. The line lay unused from 1876, and in 1885 all rolling-stock was bought by the Lough Swilly Railway. Meanwhile, the potential El Dorado around Glenariff was still being stalked by other interested parties, and in 1871 two contrasting rivals emerged, the Antrim Wire Tramway Co and the Ballymena, Cushendall & Red Bay Railway. Both aimed to reach Red Bay harbour. Within two years the Antrim company went bankrupt, and such resources as it possessed passed into Cushendall hands.

The Cushendall Railway began life with the express intention of exploiting Antrim's iron ore, which aim it proposed to achieve by running a line east from Ballymena, and building harbour facilities at Cushendall, on Red Bay. Parliament duly obliged in 1872 by countenancing construction of 22¼ miles of track 'not wider than 3 feet or narrower than 2 feet'. By the nature of things, carriage of passengers was prohibited, except by special permission from the Board of Trade. Capital was fixed at £120,000 and, of this, the Belfast & Northern Counties Railway was allowed to subscribe up to £25,000, because of its local interest. Lack of capital held up initial progress, but eventually, on 1 July 1875, the first section, Ballymena to Cargan, was opened to general traffic.

Things looked promising, and on 8 October 1876 the line opened as far as Retreat, a mere loading bank high in the Antrim mountains. Next, with 16¼ miles firmly under their belt, the Cushendall Directors addressed themselves to the task of reaching the coast. Retreat, unfortunately, lay 1,000 feet above sea level. Various plans were drawn up to combat the precipitous descent, but latterly it was conceded that even

Cushendall drivers could hardly be called upon to face a 4½-mile drop at 1 in 21, and the dream was abandoned.

Back in Ballymena, meanwhile, the B&NCR's station was only half a mile distant, and by transhipping narrow gauge loads on to its *own* standard gauge wagons, then handing them over to B&NCR care, Cushendall solved the problem of getting its minerals and merchandise to Belfast. Cushendall ambitions anent Ballymena, in fact, grew so that the company sponsored a Bill in 1877 to initiate *five* more minor railways in the area. The Bill became law in 1878, but shortage of capital ensured that the scheme never saw the light of day. In any case, within a year or two Cushendall management found it had other things to think about. Not only was the track deteriorating, but a depression was gathering on the iron-trade horizon. Time went on, Cushendall's inability to carry passengers cruelly exposed the company's utter dependence on mineral traffic, and by 1884 the recession had reached such a pitch that a despairing proposal to vest the railway within the B&NCR gained unanimous support from the Board. An appropriate Bill became law on 14 July 1884, and three months later the B&NCR, up to then a totally standard gauge concern, acquired its first narrow gauge constituent.

With a decline in mineral traffic about its own ears, the B&NCR at least had the capital required to activate passenger traffic in 'no man's land'. Permission was obtained to instigate two modest roadside tramways in the Cushendall area. Prevailing gradients, however, again baffled engineers, and the project was shelved in favour of improvements to such metals as existed. Heavier rails were laid, Cushendall's complete absence of intermediate stations was rectified, and by 5 April 1885 the B&NCR was operating a passenger service between Ballymena and Knockanally. Three years later services were extended to Parkmore, but the final 2½ miles to Retreat never bore passenger traffic. From there the B&NCR saw fit to conduct a vigorous campaign to attract tourists to the Glenariff area. It was as well, for between the years 1880 and 1894 mineral traffic from Cushendall plummetted from £11,561 a year to £2,628. Profit margin per mile shrunk accordingly from 3s 8d to 10d. Meanwhile, the fact that Glenariff was acquiring quite a reputation as a beauty spot made all the more vexing the railway's inability to drop to the coast.

The B&NCR, accepting that handicap with shrewd common sense, did the next best thing by popularizing the Vale of Glenariff, an area easily accessible by foot from Parkmore station. Special footpaths were constructed to offer holidaymakers hitherto unknown views of the Glen. Rail travellers used them free of charge, while others paid a small sum. Soon quite a considerable excursion traffic developed. The B&NCR responded by providing a number of four-wheeled one-class saloon coaches, and during summer months a normal daily service of three trains each way between Ballymena and Parkmore was duly augmented. Ironically, the station at Retreat, though it lay close to the castle from which it took its name, had no role to play in this expansion of passenger traffic. It was much too isolated. Cushendall locomotives, three in number and all 0–4–2STs, worked the line until about 1909, when other locos infiltrated.

All was not well on the B&NCR, however; by 1902 its Directors found themselves unable to resist a tempting takeover bid offered by the (English) Midland Railway. Derby, anxious to enter Irish steamship traffic, was already building a branch to Heysham harbour. So, on 1 July 1903 ownership of the B&NCR passed to the Midland Railway (Northern Counties Committee). Almost immediately a deputation representing local Irish interests urged the Committee to proceed with construction of a Retreat–Cushendall extension. The Committee, cognisant of physical difficulties, declined. It did its best, though, to improve road conditions during 1905.

During the 1914–18 war, iron ore production picked up again, though this was sadly offset by a reduction in passenger traffic. The MR(NCC), like other Irish railways, came under statutory control from 1 January 1917. Railway economics were badly affected all over the UK, and 1921 arrived ere the Government, finding individual assessment too difficult, paid out £3 million in compensation, to be divided somehow amongst the various Irish companies. By then the Partition of Ireland had brought its own problems, and the ex-Cushendall section of the NCC suffered accordingly. One train was held up and robbed by gunmen, and, amongst others, Parkmore and Retreat stations were burned to the ground. Meanwhile, as the 1920s progressed railways lost their transport monopoly, and of Ireland's narrow gauge railways only the County Donegal, with Henry Forbes at the helm, offered realistic resistance.

In Antrim retrenchment came on 1 October 1930, when Ballymena–Parkmore services were withdrawn. Parkmore's days as a tourist centre were over. Freight traffic continued to work at irregular intervals, but on 10 April 1937 the 10 miles between Rathkenny and Retreat were closed to all traffic. Came the Second World War, and Cushendall's last 6 miles, between Rathkenny and Ballymena, met a similar fate.

LOCOMOTIVES

BC&RB No	Type	Date	Makers	Maker's number	B&NCR Nos 1884	B&NCR Nos 1897	B&NCR Class	Withdrawn	Remarks
1	0–4–2ST	1874	Black Hawthorn	301	60	101A	0	1923	Rebuilt in 1907
2	,,	1874	,,	302	61	102A	0	1923	Rebuilt in 1908
3	,,	1874	,,	303	62	103	0	1911	Fitted with extended saddle tank in 1893

All three BC&RB locomotives were identical, being Hawthorn's standard type of 0–4–2 saddle tank. The first renumbering occurred when the B&NCR took over in 1884, the second when narrow gauge numbers were pushed back in 1897 to make room for increasing numbers of B&NCR standard gauge locos. The later suffix 'A' was evidence of entering reserve stock. In 1893 the saddle tanks of Nos 102 and 103 were extended flush with the smokebox front. In 1908, however, No 102's tanks were restored to their original dimensions.

From February 1920 Nos 101A and 102A spent 19 months, by Order of the Railway Executive, on construction and working of the Arigna Valley extension.

Heavily engaged in hauling coal trains, they proved very popular with Cavan & Leitrim men. After returning north in November 1921 they lay idle for over two years before being scrapped. No 103 had already been sold to a mining company after withdrawal in 1911.

By the very nature of its trade, the Cushendall Railway owned a fair quantity of wagons. The number had risen to 241 by the time the B&NCR took over, and in the absence of specific information one might reasonably assume that one-quarter were standard gauge, and the remainder narrow gauge. Two narrow gauge brake vans were purchased very early on, and one odd vehicle followed in 1877 — an eight-wheeled Directors' Saloon. The B&NCR added ten tramcar-like carriages as tourist traffic developed. Built between 1886 and 1898, most of them lasted into the early 1930s. The first of them, B&NCR No 306, saw 1954 in before it was withdrawn.

Finally, it might be added that Glenariff Land & Development Co, an immediate predecessor of Cushendall in iron ore working, owned at least five locos during its brief lifetime. The first 3-foot gauge locos in Ireland, two of them, built by Stephenson & Co in 1873, were 2–4–0Ts, with inside frames and outside cylinders. Little is known of their active life until, auctioned in 1885, they passed into Lough Swilly ownership in company with 40 wagons and a brake van. Numbered 5 and 6 on the Swilly, and known thereafter quite misleadingly as the 'Cushendalls', the two tanks were replaced in 1899, and, though renumbered 5A and 6A, were dismantled shortly afterwards. Glenariff's No 5, an 0–6–0ST built by Black Hawthorn in 1879, was sold to the Ballycastle Railway in 1882. It ended up there as No 3 *Lady Boyd*.

BALLYMENA & LARNE RAILWAY

Incorporated: 7 August 1874
Opened: 24 August 1878
Absorbed by B&NCR: 16 July 1889

All through the first half of the nineteenth century Portpatrick, in Wigtownshire and Donaghadee, in Co Down, enjoyed undisputed monopoly as 'short sea route' ports between Scotland and Ireland. Then gradually Portpatrick's lack of shelter began to tell, and towards the mid-1860s sailings faded commensurately. In Scotland, meanwhile, Stranraer was ready and willing to take Portpatrick's place. Thirty-six miles away, Larne, a small fishing village on the northeast coast of Ireland, also began to sense its time had

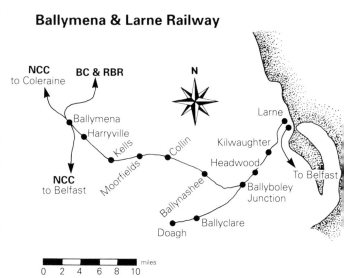

Ballymena & Larne Railway

come. One man, James Chaine, businessman and MP for South Antrim, took a particularly keen interest in Larne's welfare.

Chaine's combination of political influence and business acumen soon became something of a local legend. He built Larne Harbour, added a pier over 1,000 feet long, and joined forces with others in 1871 to found the Larne & Stranraer Steamboat Co. Five years later the newly opened standard gauge Carrickfergus & Larne Railway Co offered an important link with Belfast, and Larne's prestige swelled accordingly. Meanwhile, promotion of a Larne & Antrim Railway, again a standard gauge concept, fell by the wayside, and as other promoters rushed to fill the vacuum Chaine was found to be supporting a 12-mile-long 3-foot gauge scheme, the Larne & Ballyclare Railway. A Bill was duly submitted, and it received Royal Assent on 5 August 1873. That same year the existence of iron ore deposits was verified at Glenwirry, an area much nearer Ballymena, and, with potential mineral traffic clearly in sight, those who had promoted the L&BR hastened to sponsor a narrow gauge extension.

The result was a composite Act of 7 August 1874 which not only authorized construction of a further 7 miles of track from Ballyboley Junction, on the B&LR's present route, to Harryville, near Ballymena, but conferred a new title on the joint enterprise: the Ballymena & Larne Railway Company. Harryville, as it happened, was very near the B&NCR's standard-gauge goods station at Ballymena; but heartfelt appeals by the B&LR Board to be allowed a brief mixed gauge passage over B&NCR metals in order to tap the Cushendall Railway's mineral wealth met with a dusty response from the larger company.

The Ballymena & Larne's Act of 1874 authorized issue of capital to the tune of £136,000, and sanc-

tioned further borrowing of £45,000. After an initial flush, however, subscriptions slowed desperately, and by late 1877 only £80,000 had been collected. None the less, the Board, bit firmly in its teeth, called for construction tenders, and placed an order with Beyer Peacock of Manchester for one locomotive. Specifically requested as 'a duplicate of *The Sutherland*, Isle of Man engine', the 2–4–0 tank duly arrived in April 1877. Line construction dragged on, hampered by lack of funds, and only in June 1878 did management declare its 29-mile line 'complete'. Costs had worked out at £3,400 per mile. Subsequent inspection by the Board of Trade produced a disenchanting catalogue of faults; but after frenzied activity on the B&LR's part, the Inspector relented sufficiently to allow passenger services to commence on 24 August 1878. Disappointingly, one year's summer traffic had already gone by the board.

Still anxious to exploit Antrim's mineral resources, the B&LR had already submitted a Bill seeking permission to build no fewer than *eight* new sections of

This was Beyer Peacock's response in 1878 to the Ballymena & Larne's request for 'a duplicate of Isle of Man Railway's engine Sutherland'. *First numbered 4, the loco became No 105 under B&NCR auspices in 1889. November 1928 saw it sold to the Castlederg & Victoria Bridge Tramway, but it performed little regular work between then and eventual closure of the Tramway in October 1933.* (Author's Collection)

railway. The resultant Act of Parliament, dated 8 August 1878, chose to compromise by denying five and sanctioning three. Ostensibly the most important, the long-sought-after link with Cushendall metals, partly over B&NCR territory, was accomplished on 22 September 1880. The B&LR Directors were very pleased to receive assurances of complete Cushendall co-operation — until the unfortunate realization dawned that the Cushendall Railway, in fact, still lacked authority to run passenger-carrying vehicles! The second extension authorized by the Act, one of 1½ miles to Doagh, west of Ballyclare, was opened to all traffic in May 1884. Coal was the attrac-

Meet 'The Bruiser', the Ballymena & Larne's most powerful locomotive! Originally numbered 5, it became B&NCR No 109 in 1897. Nevertheless, it still soldiered on around Larne, specializing in handling heavy coal and freight trains. So consistent was 'The Bruiser's' performance that the 2–6–0ST finished up in 1934 with nearly 900,000 miles to its credit. (Steamchest)

Above *In 1892 Beyer Peacock constructed two quite remarkable 2–4–2 compound tank locomotives to the order of Bowman Malcolm, the B&NCR's young Locomotive Engineer. Numbered 69 and 70, then 110 and 111, they served the Ballymena & Larne section well, and four more of the class followed from York Road Workshops, Belfast, over the years 1908-1920.* (Author's Collection)

Left *Of the two original Beyer Peacock 2–4–2Ts, No 111 was the more reliable, and as a consequence No 110 was chosen in 1931 when the LMS/NCC decided to rebuild one as a 2–4–4T. The only one of its type ever to appear in the British Isles, No 110 looked impressive enough in its rebuilt form. Results, however, were not encouraging, and the modification was never repeated.* (Steamchest)

tion here. The third branch authorized, only a mile long between Larne and Kilwaughter, was never completed in its entirety.

Thus, from 1880 the B&LR at least shared station facilities at Ballymena with the B&NCR. Starting from a single through platform, both lines, standard gauge and 3 foot, crossed the Braid Water on parallel bridges ere the B&LR curved away towards the east, aiming for the coast. It had some hard climbing to do before reaching its peak at Ballynashee, 660 feet above sea level and a correspondingly steep descent culminated in a fearsome drop of 408 feet to sea level at Larne. Many a freight train was to find itself the victim of gravity on this 6½-mile section. Once Larne was reached one last mile of narrow gauge track, running towards the Harbour, cheek by jowl with standard gauge Carrickfergus & Larne metals, divided to serve a passenger platform on one side and mixed gauge sidings on the other. By 1883 the B&LR was running four daily trains each way between Larne and

Ballymena, with three on Sundays. One of the midweek trains, the 12 noon from Larne Harbour, timed to take 1 hr 5 min for its 24¾-mile journey, was featured in the B&LR's timetables as a 'Boat Express'.

In the meantime, would-be railway promoters in the Antrim were still active. An Act of 1879 sanctioned construction of a 10-mile long 3-foot gauge line, to be called the Ballymena & Portglenone Railway. This was intended to branch off B&LR metals south of Harryville, but as only £1,566 of an authorized capital of £60,000 was ever raised, the scheme never left the ground. Next came an even more ambitious plan — to link Londonderry and Larne. This would have involved narrow gauge track crossing the River Foyle by a viaduct of 44 spans; mercifully perhaps, the Londonderry & Larne Railway Bill did not survive a second reading at Westminster. More followed. In 1885 a plan for a 3-foot gauge Ballymena & Ahoghill Tramway aborted. Two more narrow gauge proposals, centred on Ardoyne and sponsored by a minor concern, the Belfast Central Railway, shared a similar fate. Itself unable to pay a dividend to Ordinary shareholders since 1883, the poor old Ballymena & Larne did rather well to survive amidst such heady activity!

By August 1884, such was the deepening trade depression that B&LR Directors felt obliged to advocate a reduction in carriage rates for iron ore. This was duly effected, but dividends still remained invisible — until 1888, when a paltry three-quarter per cent rewarded weary shareholders. The latter had also been urging economies since their 1885 Meeting; and B&LR special passenger and mail trains which up to now had suited steamer services were withdrawn on 1 January 1886. Opportunity was also taken to extend company borrowing by a further £52,000. On the operational side, total economies exercised in 1886 yielded a mere saving of £500. This amount was easily eclipsed by a fall in mineral and passenger traffic. Three years later the B&LR Directors, faced with an increasingly blank wall, moved a resolution that the line be sold to the B&NCR. At a Special General Meeting held at Larne Harbour on 1 May 1889, shareholders carrying the largest votes won the day, and the appropriate Act became law on 16 July 1889.

The B&NCR at least found absorption of the B&LR a simpler, and less expensive, operation than that of the Cushendall Railway. The B&LR track was in reasonable condition; so, too, were its six locos, 15 carriages and 347 sundry goods vehicles. None the less, the B&NCR spent an appreciable sum of money bringing the B&LR stations and buildings up to standard, and even introduced two new compound 2–4–2 tank locomotives in 1892.

Eleven years later Derby gave vent to Irish ambitions, and the B&NCR itself passed under Midland Railway (NCC) control. The one-time B&LR line, still useful as a short-cut from Larne to Ballymena and points west, continued to attract cross-channel passengers, though a Minute of February 1904 reveals that they lodged many a complaint of rough-riding. Despite that, the Midland Railway elected to spend little money on the Ballymena section between 1903 and the outbreak of the First World War.

The railway agonies of the war years, and the 'Troubles' which beset Ireland, have already been described. Even on the British mainland, individual railway companies found themselves quite impotent to combat savagely encroaching road transport. Thus the Grouping, as from 1 January 1923, brought the LMSR into being. Even as the Ballymena lines passed into LMS(NCC) ownership, road competition intensified. Rather late in the day, the LMS(NCC) started buying out rival bus companies; but, so lax was overall Northern Ireland Government policy that Antrim's narrow gauge railways obviously faced imminent extinction. The first B&LR casualty came on 1 October 1930, when the Ballyclare-Doagh section lost its passenger service. It closed entirely three years later.

The real crunch came in 1933, when a lengthy strike of railway employees in Northern Ireland provoked the LMS(NCC) into terminating all passenger services on the Ballymena narrow gauge lines. Freight traffic staggered on into Second World War years; but on 2 June 1940, Ballymena was stripped of both its narrow gauge constituents. Rails lifted from the B&LR's old Ballymena–Ballyboley section found their way to Europe for use by the BEF. This left the Larne–Ballyclare stump as sole survivor, and Ballyboley, ceasing to be a junction, withered into insignificance. 1 October 1948 arrived, and further changes in British railways saw the LMS(NCC) vanish in favour of the Railway Executive (NCC). That did not last long, for British Railways sold its NCC interest to the Northern Ireland Government for £2½ million, and on 1 April 1949 the narrow gauge line to Larne acquired yet another new master — the Ulster Transport Authority.

The final blow came in 1950, when the paper mill at Ballyclare, sold reason for the narrow gauge line's continued existence, closed down. Such a calamity faced the UTA with little option but to close the line to Larne. So, for the first time in 75 years, the County of Antrim found itself served only by standard gauge metals.

Sad to say, railway closures had by now become such a commonplace occurrence that when 2–4–2T No 42 limped into Larne station with one last train on 20 May 1950 she did so in an atmosphere almost completely devoid of emotion. It made a poignant ending to an exciting story.

LOCOMOTIVES

Before we go on to consider details of such locos as were acquired by the B&LR management and its successors, it may be of interest to note that both R. F. Fairlie of articulated locomotive fame and the Baldwin Locomotive Company of Philadelphia USA were approached in 1876, some months before Beyer Peacock was awarded its initial contract. Practical liaison with either party, alas, never came to fruition, and only our imaginations can picture what form B&LR locomotive events *might* have taken! As it was, an unbounded admiration for the Isle of Man's highly successful 2–4–0 tanks, shared jointly by James Chaine, the B&LR's Chairman, and his successor, carried the day, and ensured the little railway's total reliance on Beyer Peacock products throughout its 11 years of independent existence.

The B&LR's request to be furnished with a copy of *The Sutherland* was not quite met, for Beyer supplied, in 1877, a near-replica of *Peveril*, a later Isle of Man

LOCOMOTIVES

B&LR No	Type	Date	Makers	Maker's number	B&NCR Nos 1889	1897	B&NCR Class	Withdrawn	Remarks
1	2–4–0T	1877	Beyer Peacock	1687	63	104	P	1920	Based on IOM Rly design
2	0–6–0T	1877	,,	1700	65	106	Q	1933	
3	0–6–0T	1877	,,	1701	66	107	Q	1931	
4	2–4–0ST	1878	,,	1828	64	105	P	1928	Sold to C&VBT Co. Scrapped 1933
5	2–6–0ST	1880	,,	1947	68	109	R	1934	Nicknamed 'The Bruiser'
6	0–6–0T	1883	,,	2304	67	108	Q	1932	

B&NCR No									
69	2–4–2T	1892	,,	3463	—	110	S	1946	Rebuilt as 2–4–4T in 1931
70	2–4–2T	1892	,,	3464	—	111	S	1950	Renumbered 44 in 1948

NCC No	Type	Date	Makers	Renumberings No	Date	No	Date	NCC Class	Withdrawn	Remarks
112	2–4–2T	1908	York Road, Belfast	102	1920	42	1939	S1	1950	Rebuilt to S1 in 1928
113	,,	1909	,,	101	1920	41	1939	S1	1950	Rebuilt to S1 in 1930
103	,,	1919	,,	—	—	—	—	S	1938	
104	,,	1920	,,	—	—	43	1942	S	1954	

development. Differences, however, were largely cosmetic, and the B&LR was content to put Nos 1 and 4 to work on passenger services. No 4, the longer lived of the two, was sold to the Castlederg & Victoria Bridge Tramway in November 1928. There, fitted with skirting over its left-hand wheels and motion, it worked until 1933. The B&LR's three 0–6–0Ts were tougher little propositions, and after working on the Parkmore section of the B&NCR, at least two of them finished their days on the Ballycastle line. No 6 had the additional comfort of an enclosed cab. No 5, a unique type of outside-cylindered 2–6–0ST, was the B&LR's most powerful loco, and weighed 25½ tons in working order. Known to all who worked it as 'The Bruiser', it still put up a tremendous mileage year by year, pulling heavy coal and freight trains out of Larne; it finished up 54 years later with a cumulative mileage of just under 900,000. Not bad for a locomotive which spent its whole life on the Ballymena–Larne section!

By 1890, having absorbed the stock of two narrow gauge concerns, the B&NCR's locomotive engineer, a young man called Bowman Malcolm, found himself presiding over a fleet of nine 3-foot engines of four different types. A keen advocate of the two-cylinder compound system, and incidentally, a devotee of saddle tanks, Malcolm reacted by inviting Beyer Peacock to produce a new narrow gauge design. Typically, he even specified eight desirable requirements. Beyer, taking up the challenge, responded by constructing two handsome and quite remarkable 2–4–2 compound side tanks. Proudly hailed, they arrived at Belfast in May 1892, and both were classified 'S'. No

70 was the more successful, and worked over a million miles before being scrapped in 1950. Sister engine No 69 required general overhaul rather too frequently for comfort. Indeed, it became the subject of extensive surgery in 1931, when, under LMS(NCC) auspices, it re-emerged as a 2–4–4T, classified 'S2'. The modification, unique though it was, was not a success.

Sixteen years elapsed before Malcolm introduced a third compound tank. This time the 2–4–2T came not from Beyer Peacock, but from the York Road workshops at Belfast. So, too, did No 113, a year later. In LMS(NCC) days both were altered to take extra coal. A bunker appeared behind the cab, and they were reclassified 'S1'. At times both wandered on to Ballycastle metals, and 112, renumbered 42 by the NCC, spent its last years working between Larne and Ballyclare paper mills.

Malcolm's last two compound tanks, reverting again to class 'S', appeared fully a decade later. No 103 was unlucky enough to be made redundant in 1938, but No 104, renumbered 43 in 1942, lived longest of all, to 1954.

Finally, a word on the various renumberings. In 1889, having already rationalized numbers on its three Cushendall locos, the B&NCR continued the process by allocating Nos 63–67 to the six B&LR locos it had acquired. Discovering later that it had left insufficient low numbers to accommodate its growing stock of standard gauge locos, the B&NCR then renumbered its narrow gauge stock; and in January 1897 the 11 locos concerned were given numbers 101–111. Four of these were later renumbered 41–44 by the NCC.

PORTSTEWART TRAMWAY

Opened: June 1882
Closed: 31 January 1926
Absorbed by B&NCR: 1 June 1897

When a totally independent concern, the Ballymena, Ballymoney, Coleraine & Portrush Junction Railway, reached north in November 1855 to complete a first vital standard gauge link between Belfast and Londonderry, the short section it built was regarded at the time as a branch. One intermediate station was provided, 3 miles south-west of Portrush, at a remote spot called Portstewart. Portrush, with its comparative ease of access to Giant's Causeway, soon became a very fashionable watering place; the Belfast & Northern Counties Railway, already in command of Belfast–Ballymena metals, hastened to snap up the BBC&PJR in 1861.

Rather more unexpectedly, Portstewart also chose to blossom as a popular seaside resort. But it faced difficulties, for as its small town expanded along the sea front it became patently clear that ultimate prosperity would never be achieved while one major problem continued to exist — the B&NCR's 'Portstewart' station lay nearly 2 miles out of town. Merchants grumbled, local discontent grew, deviation of the 'main line' was considered (and hurriedly rejected on financial grounds!), and, latterly, the solution adopted by local businessmen was the promotion of a Portstewart Tramway Co. The aim was to build a 3-foot gauge single line, 1¾ miles long, between town and station.

Opened in June 1882, the tramway contained one passing loop midway, and run-round facilities were provided at each end.

Typical of the times, steam locomotion was envisaged and recourse to Kitson & Co of Leeds soon produced two examples of their well-known 0–4–0 tramway units. With bodywork totally enclosed, and motion surrounded by protective metal plates, trams Nos 1 and 2 must certainly have generated intense local curiosity as they paddled to and fro, hauling one, or a brace, of four-wheeled single-deck cars behind them. Their main task, of course, was to connect with main line trains at Portstewart station; but quite often half-way trips to Victoria Terrace were made to provide a sort of urban transport for townsfolk. Holidaymakers, no doubt, relished the facility, but winter months, alas, brought disillusionment. A decade passed, profitability continued to elude the tramway's management, and when, in 1897, general track repairs became a matter of urgency the company opted to go into liquidation. The tramway was put up for sale. The B&NCR, enterprising as ever, made a bid, and on 1 June 1897 acquired its third narrow gauge concern. The whole line was thoroughly repaired, and in 1901 there came a third, and last, tramway engine from Kitsons. Rather more powerful than its predecessors, it was given number 3.

Despite its lack of profitability, the tramway was allowed to function for another 30 years by the B&NCR and its successors. So, the three tram locos worked stolidly on. Their very age, however, and the tramway's clumsy occupation of the public highway

A fortuitous visit to York Road Workshops, Belfast, in the summer of 1950 offered a rare opportunity to have a look inside Portstewart Tramway locomotive No 2. Having survived enemy air raids during the Second World War, it was being completely renovated, and can now be seen in Belfast Transport Museum. (Steamchest)

became increasingly important factors as the track again began to deteriorate. At one time in the mid-1920s the Northern Ireland Government, reflecting on unemployment which was rife at the time, even contemplated altering the course of the LMS(NCC) main line so that it would pass through the heart of Portstewart. Varying degrees of difficulty thwarted the plan. Then, as 1926 arrived, it became clear that immediate action was imperative. It was duly taken.

The tramway was closed on 31 January 1926, and a local bus service was instituted in lieu. In 1933 the LMS(NCC) saw fit to reassert its authority. It took over the working of Portstewart's bus services, but lost control again in 1935, when all Northern Ireland railways were obliged by law to hand over their road stock to the newly formed Northern Ireland Transport Board.

LOCOMOTIVES

No	Type	Date built	Makers	Maker's number	Remarks
1	0-4-0T	1882	Kitson	T56	Preserved, but perished during the Second World War
2	,,	1883	,,	T84	Now in Belfast Transport Museum
3	,,	1901	,,	T302	Sold in 1926

Although not the first to build steam tramway locomotives, Kitson & Co had acquired a considerable reputation in that field by 1880, and was already specializing in production of four-wheeled trams to its own design. Vertical boilers, inclined outside cylinders, a modified form of Walschaerts valve gear — all were duly encased by bodywork, and a condensing system was placed on the roof. Then, after a series of trials, horizontal boilers were substituted, and the roof condensing system evolved into a series of arched transverse tubes. The latter was the type which came into the Portstewart Tramway's possession in 1882–83. With a wheelbase of only 5 feet, both locos weighed 9 tons in working order, and could generate 3,680 lbs of tractive effort. No 3, the last tramway engine built by Kitson, weighed 11 tons, and produced nearly half as much power again.

When the tramway closed in 1926, its total stock consisted of the three tram locos, one four-wheeled single-deck car, one four-wheeled luggage van, and two bogie double-deck cars. The latter had been supplied by Milnes in 1899. Loco No 3 was sold to a contractor at Castlerock, whence it worked as a stationary engine for nine more years. Locos Nos 1 and 2 were taken, meanwhile, to York Road Works, Belfast, and remained stored there for several years.

In 1939 tram No 1 moved on to Hull Museum of Transport, and there it perished in a wartime air raid. No 2 hung on at Belfast, and was also subjected to enemy air raid. Fortunately it survived to be overhauled, and, repainted in B&NCR green, it now reposes in Belfast Transport Museum. Alas, no Portstewart car exists, for all were sold in 1926 — as garden shelters!

BALLYCASTLE RAILWAY

Incorporated: 22 July 1875
Opened: 18 October 1880
Absorbed by LMS(NCC):
 11 August 1924

Much further east along the north Antrim coast the village of Ballycastle also occupied a distinctive site, in that Fair Head, nearest spot in Ireland to the Scottish mainland, lay not far away. A number of coal mines were still at work in the area, yet, from a railway point of view Ballycastle's plight was even worse than that of

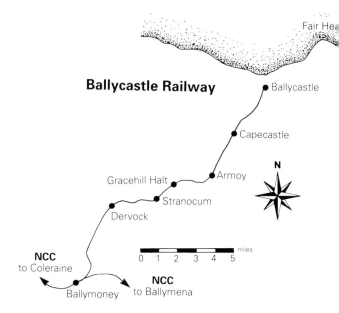

NCC No 102, the first 2–4–2T built at York Road in 1908, hustles along near Ballymoney with a typically mixed up train on 23 June 1937. Its two corridor coaches were built originally for the Ballymena & Larne boat train service, and served as such until 1928, when they were transferred to the Ballycastle branch. (F. C. Le Manquais)

Portstewart. Both were entitled to cast envious eyes at the B&NCR's Coleraine and Portrush metals. But Portstewart at least had a station within 2 miles radius of town, whereas poor Ballycastle's nearest point of rail contact was at Ballymoney, 16 miles distant. It follows that two schemes which emerged in 1876 were both designed to bring Ballycastle within the railway network. Up to then the merchants of Ballycastle relied perforce on horse-drawn transport to establish contact with the outside markets.

The first scheme envisaged a revival of Ballycastle's coal mining industry, modest though it was, and proposed transport of coal and passengers along a line to be built between Ballycastle and Ballymena. The plan was probably quite sound, but it was never put up to Parliament. Then, businessmen and landowners from the north of Antrim resolved to build a 3-foot gauge line between the same two towns. The route was surveyed, a Bill was submitted, and it received Royal Assent on 22 July 1875. The Ballycastle Railway Company was authorized to raise £90,000 in share capital and £45,000 in loans. In view of its local vested interest, the B&NCR, too, was allowed to subscribe £18,000 towards the capital, and to nominate two Directors on the Ballycastle Board.

Construction started in January 1879, and, despite delay caused by the unfortunate death of the first contractor, the line was deemed ready for inspection by 18 September 1880. A four-arched viaduct had to be built at Ballycastle, but, apart from a sharp ascent at 1 in 60/50 for 2½ miles out of that town, plus some 10-chain curves, no other engineering works of consequence were necessary. Initially, the Board, rather rashly, sought prices for 30 lb and 40 lb rails; 45 lb rail was used in the end. Colonel Rich's inspection in September produced a number of faults. But a second look in October 1880 satisfied all concerned, and

traffic commenced on 18 October.

An 'official' opening ceremony followed a week later, when a special train left Ballymoney at 12 noon, and deposited guests and VIPs on Ballycastle platform at 12.45 pm. Forty-five minutes for 16¼ miles was to remain a pretty constant speed factor in Ballycastle Railway calculations, though one fast Saturday train regularly accomplished the distance in 40 minutes. A station had to be built, of course, for Ballycastle, but at the Ballymoney end BR trains were allowed to use a bay on the town side of the B&NCR's up main platform. Three Ballycastle trains ran each way on weekdays, with one on Sundays, and Black, Hawthorne & Co supplied all three 0–6–0STs which comprised the Ballycastle's initial stock.

Having spent just under £3,000 on locomotives, the Ballycastle's Board then embarked on a £7,415 order for rolling-stock. This produced seven six-wheeled coaches, one passenger guard's van, 55 wagons, open and closed, five open cattle trucks, and one brake van. Irish passenger traffic, however, is particularly volatile, and by 1888 the BR found itself placing seats in open wagons to cope with passenger overflow on Fair Days. The practice, in fact, was to persist until 1907 or thereabouts. Then, in 1896 the BR management resolved to order a carriage 'to seat 50 passengers at a cost of £100–120'. Metropolitan Carriage & Wagon Co duly obliged — but the splendid eight-compartment bogie coach which arrived in July 1896, the largest ever seen on Irish narrow gauge

The Ballycastle's last locomotive purchases, a brace of 4–4–2Ts from Kitson & Co in 1908, cost £2,375 each, but were sad disappointments. The NCC attempted to remedy their lack of adhesion by rebuilding the locos in 1926-27. Renumbered 113 and 114, the tanks were then dispatched to the Ballymena & Larne section, though No 113 did return to Ballycastle for a brief spell during the Second World War. Chimney, boiler mountings and cab were all cut down to meet the restrictions of Ballymena & Larne bridges. No 114, seen above, was eventually sold to a contractor in 1942. (Author's Collection)

metals, cost the railway company £280. Once they had recovered their composure, the BR Directors ordered three more over the years 1897–99. Prices rose, until the very last cost £466 10s.

Meanwhile, permanent way maintenance was turning out to be as vexing a financial thorn as any. Ballycastle's light 45 lb rail had been spiked direct to the sleepers, and the boggy moorland over which a considerable part of the line passed soon played havoc with sleepers and ballast alike. Restoration work, in turn, played havoc with Ballycastle finances, and for decades the annual item of 'maintenance and renewal of way and works' occupied an inordinate proportion of total expenditure. Then came further trouble in 1908, when two remarkably ill-chosen 'Atlantic' tanks, built by Kitson, were introduced. The engines were heavy and powerful, but the BR's curves, particularly the reverse set at Ballylig, 3 miles and a steep gradient south of Ballycastle, mercilessly exposed the locos' sad lack of adhesion. As a temporary expedient the curves were eased, but 1921 arrived ere the rails were relaid. That year 22 tons of 75 lb rail were expended on Dervock, the worse curve of all. Truly, Ballycastle's initial 'economy' was proving a false one!

The real trouble was that the BR's finances were precarious from the start. £28,400 of its authorized £90,000 Ordinary stock was never taken up, and as a

consequence interest on borrowed funds featured prominently in every annual Balance Sheet. Even the rolling-stock obtained in 1880 became the subject of quarterly payments, and by 1885 the BR found itself in a near-bankrupt condition. Thanks, however, to financial juggling, and skilled guidance from its General Manager, the little railway fought its way into better times, and pacified shareholders by declaring a dividend of 1 per cent in February 1898. These dividends continued until 1900, but lapsed again when two new carriages were bought. In 1906 a dividend of 1 per cent reappeared, and was even hoisted to 2 per cent the following year. That autumn, however, the two 'Atlantic' tanks were placed on order at £2,375 apiece — and BR dividends vanished for evermore.

Like other Irish railways, the BR suffered during the First World War years. Wages and costs soared, but traffic receipts lagged far behind. Then, road competition began to exert inflexible pressures. Even the £8,000 which the BR received from the Government as war-time compensation vanished immediately, offset against working losses. Mercifully, the 'Troubles' of 1920–21 had little impact on Ballycastle affairs. But this helped little, for, so adverse was the course of Company finances that an Extraordinary Meeting of shareholders held on 8 February 1924 carried a resolution to 'discontinue the working of the line'. Sad days, indeed. Ironically, the Northern Ireland Railway Commission had already recommended in its Report of December 1922 that the LMS(NCC) should be persuaded to buy up the narrow gauge concern. The Northern Ireland Government, as always, showed little interest.

Things came to a head on 19 April 1924, when a deputation of BR Directors met an NCC committee. The NCC had already done its homework, and, having calculated that £30,000 would have to be spent to

bring the Ballycastle line up to scratch, made a flat offer of £10,000. The BR Directors, sadly disillusioned, returned home; and Ballycastle operations drifted to a complete standstill on 4 April 1924. Then, after further negotiations, the NCC increased its offer to £12,500. A thoroughly despondent meeting of BR shareholders gave reluctant consent on 2 May 1924, and the NCC, content to pre-empt lengthy legal formalities, offered locals some cheer by reopening the Ballycastle line on 11 August. Almost a year later the relevant Bill became law, and the NCC was formally allowed to 'enter into possession of the line and work it'. Long before that, however, decisions had been reached in Belfast. If the Ballycastle section was to be made viable, considerable economies would have to be effected.

The NCC was as good as its word. The BR's two surviving saddle tanks, having served 45 years, were scrapped. On the other hand, the Kitson 4–4–2Ts, *bêtes noir* though they were, were still adjudged youthful enough to merit heavy repair. After rebuild at York Road shops they were posted permanently to the Ballymena & Larne section. Vintage and well worn, Ballycastle carriage and wagon stock was auctioned off locally, and replacement vehicles were summoned from the Ballymena lines. Workshops and loco shed at Ballymoney were demolished, and a transfer siding was provided to facilitate the movement of narrow gauge stock on to standard gauge transporters. Now that Belfast was in charge, Ballymoney also surrendered responsibility for traffic operations, and local administration moved to Ballycastle. Gradually the whole section was relaid with 60 lb rail and properly fishplated for the first time. With single line working ordained throughout, various signal boxes were also eliminated. Ballycastle folk, watching the protracted rehabilitation process with barely concealed chagrin,

at least had some consolation when a handful of extremely comfortable centre-corridor bogie coaches arrived in 1928.

So, working 'one engine in steam', the Ballycastle line soldiered on through the 1930s. The train service actually increased under NCC auspices, and in summer months five weekday trains ran each way. Sundays were treated to three. The conduct of the Second World War had little effect on such an out of the way spot, and such strains and stresses as were imposed by food rationing and coal shortage were calmly absorbed. Post-war years, though, were more difficult to assimilate, for, in keeping with the Northern Ireland Government's abysmal indifference towards railway affairs, depressing events began to happen with frightening speed. The LMS(NCC) organization became the Railway Executive (NCC) on 1 January 1948. Fifteen months later, however, the British Transport Commission, unwilling to carry Irish responsibilities, sold its NCC interests to the Ulster Transport Authority for £2,668,000. Now the UTA was faced with the impossible task of running Northern Irish railways without loss. A little earlier, serious consideration had been given to converting the Ballycastle section to standard gauge; but the existence of Capecastle tunnel, with its narrow bore, proved a fatal impediment.

Almost inevitably, the public were warned early in 1950 of serious cutbacks. Some 82 miles of standard gauge track were to go, and 28 miles of narrow gauge. The latter consisted of 12 miles which still remained of the old Ballymena & Larne, plus, of course, the Ballycastle's 16 miles. Typical of the times, perhaps, no formal objection was raised in the Ballycastle area, and a last train headed by two of Malcolm's immortal 2–4–2Ts, ran from Ballycastle to Ballymoney and back on the evening of Sunday 2 July 1950. Paper chains may have decorated chimneys and smokeboxes, but a depressingly small number of people elected to travel by train that day.

LOCOMOTIVES

No	Name	Type	Date built	Makers	Maker's number	Withdrawn	Remarks
1	*Dalriada*	0–6–0ST	1879	Black Hawthorn	554	1925	Cost £1,145
2	*Countess of Antrim*	,,	1880	,,	555	1925	Cost £1,145
3	*Lady Boyd*	,,	1879	,,	513	1912	Sold for £120
3	—	4–4–2T	1908	Kitson	4565	1946	Later NCC No 113
4	—	,,	1908	,,	4566	1942	Later NCC No 114. Sold to contractor

The Ballycastle, one of Ireland's most expensively built narrow gauge railways at £5,723 per mile, suffered from classic defects: under-capitalization and failure to produce a steady income. Looking back now we can also see that no real potential ever existed. Perhaps, then, one might take a charitable view of the close-fisted tactics the Ballycastle Board often adopted in dealing with rolling-stock matters. They were probably obligatory rather than spontaneous.

Black Hawthorn, for instance, competing against Sharp Stewart and Beyer Peacock in 1879, obviously won the BR's contract for two 0–6–0STs because its tender was lowest. Yet, even at that delicate juncture, the railway company hedged on payment. Again, in 1881, when the Ballycastle's contractors offered to part with *Lady Boyd*, a similar Hawthorn loco, for £807, the BR's Directors prevaricated until they were able to buy the loco a year later for £600. £47 was then spent on minor repairs ere *Lady Boyd* emerged triumphantly from Ballymoney workshops, ready for action, bearing BR No 3. She served the company well until 1908, when, adding insult to injury, the Board shopped around for four years, seeking a selling price of £350 — and finally accepted £120. This, too, at a time when the BR chose to invest £4,750 in two massive 4–4–2 tanks!

Built by Kitson & Co to the Ballycastle locomotive engineer's specification, locos 3 and 4 turned out in the event to be sad disappointments. Certainly *Dalriada*'s generous 11 ft 9 in wheelbase had spread a few Ballycastle curves in its day. But the 6 ft 6 in wheelbase of the 'Atlantics' carried matters to the other extreme; despite an overall weight of 39½ tons, the adhesion factor of the Kitson tanks was low, and neither could tackle Ballycastle's steepest gradients without slipping fiercely. True to form, the Ballycastle Board allowed payment for No 4 to deteriorate into an embarrassing series of £500 instalments.

Once the NCC era arrived, only the 'Atlantic' tanks survived inspection. Bearing NCC Nos 113 and 114, they spent the rest of their lives working the Ballymena & Larne section. Only briefly, in 1942, did one of them, No 113, ever tread Ballycastle metals again. Ironically, it was ex-Ballymena 'Q' Class 0–6–0 tanks which took their place at Ballycastle. Then, in the early 1930s Malcolm's ubiquitous little compound 2–4–2Ts took charge, and two of them, Nos 41 and 44, shared the privilege of handling that last Ballycastle train on 2 July 1950.

Victims of Partition

Glance at a map, and note how Eire's five largest Counties dominate her western shores. Cork and Kerry command the south, Galway and Mayo take over once Galway Bay is breached. Then up looms Donegal, that clenched fist of northern Ireland which, together with Cavan and Monaghan, ultimately wrenched nearly half the province of Ulster from 'foreign' rule. Around 1840, when Ireland's population was approaching its peak, one square mile of Donegal meant 'home' to 160 people. Two decades later, thanks to the ravages of famine and emigration, that figure fell to 127. The haemorrhage was never staunched, and today only five towns in the County can muster a population of over 1,000. Railway events in Donegal follow the sad anti-climactic pattern.

LONDONDERRY & LOUGH SWILLY RAILWAY

Incorporated: 26 June 1853
Opened: 12 November 1863
Closed: 8 August 1953

Rugged, windswept, and devoid of industry, the County of Donegal had little to offer the Railway Mania of 1845. On the west bank of the River Foyle,

however, muscles were being flexed, and in 1852 a newly-incorporated company, the Lough Foyle & Lough Swilly Railway, obtained powers to build 8¾ miles of standard gauge track between Londonderry and Carrowen, a quiet spot on the shores of Lough Swilly. A year later a second Act altered the company's title to the Londonderry & Lough Swilly Railway. Capital flow still remained sluggish, construction was held up until 1860, and the first train did not run until 12 November 1863. By then a further Act of 1851 had sanctioned construction of a 6-mile extension northward along Lough Swilly shores to Buncrana. This opened on 9 September 1864, and ere long a healthy excursion traffic developed between Londonderry and this popular seaside resort.

In the meantime, railway appetites were also growing further west, in Co Donegal, and a group of landowners combined to sponsor yet another standard gauge line, running this time for 15¼ miles from Letterkenny, Co Donegal's largest town, to join Londonderry & Enniskillen Railway metals at Cuttymanhill, near St Johnstown. The Letterkenny Railway, as it was known, was duly incorporated on 3 July 1860 with an authorized capital of £57,000. Then came second thoughts, and by an Act of 1863 the proposed section between Pluck and St Johnstown

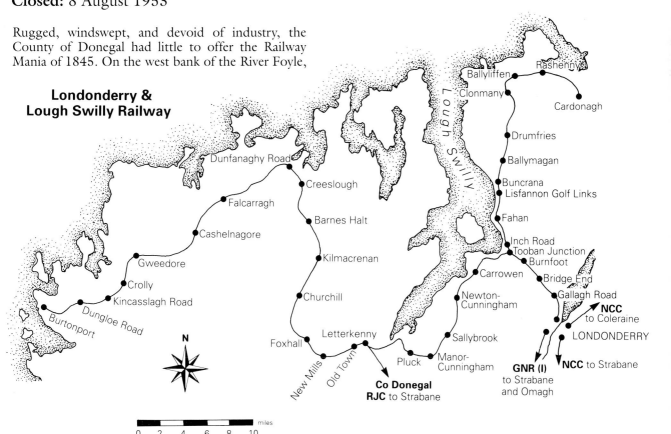

Londonderry & Lough Swilly Railway

No 4 Innishowen (*Black Hawthorn 834/1885*) was one of the Lough Swilly's early narrow gauge acquisitions. Built to work on the Letterkenny and Cardonagh extensions, the loco was renumbered 17 in 1913, and lost its name 15 years later. The rear extension to the cab must have come as a relief to the Swilly men who worked the loco up to its withdrawal in 1940. (Steamchest)

Built by Hudswell Clarke in 1901, this inside-framed 4–6–2T, No 8, was one of a pair supplied to work on the Lough Swilly's new Cardonagh Extension. Its partner perished in 1940, five years after the Extension closed, but No 8 could still be found in Letterkenny shed in the summer of 1950. (Steamchest)

was abandoned in favour of a plan to link up with Lough Swilly metals at Burt Junction. Work commenced, but trouble soon followed, for after constructing a few bridges the contractor went bankrupt. The project came to a standstill, and remained so for several years. Eventually the City of Londonderry and several Co Donegal Baronies, well aware of narrow gauge developments elsewhere in northern Ireland, offered their joint support — provided that the 15¼ miles were laid to *3-foot gauge*. Moving to meet them, the Letterkenny Railway sought, and obtained, appropriate powers on 29 June 1880. On this occasion Westminster's action also held important implications for the Londonderry & Lough Swilly Railway, for, in addition to being authorized to work the Letterkenny line, the Swilly was given permission to regauge its own metals to 3 feet.

Alas, mere implementation of a Bill did nothing to solve the Letterkenny's financial problems. Raising

capital by normal subscription proved to be an impossible task. Local authorities, it was agreed, could hardly be expected to shoulder the total burden, and, inspired, no doubt, by the kind of thinking which was later to express itself in the Tramways Act of 1883, eyes turned inevitably towards the State. Government aid was duly received. But the terms were tough; of the £85,000 advanced by the Board of Works, £50,000 was directly secured by mortgage on Letterkenny Railway assets. The balance was carefully protected by local authorities' joint guarantee. Mortgage and loan both attracted interest at 5 per cent, and the lot was to be refunded from railway revenue in 40 annual instalments. The Letterkenny management pressed on, and the line was opened to traffic on 30 June 1883. For reasons of its own, the Lough Swilly deferred conversion to narrow gauge until 28 March 1885, when rails between Londonderry and Buncrana were deftly switched in one weekend opera-

Crolly Station, which was eight miles from Burtonport, the most westerly limit of Lough Swilly metals. The bare countryside is symptomatic as 4–6–0T No 3 waits fruitlessly on 21 June 1937 for passengers. People in this modest community did their best in 1940 to prevent wholesale demolition of the rail link to Letterkenny, but met with final defeat in 1947. (F. C. Le Manquais)

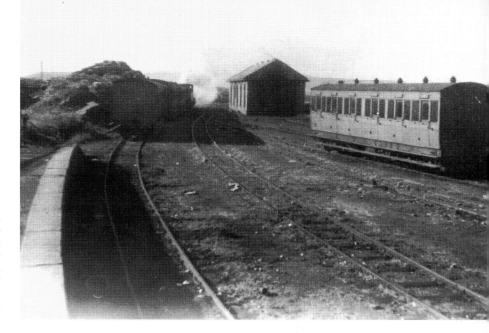

The desolation of the 49³/₄-miles-long Letterkenny and Burtonport Extension is again emphasized by this view, taken from Burtonport station platform on 19 June 1937. If the departing train is bound for Londonderry, its 74¹/₂ mile journey will take over four hours. (F. C. Le Manquais)

tion. Rather proud of itself, the parent concern was now responsible for working 31 route miles.

Two years later chickens came home to roost, when the Letterkenny Railway found itself unable to meet mortgage interest payments. The Board of Trade had no option but to assume nominal ownership of the railway. The Lough Swilly co-operated by continuing to work the line in exchange for a share in gross traffic receipts. When this 30-year agreement, incidentally, duly expired in 1917, working arrangements were calmly renewed!

Long before that, however, further railway events had materialized in Co Donegal. In 1897 the L&LSR undertook the working of an 18¹/₂-mile extension between Buncrana and Cardonagh, in the 'far north'. By now the Government's Railways (Ireland) Act of 1896 had introduced a much more liberal attitude towards the construction of new light railways, and Free State Grants were reducing the burden on local

Baronies to more humane proportions. The L&LSR, intervening quietly, took up £18,000 in the new venture. Arrangements were made whereby the L&LSR and the Public Works Loan Commissioners would share any gross receipts which ventured over £3 10s per mile per week, and the Buncrana–Cardonagh branch opened on 1 July 1901. That brought the Lough Swilly's total route mileage to just under 50 miles.

One last major railway work came in 1898, when an Order, again issued under the 1896 Act, came to the rescue of the scattered population who lived in Co Donegal's wild north-western region. Finance for the 49¹/₂-mile-long Letterkenny & Burtonport Extension Railway originated largely as before: the Government supplied a Free Grant of over £300,000, and the Baronies offered nominal support. Opened for traffic on 9 March 1903, this new acquisition was worked by the L&LSR on the same terms as the Cardonagh

extension. Thus, with 99½ route miles under its control the Lough Swilly became Ireland's second largest narrow gauge railway. Ironically, as with the largest, the County Donegal RJC, size counted for nothing when Partition descended in 1921. Both railways, though built to serve Co Donegal, happened to stray over the Border for a mile or two, and, shunned by North and South railway groupings, they were left to find their own salvation.

In an area like Co Donegal, where roads were few and far between, and badly surfaced to boot, it was not difficult for railways to establish a virtual traffic monopoly. The L&LSR, by paying consistent annual dividends of 7 per cent on its Ordinary stock between the years 1896 and 1916, appeared prosperous — until second thoughts reminded one that Ordinary stock formed only a minute proportion of gross capital expended. Underneath that surface, in fact, lay considerable financial anxiety. From a passenger's point of view, too, travel on the Lough Swilly hardly represented the acme of comfort. Trains were never steam-heated in winter, and a third class passenger reckless enough to undertake the through 74½-mile trip from Londonderry to Burtonport, that desolate outpost on the Atlantic shore, paid an uncomfortable four-hour penance on wooden seats. Yet, up to 1914 three trains a day left Graving Dock, Londonderry, on

such a wild mission. Even as early as 1905 the conditions under which the Burtonport extension was being worked began to attract attention from the Irish Board of Works. The Board commissioned an inquiry by Joseph Tatlow, the MGWR's manager. That gentleman reported adversely, and the L&LSR was instructed to mend its ways.

Poor Lough Swilly, little did it know that was just the start of a catalogue of woes where the Burtonport extension was oncerned! On 22 February 1906 hurricane force winds blowing across Owencarrow Viaduct, the line's principal engineering feature, 380 yards long and 30 feet high, succeeded in derailing two coaches. No one was seriously injured. But neither did anyone absorb the lesson, for in the decade which followed working practice on the Burtonport line steadily accrued unenviable distinction for its slovenliness. Things came to such a head by 1917 that

The last Lough Swilly engine to be given a name, 'Small' 4–6–2T No 10 Richmond, *was supplied by Kerr Stuart in 1904. The name, that of a Lough Swilly Director's residence, was later removed; but No 10 was still working on the Cardonagh Extension when it was photographed at Buncrana.* (Steamchest)

the Board of Works, deciding to invoke the Act of 1896, instituted a second, and urgent, inquiry. Mr Tatlow's services were again employed. This time his Report was so damning that the Board of Trade removed management of the extension from Letterkenny hands, and placed it under the personal care of Mr Henry Hunt, the newly-appointed General Manager of the L&LSR. Even so, Burtonport's greatest calamity was yet to come; it arrived on 30 January 1925, when a train was blown completely off Owencarrow Viaduct. Four out of 15 passengers were

The last new engines ordered by the L&LSR were two massive 4–8–4Ts, Hudswell Clarke's tank equivalent of their earlier 4–8–0 tender engines. No 6, seen here at Pennyburn in 1926, was originally an L&BER loco, but together with No 5 it later joined the L&LSR ranks in exchange for a brace of 4–6–2Ts. (Steamchest)

The traditional pea-green livery of L&LSR locomotives gave way to plain black early in the 1920s. Then, in the 1940s, a few locos were again given green livery, with yellow lining. A diamond-shaped emblem enclosing the letters 'LSR' now replaced the former L&LSR lettering. 4-6-0T No 3 is seen in this form at Pennyburn on 19 May 1950. (Steamchest)

killed, and five injured. One result of the inquiry which followed was that the L&LSR was instructed to follow the West Clare's example by installing an anemometer at Dunfaghy Road station.

The Lough Swilly management may have enjoyed halcyon 7 per cent dividend days from 1896 onwards, but the outbreak of the First World War, with its sub-sequent imposition of Government control over all Irish railways from 16 December 1916 to 15 August 1921, brought problems which were never to be truly resolved. Railway fares increased by 100 per cent. Then Government-ordained wage increases more than matched them at 250 per cent; and, as the Swilly management watched working costs soar, road trans-port nipped in to erode any possible recovery. L&LSR rolling-stock, too, had been allowed to run down, and the Burtonport extension provided another major headache. Far too many stations there were situated miles from the localities they were meant to serve. All in all it was an expensive luxury.

By the early 1920s two painful truths emerged. Road competition was clearly Enemy No 1, and the L&LSR was rapidly approaching insolvency. The lat-ter point was rammed home when the Lough Swilly's 1924 operations produced a net loss; from there on only substantial grants from both Irish Governments kept the railway going. How, though, was the ever-increasing menace of road transport to be tackled?

The Lough Swilly's great rivals, the Co Donegal RJC, opted boldly in 1926 to meet the challenge by turning to petrol railcars. The Swilly management took a different view, by deciding to match like for like. After all, the L&LSR was already operating steamboats on Lough Swilly itself, and probably saw nothing amiss in acquiring its own fleet of motor buses and lorries. But where railway transport was concerned Lough Swilly's tryst with steam remained unbroken to the very end.

In the bitter road-versus-rail battle which ensued, the CDJRC contrived to hold out a little longer and stronger, but both companies were doomed to face a lingering death. The first major casualty came Lough Swilly's way when the Buncrana–Cardonagh section had to be closed on 2 December 1935. Symptomatic of the times, the rails which were lifted went, not for scrap, but to repair the Burtonport extension. Meanwhile, Lough Swilly metals between London-derry and Buncrana still carried freight traffic all year round, though passenger traffic was confined to a twice weekly service during summer months only. Fuel shortages during the Second World War saw a full passenger service restored in 1943, but by 1948 this was again reduced to weekend excursions. A desultory kind of traffic dragged on, until the line was closed completely on 8 August 1953.

While all this was happening, the L&LSR cut its losses on the Burtonport extension by effecting a compromise. On weekdays one train from London-derry travelled all the way. Another worked between Burtonport and Letterkenny, whence passengers trav-elled on to Londonderry by bus. Then, on 3 June 1940, Lough Swilly buses took over the whole route, and all rail passenger traffic ceased. That year the rails between Burtonport and Gweedore were lifted, and the dismantling process would no doubt have spread further east, had not the good folk of Crolly uttered vigorous protest. Buses continued to rule the roost until March 1943, when fuel shortages persuaded the L&LSR management to offer brake coach accommodation on the one daily goods train to Gweedore to such passengers as were prepared to accept delay and discomfort rather than travel by bus. This state of affairs continued until 6 January 1947, when the Letterkenny-Gweedore section was finally closed.

Things were no different on the Londonderry–Letterkenny section. After 1940, when buses ran all the way to Burtonport, only a nominal goods service survived; though, once again, passengers who preferred to cling to steam were allowed to do so under rather primitive conditions. Alas, even that modest privilege vanished on 1 July 1953, when all rail traffic ceased between Londonderry and Letterkenny. The internal combustion engine had won its final victory.

LOCOMOTIVES

The 5 ft 3 in gauge years, 1863–1885

No	Name	Type	Date built	Makers	Maker's number	Withdrawn	Remarks
1	–	0–6–0T	1862	Gilkes, Wilkinson	141	1885	Auctioned 7 May 1885
2(3)	–	,,	1862	,,	142	1883	Sold to Belfast Central Railway
3	–	,,	1864	R. Stephenson	1609	1869	Sold to Londonderry Port & Harbour Commissioners
4(2)	–	,,	1864	,,	1610	1883	,,
4	*St Patrick*	,,	1876	Sharp, Stewart	2645	1885	Auctioned 7 May 1885
5	*St Columb*	,,	1879	,,	2836	1885	,,

During its 90-year lifetime, the L&LSR bought 28 locomotives, and only two of these were second-hand. Looked at from another angle, six Swilly locomotives were built to the 5 ft 3 in gauge, and the remainder were narrow gauge. Construction dates, however, fall into well-defined groups, and these match three broad phases in L&LSR's history. First came the 5 ft 3 in gauge years — 1863–1885 — and all the locomotives, it will be noted, were 0–6–0 side tanks, though each pair introduced detail differences. Nos 1 and 2, outside cylindered, weighed 26 tons and had coupled wheels 4 feet in diameter. Nos 3 and 4, inside-cylindered and altogether smaller, had 3 ft 6 in coupled wheels. The Sharp Stewart engines brought a further combination: inside cylinders, 4 ft 6 in wheels, and a working weight of 31 tons. When the L&LSR switched to the 3-foot gauge, and auctioned its remaining three engines in May 1885, No 1 went to a contractor in Dublin. The Sharp Stewart pair were snapped up by the Cork & Bandon Railway, where, renumbered 14 and 15, they were eventually rebuilt as 4–4–0Ts. The L&LSR also disposed of 12 passenger coaches and 34 assorted freight vehicles that day in Londonderry.

The Letterkenny and Cardonagh extensions, 1883–1901

No	Name	Type	Date built	Makers	Maker's number	Withdrawn	Remarks
1	*J. T. Mackay*	0–6–2T	1882	Black Hawthorn	684	1911	For use on Letterkenny Railway
2	*Londonderry*	,,	1883	,,	742	1912	
3	*Donegal*	,,	1883	,,	743	1913	
4	*Innishowen*	0–6–0T	1885	,,	834	1940	Renumbered 17 in 1913. Name removed, 1928
5 (5A)	—	2–4–0T	1873	R. Stephenson	2088	1900	Bought secondhand from Glenariff Land & Dev, 1885
6(6A)	—	,,	1873	,,	2089	1900	
5(15)	—	4–6–2T	1899	Hudswell Clarke	518	1954	Renumbered in 1913
6(16)	—	,,	1899	,,	519	1953	,,

The Letterkenny and Burtonport Extension Railway, 1903

No	Name	Type	Date built	Makers	Maker's number	Withdrawn	Remarks
7	*King Edward VII*	4–6–2T	1901	Hudswell Clarke	577	1940	Named in 1903
8	—	,,	1901	,,	562	1954	
9	*Aberfoyle*	,,	1904	Kerr Stuart	845	1928	Name later removed
10	*Richmond*	,,	1904	,,	846	1954	,,
11	—	4–8–0	1905	Hudswell Clarke	746	1933	
12	—	,,	1905	,,	747	1954	
13	—	4–6–2T	1910	Hawthorn Leslie	2801	1940	Later transferred to L&BER stock
14	—	,,	1910	,,	2802	1943	
5	—	4–8–4T	1912	Hudswell Clarke	985	1954	Originally L&BER stock, but
6	—	,,	1912	,,	986	1954	exchanged for Nos 13 & 14
L&BER locomotives							
1	—	4–6–0T	1902	Barclay	933	1940	All four locos were lettered
2	—	,,	1902	,,	934	1954	'L&BER', though given
3	—	,,	1902	,,	935	1954	L&LSR running numbers
4	—	,,	1902	,,	936	1953	

Its next task was to prepare for 3-foot running. Faced with the task of working the Letterkenny Railway, the L&LSR ordered its first narrow gauge locos, three outside cylindered 0–6–2Ts from Black Hawthorn. Details differed slightly, in that Nos 2 and 3 carried 600 gallons of water, No 1 only 500. The L&LSR's Chairman also became contractor for the Donegal Railway's Glenties branch; so *J. T. Mackay* worked there awhile on ballasting duties in 1891.

No 4 arrived once the L&LSR re-gauged its own metals between Londonderry and Buncrana, and it was supplemented in its duties by the two second-hand Glenariff tanks. Fourteen years later came two large, powerful 4–6–2 tanks, probably designed by their makers, Hudswell Clarke.

The years 1901 to 1912 produced a rare miscellany of L&LSR locos. Nos 7 and 8, which, incidentally, embodied Ireland's sole use of Allan straight-link motion, were built ostensibly for use on the Cardonagh extension. Gradually, however, the Lough Swilly began to use all loco types on all parts of its system. No 7 received its name when it handled a Royal train between Buncrana and Londonderry in 1903.

Next to arrive were four Barclay 4–6–0 tanks, specifically designed for use on the Burtonport extension. In light of their special duties these engines bore 'L&BER' lettering, and, despite rather limited coal and water capacity, they proved more than equal to their arduous task. The year 1904 saw a brief deviation to Kerr Stuart, who supplied a pair of 'Pacific' tanks, not dissimilar to Nos 5 and 8 of 1899 and 1901. They were named afer L&LSR Directors' residences, then rendered nameless some years later.

Next came an astonishing development. In 1905 the L&LSR commissioned two eight-coupled tender locomotives for mixed traffic work between Londonderry and Burtonport, a formidable haul of 74½ miles. Hudswell Clarke's response was massive by any standards, for each engine and tender weighed 58¼ tons. These 4–8–0s were, incidentally, the only tender engines to run on Irish narrow gauge metals. No 11 was scrapped in 1933, but No 12 served on the Burtonport Extension to the end. Two years later another pair of 4–6–2Ts emerged from Hawthorn Leslie's Newcastle works. Rather more powerful than the previous 'Pacifics', they carried L&LSR running numbers, but were later transferred to L&BER stock in exchange for two massive 4–8–4 tanks which appeared in 1912, and were also originally intended for Burtonport Extension use. The only example of their kind in the British Isles, they were really a tenderless version of Hudswell's 4–8–0s. At 51 tons, though, they were little behind in weight, and their tractive effort even exceeded that of the tender engines by 350 lbs. After relinquishing Burtonport duties they spent their latter years working Buncrana excursions.

The great pity was that neither eight-coupled design lived long enough to be rescued by the Irish railway preservation movement. Alas — for that matter neither did any representative of Lough Swilly's magnificent steam stud.

COUNTY DONEGAL
RAILWAYS JOINT COMMITTEE

Incorporated: 1 May 1906
Closed: 31 December 1959

Seeds of what was to become in due course the largest narrow gauge system in Ireland were planted on 7 September 1863, when the Finn Valley Railway Company opened Co Donegal's first venture of the Railway Age: 13¾ miles of standard gauge single track between Strabane and Stranorlar. There were no intermediate stations. The occasion, naturally, generated considerable local excitement. Yet one would have looked in vain for evidence of FVR rolling-stock, for construction costs, confidently predicted at the outset not to exceed £3,000 per mile, had, in fact, emerged at £5,300. The resultant financial drain left the FVR management with little

option but to entrust the working of its line to a more affluent neighbour, the Dundalk & Enniskillen Railway. Happy to oblige, for it was already performing a similar service between Londonderry and Strabane for the Londonderry & Enniskillen Railway, the D&ER subsequently sought, and obtained, Parliamentary permission to assume a new, and grander, title — the Irish North Western Railway.

The Finn Valley paid dearly for its innocence. By a ten-year agreement 35 per cent of its future revenue was pledged against INWR running costs, and an additional fixed annual rent of £375 was levied for the privilege of sharing Strabane station, and approaching it over less than half a mile of 'foreign' track. Maintenance costs were another burden to be borne,

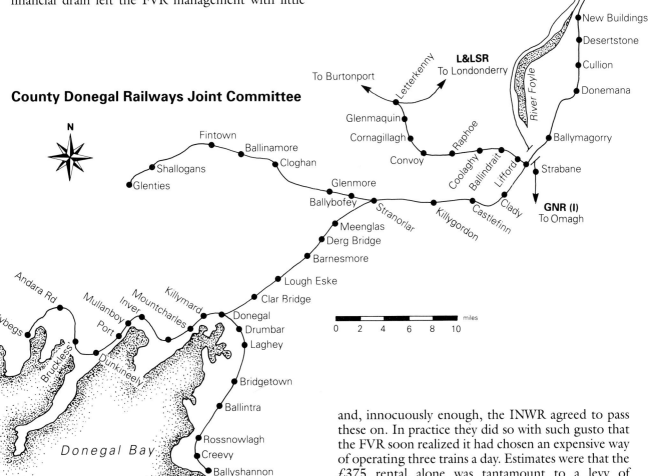

County Donegal Railways Joint Committee

and, innocuously enough, the INWR agreed to pass these on. In practice they did so with such gusto that the FVR soon realized it had chosen an expensive way of operating three trains a day. Estimates were that the £375 rental alone was tantamount to a levy of 2s 2d per train mile.

Years passed; relations between the two Companies grew ever testier. Then 1872 approached, and the FVR management was free at last to negotiate fresh terms. Tired of INWR collusion, yet wary of its own

Top *The Co Donegal's original* Meenglas *was one of half a dozen outside-framed 4–6–0Ts supplied to the Donegal Railway Co by Neilson & Co in 1893. Coal capacity was limited, as can be seen. So, too, was water capacity; but they were tough little tanks.* (Author's Collection)

Above *Coal and water shortcomings were eliminated when No 14* Erne, *one of four Nasmyth Wilson 4–6–4Ts, came on the Donegal Railway Co scene a decade later. Named after local rivers, these powerful tanks were further improved in later years when superheaters were added.* Erne *was renumbered 11 in CDRJC stock in 1937, and lived to be auctioned off in 1961.* (Steamchest)

inexperience in locomotive matters, it compromised in the end by reducing INWR aid to that of providing motive power only. Carriages were ordered, new grades of FVR staff were recruited, and from 1 November 1872 FVR passengers at least had the satisfaction of travelling in appropriately mono-grammed stock. Four years later the INWR succumbed to merger, and the GNR(I) graduated as FVR's new paymasters at Strabane.

While all this was happening, several of the FVR's more percipient shareholders had long been urging

extension from Strabane into Donegal itself. Thanks to the company's costly flirtation with the INWR, times had never been propitious for such an adventure. Certainly, current finances were in no shape to withstand further depredation. None the less, arguments in favour of the proposition persisted, and latterly found expression in the formation of a new, and separate, company, the West Donegal Railway Company. Although, rather ominously, one-third of its £150,000 capital had to be borrowed, the new Board, again under command of Lord Lifford, the FVR's influential Chairman, pressed vigorously ahead. Contemporary railway developments elsewhere in northern Ireland had been noted, and, on 21 July 1879, the WDRC's application to build the requisite 18 miles on a *3-foot gauge* basis received Parliamentary approval.

Construction commenced 12 months later. So, too, did further heavy borrowing; for bad weather, plus unforeseen difficulties, in bridging Barnesmore Gap, played havoc with the WDRC's original budget. Soon funds ran out, and a disappointed Board had to resign itself to calling a halt at Druminin, 4 miles short of Donegal. The FVR, deeply involved by now, agreed to work the line. The WDRC purchased the necessary hardware — three narrow gauge locomotives, 14 coaches, and some 40 wagons — and on 25 April 1882 an inaugural train ushered in a 40-minute, thrice daily, service between Stranorlar and Druminin. The 'temporary' nature of the latter's existence as a terminus lasted somewhat longer than was anticipated; for the next *seven* years passengers were solemnly ferried to and from Donegal in horse-drawn cars at 6d a time! Meanwhile, quite in accordance with this rather madcap situation, the FVR's prime activity consisted of working the WDRC's traffic, while the GNR(I) worked theirs . . .

The WDRC eventually reached Donegal by 1889. But even at that late date it was apparent that Co Donegal itself had gained little from the Railway Age. Fortunately, Westminster was aware that such anomalies existed in Ireland, and tabled improved legislation that same year. Free Grants of nearly £¼ million flowed Co Donegal's way, and with this help the WDRC was able to construct 19 miles of narrow gauge line between Donegal and Killybegs. The FVR, also striking east, tackled the 24 miles to Glenties. Events followed a logical course on 27 June 1892, when the two companies received Parliamentary blessing to amalgamate under a new title, the Donegal Railway Company.

Faced now, as was the Lough Swilly Railway seven years earlier, by the problems of dual gauge, the DRC's new management not only adopted a similar solution, that of re-gauging the Finn Valley section to 3 feet, but even felt confident enough to tackle the GNR(I)'s overlord status by building a new bridge and station at Strabane. From there on things began to hum. Changeover of gauge was smartly effected one weekend in July 1894, the Finn Valley's broad gauge stock was sold to the Dublin, Wickford & Wexford for £1,000; and, by the time the Glenties branch came into operation the following year, the DRC, with 75 miles under its belt, found itself the largest narrow gauge operator in the country.

Came 1896. Westminster, it seemed, was still dissatisfied with Irish railway progress, and DRC ambitions, now riding high, sharpened appropriately as a new Railways Act appeared on the Statute Book. Unfortunately, such projects as were sponsored by the Free Grants again received by Co Donegal confined

This photograph of CDRJC stock was taken at Ballyshannon on 16 June 1937. The coaches, built in 1893, are of typically British pattern, and were originally tri-composite. (F. C. Le Manquais)

Class 5 2–6–4T No 8 Foyle, *once No 20* Raphoe, *prepares for duty outside Stranorlar shed in May 1950. Withdrawn in 1950, at least it escaped the ignominy of public auction.* (Steamchest)

One of Henry Forbes's Derwent Valley 'bargains', and regauged to 3 feet, the CDRJC's petrol-driven railcar No 2 was caught on an 'off' moment at Fintown on 23 June 1937, ten years after purchase. (F. C. Le Manquais)

The importance of Stranorlar as the CDRJC's headquarters was truly reflected in the substantial nature of the station there. This view, looking east, was obtained on 23 June 1937, and shows one of the CDRJC's Nasmyth Wilson 'Baltic' tanks waiting to proceed. Everything is tidy, and as always, Stranorlar's elegant clock tower draws the eye. (Steamchest)

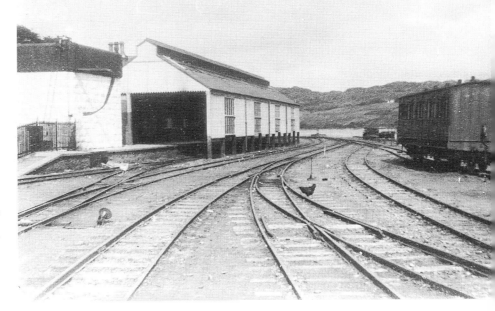

Killybegs, an isolated locality 19 miles from Donegal, lay on the north bank of Donegal Bay, and was as far west as the CDRJC ventured. Even then, Killybegs station was trim, as can be seen from this 1937 view, and water column, turntable, and loco shed facilities were available. Extension of narrow gauge metals from Donegal to Killybegs, made feasible by Free Government Grant, was completed in 1893. (F. C. Le Manquais)

themselves to the extreme north of the County. Two major railway sections were built — Buncrana–Cardonagh and Letterkenny–Burtonport — and, not unreasonably, their working was entrusted to the Lough Swilly Railway. Undismayed, the DRC pressed on independently, and in 1900, despite initial objection from the GNR(I), 14½ miles of new track were added between Strabane and Londonderry. A complementary 15½-mile extension from Donegal to Ballyshannon fell foul, however, of an old complaint, shortage of capital. A second Act had to be obtained to revive lapsed powers, and September 1905 arrived ere operations commenced.

Ironically, it was just at this juncture, when the DRC's system reached its peak of 105½ miles, that finances again began to lag. Victoria Road, the company's Londonderry terminus, happened to adjoin that of the NCC at Waterside; and the latter's masters, the Midland Railway, sparked off the next move by offering to buy out its narrow gauge neighbour. Obviously absorption of the B&NCR in 1903 had whetted the English Company's Irish appetite! The GNR(I), of course, was scandalized at the intrusion, and promptly lodged vigorous objection. In the end agreement was reached, and purchase of the DCR was borne jointly by the two major companies. A new Administrative Board of six members was drawn equally from MR and GNR(I) sources, and, as from 1 May 1906, the DRC passed into possession of the County Donegal Railways Joint Committee. Headquarters remained at Stranorlar. The Midland retained possession of the 14½ miles between Strabane and Londonderry, but the section was worked by the CDRJC.

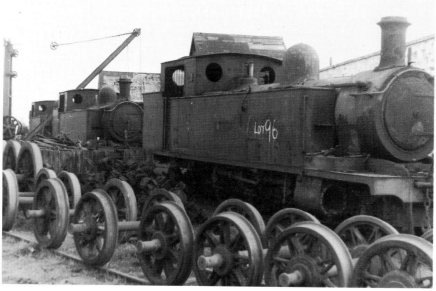

Left *'Lot 96' – what a way to end up after decades of service under Henry Forbes! County Donegal locos make a sad sight as they are lined up for public auction on 1 March 1961. An American, Dr Ralph Cox, made a valiant bid to save a deal of CDRJC stock from destruction. Alas, much of what he salvaged has deteriorated badly since.* (Steamchest)

Below *Four years after auction,* Drumboe *and* Meenglas *(left), two of the CDRJC's once proud Class 5 2–6–4Ts, await salvation in Strabane station yard, together with a considerable variety of other Donegal stock. Over the next 20 years vandalism and long-term exposure reduced Dr Cox's collection to near dereliction.* (Steamchest)

Thus strengthened, the company was able to offer financial support to the Strabane, Raphoe & Convoy Railway, a project which had been formed in 1903 with the intention of tapping the hinterland which lay between the DRC and the Lough Swilly Railway. Latterly, the new company extended its sights, altered its name appropriately to the Strabane & Letterkenny Railway, and, on 1 January 1909, 19¼ miles of 3-foot track were opened between the two towns. It was as well that the S&LR had major backing — for construction costs settled at a hair-raising £11,500 per mile! From its inception the new line was worked by the CDRJC, the total working mileage of which now rose to 124½. Separate stations were, rather aloofly, maintained at Letterkenny by the CDRJC and the Lough Swilly, and relations between the two companies were no warmer than before. Any likelihood of improvement in that direction certainly vanished around 1910, when Henry Forbes took up his appointment as Secretary to the CDRJC.

Forbes was one of nature's classic railwaymen. Hungry for traffic, and prepared to take risks to obtain it, he also demanded from others the total dedication he himself evinced in advancing his company's welfare. Fortunately, in R. M. Livesey, a son who succeeded father as CDRJC Locomotive Superintendent in 1906, he found a worthy lieutenant. Between them the two men worked wonders. Permanent way was improved, Stranorlar's workshop capacity was extended, rolling-stock was increased, additional passenger halts were introduced. Traffic so bloomed as a result that the CDRJC found itself better placed than most as the strains of the First World War began to impinge on Irish railways. Taking due cognisance, the Irish Railways Executive Committee leaned heavily on Forbes and his men during the war years. Even the Lough Swilly received help from Stranorlar in the form of repairs to one locomotive and the loan of five coaches. The Cork, Blackrock, too, had cause to be grateful.

Also photographed in Strabane yard in June 1965, railcar No 18, one of five built by Walker Bros for the CDRJC over the years 1935-40, enjoyed a better fate. Placed in the care of the North West of Ireland Railway Society, it and several other items of County Donegal stock are now static exhibits at Shane's Castle, Antrim.
(Steamchest)

The Armistice was no unmitigated blessing where Irish railways were concerned. The CDRJC received £60,613 from the Government in the way of compensation, but this went little way towards restoring rolling-stock and permanent way to pre-war standards. More menacing still was the emergence of road competition and national political turmoil. The CDRJC had its fair share of both, and during this period of trial Forbe's devotion, and the genius he displayed for improvization, thoroughly warranted the increased responsibilities his Committee asked him to assume. Contrast soon emerged between the CDRJC's, ie Forbes', handling of the post-war situation and that of the Lough Swilly. By 1929 the latter owned 19 engines of eight differing types, and Henry Hunt, its General Manager, keen to rationalize, was anxious to assess the value of the Nasmyth Wilson tanks which had served the CDRJC so well. He wrote to Forbes, suggesting that one of the locos might be tested on Lough Swilly territory. Forbes replied very cagily, declining rapport. Seven years later the Lough Swilly, wincing from a series of annual deficits, was reduced to asking the CDRJC to take over its line. The prospect of a unified narrow gauge system of 223½ miles was tempting; but, so menacing had road competition become by now, that the Joint Committee declined.

Improvements to Co Donegal's hitherto poor system of roads had, of course, released a veritable flood as small bus and lorry operators rushed in to compete against the railways. Unhappily, the latter were statutorily incapable of responding in kind. The Lough Swilly met the problem head on by buying out competition and becoming bus-owners themselves. The CDRJC hung back, but latterly even it felt obliged to hire four second-hand buses from the GNR(I). Four lorries followed from the same source. But Forbes, railwayman to the core, still refused to yield in his conviction that rail services *could* meet local demand — provided maximum flexibility was introduced in setting down and picking up passengers.

Railcars were his answer. In 1926 the Derwent Valley Light Railway happened to be disposing of two petrol-engined cars. Forbes moved quickly to Yorkshire to snap them up, at a bargain price. Their use proved his point, and within two years the CDRJC had six in regular operation. Diesel-engined cars arrived to swell the fleet, and by 1941 14 railcars were bustling around Co Donegal, winning the hearts and support of local people. Meticulous as ever, Forbes took immense pains to instruct his staff in the art of retaining that goodwill. His death in 1943 came as a grievous loss to the Committee.

Next came the Second World War. Partition had, of course, left the CDRJC almost exclusively in Free State territory, and, as such, the railway escaped British Government control during the hostilities. This, however, did not hinder operating costs from rising as relentlessly as those across the Border. Passenger receipts held up remarkably well, but by 1947 the all too familiar spectre of road competition again assumed deadly proportions. The Glenties branch was first to surrender, and in March 1952 all traffic ceased thereon. Next came the Strabane–Londonderry section, on 31 December 1954. By now, too, the MR's original half-share in the CDRJC had passed, through the LMS, then the Railway Executive, to the British Transport Commission. In similar fashion the remaining half-share in the CDRJC had been bequeathed to a sorely-harassed GNR(I) Board. The latter's travails were already such that both Irish Governments had had to assume joint responsibility for its survival. Meanwhile, over the ten years to 1958, traffic losses on the CDRJC grew to a total of £137,000. Particularly heavy losses incurred on the Ballyshannon branch during 1957 clearly presaged future events, and few could have been genuinely surprised when, in May 1959, the Committee sought formal permission to bring its railway activities to a close.

The end came on New Year's Eve 1959. A special steam train had to be laid on in lieu of the normal railcar to accommodate those who wished to say farewell. So, back and forth between Strabane and Stranorlar that night trundled five crowded coaches, with a Nasmyth 2–6–4 tank, No 5 *Drumboe*, at their head. Rain fell, detonators exploded, and a great deal of sentiment was expressed.

One thing is certain. Had Henry Forbes been present, he would have been a very proud man.

LOCOMOTIVES
West Donegal Railway

No	Name	Type	Class	Date built	Makers	Maker's number	Withdrawn	Remarks
1	*Alice*	2–4–0T	1	1881	Sharp Stewart	3023	1926	Cost £1,195 each. *Alice*, lent to the Cork, Blackrock, worked special Admiralty trains between 1918 and 1921
2	*Blanche*	,,	1	1881	,,	3021	1909	
3	*Lydia*	,,	1	1881	,,	3022	1910	

Donegal Railway Company

No	Name	Type	Class	Date built	Makers	Maker's number	Withdrawn	Remarks
4	*Meenglas*	4–6–0T	2	1893	Neilson	4573	1935	Water and coal capacity rather limited, but they could handle heavy loads
5	*Drumboe*	,,	2	1893	,,	4574	1931	
6	*Inver*	,,	2	1893	,,	4575	1931	
7	*Finn*	,,	2	1893	,,	4576	1931	
8	*Foyle*	,,	2	1893	,,	4577	1937	
9	*Columbkille*	,,	2	1893	,,	4578	1932	
10	*Sir James*	4–4–4T	3	1902	,,	6103	1933	A surprise reversion to four-coupled type, and the only 4–4–4s in Ireland
11	*Hercules*	,,	3	1902	,,	6104	1933	
12	*Eske*	4–6–4T	4	1904	Nasmyth Wilson	697	1954	Renumbered 9 in 1937
13	*Owenea*	,,	4	1904	,,	698	1952	Renumbered 10 in 1937
14	*Erne*	,,	4	1904	,,	699	1961	Renumbered 11 in 1937
15	*Mourne*	,,	4	1904	,,	700	1952	Renumbered 12 in 1937

County Donegal Railways Joint Committee

No	Name	Type	Class	Date built	Makers	Maker's number	Withdrawn	Remarks
16	*Donegal*	2–6–4T	5	1907	Nasmyth Wilson	828	—	Became 4 *Meenglas* in 1937
17	*Glenties*	,,	5	1907	,,	829	—	Became 5 *Drumboe* in 1937
18	*Killybegs*	,,	5	1907	,,	830	—	Became 6 *Columbkille* in 1937
19	*Letterkenny*	,,	5	1907	,,	831	1940	Became 7 *Finn* in 1937
20	*Raphoe*	,,	5	1907	,,	832	1955	Became 8 *Foyle* in 1937
21	*Ballyshannon*	,,	5A	1912	,,	958	1961	Became 1 *Alice* in 1928
22	*Stranorlar*	,,	5A	1912	,,	956	1959	Became 2 *Blanche* in 1928
23	*Strabane*	,,	5A	1912	,,	957	1961	Became 3 *Lydia* in 1928

The West Donegal's three locos were named after members of Lord Lifford's family. Their coal and water capacity, though limited, was sufficient to enable them to work between Stranorlar and Druminin, and during this seven-year period they averaged some 7,000 miles apiece per year. Once the Donegal Railway took over, however, six-coupled tanks were considered necessary, and the tough little Class '2s' came into being. R. H. Livesey's reversion, on the other hand, to four-coupled tanks in 1902 proved a retrograde step, and the heavy axle loading of these Class '3' engines confined them for many years to the Londonderry–Stranorlar section, where the rails were heavier. Both were named after members of the Board. Livesey's final contribution, the 'Baltic' tanks, reflected the growth of freight traffic on the DRC. Named after local rivers, they could handle heavy loads, and this capacity was improved in later years as superheaters were fitted. The 2–6–4 tanks introduced by the CDRJC in 1907 were a vast improvement, and their outside bearings and Walschaerts valve gear marked a radical departure from previous practice. So successful were they that an improved version, built with superheater and 1,500 gallon tanks, emerged in 1912. Still only costing £2,500 apiece, these Class '5A' tanks easily qualified as the most advanced narrow gauge locomotive design in Ireland.

By 1937 only locos from Classes '4', '5' and '5A' survived, and the opportunity was taken to renumber the CDRJC stock. Half a dozen old WDR and DRC names were also revived, and an attractive new livery, known as 'geranium red', was adopted. Even though railcars were rapidly being introduced, County Donegal steam still had two decades of work ahead. When the end did come, No 2 *Blanche*, destined for the breakers in 1959, was salvaged by the Belfast Museum of Transport, as were Nos 4 and 5, *Meenglas* and *Drumboe*, by Dr Ralph Cox, an American. At a

public auction of DCRJC effects, held in 1961, Dr Cox was again in the forefront, and bid successfully for Nos 6 and 11, *Columbkille* and *Erne*, together with considerable quantities of coaches, wagons and track.

Today, 25 years later, the preservation situation is not quite so rosy. *Blanche* still resides safely at Belfast Museum, as do three ex-CDRJC railcars. No 6 *Columbkille*, Nos 12 and 18 (two ex-CDRJC diesel railcars), one coach, one wagon and five coach underframes — all part of Dr Cox's booty — are cared for, in static form, at Shane's Castle Railway, Co Antrim. The remaining items purchased by Dr Cox have fared less well. Dumped in Strabane station yard in 1961, they were later offered, fruitlessly, for sale. Two and a half subsequent decades of exposure to weather and vandalism have created a sad vista of dereliction. *Meenglas* and *Drumboe* continue to lie there, rusting away. Four ex-CDRJC composite coaches and a passenger van have been stripped to their underframes, and *Erne* appears to have sunk without trace. An additional cache of CDRJC buses, lorries and rail wagons has long since gone — despite Dr Cox's gallant initiative.

The CDRJC's enthusiasm for railcars was unequalled anywhere else in the UK; 23 vehicles in all passed through its hands over a period of 45 years. Eleven were petrol-driven, and 12 were diesels. The GNR(I) supplied bodies for 11 cars, and the remainder were a heterogenous collection.

After experiment in 1906 with a tiny four-wheeled inspection car there was a lapse of two decades before Forbes invaded the Derwent Valley, and returned with his two 'bargains'. Thereafter, with the collusion of the GNR(I) works at Dundalk, a lengthy sequence of cars followed. Nos 4, 5 and 6 were petrol-driven, and the first diesels, Nos 7 and 8, came into use in 1931. The year 1933 saw an interruption in the form of two ex-GNR(I) petrol-driven bus conversions, but, a few

CDRJC railcars, bought new

No	Builder	Date introduced	Power	Cost	Remarks
1	Allday & Onions, Birmingham	1906	Petrol, 10 hp	£237	Preserved at Belfast Transport Museum
4	O'Doherty	1928	Petrol, 36 hp	£522	Lent to CVR 1932. Scrapped 1947
5	O'Doherty/Knutsford	1929	Trailer	£318	Scrapped 1960
6	GNR(I)/O'Doherty	1930	Petrol, 32 hp	£900	Rebuilt as trailer, 1945. Scrapped 1958
7 & 8	,,	1931	Diesel, 6.L.2	£2,086	First in British Isles. Scrapped 1949
12	GNR(I)/Walker Bros	1934	Diesel, 6.L.2	£2,281	First power bogie type on CDRJC. Bought by Dr Cox
14-18	,,	1935/40	,,	£2,500	No 18 bought by Dr Cox
19	,,	1950	Diesel, 6.L.W	£8,176	Sold to Isle of Man Railway, 1961
20	,,	1951	,,	£7,885	,,

second-hand acquisitions apart, the CDRJC dealt exclusively in diesel cars from 1935 onwards.

No 17 was destroyed in a collision near Donegal on 29 August 1949. No 18 looked like following suit when it was accidentally damaged by fire at Sessiaghoneill on 7 November that same year. Rebuilt at Dundalk works, however, it returned to service in June 1950, and contrived to complete 641,694 miles in all. Walker/GNR(I) diesel cars Nos 19 and 20 continue to serve on the Isle of Man Railway. Both were given a major overhaul in 1982.

CDRJC railcars, bought second-hand

Nos	Source	Date introduced	Power	Cost	Remarks
2 & 3	Ex-Derwent Valley Light Railway	1926	Petrol, 22 hp	£314	Converted from 4 ft 8½ in gauge. No 3 preserved at Belfast Transport Museum
9 & 10	Ex-GNR(I) buses	1933	Petrol, 36 hp	—	Scrapped 1939 and 1949
11 (*Phoenix*)	Ex-Clogher Valley Railway	1933	Diesel, 6.L.2	—	Preserved at Belfast Transport Museum
2	Ex-Castlederg & Victoria Bridge	1934	Petrol, 22 hp	—	Rebuilt as Trailer, 1944
3 & 13	Ex-Dublin & Blessington Tramway	1934	Petrol, 35 hp	—	No 13 rebuilt as Trailer, 1934
10	Ex-Clogher Valley Rly	1942	Diesel, 6.L.2	—	Preserved at Belfast Transport Museum

Lost causes

DUBLIN & LUCAN TRAMWAY

Incorporated: 11 November 1880
Opened: 2 July 1883
Closed: 29 January 1925
Gauges: 3 ft 0 in and 3 ft 6 in

Where the matter of integrating transport systems was concerned, Cork was not the only perverse city in Ireland. Dublin ran it a close second, with its strange, and quite illogical, peripheral Tramway system. For, despite the fact that a 5 ft 3 in gauge tramway system operated by Dublin United Tramways, presently horse-drawn but due for electrification in 1898, was already serving the city, neither of two new roadside tramways which opened in the 1880s devoted much thought to the prospect of through passenger running. The Dublin & Blessington Tramway, opened on 1 August 1888, adopted the 5 ft 3 in gauge and opted for steam operation. The Dublin & Lucan Tramway, reaching out for 7 miles to the picturesque village of Lucan, deviated even more markedly from precedent by choosing both steam and a 3-foot gauge.

Opened as far as Chapelizod (1¾ miles) by June 1881, the Dublin & Lucan Tramway finally reached Lucan on 2 July 1883. Further extensions to Celbridge (3¾ miles) and Clane (7 miles) were mooted by a new company, the Lucan, Leixlip & Celbridge Steam Tramway, but only a modest section

of just under 2 miles to Leixlip ever materialized. By and large the D&LT followed local road contours, and short severe gradients were sanguinely embraced. The first locomotive employed was a double-decked 2–4–2 steam car, designed by Edward Perrett and built by Manlove Alliott & Fryer of Nottingham in 1881. Due, however, to the adverse effects of prolonged standing time, its functional life on the Dublin & Lucan was short, and over the years 1882-87 Kitson & Company's Airedale Foundry at Leeds provided six of their more conventional 0–4–0 enclosed steam tram locos. These normally hauled bogie tramcars, but were sometimes used to handle composite trains. One more steam loco, a two-cylinder von Borries compound built for the Leixlip extension, arrived from Thomas Green & Son, also of Leeds, in 1892.

This complement of steam locomotives sufficed to meet the D&LT's requirements, with varying degrees of success, until a new chapter opened up in 1896 — when Westminster, in its wisdom, embraced a new Bill concerning the tramway's future. The terms of the Act sanctioned conversion to electric traction; thus, appropriately enough, the title of the tramway was altered to the Dublin & Lucan Electric Railway. The Act also authorized deviation from the 3-foot gauge, but for some reason the new company chose to adopt a 3 ft 6 in gauge, instead of seizing a heaven-sent opportunity to link up with the Dublin United Tramways' 5 ft 3 in metals. Probably lack of finance dictated this course of action. Whatever, commencing in 1899 the Kilmarnock firm of Dick, Kerr & Co Ltd supplied conventional double and single-decked tramcars. An additional electric

Over a period of five years, Kitson & Co of Leeds supplied the D&LT with their well-known 0–4–0 enclosed steam tram locos. This Works photograph is of No 6, the last to be supplied, in 1887. Nos 1–3 were scrapped when electrification was introduced in 1899. Nos 4–6 somehow contrived to survive to 1912. (Kitson & Co)

locomotive was obtained to handle goods traffic.

Expectations may have been high, but, again, it was a case of too little, too late. The onslaught of bus competition which developed in Dublin, and elsewhere, immediately after the First World War threw merciless light on the slow and inconvenient nature of the D&LER's contact with the city. The end was inevitable, and it came with the closure of the tramway on 29 January 1925.

Ironically, Dublin United Tramways, stepping in to fill the vacuum, relaid new metals on the one-time narrow gauge trackbed, and reopened a 5 ft 3 in gauge tramway service on 27 May 1928. Twelve brand new electric cars, specially built at their Inchicore works, resumed service between Dublin and Lucan. Equally ironically, it was the double-decker bus service which this time sounded a death knell; the Lucan tram service was finally abandoned in April 1940.

Adding yet another element to the essentially Irish nature of the Dublin & Lucan saga, the flat-bottomed 5 ft 3 in gauge track was duly salvaged. The Great Southern Railway acquired it later, and part of it was relaid on the Clonakilty branch. The remainder found employment in the Limerick–Newcastle area.

LOCOMOTIVES

No	Date built	Makers	Maker's number	Withdrawn
1	1882	Kitson	T57	1899
2	1883	,,	T74	1899
3	1883	,,	T81	1899
4	1884	,,	T104	1912
5	1884	,,	T108	1912
6	1887	,,	T224	1912
7	1892	T. Green	169	Sold 1896

LISTOWEL & BALLYBUNION RAILWAY COMPANY

Incorporated: 16 April 1886
Opened: 29 February 1888
Closed: 14 October 1924

Legend has it that the idea of a monorail occurred to Charles Lartigue, a French inventor, as he stood in an Algerian desert one day and watched a camel train go by. Their beautifully balanced pannier loads, it seems, intrigued him. It offers no explanation, however, as to why, after tentative experiment in France, the Lartigue Construction Company should choose a remote corner of Ireland as a suitable venue for further practical demonstration. The impact of the French upon the Irish must have been interesting — to put it mildly. As they watched the bizarre project take shape in 1887, one can assume the good folk of Ballybunion, a quiet seaside resort on the mouth of the River Shannon, harboured many an emotion — including that of sheer amazement. Yet why should they not welcome contact with main line W&LR metals at Listowel? To them it opened up the whole of Ireland.

The Act of Incorporation established L&BR capital as £22,000; and, commendably, its 9½-mile length was completed in nine months at a very reasonable cost of £26,300. Provision of rolling-stock added a further £6,500, and, true to their word, the French company footed the entire bill. Appropriately, the slightly mad operation opened in Leap Year.

Was the L&BR a monorail in the true sense of the word? Purists would say 'no'; for, although single rails were employed, and were laid in 31-foot lengths along A-shaped trestles, important guide rails ran along either side, 2 feet nearer the ground. They provided stability. No ballast was required, of course, and the line was single, except for a passing loop at Liselton, one of only two intermediate stops between Listowel and Ballybunion. Points were simulated by mounting sections of the line on turntables, whence a few vehicles were handled at a time. At level crossings recourse was made to drawbridges. Passengers, meanwhile, had problems of their own to solve. Steps were provided to facilitate transfer within a coach; but 'regulars', it seems, treated such luxury with disdain, and soon cultivated their own habit of crawling over or under the main rail itself.

Odder still were the three locomotives built specially by Hunslet of Leeds. Each had twin boilers, working at 150 lbs pressure, and may be best described as 0–3–0s; for although three coupled

Above *Faced with the unusual demands of the 'Lartigue Single Rail System', the Hunslet Engine Co of Leeds rose to the occasion in 1887 by producing three of the most novel engines they ever built – Nos 1, 2 and 3 of the Listowel & Ballybunion Railway. Evidently undaunted by the peculiar duties they had to perform, the crew of No 1 pose cheerfully enough for the photographer before setting out on another extremely bumpy 9½-mile ride. (Author's Collection)*

Right *One of three daily trains, ready to leave Ballybunion terminus for Listowel, sports three coaches, one 'bridge', and two sand wagons. There seems, however, to be a marked absence of passengers! Note, too, the fishplated 'permanent way' in the foreground. (Author's Collection)*

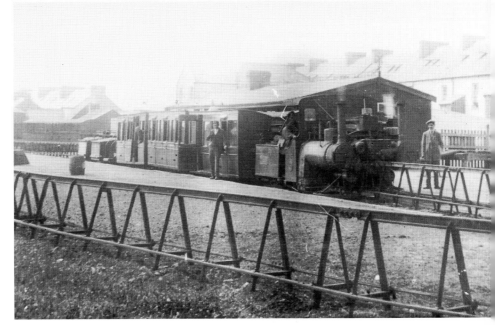

Right *A closer look at the 'bridge'. This mobile platform, buffered up between coaches and sand wagons in the previous picture, constituted the L&B passengers' 'official' way of crossing the line. Quite often, though, patrons opted to dive through under the rails. Being Ireland, nobody worried too much. (Author's Collection)*

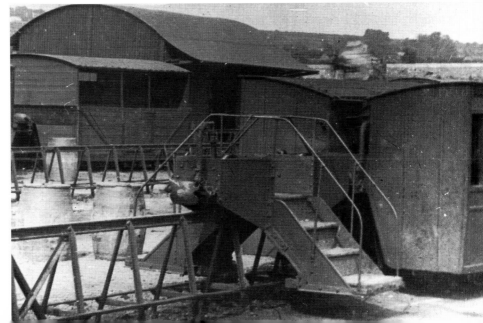

wheels, 2 feet in diameter, ran between the boilers on the master rail, only the central one was driven. Alternatively, the locos might be deemed 0–3–2–0s, for two-wheeled steam tenders were also fitted. Each operated on two separate cylinders, though latterly these were removed. Archibald Sturrock, of Doncaster, could have told them steam tenders were not 'on'! Engine and tender, weighing 6 and 4 tons respectively, were both equipped with the Westinghouse brake, and the fact that duplicate cab controls were also fitted did not spare the driver the gratuitous task of firing one of the boilers. In theory, the locomotives were capable of attaining speeds of up to 27 mph. In practice, a speed limit of 17 mph was always observed.

Coaches and wagons were equally unconventional, for their single pair of wheels also ran on the monorail — although, like the engines, ancillary wheels contacted the guide rails below. Noise and vibration suffered by passengers can be imagined. Nevertheless, at the height of its career the L&BR carried 1,400 passengers a day. Most, of course were summer visitors. At the Listowel end, the W&LR's station was within easy walking reach, and a connecting service of trains was devised. Midweek, three monotrains ran daily, and the through trip took 45 minutes. Incidence of passenger traffic on the L&BR is clearly indicated by the fact that the company's ratio of goods vehicles to passenger was only 2:1, as opposed to Irish light railways' normal ratio of 5:1. Mixed trains were the order of the day, for traffic in sand provided a useful revenue, and some 10,000 tons a year were transported from Ballybunion's dunes. Quite often passengers had to wait at intermediate stops while sand wagons were being added or detached.

Despite its popularity, the L&BR was never really a viable proposition, and as early as 1897 such assets as it possessed passed into the hands of the Official Receiver. Even then it still contrived to declare dividends in 1907, largely from the carriage of sand. During the first 25 years of its life, however, the L&BR failed on eight occasions to earn its working expenses. Shortage of coal during the First World War saw turf used experimentally as locomotive fuel. But the 1917 venture was a brief one, and, try as they might, the compromise never met with success in Ireland. By early post-war years rising costs and increasing competition from road transport were exerting intolerable pressures. The year 1922 saw a record loss on the L&BR of £1,525, and it was revealed that working expenses, once absorbing some £2,600 annually, had soared now to £4,588. Understandably, the newly formed Great Southern Railways declined to saddle themselves with such a highly speculative and loss-making concern. Thus, on 14 October 1924 the line was closed. Very soon after,

70 tons of track were lifted, and were sold as scrap, like everything else.

GIANT'S CAUSEWAY, PORTRUSH & BUSH VALLEY RAILWAY & TRAMWAY COMPANY
Incorporated: 26 August 1880
Opened: 29 January 1883
Closed: 30 September 1949

The title was an imposing one. Yet it was not assumed lightly, for in 1880 the company had every intention of linking Portrush with Bushmills, 6 miles away, by a 3-foot gauge tramway. The intention then was to push on to Ballycastle over 7¾ miles of new light railway. Capital of £45,000 was dedicated to the purpose, and, indeed, the tramway opened in 1883. Then came a change of heart. Under legislation passed against fierce opposition in August 1885, fresh capital of £5,000 was introduced. The light railway project was abandoned, and work commenced instead on a 2-mile extension of the tramway, from Bushmills to Giant's Causeway. Mainsprings behind the scheme were two Irish brothers, Arthur and William Traill, and a German electrical inventor, William Siemens. To them really, and not to Ireland, should be accorded the distinction of operating the first major electric railway in the UK. Volk's Electric Railway also opened in Brighton during 1883, but it was a much more modest concern. Interestingly, Siemens' dynamo was again employed.

As far as electric working was concerned, Volk's Railway, in fact, won the race by a margin of eight weeks, for a delay in completing the hydro-electric plant at Bushmills obliged the Irish company to commence operations by steam. Two steam trams, originally earmarked for employment in Portrush only, were accordingly conscripted for use throughout the system. Eventually, electric trams took over on 28 September 1883.

The Irish method of operation attracted great interest at the time. Power came from Bushmills, where it was generated by water turbines on the River Bush. It reached the cars via conductor rails which, pitched 1½ feet above ground level, were strictly confined to the far side of public highways, for obvious public safety reasons. Conductor rails could not be tolerated, however, in the busy streets of Portrush, and it was here that the brace of steam trams already mentioned were meant to operate. Use

of the overhead trolley system provided an obvious answer, and, once an auxiliary power station was opened at Portrush, this was adopted in 1899.

As might be expected, the tramway became very popular with tourists, and during the high season all four steam tram locos the company finally acquired were kept fully employed in helping to relieve the hard-pressed electric cars. This state of affairs lasted until 1915, when additional electric motive power was provided and steam was pensioned off. The company's activities were remarkably self-contained. All repairs and maintenance were undertaken locally, and drivers and conductors joined in during the winter months when the system closed down. The tramway's single track often wound along cliff tops, and large flags were used to indicate safe conditions to drivers. There can be no doubt that this kind of family activity, plus clever and resourceful management by the Traill brothers, kept the concern going through many a lean year. By 1923 five electric locos and 18 coaches were in operation.

Portrush, 17 May 1937, and Car No 2, complete with trailer, is ready to leave at 12.20 pm on its seven-mile journey to Giant's Causeway. Although the Tramway survived the onslaught of both road transport and the Second World War, the Ulster Transport Authority could not see its way to finance post-war rehabilitation, and, regrettably, this popular holidaymakers' facility was terminated in September 1949. (F. C. Le Manquais)

Though it had to combat considerable road competition during the 1930s, the tramway kept going at a modest profit all through the Second World War. By 1949, however, the whole track badly needed renewing. In the event the Ulster Transport Authority was asked to save the tramway. They did, in fact, carry out a careful examination, but were forced to a reluctant conclusion that salvage was not economically feasible. Closure came in September 1949, and over the next 18 months every existing item of equipment was garnered for ultimate public auction at Belfast.

LOCOMOTIVES

No	Name	Type	Date built	Makers	Withdrawn	Remarks
1	—	0–4–0	1883	Wilkinson	1910	One of these two locos bore the name
2	—	,,	1883	,,	1899	*Wartrail*
3	*Dunluce Castle*	,,	1886	,,	1930	Both locos were sold
4	*Brian Boroihme*	,,	1887	,,	1930	

Four steam tram locos found early employment, while the electric stock ultimately owned amounted to six motor-cars and 12 trailers. The latter were four-wheeled, and mostly open, with toast-rack seating.

Livery was red and cream, and this was well looked after in the workshops at Portrush.

Trailer car No 2 is now a static exhibit at the Ulster Folk Museum, at Craigavad, Co Down.

BESSBROOK & NEWRY TRAMWAY

Incorporated: 26 May 1884
Opened: October 1885
Closed: 10 January 1948

Of all the 32 Counties in Ireland, Armagh, with its bustling population of 500 to the square mile, least required the stimulus of the 1883 Tramways Act. The introduction of the Steam Age within the County had already witnessed rapid development of both railways and industry. Yet, curiously, the manufacture of jute, Armagh's strongest card in Ulster's bid for industrial prosperity, produced one modest applicant amongst the many concerns which jostled for registration under the Act. In this instance, however, no supporting Guarantee was sought from Authority, for the motive which prompted the tramway's construction was primarily industrial. In the latter half of the nineteenth century Bessbrook's flax mills had blossomed into an important industrial complex, and, as time went on, the prospect of transporting raw materials and finished products by rail to and from

20 July 1933, and an electric car prepares to uncouple a van at Bessbrook car depot. The bogie trailer was one of those purchased in 1928 from Dublin & United Tramways, ex-Dublin & Lucan Tramway. The car depot lay immediately behind the camera, alongside the Tramway's Bessbrook station platform. (Steamchest)

Newry, where GNR(I) metals invited facile distribution, assumed an irrestistible attraction.

Although a steam tramway was originally envisaged, the Bessbrook & Newry, in fact, followed the Giant's Causeway footsteps by employing hydro-electric power. It even pre-empted that concern by adopting the third rail principle from inception. Certainly, once powers were granted at Westminster construction went ahead without delay, and the 3-mile line, built at a cost of £5,000 per mile, was ready for use by October 1885. The nerve centre, as it were, was located at Bessbrook, and rendezvous with the GNR(I)'s main Londonderry line was made via a small platform adjacent to the latter's station at Edward Street, Newry.

Some interesting idiosyncrasies were to be found in the Bessbrook rolling-stock. Its bogie power cars, for example, were strangely limited, in that they could be driven from one end only. This defect was somewhat clumsily countered by the provision of run-round loops at both ends of the line. At one spot near Bessbrook the tramway was obliged to cross a public highway. Here, for a matter of 50 yards, the third rail was, perforce, abandoned, and cars collected current overhead. Mill workers and public alike used the tramway, and during 'rush hours' bogie trailers were added to provide additional passenger accommodation. To meet all-important industrial demands, a miscellany of good vehicles, open and closed, was also maintained. Designed with flangeless wheels, so that they could be put to economic use on either road or rail, when they ran on the 3-foot metals ingenious

use of lower outer rails ensured that wagon wheels were kept firmly in check.

In its heyday the tramway was very popular indeed with mill workers. It offered a convenient and reliable hourly service 'twixt town and mill. The service was duly augmented at strategic intervals, and, considering the frequency of stops, a time of 20 minutes for the 3-mile trip was not unreasonable. This healthy amalgam of passenger and freight traffic successfully surmounted the hazards of 1914–18. By the end of the Second World War, however, the superior mobility of lorries and buses was posing questions which could not be answered. The struggle for post-war existence was very brief — and terminated on 10 January 1948.

At its peak the Bessbrook & Newry owned four bogie power cars, five assorted trailers, and 27 goods vehicles. Bogie car No 2, built by Ashburys in 1883, was preserved by the Bessbrook Spinning Company. All else went for scrap.

CASTLEDERG & VICTORIA BRIDGE TRAMWAY

Incorporated: 16 July 1883
Opened: 4 July 1884
Closed: 3 October 1933

When, early in 1883, three northern Baronies took positive steps to support the C&VBT by joining in a Guarantee for £13,000, they unwittingly penalized their ratepayers to the tune of £260 per annum for 30 years to come. The Viceregal Railway Commission of 1906 acknowledged the fact when it observed that if the Baronies' action had been deferred until the Tramways Act was passed a little later in the year, annual Treasury relief of up to 2 per cent of the tramway's capital would have come their way. Accordingly, the Commission's Report of 1910 recommended that a Grant of £6,000 be awarded as compensation. The intention was good; but the Grant was never made.

The C&VBT's mission in life lay in bridging the 7¼-mile gap which lay between Castlederg, a small town in Co Tyrone, and its nearest point of railway contact, the GNR(I)'s main Londonderry line at Victoria Bridge. Once the tramway was built, its steam tram locos were allowed 40 minutes to complete the journey. They ran in such sequence as to make convenient main line connection, and invariably mixed in character, a handful of tram trains sufficed to meet weekday requirements. None ran on Sundays. Like its contemporaries, the Giant's Causeway and the Bessbrook & Newry, the tramway was earnestly and most efficiently run. Offices and workshops were conveniently grouped at Castlederg, and there light repairs to rolling-stock and locomotives could be comfortably contained. Only twice were ouside resources utilized, when No 4, the C&VBT's largest locomotive, underwent heavy repairs at the GNR(I)'s Dundalk Works.

Castlederg trams stopped anywhere on request,

No 5, a conventional 0–4–4T supplied by Hudswell Clrke in 1912, was still required to work with nearside motion shielded, tramway fashion. Note, too, the jack on the running plate. The loco was scrapped in 1935, some two years after the Tramway finally closed. (Steamchest)

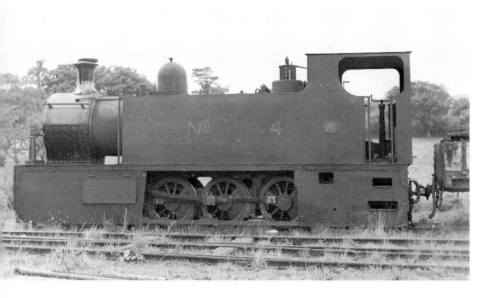

2–6–0T No 4 was also a Hudswell Clark engine, and was, in fact, the Castlederg's biggest loco. Saved from demolition when the Tramway closed, it was bought later from a scrap merchant by the Clogher Valley Tramway, who found the locomotive very useful indeed. No 4 is shown here at Castlederg in the early 1930s. (Steamchest)

The same locomotive, rebuilt as a 2–6–2T, is proudly displayed, with an immaculate clerestory-roofed coach, by the Clogher Valley Tramway. In obligatory CVR fashion, the engine has been given a large headlight. But at least CVR No 4 could operate consistently in forward gear on Clogher metals. (Steamchest)

and thus offered a valuable social service to the inhabitants of the few villages scattered near, or along, the line. Certainly, public response kept the company solvent, until, that is, the First World War arrived to introduce inevitable difficulties. In post-war years road competition erupted in crippling fashion. The Castlederg area was particularly vulnerable, and, as rail traffic reached its nadir in the mid-1920s, the C&VBT's Locomotive Superintendent was driven to devise a home-made 20 hp paraffin-driven railcar in a desperate bid to introduce maximum economy. His efforts were not in vain, for steam working was reintroduced a few years later. It seemed as if the crisis had been overcome.

Alas, the year 1933 witnessed a massive railway strike in Ireland, and this proved more than the company could withstand. Even after the dispute was resolved, Castlederg services were never able to resume, and official closure of the tramway followed in October of that year. Workshop equipment and rolling-stock were sold to a Glasgow firm; though, as we shall see presently, quite a quantity escaped the breakers, and lived to fight another day.

LOCOMOTIVES

In accordance with Board of Trade requirements, Nos 1 and 2 were 'totally enclosed' trams, though wheels and motion, in fact, required guarding only on the near side of each locomotive — for the Castlederg owned no turntable, and the line kept to one side of the public highway. Both locos were originally fitted with condensing apparatus, but this was later

No	Name	Type	Date built	Makers	Maker's number	Withdrawn	Remarks
1	*Mourne*	0–4–0T	1884	Kitson	T106	1904	} Named after local rivers
2	*Derg*	,,	1884	,,	T107	1912	
3	—	0–4–0T	1891	,,	T257	1928	Improved type of tram
4	—	2–6–0T	1904	Hudswell Clarke	698	1933	Sold eventually to Clogher Valley Rly
5	—	0–4–4T	1912	,,	978	1933	
(6)	—	2–4–0T	1878	Beyer Peacock	1828	1933	Bought from NCC in 1928
Railcar			1925	CVBT Workshops	—	1928	Ran 30,000 miles

removed. No 3 was an 'improved' tram. Somewhat larger, it boasted a form of Walschaerts valve gear, and, taking advantage of relaxed regulations, only wheel guards were fitted. Getting away from the tram format, Nos 4 and 5 were much more conventional steam engines. They appear to have coped quite adequately with traffic requirements right up to the date of closure, which rather suggests that purchase of the Beyer Peacock 2–4–0T from the NCC in November 1928 was strategic, rather than practical. Whatever, this curious acquisition came at a time when the Castlederg's paraffin railcar was approaching the end of its working life, and thought was being given to the resumption of steam working. In the last analysis the 2–4–0T did little regular work, and seemed to function largely as a spare engine. Both it and No 5 met melancholy ends soon after the tramway closed in 1933. No 4 would have followed suit, but for the fact that the Clogher Valley Railway intervened. Rebuilt there as a 2–6–2 tank, it celebrated its reprieve by yielding eight more years of useful service on Clogher Valley metals. Many of the Castlederg's 31 vans and wagons also found their way to Auchnacloy.

The fate of the paraffin railcar is particularly interesting. Withdrawn by the C&VBT in 1928, it lay out of use for a number of years, and latterly the engine was removed. Henry Forbes, of CDRJC fame, purchased the remains at knockdown price in 1934, whence Stranorlar works attended to her transition, by fitting a new body and a 22 hp Reo engine. Though converted to a trailer in 1944, she never the less served until 1959.

With all else gone, one Castlederg saloon coach of 1883 vintage eventually found its way into the Ulster Folk Museum.

CLOGHER VALLEY TRAMWAY

Incorporated: 17 May 1884
Opened: 2 May 1887
Closed: 31 December 1941

Railway promotion was a popular pastime in Ireland around 1845, and that year at least one pair of proposals, neither of which came to fruition, evinced

A typical mixed train for Maguiresbridge, with No 3 Blackwater at its head, halts at Aughnacloy station. The loco is working cab-first in traditional style, and her driver is examining a warm bearing. His fireman is on top, tidying up a consignment of coal just received from the overhead hopper. The CVR's locomotive and carriage workshops were also located here. (Steamchest)

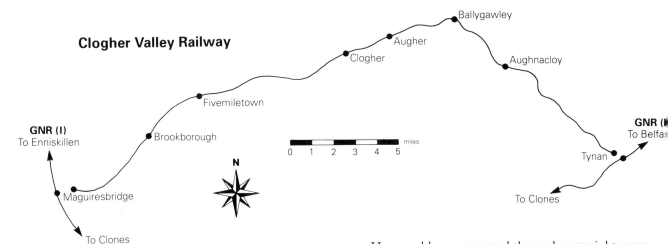

Clogher Valley Railway

Ballygawley

Augher

Clogher

Aughnacloy

Fivemiletown

GNR (I)
To Belfast

Brookborough

GNR (I)
To Enniskillen

miles
0 1 2 3 4 5

N

Maguiresbridge

Tynan

To Clones

To Clones

a lively interest in the welfare of Auchnacloy and Clogher, modest country towns, both just inside Co Tyrone. Even after the Railway Mania subsided, kindred propositions persisted at regular intervals, and five more fell by the wayside ere the Clogher Valley Tramway finally obtained powers to proceed. Its sponsors put forward a plan which appeared to be simplicity itself. Capital would be fixed at £150,000, and Tynan would be linked to Macguiresbridge by 37 miles of narrow gauge metals. The fact that ready-made GNR(I) station facilities already existed at *both* ends of the proposed line spared the thought, and expense, of building CVT terminals.

The first to advance under the 1883 Tramways Act, the CVT Directors soon sampled its legal intricacies. Early in the day, for instance, they found themselves obliged to submit detailed plans in turn before two Grand Juries, four Baronies, and a brace of inspecting engineers. The time and energy consumed can be imagined. After that hurdle was cleared, and Baronial Guarantees were secured, came the thorny question of raising capital.

Here problems presented themselves straight away. The local populace were enthusiastic to a man; but, not unnaturally, few in their ranks were capable of following the financial lead of a handful of landed gentry. Thus, local subscriptions were slow, and disappointing. Meanwhile, construction costs were gobbling funds as fast as they could be provided, and a positive crisis arose in March 1886, when a Finance House reneged on its offer to purchase unsold CVT stock. Possibly a figure of £70,000 was more than they had bargained for!

Three months later, CVT fortunes received a second damaging blow, when Gladstone's Home Rule Bill met with defeat at Westminster. The climate of English investment, already cool enough towards Irish affairs, promptly dropped to zero. Appeal to the Board of Works merely produced a reminder that the CVT was already heavily indebted to local authorities, and, latterly, only a pledge of guaranteed shares, under the Public Loans Tramways (Ireland) Act of 1896, conjured up a sorely needed loan of £44,000. Even then, the CVT Directors had to move heaven and earth to persuade the Treasury to drop the interest rate from 5 to 4 per cent.

Clogher Valley diesel railcar No 1 stands by at Fivemiletown station on 15 June 1937. Built by Walker Bros in 1932, it later became No 10 on the County Donegal, and is now an exhibit in Belfast Transport Museum. Significantly, not a passenger or member of staff can be seen in this 1937 view. (F. C. Le Manquais)

The CVR's 'white elephant', the steam tractor supplied by Atkinson-Walker of Preston in 1929, lay derelict in Aughnacloy yard for years before Henry Forbes, of County Donegal fame, bought it, minus the steam engine. Fitted with a Gardner oil engine, and with one tank used for fuel oil and the other for water, the new unit, named Phoenix *because it had literally risen from its ashes (!), and numbered 11, subsequently handled a deal of light traffic in the Strabane locality; it now rests in Belfast Transport Museum. This view of* Phoenix *in action was taken at Strabane on 16 June 1937.* (F. C. Le Manquais)

Despite these alarums and excursions, the tramway was made ready for public use by mid-1887. For most of its course it shared public highways, either running alongside, or diving through narrow village streets. Only occasionally, in a bid to avoid undesirable gradients, did it hive off across fields. Thirty-seven stations and halts were crammed into its length, and for reasons of safety the Board of Trade inflicted 19 further 'absolute stops' at road crossings. Add speed restrictions of 4 mph at the 13 other hazards, and it will be understood why a passenger determined to travel from Tynan to Macguiresbridge had to be prepared to mortgage at least 3 hours of his time. Generally speaking, the tramway was well built, though some felt its major stations had a grandeur about them which seemed incompatible with the amount of traffic they were likely to attract.

Opening day appeared to invoke similar overtones, for public response was less than generous. Nor, as the years went by, did CVT traffic have much comfort to offer those who footed the bill. Fair Days were brisk enough, though, and traffic on the occasion of the Orangemen's Annual Demonstration was positively frantic. Payment of dividends, however, was the crucial factor, and the penalty suffered by local ratepayers, even after Treasury relief, shows clearly in the returns for the first eight years, which are tabulated below.

As might be expected, such a melancholy procession of figures gave the CVT Directors food for thought. Convinced that the designation 'Tramway' was an inhibiting factor, they duly deliberated; and, on 16 July 1894, a new title was officially adopted. From now on the Clogher's venture would be known as the Clogher Valley Railway Company Limited. Efforts were also made to join with the Cavan & Leitrim Railway in creating a grandiose 234-mile network of 3-foot metals across the breadth of northern Ireland. Mercifully, neither concern proved capable of implementing its dream.

Tramway or Railway, the discomfiture of the four Baronies behind jthe Guarantee lessened none from 1894 onwards. Twenty-seven subsequent years yielded 20 deficits. Indeed, in 1916, when a record loss of £1,479 was notched up by the CVT, local liability soared with it to £5,179. Government

Year	Working Profit (£)	Working Loss (£)	Dividends (£)	Total Baronial contribution (£)	Less maximum Treasury relief ie 2% of capital (£)	Net local loss (£)
1887	28	—	5,854	5,826	2,466	3,360
1888	27	—	6,018	5,991	2,466	3,525
1889	—	538	6,342	6,880	2,466	4,414
1890	—	786	6,339	7,125	2,466	4,659
1891	—	78	6,339	6,417	2,466	3,951
1892	222	—	6,339	6,117	2,466	3,651
1893	148	—	6,208	6,060	2,466	3,594
1894	—	223	6,079	6,302	2,466	3,836
					Total net deficit	£30,990

Aughnacloy station, looking towards Tynan in June 1937. Note the broad platform, gas lamps, and profusion of advertisements. The number 63 on the nearest wagon suggests that the CVR was equally lavish in its provision of freight-rolling stock. (F. C. Le Manquais)

control during the First World War, with its consequent demands for higher wages, punished CVT fortunes in a way that post-war compensation of £16,732 could not mend. As a consequence, immediately control ended in August 1921, the CVR, in common with all other Irish railways, imposed wage cuts.

The next torment to arrive on the scene was the Partition of 1921. The CVR metals lay entirely within Northern Ireland. Thus they escaped the direct impact of the 'Troubles' which followed. Not so the GNR(I). Its highly vulnerable Dundalk–Enniskillen line received such attention from Irregulars that it was forced to close for six months. This, of course, left the CVR and Macguiresbridge whistling for passing traffic. Came 1922, and a Northern Ireland Railway Commission, charged with the consideration of Ireland's new railway geography, produced conflicting Reports. A Majority stood firmly behind continuation of private railway management, and only deviated momentarily to recommend that the CVR be absorbed by the GNR(I). A Minority plumped for public ownership. Stormont solved the conumdrum in all too familiar a fashion by taking no action. The GNR(I), too, declined with thanks.

So the CVR tottered on through the 1920s. Soon, the menace of road transport began to bite. By 1925 even the CVR Directors were alarmed, and at a Board Meeting in December a motion was tabled by one Director calling for an end to the railway. It failed to attract a seconder, and a programme of economies was drawn up instead. These merely anticipated a series of more stringent cuts which were recommended by yet another Committee of Inquiry the following year.

This time the Government's eye remained fixed on the CVR. The findings of the Abbott committee were accepted; and, under appropriate legislation in 1928, the railway passed under the jurisdiction of a Committee of Management, drawn from County Council and Ministry of Commerce nominees. No

question arose of shareholders being bought out. They would continue to receive guaranteed dividends as before.

The Committee of Management was fortunate, in that both Government representatives, Robert Darragh and Henry Forbes, were experienced railwaymen. To the enthusiasm of the latter, in particular, can be attributed the continuation of passenger services on the CVR. From 1 September 1928, first class travel was abandoned, as, too, was the practice of running mixed trains. Further wage cuts were also imposed. Then, in January 1929, largely on the strength of the Abbott Committee's proposals, an Atkinson-Walker steam tractor was introduced as an experiment. The choice of vehicle proved an unhappy one, and, fortunately for the CVR, no money changed hands ere the firm went bankrupt that same year. For years the tractor lay forgotten in Auchnacloy yard.

Possibly the steam tractor fiasco weakened the CVR's faith in steam. Whatever, Forbes, enthusiastic as ever, arranged a trial run, in May 1932, with one of his smaller CDRJC railcars. Success on this occasion inspired the CVR to order an articulated diesel vehicle. By December 1921 it was in service, and very satisfactory it proved to be — albeit subsequent purchase of a smaller diesel tractor proved less beneficial. Curiously, the CVR's last purchase was a steam locomotive, obtained, in 'bargain' circumstances, from a firm of Glasgow scrap merchants in 1934.

Despite the Committee's most valiant efforts, the economic depression of the early 1930s clearly presaged the CVR's inability to survive. A Pole Report in 1934 bluntly recommended closure; but, so loud was the cry this raised locally that the Government saw fit to shelve the issue. Payment of dividends, however, continued to inflict its worrying toll, and, once the Second World War descended, even the County Councils decided they had had enough. A Government Order of December 1941 confirmed closure, and the following year all movable assets of the CVR were disposed of by tender and public auction. No one, surely, could have grudged the measure of poetic justice whereby Henry Forbes secured both diesel items, and other bargain lots, for his beloved County Donegal Railway. That year, too, the CVR's ubiquitous 2–6–2T, No 4 was purchased by the Turf Board of Eire.

LOCOMOTIVES

No	Name	Type	Date built	Makers	Makers number	Withdrawn	Remarks
1	*Caledon*	0–4–2T	1886	Sharp Stewart	3369	1923	Name derived from local village
2	*Errigal*	,,	1886	,,	3370	1942	Name derived from local parish
3	*Blackwater*	,,	1886	,,	3371	1942	Name derived from local river
4	*Fury*	,,	1886	,,	3372	1929	,,
5	*Colebrooke*	,,	1886	,,	3373	1936	Name derived from local village
6	*Erne*	,,	1886	,,	3374	1942	Named derived from lough
7	*Blessingbourne*	0–4–4T	1910	Hudswell Clarke	914	1934	Name derived from CVR Chairman's residence
4	—	2–6–2T	1904	,,	698	1942	Obtained from C&VB Tramway in 1934
Diesel railcar No 1			1932	Walker Bros		1941	Purchased by CDRJC when CVR closed
Diesel tractor No 2			1933	,,		1941	,,

The CVT's first six locos, destined as they were for tramway use, arrived from the Atlas Works equipped with cow-catcher, bell and skirted wheels. The condensing gear which they also bore was later removed as Board of Trade regulations were relaxed. Weighing 24 tons fully laden, these engines worked cab-first at all times, and large oil lamps were mounted high between the rear windows of the cab. Later, the lamps were lowered, and, later still, small acetylene-burning lamps were substituted. The CVT's wet, steep track demanded wheel sanding, and, after experiment, gravity, it was found, gave the best results. New boilers were fitted to the locos over the years as occasion demanded.

The only other steam locomotive ordered new, No 7, was built to the specification of Gustav Akerlind, the CVR's longest-serving Locomotive Superintendent (1889–1922). Introduced in 1910, the 0–4–4 tank proved a dismal failure. Adhesion was sadly lacking, and CVR men hated her, so much so that in 1925 she put in only 188 miles. In 1926 matters improved little at 733 miles, and she was put up for sale. No bids were ever made, and *Blessingbourne* lay idle in Auchnacloy yard for years to come. Latterly, she and a completely worn out *Caledon* were swopped for a Castlederg & Victoria Bridge Tramway engine.

The latter was a particularly interesting acquisition. When the Castlederg closed down early in 1933, the CVR management, in a flash of inspiration, offered their two 'albatrosses' in exchange for a 2–6–0T that Messrs Arnold Young & Co Ltd of Glasgow had bought for scrap. Once the deal was struck, the loco travelled by GNR(I) well-wagon from Victoria Bridge to Macguiresbridge, whence she proceeded to Auchnacloy under her own steam. There, the CVR workshops attended to her renovation, and she re-emerged as a 2–6–2 tank, still bearing her Castlederg number, 4, and still nameless. The one-sided skirting previously carried had been removed, and a new bunker had been fitted in lieu of the boiler–top coal hoppers which the CVR normally employed. With the improved visibility this offered to drivers, No 4 was thereafter usually driven in forward gear. A considerable asset, it served the CVR well to the bitter end.

So, too, did the diesel car acquired by the CVR in 1932, notwithstanding its involvement in two (minor) accidents in its time. Through its employment considerable economies were effected, and by January 1939 it completed 304,000 miles. The CDRJC squeezed a further 348,977 miles from it before events there terminated in 1960. The CVR's second diesel purchase, the rail tractor, proved rather more limited in application. But it, too, passed ultimately to the CDRJC, and there it enjoyed a new lease of life.

The CVR's diesel railcar No 1 lingered long enough after the CDRJ closed down to find a home in the Belfast Transport Museum.

Industrial

Despite its partiality for 3-foot gauge metals, Ireland was never able to develop industrial narrow gauge railways at a commensurate pace, for, thanks to a historic paucity of investment capital from the mainland, particularly where Southern Ireland was concerned, the country was largely left to make the most of its agricultural origins.

Yet, interestingly, one of Ireland's oldest industrial narrow gauge lines could claim a pedigree much akin to that of one of Wales' larger slate-carrying railways; for, when it first commenced operations in August 1854, the Carnlough Limestone Railway, on the Antrim coast, employed both horses and a cable-operated standard gauge main line. Later, a 3 ft 6 in gauge section, introduced between Carnlough Harbour and Tullyaughter Quarries, found a use for steam traction; whence a solitary 0–4–0T, known as *Otter*, was supplied by Andrew Barclay Sons & Co of Kilmarnock in 1898. Sad to say, the Welsh analogy persisted, and mineral productivity petered out early in the twentieth century.

Next, a more recently acquired industrial concern, the British Aluminium Company, chose to employ narrow gauge metals to convey ore from factory to quayside. Its 3-foot gauge line to Larne Harbour opened in 1900, and three small Peckett 0–4–0Ts — later listed by their makers, incidentally, as their 'Aluminium' Class — pursued busy lives. The last narrow gauge railway in Co Antrim to use a steam locomotive, in fact, the BAC line closed in 1960. Fortunately, 0–4–0T No 1 (Works No 1026/1904) survived to pass into private hands, and now functions happily on Shane's Castle Railway as *Tyrone*. No 2 (1097/1906) resides in the Belfast Transport Museum.

Then, in 1925, a much more extensive deployment of narrow gauge steam came the Irish Free State's way when a consortium of German firms undertook construction of a massive hydro-electric scheme on the River Shannon, at Ardnacrusha, near Limerick. The network of 600 and 900mm metals which was subsequently laid, and the locomotives which worked thereon, were, not unnaturally, German. Consequently, everything vanished once the project was completed in 1930.

In many parts of Ireland peat has long been a traditional source of domestic fuel. Irish railways, too, have dabbled from time to time with the feasibility of operating peat-burning locomotives. But it took the effects of the Second World War to see an Irish Peat Commission, the Bord na Mona, firmly established in 1946. Initially, large existing bogs at Glenties, Co Donegal, and Clonsast, Co Offaly, were developed. Soon many other areas were being exploited, and over a period of years the Bord na Mona created a positive web of 3-foot gauge lines to assist in the process of transporting turf from bog to processing plant. Although most were operated by diesel locomotives, there was one notable exception, in Co Offaly, where three turf-burning 0–6–0WTs, obtained from Andrew Barclay Sons & Co in 1949, worked between peat bogs and the ESB power station at Portarlington. Needless to say, diesel locomotives have since taken over. A second major Irish industrial process, that of processing sugar beet, chose to rely on standard gauge metals.

But to find the most astonishing of Ireland's narrow gauge ventures one had to venture further east, into what was to become Eire's capital city.

GUINNESS BREWERY, DUBLIN

Opened: 1874
Closed: 1947
Gauge: 1 ft 10 in

The Brewery belonging to Arthur Guinness Son & Co Ltd remains almost an industrial monument in Dublin, for, as far back as 1874 an extensive narrow gauge railway network was laid within its precincts. A spiral tunnel, frequent triangular junctions, and 12-hour working were all early manifestations of today's 'merry-go-round' industrial practice. Then, in 1878, Westminster sanctioned extension of Guinness railway metals into adjoining streets. Thus, the transfer of brewery products over standard gauge track to the Great Southern system became feasible.

The first loco to tread Guinness' narrow gauge metals was an 0–4–0T which was supplied by Sharp Stewart (Works No 2477) in 1875. Then, in 1876, came two, typically eccentric, geared 0–4–0Ts from Stephen Lewin, of Poole. Numbered 2 and 3, they bore the appropriate names of *Hops* and *Malt*. (Similar locomotives are described elsewhere in this book in the section on the Great Laxey Mining Company Tramway.) Within a decade, however, the Brewery's engineer, Samuel Geoghehan, tired of the maintenance problems posed by the Lewin locomotives — the valve gear was much too near the ground and attracted both dirt and damage — and was moved to design a remarkable little 0–4–0, wherein the cylinders and crankshaft were positioned horizontally above the boiler. A coupled wheelbase of only 3 feet also facilitated negotiation of the sharp radius curves which abounded throughout the Brewery. In the prototype, which was built by the

The Guinness Brewery's 18 little 1 ft 10 in gauge steam locos, built in Dublin, soon developed even more remarkable characteristics by being able to be employed in broad gauge wagon shunting activities. No 15, seen here, was supplied by W. Spence of Dublin in 1895, and is now preserved at Stradbally, Co Laois. When built, the loco carried running number 21. (Steamchest)

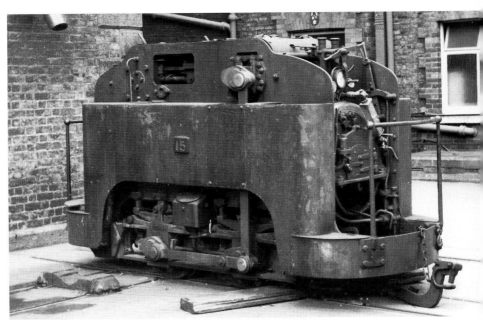

Avonside Engine Co in 1882, steam brakes were fitted, and a modest Ramsbottom boiler, with circular firebox, worked at a pressure of 160 psi. The locomotive weighed only 7 tons 8 cwt, the side tanks held 80 gallons, and the coal capacity was 3½ cwt. The only pity was that the poor driver's operating stance placed him plumb on top of the coal!

Next, Geoghehan unearthed a Dublin ally in William Spence, whose Cork Street Foundry & Engineering Works turned out 18 more of these little locos over the years 1887–1921. They formed, incidentally, the Foundry's entire output of steam locomotives. A little later Spence followed up another ingenious Geoghehan idea by building four very special, though ostensibly quite elementary, standard (5 ft 3 in) gauge haulage trucks. Two were produced in 1888, and one each in 1893 and 1903. Using these, motive power was provided on Brewery 5 ft 3 in tracks simply by employing a hydraulic (later, electric) hoist to lower a narrow gauge engine into a haulage truck frame. The flanges of the loco's wheels then engaged on rollers, which, in turn, meshed with

gears mounted on the truck axles. A gear ratio of 3:1 ensured that narrow gauge loco power sufficed to conduct main line shunting, etc. The whole principle was quite unique, and no similar application has ever been known throughout railway history.

Thus equipped, the Guinness Brewery pursued its peaceful way for decades more. In post-Second World War years, ominously enough, a few diesel locos were also introduced. Then came the crunch, in 1947, when road transport took complete command, and prompted abandonment of the internal railway system. The *coup de grâce* finally came in May 1965, when the 5 ft 3 in link with the GSR's Kingsbridge Yard was also severed.

LOCOMOTIVES

Like many of the Welsh quarry engines, the Guinness locos attracted a great deal of affectionate interest from the railway preservation movement, and six remain intact to this day. Details are given in the accompanying table.

Guinness Brewery — preserved locomotives

No	Built	Withdrawn	Current location
13	1895	1956	Talyllyn Railway Museum, Towyn
15	1895	1957	Irish Steam Preservation Society, Stradbally, Co Laois
17	1902	1962	Guinness Brewery, Dublin
20	1905	1956	Belfast Transport Museum
22	1912	1962	Winn Technology Ltd, Kilbrittain, Cork
23	1921	1965	Amberley Chalk Pits Museum, Sussex

PART 3

English narrow gauge railways

The 19¼-mile journey between the two termini of the Lynton & Barnstaple Railway required 1½ hours, and the gentle nature of travel on the L&BR is beautifully exemplified by this portrait of No 761 Taw as the little Manning Wardle chuffs its way past the foothills of Exmoor en route to Lynton. (Steamchest)

England never *relied* on narrow gauge railways as did Ireland and Wales, for her commercial, geographical and social circumstances were quite different. It follows that almost every English narrow gauge railway was built for its own peculiar reason; though, of course, in the last analysis these reasons lend themselves to broad categorization.

Take one, that of industrial need. It required the Industrial Revolution to stimulate such basic mineral deposits, coal apart, as England possessed; and with it came the Age of Steam. But, in England, George Stephenson's persuasive advocacy of the 4 ft 8½ in gauge, plus ready provision of capital throughout the country, ensured that the battle of the gauges emerged not as one between standard and narrow gauge, but as a comparatively short-term contest between standard and broad gauge metals. Brunel lost the battle and, almost without exception, England's coal mines, iron foundries and mineral workings gratefully accepted inclusion in the maze of standard gauge metals which subsequently evolved.

The lone industrial exceptions form the first category in this consideration of English narrow gauge. Cornwall and Devon mined copper and clay long before railways existed, and, like Wales, they had developed their own system of crude horse-drawn tramroads. As the terrain was less mountainous, however, a sub-standard gauge of around 4 feet, the 'Dartmoor' gauge, generally sufficed. Conversely, the few mine workings which advanced to the use of steam chose that occasion to think afresh. The result, both in Cornwall and Devon, was a positive miscellany of gauges, ranging from 1 ft 11½ in to 4 ft 2 in! Two of England's narrowest railways, the Snailbeach and the Ashover, aiming to transport lead and stone to their nearest standard gauge outlet, exercised economy to the nth degree, and, inspired by Colonel Stephens, even tried to keep afloat by purchasing ex-WD equipment after the First World War. Inevitably, fate was unkind. And so it was to all nine railways in this category. Their case histories vary so widely, however, that each is best left to tell its own story:

English industrial narrow gauge railways

Name	Traction		Railway closed	Main mineral handled	Standard gauge railhead	Gauge (ft in)	
	Horse	Steam					
Peak Forest	1800	—	1926	Limestone	Canal at Bugsworth	4	2
Severn & Wye	1809	1864	1883	Coal	Lydney	3	8
Redruth & Chasewater	1824	1854	1915	Copper and coal	Devoran	4	0
Stratford & Moreton Tramway	1826	—		Coal and stone		4	0
Pentewan	1829	1874	1918	Clay	St Austell	2	6
Caldon Low Quarries	1847	1877	1934	Limestone	Caldon Junction	3	6
Snailbeach	—	1877	1947	Lead	Pontesbury	2	4
Marland Light Railway	—	1881	1970	Clay	Torrington	3	0
Ashover	—	1925	1950	Stone	Clay Cross	1	11½

In England, more than anywhere else in the UK, the Industrial Revolution brought unique financial prosperity to masses of working class people. Certainly, in the last quarter of the nineteenth century steady employment meant regular wages, and people's appetites expanded accordingly to meet this new phenomenon. Pleasure trips to quite distant parts, even

holidays, could be undertaken for the first time; and England's numerous railway companies were ready and willing to meet this new demand. Trips to the coast, too, offered hitherto untold delight, and, so popular did the habit become that a new breed of pleasure-giving, passenger-carrying narrow gauge lines opened up to meet the new boom. Some used steam; others, more daring, went electric. Whatever, six of these narrow gauge ventures form the second category, and three more, rather different in calibre — the Wolverton & Stony Stratford Tramway, the Lynton & Barnstaple and the Leek & Manifold Railways — have been added. The first pair, while quite happy to function as common carriers of both goods and humans, were undoubtedly born of human need. The Leek & Manifold succeeded, rightly or wrongly, in transporting narrow gauge comfort to extraordinary heights. All, of course, traversed routes where the introduction of standard gauge metals would have been a financial impossibility. But, again, generalization is misleading. Let each account for itself:

'Pleasure abounding'

Name	Opened	Closed	Standard gauge railhead	Gauge (ft in)	
Southwold	1879	1929	Halesworth	3	0
Volk's Electric	1883	Still extant	Brighton	2	8½
Alford & Sutton Tramway	1884	1889	Alford	2	6
Wolverton & Stony Stratford Tramway	1887	1926	Wolverton	3	6
Southend Pier	1890	1978 (Re-opened 1986	Southend	3	6
Rye & Camber	1895	1940	Rye	3	0
Brighton & Rottingdean	1896	1901	Brighton	2	8½
Lynton & Barnstaple	1898	1935	Barnstaple	1	11½
Leek & Manifold	1904	1935	Waterhouses	2	6

A third, and final, category, smaller in number but just as diverse in composition, emanated from the art of war rather than peace. Contained therein is the narrow gauge element of a considerable domestic track mileage which, for over a century from 1824 onwards, was exclusively operated by Army and Navy personnel.

Naval and military

Name	Opened	Closed	Standard gauge railhead	Gauge (ft in)	
Royal Arsenal Railway, Woolwich	1824	1969	Plumstead	1	6
Chatham Dockyard Railway	1871	Late 1930s	Gillingham	1	6
Hoo Ness Island Railway, Admiralty	c1890	—	—	2	6
Chattenden & Upnor Railway, Admiralty	1898	1961	—	2	6

Industrial

PEAK FOREST TRAMWAY

Opened: 1800
Closed: 1926
Gauge: 4 ft 2 in

Long before the Railway Age exploded throughout the length and breadth of England, the Peak District of Derbyshire was experiencing its own difficulties in transporting limestone to much more affluent surrounding areas. Coalfields, agricultural oases and textile mills all lay nearby, offering tempting markets; but humping limestone down from the heights remained a well-nigh insuperable problem. Then, towards the turn of the century, came not one solution, but two. The Cromford Canal was opened in February 1792, and, on the north-west side, the Peak Forest Canal followed on 1 May 1800. Between the two canals, however, there still lay another problem — a valuable stretch of high lime-stone country which was totally unsuitable for further canal development.

In the event two railways came to the Peak District's rescue, a standard gauge concern known as the Cromford & High Peak Railway, and the 4 ft 2 in gauge Peak Forest Tramway. Only 6 miles long, as opposed to the C&HPR's 34 miles, it is the tramway alone which concerns us. Let one more analogy, however, throw light on their respective histories. The C&HPR, an independent company, had to fight its own way towards profitability; the PFT, born as part of the Peak Forest Canal undertaking, was less concerned with things financial.

The date of the Peak Forest Tramway's origin has been lost in the mists of antiquity. All we know is that it was not the first tramroad in Derbyshire, and that its single track was probably completed by the time the Peak Forest Canal opened in 1800. Except for portions which passed under a bridge, and through a 100-yard tunnel at Chapel Milton, its whole length was relaid double in 1803. The original rail, L-shape in section, weighed 56 lbs to the yard, and was laid in 3-foot lengths. Iron slippers, pegged to stone sleepers, held the rails in place. Then, in the

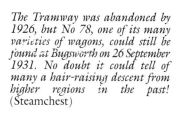

A quiet Sunday morning at Bugsworth Basin. Peak Forest Railway wagons which did not enter the loading shed on the right, whence their contents were discharged into waiting barges below, were dealt with by the circular tipper on the left. It all seems rather primitive, yet the arrangement was capable of handling 2,000 tons of limestone per day. (Steamchest)

The Tramway was abandoned by 1926, but No 78, one of its many varieties of wagons, could still be found at Bugsworth on 26 September 1931. No doubt it could tell of many a hair-raising descent from higher regions in the past! (Steamchest)

1860s, the lot was replaced by 9 ft-12 ft lengths of steel rail. Produced at the Manchester, Sheffield & Lincolnshire Railway Company's works at Gorton, the new rail was of the same section and weight as its cast-iron predecessor.

Running south-east to north-west, the tramway consisted of two sections, and horse traction was always the order of the day. The first section, or Bottom Line as it was known, ran from the Canal basin at Bugsworth and, after 3 miles of steady gradient, it reached the village of Chapel-en-le-Frith. Then came the Plane, a 512 yard 1 in 8 incline which lifted the line another 209 feet. At the top of this incline sidings were built to hold loaded wagons as they arrived from various quarries, 1,100 feet and more above sea level. On the Plane wagons heading for the canal were selectively released downhill by means of a large wooden drum and winding gear. A hemp rope line was first used, but this was replaced in 1809 by a 1,075-yard-long chain, and again by endless wire rope in the 1870s. How many casualties occurred as trains of wagons, with their rudimentary braking system, negotiated four overbridges and six level crossings will never be known. At the bottom of the Plane, the wagons were reassembled into trains, and horse teams hauled them down to Bugsworth basin.

Peak Forest metals were doubled by 1803, except for a section through Stoddart Tunnel, bear Chapel-en-le-Frith. The resultant bottleneck caused considerable congestion at both ends of the Tramway, and safety regulations were often flouted, with unfortunate results! This photograph of the trackbed was taken in September 1931. (Steamchest)

Peak Forest wagons, roughly made of iron plates, could carry 45 cwt of limestone, and as each arrived at Bugsworth it was diverted in one of two directions. Either it entered a large loading shed, whence its contents were shot into barges below, or it was moved on to a jetty, where a circular wooden wagon tipper guaranteed the stone a similar fate. In the early days some 2,000 tons of stone per day were moved thus. Towards the end of the century traffic dropped to 750 tons. A quarter of a mile before Bugsworth a branch left the main tramway, and plunged through a narrow tunnel, 200 yards long, to service a local stone quarry. Despite its limitations, this branch remained in use until 1915. Beyond the Canal Basin another branch passed on through Bugsworth village before terminating at some old limekilns.

At Chapel-en-le-Frith several branches fanned off to serve an iron foundry and sundry warehouses. From here to the summit the rule was 'coal in, stone out'. The Top Line commenced after the Plane was ascended, and a further climb, mostly at 1 in 200, took the tramway 2½ miles on to Dove Holes Dale, the region of limestone quarries. Top Line horses were stabled here, and Bottom Line horses at Chapel-en-le-Frith. The Plane apart, five-horse teams handled empty or coal-laden wagons, and two-horse teams were used for loads of corn, provisions, and other lighter goods. A waggoner, plus a boy, conducted horse-drawn loads up the line. On the return journey the waggoner rode down with a gravity train, and the horses descended on foot under the care of the 'nipper' boy. No free horse rides here!

The only type of signalling used was a rather crude form of coloured disc on the Plane itself. Yet, despite that, and its complete forswearance of mechanical traction, the Peak Forest Tramway lasted

well into the twentieth century. In 1830, Peak Forest Canal shares held a value of £88, and each attracted a dividend of £3. Then, as railways in the area expanded, full control of the Canal Company passed to the Manchester, Sheffield & Lincolnshire Railway on 2 August 1863. This became the Great Central Railway in August 1897, and so matters remained until Grouping in 1923.

One year later the Top Line between Dove Holes and Chapel Milton was closed. By 1926 the Tramway was completely disused, and in 1936 T. W. Ward of Sheffield was given the task of lifting the track. Considerable parts of the tram route were sold to private individuals by early post-war years, but subsequent research into the Peak Forest Canal by voluntary societies has since seen major parts of the canal, at least, restored to near original condition. Several relics of the tramway have been unearthed in the process, and the National Railway Museum at York today houses an example of tramway track, together with a small wagon.

SEVERN & WYE RAILWAY & CANAL COMPANY

Opened: 1809 (Converted to broad gauge in 1869)
Gauges: 3 ft 6 in and 3 ft 8 in

The Forest of Dean is still a remarkable area of 27,000 acres, and many people living in and around it still hold tightly to such traditional privileges as the right to hew wood and cut stone. Beneath the Forest, too, is a coalfield covering thousands of acres, and a few mines are still worked. Nearly two centuries ago human endeavour in winning coal from the Forest area grew so in intensity, and was so hindered by bad roads that the concept of horse-drawn tramroads gained ready acceptance. Much argument ensued, various schemes were preferred, but eventually, on 10 June 1809, the Lydney & Lydbrook Railway Act received Royal Assent.

The plan was to build a tramroad from Lydbrook, near the River Wye, to Lower Forge, which lay not far from Lydney and the mouth of the Severn. Eight short associated branches were also incorporated. A further Act of 21 June 1810 changed the undertaking's name to the Severn & Wye Railway & Canal Company, and authorized introduction of further facilities. These included the construction of a canal and harbour at Lydney. Contracts for the various sections were duly awarded, and it was established that a desirable gauge would be 3 ft 6 in. Operational prac-

tice would be simplicity itself: The railway company would provide the track and collect tolls; hauliers would find their own horses and wagons. The Act made no mention of passenger traffic.

As can be imagined, such a primitive combination of tramroad and punitive rules hardly made for a life of peace. Over the next decade or two hauliers grumbled, and frequently offended Authority by committing such offences as allowing their horses to trot. This had an adverse effect on the track. Quite often, too, the railway company's weighing scales were a source of argument and complaint. Certainly, the company's legal ability to recover unpaid tolls by confiscating wagons and contents hardly endeared itself to hard-pressed hauliers.

Again, the track itself was fragile. Its flanged cast-iron plates rested on stone blocks, and gave such trouble that by 1848 'a change of line for heavy traffic' saw wrought-iron plates introduced. The gauge had already been increased to 3 ft 7 in in 1840; and three years later it crept further to 3 ft 8 in. Traders naturally had difficulty in providing wagons which rode accurately. Increasingly, too, the merits of steam locomotion were being urged upon those who ran the tramroad. They, in turn, shrank from the expense and difficulty of converting miles of steep and intricate branchways. Latterly, a Commons Committee on Woods and Forests, deluged with complaints of needlessly high tolls, urged reformation; and, at a meeting held on 22 October 1852, Severn & Wye shareholders approved a proposal that the company should become carriers, and use steam locomotives. An appropriate Act was secured on 15 August 1853.

Even then the Severn & Wye dragged its feet, and 1864 arrived before the first of five 0–4–0 well tanks arrived at Lydney. All were built by Fletcher Jennings to a patent design. Figures issued in 1869 indicate that, collectively, the S&W locos worked about 50,000 tons of coal per year down to Lydney, ie some 70 wagon loads a day. By that date, however, S&W affairs had taken yet another grotesque twist, for, under pressure from the Great Western Railway, broad gauge track was introduced in 1868. Part of the line was converted by April 1869, by which time loco No 5 had been widened accordingly. A new broad gauge convertible 0–6–0T followed from Fletcher Jennings in November 1868, and during 1869 tramroad tanks Nos 2 and 3 were also altered to the broad gauge.

One final change overtook the S&W's remarkably complicated career in May 1872, when, following the example of the GWR's South Wales line, the Severn & Wye management decided to adopt standard gauge. For a while standard and broad gauge tracks functioned together in places. Then, ultimately, conversion was completed — a 3 ft 8 in gauge tramroad faded steadily into legend.

LOCOMOTIVES

No	Type	Date built	Makers	Maker's number	Cost	Remarks
1	0–4–0WT	1864	Fletcher Jennings	45	£695	Withdrawn 1879. Served as motive power for a canal dredger thereafter
2	,,	1865	,,	53	£720	Both converted to broad gauge (1869), then standard gauge (1872). Later sold
3	,,	1865	,,	54	£720	
4	,,	1865	,,	55	£720	Sold in 1872 as 3 ft 8 in gauge tramway loco
5	0–6–0WT	1865	,,	60	£1,008	Converted to broad gauge (1868), then standard gauge (1872). Later sold

Locos Nos 2 and 5, when converted to standard gauge in 1872, were given the names *Little John* and *Forester*. Once the Severn Bridge Railway was opened on 17 October 1879, the two companies amalgamated to form the Severn & Wye and Severn Bridge Railway Company. A Receiver had to be appointed by 1883, whence the undertaking became a joint line of the Midland and Great Western Railway companies.

REDRUTH & CHASEWATER RAILWAY

Opened: 30 January 1826
Closed: 25 September 1915
Gauge: 4 ft 0 in

Long before it became a happy hunting ground for tourists, Cornwall was a hive of mining and industrial activity. Tin was mined at first, but by the mid-nineteenth century Cornwall's output of copper ore, sent perforce for smelting to South Wales, where coal was readily available, had captured world markets. Inevitably, transport of copper ore to the coast for shipment, and the reciprocal carriage of coal inland to feed Cornwall's growing army of steam pumping engines, demanded the introduction of horse-drawn tramroads. Thus evolved Cornwall's first public railway, the Poldice Tramway, a primitive plateway built by a group of Cornish mine and land owners. Opened in 1809, it linked copper mines inland, including one called Poldice, with Portreath, a thriving little port on the north coast. An earlier proposition had postulated a canal; but no doubt the sponsors' close business association with the colliery trade in South Wales, where tramroads were by now firmly entrenched, influenced the final choice of rail.

The horse-drawn tramway was such a commercial success that others were bound to follow. One copper group in particular, Consolidated Mines, was increasing production at such a rate that conventional transport by pack horse could no longer cope. All signs were therefore propitious when a group of Cornish mining adventurers decided to meet in London in January 1824. They ended the meeting resolved to pursue installation of a mineral tramroad, some 10 miles long, between Redruth and Chasewater.

Capital of £20,000 was readily subscribed, and Royal Assent was duly given on 17 June that year. A gauge of 4 feet, once common in South Wales, but latterly superseded by standard gauge, was chosen; and, after official opening celebrations in 1826, the primitive tramroad, with its wrought-iron rails, cast-iron chairs, and rough granite blocks, was put to work. Teams of horses, on a ratio of one horse per 2-ton wagon, were the order of the day. The line was single-tracked, with frequent passing loops, and it contained gradients of 1 in 35 in its drop to the coast.

Eventually, and rather significantly, the carriage of coal began to approach that of copper in importance, and, so satisfactory were profits that the proprietors were quite happy to march with the times by introducing locomotive haulage. An appropriate Act was passed on 9 May 1853, and relaying with heavier bullheaded rail commenced without delay. During that year Redruth's horses finished in a blaze of glory, by handling a total of 94,764 tons of copper and coal — even while relaying was in progress.

Midway through the summer of 1854 two 0–4–0 saddle tanks arrived from Glasgow. Extremely crude in appearance, each was devoid of running plate and cab, and sported huge wooden dumb buffers. Square saddle tanks were topped by a clumsy toolbox and chimney of inordinate length. Nevertheless, with new 5-ton wagons also provided, they proved themselves capable of handling 50-ton loads. By 1857, however, intensive daily working of the two locomotives, with consequent difficulty of maintenance, made provision of a third loco imperative. *Spitfire*

Once Spitfire, *Redruth's most powerful engine, arrived on the scene in 1859, at the quite considerable cost of £1,340, it concentrated on heavy work – delivering coal to the copper mines inland, and returning with wagon-loads of copper ore. These were dealt with at harbour level by the Redruth's two smaller 0–4–2STs.* (Author's Collection)

arrived in 1859, at a cost of £1,340, again a Neilson saddle tank, but six-coupled this time. The new loco's additional power was promptly deployed on the steeper section of the line above Nangiles, and the smaller engines took to marshalling trains at the lower level. Coal went up to the mines — copper ore came back. Passengers were never carried, though miners scrounged many a dangerous lift. Meanwhile, the railway company's engagement in local shipping was largely discarded in 1863. It had never been a success.

Business flourished. The year 1865 brought a new peak in railway traffic, and the company set about tidying its locomotive affairs. New workshops were built at Devoran, and the two smaller engines were overhauled, *Miner* to the extent of re-emerging as an 0–4–2 saddle tank. Then, within a year, the world copper boom began to fade. Soon many once prosperous mining areas of Cornwall were reduced to deserts of unemployment. Miners emigrated by the thousand. R&C traffic held firm for a while, but closure of an important local copper mine in 1870 had devastating effects. The shipment of copper ore plummeted to unheard of depths, and the only other source of income, that of handling coal, dropped uncomfortably. Attempts were made to stimulate production of both tin and china clay in the area, but these were totally offset by floods in 1876–77 which completely silted Devoran's all-important shipping channel.

Prospects were now so bleak that the R&C opted to go into Receivership in December 1877. By now one locomotive was handling the line's total traffic throughout the 1880s, and all through this period *Smelter* was usually to be found at the back of Devoran loco shed. By 1890 the amount of copper handled fell to derisory levels. Fortunately, coal continued to provide railway employment. By 1900, however, R&C receipts were barely covering expenses. Debenture interests payments had already been suspended, and when coal tonnage fell disastrously in 1915 the decision was made to close the line. Thus, on 25 September 1915, *Miner* worked a last train down to Devoran. Despite her old domed haycock firebox and rough and ready look, she had given 60 years of faithful service.

Permission to abandon the railway was granted on 19 April 1918, and within two months everything went by tender. The faithful *Miner* was used to lift the rails. Thence she and her other, less reliable, colleagues were reduced to scrap. So, too, was Devoran's function as a port. As if the death of the Redruth & Chasewater Railway were not enough a steady decline in coastal shipping made doubly certain of that.

LOCOMOTIVES

Name	Type	Date built	Makers	Scrapped	Remarks
Miner	0–4–0ST	1854	Neilson	1918	} Both altered to 0–4–2ST within a year or so
Smelter	,,	1854	,,	1918	
Spitfire	0–6–0ST	1859	,,	1918	

STRATFORD & MORETON TRAMWAY

Opened: 5 September 1826
Closed: *circa* 1889
Gauge: 4 ft 0 in

The Stratford & Moreton Tramway was incorporated on 28 May 1821, and once work got under way its 4-foot gauge line was constructed under the direction of Thomas Telford. Primitive fish-bellied cast-iron rails were laid on stone blocks at 1 yard intervals along its 17-mile length. The tramway opened for traffic on 5 September 1826, and, worked entirely by horse traction, it was used to supply coal and stone between the Stratford-on-Avon and Moreton areas, while agricultural produce was ferried back in return. Then, in 1847 the Oxford, Worcester & Wolverhampton Railway took possession of the tramway, and it was practically abandoned by the year 1859. Passenger traffic into Stratford ceased that year.

The following year, on 1 July, the West Midland Railway was formed by the amalgamation of the OW&WR with two other companies. Three years later, on 1 August 1863, the West Midland was itself officially absorbed by the Great Western Railway, and in 1889 a part of the old Stratford & Moreton Tramway was converted to a steam-operated branch — that between Moreton-in-Marsh and Shipston-on-Stour. The tramway track went for wartime salvage in 1918.

Despite the conversion, the Shipston-on-Stour branch of the GWR carried many a relic of tramway days. Although closed to passenger traffic from 8 July 1929, goods traffic continued. The year 1946

The last wagon to see service on the Stratford & Moreton Tramway survived to be placed on a short section of original track and exhibited publicly at Stratford-on-Avon. It is seen here on 27 October 1962. (Steamchest)

found the branch being laid with heavier track, presumably to permit the passage of heavier locomotives, and even at that late stage several of the stone blocks on which the tramway rails had been laid could still be seen at places where the GWR branch deviated from the old tramway route. Remarkably, the old route was still marked by GWR boundary posts, quite often some distance removed from the branch.

PENTEWAN RAILWAY

Opened: 1 July 1829
Closed: 2 March 1918
Gauge: 2 ft 6 in

Even in 1739 ecological problems were being identified in Cornwall; one writer of the period laments 'the obstruction being caused in the pretty little port of Pentewan by the bar of sand brought down from the tin works'. By 1830, however, many of the smaller tin mines had closed, and Pentewan, hitherto a victim of industry, suddenly found itself the possible beneficiary of a new trade — clay mining. Large deposits of kaolin or china clay, a decomposition of granite, had been discovered in the St Austell area. Prospects, in fact, were such that a prominent landowner, Sir Christopher Hawkins, saw fit to invest

Narrow gauge tender locomotives were a rare enough phenomenon in England, but Pentewan's bizarre appearance exceeded all normal limits. Both loco and tender were outside-framed, and the outside cylinders were a mere 7 inches ×12 inches. A chimney of outsize length dominated a domeless boiler and raised firebox. The total heating surface was only 126.5 sq ft, and the wheels were of 20-inch diameter. No cab, of course. (Author's Collection)

Trewithen, *a second version supplied by Manning Wardle in 1886, had slightly larger cylinders and boiler. Local complaints, however, must have been heeded, for a capacious cab was fitted. Both locos only lasted some 25 years in Pentewan Railway service* (Author's Collection)

£22,000 in the construction of a new harbour at Pentewan. Once the harbour was completed in 1826, plans were immediately launched to establish a tramroad link between Pentewan and St Austell. Parliamentary sanction would not be necessary.

In the event, the 4-mile tramroad cost £5,732 to build. A public notice, dated 1 July 1829, intimated the railway's readiness to serve. Presumably this post-dated actual operations, for a boy was killed on the line two days earlier. Fortunately, this was the Pentewan's one and only fatality. The gauge chosen, 2 ft 6 in, was a curious one for Britain, though, oddly enough, it was later to achieve considerable popularity elsewhere in the British Empire. Pentewan's line, meantime, was part gravity-worked, part horse-drawn. Ironically, sand, this time from the new china clay workings, still continued to create

problems as it piled up at Pentewan. Resolute attempts were made in 1843–44 to clear the harbour, but the problem was never satisfactorily resolved.

For its first 45 years the Pentewan Railway pursued an undistinguished career. Plagued from time to time by silting, flooding, and intrusion by the broad gauge Cornwall Railway, it eventually re-surfaced under new management, on 20 February 1873, as the Pentewan Railway & Harbour Company Ltd. Fresh capital of £30,000 was raised, the dock and railway were leased from the Hawkins family, and an intriguing name appeared when J. B. Fell, well-known exponent of central-line adhesion, was appointed temporary Engineer. Later that year work began on conversion from horse tramway to locomotive worked railway.

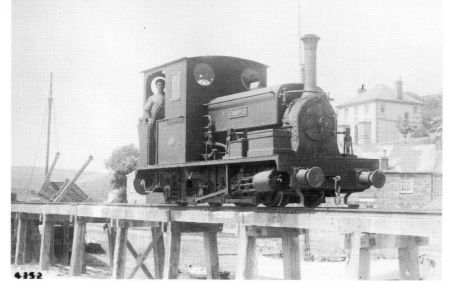

The undoubted favourite of Pentewan loco men was Canopus, *a much more conventional 0–6–2T supplied by Manning Wardle in 1901. Outside frames and long chimney still applied, however.* Canopus *received the melancholy distinction of handling the demolition train when Pentewan tracks were lifted in 1918.* (Author's Collection)

4352

The Pentewan's first locomotive, similarly named, arrived at St Austell around February 1874, though a petition to the House of Lords by rival interests, headed by the Cornwall Railway, successfully denied her immediate début on Pentewan metals. Eventually, however, by 7 August 1874 the company was formally reconstituted as the St Austell & Pentewan Railway Harbour & Dock Company, and the requisite Bill also sanctioned introduction of passenger traffic, plus construction of two northward extensions. As it happened, neither event ever materialized, for the company had trouble enough scraping initial capital together. Nor did its troubles end there. In 1877 the GWR, having taken over the working of its two major Cornish rivals, created further havoc in the Pentewan's economy by sponsoring cheap export of clay via Fowey. As a direct consequence of this unfriendly act, the Pentewan Company gradually faded out of existence. Thus, in November 1881, the dock and railway reverted to Hawkins family possession in lieu of unpaid rent.

One can only presume that the Pentewan concern lowered its rates subsequently to meet a still expanding china clay industry; for, after a period of comparative inactivity in the early 1880s, things began to undergo a change for the better — and even culmi-

nated in a profit of £1,206 for the year 1889.

Human nature being what it is, the very first sign of recovery sparked off a miscellany of new and optimistic schemes. The old extension *would* be built, the line would be electrified by central rail, and a new gauge of 3 feet adopted! Despite fierce opposition from the GWR and its associates, a new company was actually formed to implement these proposals. In a positive fever of excitement, capital was pitched at an absurdly high figure of £80,000. In reality, only £1,131 was raised by the end of 1890, and in 1892 a second Act was quietly passed authorizing abandonment of the project. The Pentewan Railway, left to pursue the even tenor of its way, soldiered on, shipping clay. The only passenger traffic it ever conducted had emerged by now in the shape of annual free Sunday School excursions between St Austell and Pentewan. On such occasions the chil-

The Pentewan Railway's last acquisition, Pioneer, *came from the Royal Navy in 1913. Included in this photograph, taken at Pentewan Harbour, is the 1873 saloon coach which was strictly reserved for use by Sir Christopher Hawkins' family. Children on the Pentewan's annual free Sunday School picnics travelled in open wagons.* (Author's Collection)

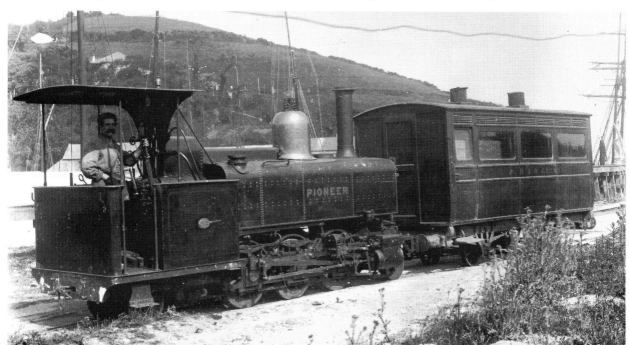

dren were carried in open wagons. The company's lone carriage, built in 1873, remained stoutly reserved for private use by the Hawkins family.

By the turn of the century a new trade in sand arrived providentially to bolster a slightly declining clay traffic, and *Trewithen*, a locomotive which had replaced *Pentewan* in 1886, was, in turn, pensioned off in favour of *Canopus*, a large 0–6–2 tank, again from Manning Wardle. Powerful and sturdy, *Canopus* was able latterly to replace horse traction on the upper section. By now even the harbour was in good fettle, though still susceptible to silting when gales raged. 1913 arrived, and the Pentewan acquired its last locomotive, *Pioneer*, a rather unconventional second-hand 2–6–2 saddle tank.

Alas, the year 1913 also ushered in grave events, for the combination of a clay workers' strike that very year, plus the outbreak of war in 1914, sufficed to decimate the Pentewan's clay traffic. Even coal

traffic to the St Austell Gas Co ceased after 1915. Pentewan Harbour, meanwhile, was incapable of expanding, or rectifying its periodic hazards, to meet wartime demands. Thus, exactly like Devoran, it slowly perished. The end came in 1918 when a final load of clay travelled to the coast on 29 January. Five weeks later the Pentewan's very last train carried eight tons of sand to a once bustling little harbour.

Concurrently came an 'urgent request' from the Government to sell all Pentewan equipment for use in the field of battle. Little time elapsed ere the two locos, wagons and track were despatched to Sunbury, ostensibly *en route* to France. But it was all rather late in the day, and local opinion in St Austell still insists that no part of the booty ever crossed the English Channel. Whatever did happen to the Pentewan rolling-stock, at least the railway had one consolation: it was spared the agony of facing the post-war years.

LOCOMOTIVES

Name	Type	Date built	Makers	Maker's number	Withdrawn	Remarks
Pentewan	0–6–0	1873	Manning Wardle	461	1896	Cost £925
Trewithen	0–6–0	1886	,,	994	1901	
Canopus	0–6–2ST	1901	,,	1547	1918	Cost £1,051
Pioneer	2–6–2ST	1903	Yorkshire Engine Co	757	1918	From Royal Navy's Chattenden & Upnor Railway

The Pentewan first locomotive was distinctive on several counts. To begin with, tender locomotives were a rarity on the British narrow gauge; secondly, *Pentewan*'s chimney was inordinately long, half the overall height of the engine, and her long low boiler was domeless. A tall thin pipe over the firebox conducted steam away from the driver — which was just as well, for not a scrap of protection was provided for the locomotive crew. So unconventional, in fact, was *Pentewan*'s design that one has only to remember that J. B. Fell was Company Engineer at the time to suspect that ultimate conversion to Fell's patented horizontal guide-wheel system may well have been in mind. In any case, neither *Pentewan* nor her sister locomotive, *Trewithen*, lasted very long on the Cornish railway's rough track; and the arrival of a much more conventional 0–6–2ST, *Canopus*, in 1901 must have come as a welcome relief to Pentewan's enginemen, tired of trying to maintain water levels in a desperately shallow space over the firebox. Even *Trewithen*'s roomy cab hardly helped solve *that* problem!

The Pentewan's fourth locomotive was again a complete departure from precedent. Built originally

for use on the Royal Engineers' Chattenden–Lodge Hill instructional line, near Rochester, *Pioneer*'s transition to Cornish metals occurred some years after the Navy took over at Chattenden. There is no reason to suppose that the Pentewan Railway really required a reserve engine, and one can only assume that a rare opportunity to buy a second-hand 2 ft 6 in gauge loco proved too tempting to resist. *Pioneer* herself was an odd mixture of bar frames, scanty cab, and square saddle tank, while at ground level a miscellany of Walschaerts valve gear, springs and frame almost hid her driving wheels from view. In practice her performance proved superior to the track she was obliged to run on, though the more her capacity for speed occasioned derailments, the more Pentewan men's hearts warmed to dear old *Canopus*.

When the end came in 1918, *Canopus* was selected to haul the demolition train, before being sent to Sunbury. Years later, on 27 January 1924, she was spotted standing disconsolately at a power plant in West Drayton, with lot numbers chalked on her tank sides. Within weeks, she disappeared. *Pioneer*'s history after returning to Sunbury in 1918 still remains an untold story.

CALDON LOW QUARRIES TRAMWAY

Opened: 1847
Closed: 1934
Gauge: 3ft 6 in

On 13 May 1776 the proprietors of the Trent & Mersey Canal Company obtained Parliamentary powers to build a railway, or plateway, from limestone quarries at Caldon Low to a proposed canal basin at Froghall, 684 feet below in the Churnet Valley. Both the canal and the 4-mile-long railway opened on 1 May 1777, and the canal, 93 miles long and built at a cost of £300,000, proved an enormous success. It paid handsome dividends for decades to come, and became, in fact, a vital artery where the welfare of the Potteries was concerned.

Record has it that the course of the original tramroad route was changed in 1783, and that a new route was sought again in 1802, when the Canal Company received powers to construct a double-lined plateway. Five inclined planes were incorporated in its length, and all were worked by the weight of descending wagons. Matters remained thus until the North Staffordshire (Pottery Line) Act of 26 June 1846 saw the Trent & Mersey Canal vested in the North Staffordshire Railway. In the opinion of the NSR's consulting engineer, G. P. Bidder, this simple annexation saved the railway company incalculable expense; and, well aware of the value of the Caldon Low's limestone, and its tramway, the railway undertook a third change of route in 1847. The tramway now consisted of three inclines, and was of 3 ft 6 in gauge. Decades later two 0–4–0 saddle tanks, built by H. Hughes & Co in 1877, arrived on the scene to work the tramway. A Bagnall-built 0–4–0ST followed

at the turn of the century.

The next narrow gauge development in the area came when the Leek & Manifold Valley Light Railway opened in 1904 under Light Railway Act auspices. The NSR, in accepting responsibility for running the L&M, also undertook construction of several associated standard gauge lines. These included a 61-chain branch from Caldon Junction, south of Waterhouses, to Caldon Low quarries. New stone works were about to be started, and the standard gauge branch would offer better outlet facilities than the cable incline to Froghall. When, in fact, the first L & M sod was cut by the Duke of Devonshire, the official NSR party which attended the ceremony used the Caldon Tramway to reach the spot. Once the Waterhouses branch was completed, the NSR management, very typically, began to exploit it to its full advantage. The Railways (Electrical Power) Act of 14 August 1903 enabled power to be used at Caldon Quarries as a tourist attraction, and a cave, opened in 1906, was illuminated by electricity for the purpose of viewing stalactites and stalagmites. The words 'Alight for Froghall Quarries' were added to Waterhouses station nameboard. Froghall was still the official name for the quarry; though one observes the following item which appeared in an NSR public advertisement dated 1909:

'WATERHOUSES, for the Caldon Low Limestone Quarries, the happy hunting ground of the geologist.'

In strange contradiction to the NSR management's proverbially stuffy attitude to Leek & Manifold affairs, so, too, did the following:

MANIFOLD VALLEY TOY RAILWAY — 2 ft 6 in gauge — runs along the Valley of the Manifold

Toad, *one of the twin 0–4–0STs built by Hughes & Co in 1877, looks in good enough condition as it rests at Caldon Low shed. Unnumbered by either the NSR or LMSR, all three Caldon Low locos bore North Staffordshire Railway livery when they were scrapped in situ in 1934.* (Steamchest)

to a point where it sinks into the earth, to reappear at Ham, 4 miles away — the most beautiful scenery in Staffordshire.'

The 'Toy Railway' reference was unkind; but the NSR really meant business when it came to advertising!

The Caldon Low Cable inclines were eventually closed, on 25 March 1920, and from there on all quarry traffic passed to the outside world via Caldon Junction and Waterhouses. By then the quarries were employing some 100 four-wheeled wagons. Their low-fixed sides were flush with the solebars which extended to form dumb wooden buffers. All wheels had inside bearings, and brakes were fitted on one side only. The three saddle tanks worked within the confines of the quarry, and their small loco shed came under the supervision of the shed foreman at Stoke.

Railways were flagging as Grouping approached in the early 1920s. So, too, was Caldon Low limestone traffic, for the NSR registered a loss of £1,180 there during its last year of operation. When the LMS took over, it attempted to revive the Caldon Low's fortunes, but £42,000 spent in 1923 only produced a profit margin of £3,000. The trouble was that ICI Ltd closed its Brummer Mond works at Sandbach in 1920 — and Brummer used to absorb most of Caldon's daily limestone output of 1,000 tons. ICI was now quarrying for itself at Tunstead, near Buxton; and with this, and other, bleak prospects in permanent view, the LMS decided to relinquish ownership. Caldon Low Quarry was accordingly leased to a Sheffield firm in 1934, and the tramway was closed. Four years later the old NSR/LMS link with the Caldon Low was revived at a ceremony held on 12 July 1938 to launch the building of the new Euston station. The LMS Chairman, Lord Stamp, pressing a button, fired a blast at Caldon which yielded 100,000 tons of limestone. Indeed, part of the latter provided a foundation stone for the new LMS terminus.

The Caldon Junction branch to the quarries, originally part of the Leek, Caldon & Hartington Light Railway as authorized in 1899, finally closed for traffic on 1 March 1943. The rails remained, however, and, nearly ten years later, a group of railway enthusiasts took great delight in running a first passenger train over Caldon Low metals.

LOCOMOTIVES

No	Type	Date built	Makers	Remarks
Frog	0-4-0ST	1877	H. Hughes	Not a great deal is known of Caldon Low's three tanks, except that all had 2 ft 3 in diameter wheels and outside cylinders were 7 in x 12 in. All three were scrapped at Caldon Low shed in 1934, still in NSR livery.
Toad	,,	1877	,,	
Bobs	,,	1901	Bagnall	

SNAILBEACH DISTRICT RAILWAYS COMPANY

Opened: 1877
Closed: 14 April 1947
Gauge: 2 ft 4 in

Lead mining in the Stiperstones, a chain of hills south-west of Shrewsbury, had a venerable history which can be traced right back to Roman times, though, of course, for centuries it was conducted on a very modest scale. Poor roads and lack of adequate transport made sure of that. Yet, even when the Railway Mania swept through England the Stiperstone area failed to benefit *per se*, and in 1872 a group of local mining concerns, led by the Snailbeach Mine Co Ltd, resolved to help themselves by sponsoring a narrow gauge railway. In the event an appropriate Act of Parliament in 1873 sanctioned construction of *two* railways, each of 2 ft 4 in gauge. One, 3¼ miles long, was to link Pontesbury, where the GWR and LNWR shared a joint station, with Crowsnest, near Snailbeach village. The other, nearly 2 miles in length, was to carry on from Crowsnest and serve a lead mine at Pennerley. The latter was never built.

Raising the authorized capital of £20,000 for Scheme No 1 alone proved difficult enough. Only those lead mines which were likely to benefit cared to subscribe, while, not surprisingly, the general public evinced little interest in a non-passenger-carrying railway. Meanwhile, Snailbeach Mine, the main beneficiary, was inhibited by law from subscribing more than £2,000; but, thanks to extramural exertions from that direction, and the raising of a £4,000 loan,

work eventually got under way.

The line was opened for traffic in the autumn of 1877. Soon after leaving Pontesbury Junction, where transhipment sidings were located, it took on a 2-mile climb of 1 in 38, before easing slightly as it curved towards Snailbeach. The last half-mile to Crowsnest, where a siding and loading area were collectively dubbed Snailbeach station, was straight. The 40 lb rails were spiked to sleepers, and as the railway was run on a 'one engine in steam' basis, signals were neither provided nor required. Two small saddle tanks were acquired, in 1877 and 1881 respectively.

During its first five years the Snailbeach Railway prospered, with mineral traffic averaging 14,000 tons a year. But once some of the mines closed in 1884 the annual tonnage dropped to 5,500, and payment of 3 per cent on the railway company's Ordinary shares became untenable. By 1887 the Snailbeach directorate were only too glad to hire both their locomotives out to the Glyn Valley Tramway, when that august concern embarked on complete reconstruction of its permanent way. Latterly, anxious to initiate additional income from other, more remote, mines, the Snailbeach Directors resolved to tackle that problem by extending rail services deeper into the Stiperstones area. Proposals for an ambitious extension of 11 more miles, starting beside the parent line at Snailbeach village, were put up to Westminster; the Shropshire Minerals Light Railway Act received Royal Assent on 5 August 1891. Alas, it was too late in the day. Not only was capital impossible to find, but lead mining was slowly dying on its feet.

The SDR management had no option but to shrug off disappointment and soldier on. By the turn

Above *A view, taken near Minsterley on 8 July 1925, of Snailbeach metals as they dived through a very short and rather crudely constructed tunnel.* (LCGB, Ken Nunn Collection)

Below *Snailbeach locomotive shed, also seen in July 1925, was not a model of elegance either. One would never guess from the woebegone appearance of Baldwin 4–6–0T No 3 that Colonel Stephens' comparatively recent arrival had generally smartened up Snailbeach affairs!* (LCGB, Ken Nunn Collection)

of the century annual losses worsened, and seemed certain to spell extinction. Then, quite suddenly, both fortunes and traffic changed. The Ceirog Granite Company opened a quarry at Eastridge, and by the simple expedient of constructing a short branch thereto, the SDR found itself able to offer the granite company an excellent outlet to Pontesbury, 2 miles away. The benefit proved truly mutual, for within a year of opening the branch in 1905 the Snailbeach was conveying record quantities of mineral traffic — so much so, that management's mind turned with relief to the matter of providing additional locomotive power.

The Snailbeach Directors hardly acted with reckless abandon. First, wheels within wheels, the Glyn Valley Tramway lent a Beyer Peacock 0–6–0T for trials. The exercise, unfortunately, proved abortive, for the Glyn Valley engine's 2 ft 4½ in axles did not take kindly to the Snailbeach's slightly narrower gauge track, and the loco was soon returned, with thanks, to its owners. Summoning courage, the SDR then purchased a brand new six-coupled tank from W. G. Bagnall of Stafford. It was named *Dennis* as an appropriate gesture to Sir Henry Dyke Dennis, who was on the Board of both the SDR and the Glyn Valley.

At first the SDR's locomotive purchase seemed totally justified, and during 1909 a new peak was reached, when 38,000 tons of minerals were handled. Then trade dipped again, and latterly even the Snailbeach Debenture interest fell into arrears. This was no temporary lull, and during the First World War stone traffic ceased entirely. Post-war years brought no respite, and by 1920 the SDR would undoubtedly have been wound up had not Colonel H. F. Stephens arrived on the scene.

Whatever his faults, Stephens certainly introduced a personal briskness into railway management wherever he went. Taking over on 1 January 1923, despite inheritance of debts to the tune of £4,531,

the new-broom Directorate immediately set to work. The Eastridge branch rails had already been lifted in 1922. But, elsewhere, most sleepers were replaced, using half-width standard gauge wood, and a section of the line from Pontesbury was relaid with heavier 45 lb rail. Typical, too, of Stephens' opportunism, 30 wagons were purchased, second-hand, from Government sources. *Dennis*, by now in poor condition, was laid aside for thorough overhaul (a service, incidentally, she was never destined to receive!), and in her place came No 2, an 0–4–2 tank from E. C. Cornforth of Stoke. Already 20 years old, it had been built by Kerr Stuart in 1902. Two rather more doubtful acquisitions followed, in the shape of Nos 3 and 4. These were Baldwin-built 4–6–0 tanks, veterans of war service in Europe, and reconditioned by Bagnalls in 1918.

Hearteningly, Stephens' efforts to improve SDR efficiency were not in vain. Traffic blossomed, and reached 26,532 tons in 1938. Lead traffic no longer existed, but a new granite quarry which opened on Callow Hill contrived to produce enough chipped stone to keep the SDR locos fully occupied. Then, gradually, as road lorries intervened, came a decline, and the Snailbeach services waned. Such was the trend that steam working ceased in July 1946, and a hired Fordson tractor, its wheels straddling the 2 ft 4 in track, took over the handling of empty wagons between Pontesbury and Callow Hill, the sole source of traffic.

Truly, the writing was on the wall, and from 14 April 1947, when the Pontesbury–Callow Hill section was leased to Shropshire County Council, the Snailbeach Railway, bowing the knee, ceased to operate any service whatever. For many years its engines, shed and track lay rusting and desolate — as if asleep, and merely awaiting salvation. Alas, the Colonel Stephenses of this world, were they to return, would find little sympathy in our modern industrial society.

LOCOMOTIVES

No	Name	Type	Date built	Makers	Maker's number	Remarks
—	*Belmont*	0–4–2ST	1870s	T. Hughes	—	
—	*Fernhill*	0–6–0ST	1875	Lennox Lange	—	
1	*Dennis*	0–6–0T	1907	Bagnall	—	Withdrawn 1936
2	—	0–4–2T	1902	Kerr Stuart	802	
3	—	4–6–0T	1916	Baldwin	44383	
4	—	4–6–0T	1917	,,	44572	

Light railways built for purely industrial purposes tend to inherit a miscellany of locomotive types, and, as can be seen, the Snailbeach was no exception.

Only one of its five engines was delivered new.

The history of the first two is positively obscure. Perhaps the best that can be said is that *Belmont* appears to have been built during the early 1870s by Hughes Locomotive & Tramway Engine Works Ltd, of Loughborough. Like *Tal-y-llyn*, of Welsh fame, she probably emerged from the workshops as a four-coupled saddle tank, and was later fitted with trailing wheels for stability's sake. *Fernhill*, on the other hand, is reputed to have been supplied by Lennox Lange, of Glasgow. But since research reveals that his firm only *dealt* in locomotives, as opposed to building them, one is inclined to accept an alternative theory that *Fernhill* was, in fact, built by Stephen Lewin in 1875, and, re-gauged from 2 ft 6 in, was later *traded* to the SDR by Lennox Lange.

No doubt, however, hovers around *Dennis*, a straightforward, and very neat, new purchase from W. G. Bagnall Ltd of Stafford in 1907. Bagnall was by then long experienced in industrial locomotive production, despite its comparatively recent origin in 1875. Undoubtedly, lack of attention was the cause of the poor mechanical condition in which Stephens found her when he beamed a critical eye in 1922. After being taken out of service, ostensibly for overhaul, *Dennis* lay for years, unattended, outside Snailbeach shed, and was eventually withdrawn officially in 1936. Her replacement, No 2, though purchased second-hand, arrived with an equally impeccable pedigree, having been built by Kerr Stuart & Co Ltd of Stoke. Originally destined for 2 ft 6 in gauge, her outside framing permitted easy conversion for Snailbeach use. No 2 and *Dennis*, though from different stables, were very similar in appearance.

SDR Nos 3 and 4, typically American in outline, and ruggedly built to withstand the rigours of war service, were rough riders, but, together with No 2, they served their masters faithfully to the end. In Stephens' day instructions were issued that all three engines should be used in careful rotation over 2-3 week periods, and this precaution at least ensured that they were kept in reasonable running order. The only adverse effect of the practice was that all three became unserviceable about the same time, albeit long after Stephens' death in 1931. Faced, therefore, with three unworkable locomotives, and short of both staff and cash, it is no surprise that the SDR management opted to terminate steam working in 1946.

Early SDR wagon stock invariably hovered around the 50 mark. The ravages of the First World War, however, pruned this number severely, hence Col Stephens' alacrity in purchasing 30 more from Government sources in 1922. After that, all SDR wagons were numbered in orderly numerical sequence. One survives to this day, in the safe-keeping of the Welsh Highland Light Railway.

MARLAND LIGHT RAILWAY

Opened: 1 January 1881
Closed: November 1970
Gauge: 3 ft 0 in

For the past three centuries, dead-lake deposits of ball clay, a unique type of mineral found almost exclusively in Devon, have been exploited; and today, the high-quality mineral still finds ready markets all over the world. Certainly North Devon people who lived in the valley of the River Torridge from 1680 onwards were well aware of the phenomenon, and, as the nineteenth century progressed, the sight of horse-drawn carts, full of clay, labouring towards the Torridge Canal became a familiar one. At Town Mills, near the little town of Torridge, the carts were emptied into barges which then carried the valuable cargo on to Bideford and the open sea.

Eventually, in 1880, there came a change, when the North Devon Clay Company, the largest employers in the area, obtained powers to construct a light railway, 3 feet in gauge, between its Peter's Marland works and Torrington, 6 miles away. The line was soon opened, and, interestingly, the Engineer in charge was J. B. Fell, of 'Fell centre rail' and Mont Cenis Railway fame. Fell was 65 years old at the time. A subsequent proposal in 1895 to construct a standard gauge Torrington & Okehampton Railway, which would absorb the route of the narrow gauge railway, failed for financial reasons. Thus, the Marland Railway was left to function unhindered for 25 more years.

Short line though it was, construction of the Marland Railway was not easy, for with the Mere Valley lying between it and its objective, the single narrow gauge line had no option but to accept a stiff climb at 1 in 50 to a point called Summit. Here a passing loop was provided, and after that came a comparatively easy descent of 1 in 45 towards Torrington. Before the latter could be reached, however, a spidery wooden fan viaduct had to be built across the River Torridge. So flimsy was the viaduct that two six-coupled tanks which monopolized all traffic north of Summit were designed with an extra-long wheelbase to ensure that the weight of the locomotives was spread over two supports of the wooden structure. Traffic between Peter's Marland and Summit was handled by a miscellany of smaller tanks which will be described presently.

Not far from Summit, deep in the heart of the Devon countryside, lay a row of terraced houses built by the Clay Company for its workers. They, therefore, travelled to and from Peter's Marland by rail each day. At first, transport was simply a converted form of clay wagon, covered and enclosed, with

Seen in the background of this shunting scene, Marland's 145-foot viaduct across the River Torridge was so flimsy in construction that extra-long wheelbase locomotives were used, in order to spread the weight over two wooden supports. A passing loop was also provided at this spot. (Steamchest)

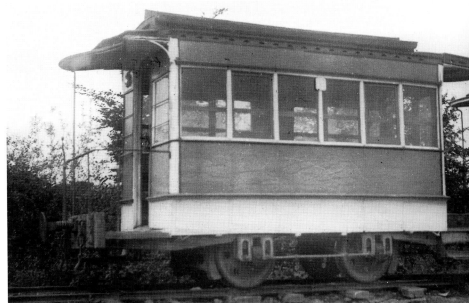

Stylish travel for Clay Company workers on the Marland Light Railway! Many lived in Company houses near Summit, and latterly the problem of transporting them to work at Peter's Marland was resolved by the purchase of two formerly horse-drawn four-wheeled coaches from London's North Metropolitan Tramway. They are seen at Marland on 5 July 1912. (LCGB, Ken Nunn Collection)

Also seen at Marland in July 1912 was this typical Stephen Lewin product, No 3 Peter, as supplied in 1871. The presence of a central buffer with wooden dumb buffers behind suggests that some rough shunting took place on the Marland Light Railway. (LCGB, Ken Nunn Collection)

small end windows. Such was the discomfort that the men preferred to switch to open trucks in summer. Then, latterly, two four-wheeled coaches, one-time horse-drawn tramcars on the North Metropolitan Tramway, were obtained; and, with one painted blue, and the other yellow, Marland's workmen travelled to work exactly as they might have done in London — except they had a *steam* horse in front! The line had no signals, but no accident of consequence seems ever to have occurred.

At the Peter's Marland end the single track, constructed of 30 lb rail, fanned into various sections of the clay works. A small locomotive shed was to be found there, and much later, in 1924–25, two standard gauge locomotives were acquired to work a transhipment siding. At first clay was obtained from open pits. Then, as these became exhausted, a gradual development through shallow timbered drifts culminated in underground working. Men and clay were lifted to the surface by winding gear, exactly as in coal mining.

It will be recalled that the abortive Torrington & Okehampton Railway proposed to utilize the Marland Railway's route along part of its way, in return for which the standard gauge railway would have obliged itself by law to convey Marland workmen at reasonable times and fares. Abandonment of the project in 1907 cancelled such arrangements, of course. But its very postulation had fired local appetite for conventional railway facilities, and enthusiasm remained remarkably undamped. Latterly it found new expression, when, in 1914, promoters of a North Devon & Cornwall Junction Light Railway received Light Railway Order permission to build a 20½-mile standard gauge railway which would link Torrington with Halwill Junction, on the L&SWR's North Cornwall line. Back, too, came an old proposal: the first 5½ miles of the new railway would follow the present line of the Marland Light Railway.

The outbreak of war in 1914 successfully precluded practical progress being made. But powers were not allowed to lapse, and, after further Parliamentary action in 1922, the new railway company found itself ready to proceed. By now it had appointed Colonel H. F. Stephens as Engineer in charge of construction, and that gentleman was astute enough to appreciate that the Marland works offered a ready-made clay traffic of 40–50,000 tons a year. The only problem left was the provision of capital. With post-war unemployment rampant in the West Country, local Councils, however, were only too happy to lend financial assistance. They raised £63,000, the Ministry of Transport was asked for a Grant of £180,000, and even the North Devon Clay Co subscribed £9,000 towards an ultimate capital of £300,000.

So, 5½ miles of the Marland's track disappeared to form a trackbed for standard gauge metals. The Torridge viaduct, quite incapable of bearing heavier loads, was also abandoned, and a new viaduct was painfully constructed alongside. There were even riots caused between navvies and locals, but Stephens' line eventually opened on 27 July 1925. The junction between the standard gauge and the surviving narrow gauge metals became known as Dunsbear Halt, and work continued at Peter's Marland as before. The North Devon Clay Co survived the depression of the 1930s, and the Second World War. But towards the end of the 1960s profitability began to flag, and the Marland works passed on to a Newton Abbot firm which was prepared to invest further capital. Output subsequently soared to 100,000 tons per year, but increased mechanization, plus energetic incursion by road transport, saw the 3-foot gauge line close in November 1970. By then, of course, steam had, in any case, vanished from the scene.

LOCOMOTIVES

The accompanying list of Marland motive power underlines the remarkable changes which have embraced the locomotive scene over the last century. *Peter* was a typical Lewin product, cabless and high-chimneyed; *Mary* had a high chimney and box-like cab; while *Marland* looked modern by comparison. All were painted dark green, unrelieved by lining. The three tanks from Jersey originally bore the names *David*, *Goliath* and *Merton*, and lay derelict at St Helier for some years before being sold to the North Devon Clay Co. They were, however, found to be too heavy for Marland's metals, and were subject to an ingenious rebuild by Hodges of Exeter in 1914, 1915 and 1910 respectively. The saddle tanks were removed from the boilers, and placed on four-wheeled wagon trailers. Thus, in effect, they were transformed into tender engines. At a later stage *Merton*'s tender was further converted, when the saddle tank was replaced by an old boiler. The loco remained serving in this form until 1951. After that date, diesel locomotives took over both narrow gauge and standard gauge working at Peter's Marland.

Two additional steam locomotives were acquired during 1924–25 to work the standard gauge link with the North Devon Railway. *Mersey*, a Hawthorne 0–4–0ST of 1902 vintage, was rebuilt by Cudworth & Johnson before reporting for duty in 1925. It was scrapped in 1953. The other loco, No 79, was a Manning Wardle 0–6–0ST veteran of 1888, which met its end in 1946. Two Fowler 0–4–0 diesels which replaced them carried on under British Railways auspices, shunting wagons to and from the loading sheds.

No	Name	Type	Date	Makers built	Remarks
1	*Mary*	0–6–0ST	1880	Black Hawthorn	Scrapped 1925
2	*Marland*	0–6–0T	1886	Bagnall	,,
3	*Peter*	0–4–0T	1871	Stephen Lewin	,,
11	—	0–6–0ST	1901	Avonside	,,
4	*Merton*	0–4–0ST	1875	Fletcher Jennings	Formerly employed on construction of break-water at St Helier, Jersey.
	Jersey No 1	0–4–0ST	1873	,,	Purchased by Marland Light Railway in 1908.
	Jersey No 2	,,	1873	,,	
Nos 5 to 10 were allocated to winding engines					
–	*Forward*	60-66 bhp Diesel		John Fowler	Scrapped 1970
–	*Advance*	40 bhp Diesel		,,	Withdrawn 1963
–	*Efficiency*	,,		,,	Scrapped 1970
	—	0-4-0 Diesel		Ruston & Hornsby	Withdrawn 1970
	—	,,		,,	Scrapped 1970

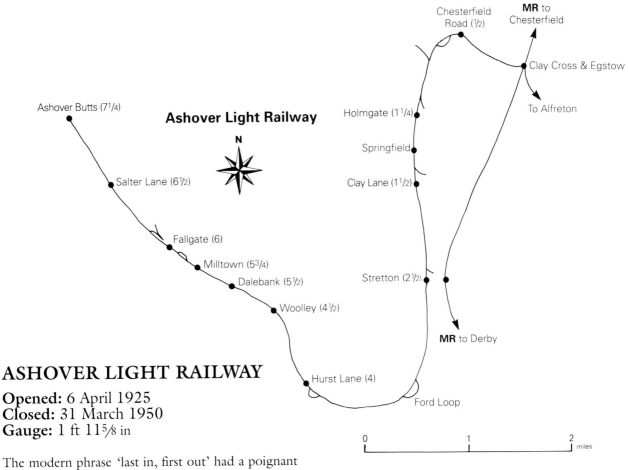

Ashover Light Railway

ASHOVER LIGHT RAILWAY

Opened: 6 April 1925
Closed: 31 March 1950
Gauge: 1 ft 11⅝ in

The modern phrase 'last in, first out' had a poignant significance for this little Derbyshire railway, for, opened as late as 1925, it did not live to celebrate its silver jubilee. One might have thought its pedigree

deserved a better fate, for the railway was sponsored by the Clay Cross Company of Derbyshire — and the first two Chairmen of that concern were George Stephenson and his son, Robert. Traditionally, Clay Cross processed minerals for a living, and when a large local estate came up for sale in 1918, prospects of adding limestone, gritstone and fluor-spar to the list loomed realistically. So, the company bought the estate, and set about building a single track railway, 7¼ miles long, to link quarries and processing plant. The Ashover Light Railway was eventually incorporated under a Light Railway Order of 4 December 1919, and the ubiquitous Lt Col H. F. Stephens, fresh from military service, was appointed constructional Engineer. Further powers were obtained under subsequent LROs of 1922 and 1924.

With mineral traffic seemingly assured, the ALR management, possibly encouraged by Stephens, was persuaded to exploit the natural beauty of the Derbyshire countryside by thinking also in terms of tourist traffic. Certainly one senses the direct influence of Col Stephens in the ultimate choice of a 1 ft 11⅝ in gauge, though, optimistically, clearance was left so that standard gauge metals could be substituted as or when required. Typical of Stephens' opportunism, too, four ex-WD Baldwin 4–6–0 tanks were obtained at a disposal sale in Darlington, and all were used during construction of the line. Two more Baldwins followed from T. W. Ward of Sheffield in 1925, in readiness for opening day. So, too, did four tramcar-type coaches, built by the Gloucester Railway Carriage & Wagon Co Ltd. Just over a year later eight 24-seater coaches were snapped up from the Wembley Exhibition's 'Neverstop Railway'. The ALR's first 40 wagons were also ex-WD.

In the matter of construction the configuration of the land was such that severe curves and gradients could not be avoided. The ALR line started from Clay Cross and Egstow station, which, although ¾ mile from the town itself, at least afforded useful

transhipment facilities with the LMS nearby. Climbing straight away at 1 in 37, the line then executed the first loop of a figure 'S', before crossing a substantial girder bridge and entering Chesterfield Road station. The latter was to prove a popular boarding spot for excursionists in the railway's heyday, as were two other halts further down the line — Springfield and Clay Lane. At Stretton (2½ miles) contact with the LMS was again so close that ALR trains often loitered there to harvest passengers from incoming main line trains. Thereafter, the two railways ran abreast for a mile or so, before the ALR metals turned inland up the River Amber valley. At 6 miles came Fallgate Quarry, and here, illustrating the importance of limestone traffic, the ALR divided into four parallel tracks, and several sidings clambered off to service the various working faces. On went the ALR track, still clinging to the bottom of the valley, and only climbing where necessary, until the terminus, Ashover Butts, was reached. This may have been Mecca to the tourists, but it was the existence of Butts Quarry nearby which provided the ALR with what seemed to be an even more reliable source of income; particularly later, when the LMS placed an important standing order for the supply of rail ballast.

With construction work commencing on 22 December 1922, the line was built to typical Colonel Stephens standards. In short expenditure was kept to a minimum. 30 lb rails were spiked directly on to wooden sleepers, scotch blocks served as buffer ends at all sidings, and most points were worked by hand. Traffic was worked by a staff system, and only after passenger traffic ceased in 1936 was reversion made to 'one engine in steam'. The opening ceremony was a cheerful, and quite colourful, occasion, and expectations soared as over 5,000 passengers travelled during the first week. Eight trains ran each way on weekdays, and weekend traffic was brisk. Alas, the coal strike of 1926 brought traffic to a standstill; such passenger services as were resumed in 1927 not only reflected the general economic unease of the country, but ran up against new deadly competition from buses. Easter 1931, in fact, was the last occasion on which two ALR passenger trains operated simultaneously over the line, though a desultory service excursion or two ran as required.

Mineral traffic, meanwhile, was just hanging on at one train a day. Stone traffic was on the wane, and the opening of a new coal outcrop near Clay Cross in 1922 must have come as a considerable relief to a harassed ALR management. By now Clay Cross Works had built a diesel-electric locomotive to relieve the ALR's stock of ageing steam engines. Ironically, the diesel needed heavy repairs by mid-1942, and steam came once more to the rescue. But the whole situation was only a temporary relief, for later that year the opencast coalfield was found to be exhausted. The sidings were removed, and the ALR had no option but to revert to its previous precarious existence: one train a day.

The track was deteriorating badly. So, too, were the steam engines; yet the crews still preferred them to the diesel. Even the 11 trucks which comprised the daily freight train were beginning to prove overmuch for one engine over the steepest gradients, and had to be divided some 4 miles from Clay Cross. By 1949 only one steam loco remained usable, and a Planet-type diesel was purchased. Steam men must have smiled when it was found that even the diesel could not take a loaded train to Clay Cross without dividing!

Guy rests on his laurels at Ashover Butts. Typical of Colonel Stephens' light railway practice, a rough wooden side shelter and rear extension have been added to the cab. (Steamchest)

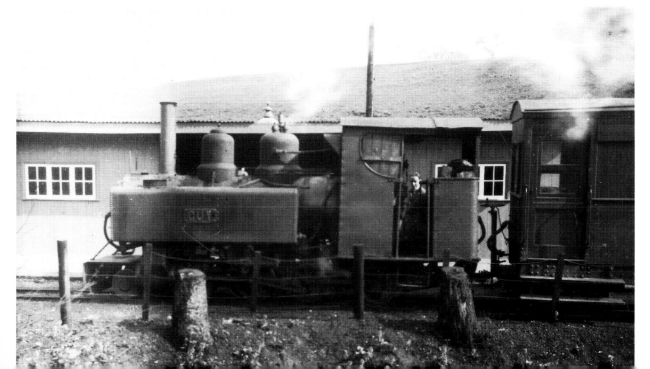

The final blow came early in January 1950, when the Railway Executive cancelled its standing order for limestone ballast. Ashover Butts Quarry closed as a consequence, and with it went the *raison d'être* for the ALR's continuing existence. Permission was sought to close the line, and the sad event took place on 31 March 1950. Two months later, the company was officially wound up. Track-lifting commenced in October of that year, and all four remaining steam locos were reduced to scrap as they stood at Clay Cross yard.

LOCOMOTIVES

Name	Type	Date built	Makers	Maker's number	Out of use	Withdrawn	Cut up
Hummy	4-6-0T	1916	Baldwin	44370	1946	1950	1951
Guy / Georgie	,,	1917	,,	45227	1937	1939	1942
Joan	,,	1917	,,	44720	1948	1950	1951
Peggy	,,	1917	,,	44743	1949	1950	1951
Bridget	,,	1917	,,	44737	1945	1947	1951
Guy	,,	1917	,,	44695	1936	1943	1943

Baldwin tanks, built by the hundred for First World War service in Western Europe, were never popular when translated to British narrow gauge use. Certainly the quartet which the ALR purchased at Darlington exemplified the usual faults of rough riding and poor steaming, and even a pair received later, though freshly overhauled by T. W. Ward of Sheffield gave crews many an anxious moment. During the lifetime of the Baldwins, considerable swopping of parts, even cannibalization, took place, and the only thing which seems certain is that all were named after members of the Jackson family, whose sire, General Thomas E. Jackson, was Chairman of the Clay Cross Company. In one instance, that of *Georgie*, nameplates were cast but never borne. Generally, the Baldwins wore badly, and by 5 July 1949 only *Peggy* remained workable. She it was, therefore, who worked the last steam train out of Clay Cross. Several internal combustion locomotives functioned on and around ALR metals from 1927 onwards. These, however, were owned by the Clay Cross Company, and did not appear on ALR lists.

The ALR's 12 coaches have already been mentioned. The Wembley lot were unusual, for, originally built on steel frames, they were rebuilt at Clay Cross on wooden frames. One side was left completely open, for passengers to board or alight, the other was covered with wire netting; excursionists, it is recorded, enjoyed the combination of fresh air and good views! Most of the ALR's coaching stock, however, was stored in the open, and little was left by the time scrap merchants descended in 1951. Yet, miraculously, two of 1925 vintage survived, and, fitted with leather upholstered seats from Glasgow, Leeds and Liverpool tramcars, they now serve on the 60cm gauge Lincolnshire Coast Light Railway at Humberston, near Grimbsy.

The total wagons used on the ALR, again largely ex-WD, were numbered 1–70. A potentially interesting link with the Leek & Manifold Railway was forged in 1935, when an old 2 ft 6 in bogie transporter wagon was purchased, with a view to eliminating transhipment of coal at Clay Cross. The wagon was duly re-gauged at Clay Cross Works. In the event it proved totally unreliable, and was soon abandoned.

Pleasure abounding

SOUTHWOLD RAILWAY

Opened: 24 September 1879
Closed: 11 April 1929
Gauge: 3 ft 0 in

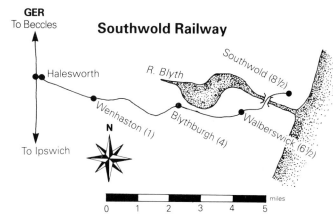

When, in 1862, East Anglia's five major railways joined forces under the common title of the Great Eastern Railway, one might have thought the resultant unification offered the thinly spread population of the County of Suffolk a reasonably satisfactory railway service. Apparently, however, the good folk of Southwold, a rapidly developing centre of sea bathing, south of Lowestoft, saw things differently, for at a Southwold Town Council meeting held on 19 October 1871, one important item on the agenda was an application from the Lowestoft, Yarmouth & Southwold Tramway Co Ltd to build a tramway between Lowestoft and Southwold. After careful consideration, and insistence on minor alterations, the Council agreed. Despite that, the tramway never materialized.

Nevertheless, Southwold had made its point, and local agitation, thrusting aside its tramway disappointment, soon refocused on an even more ambitious proposition — that of linking up with the GER main line metals at Halesworth, less than 9 miles inland. Public meetings, presided over by prominent landowners, waxed vigorously at both towns during October 1875, and as a result the Southwold Railway Company was incorporated by Act of Parliament on 24 June 1876. Apart from containing authority to construct a line 8 miles and 63 chains long betweeen Halesworth and Southwold, the Act also sanctioned the provision of short branches at each end. The intention here was to reach navigational waters. That brought the total length to 9½ miles. Capital emerged at £67,990, and, with an eye

fixed on extra carrying capacity, a gauge of 3 feet was chosen in preference to the more conventional 2 ft 6 in. Construction work commenced on 3 May 1878.

30 lb flat-bottomed rail, spiked to wooden sleepers, was laid throughout. But, although the line was single, with but one passing place at Blythburgh, room was carefully left for doubling, should such contingency arise in future years. Thus, the Southwold's 18 bridges were quite substantial affairs, none more so than a timber-piled swing bridge which was built over the River Blyth at Blackmore. Gradients presented no great problem, for the steepest was 1 in 53. Intermediate stations were provided at Wenhaston, Blythburgh and Walberswick, charming villages all; in the interests of economy, low platforms were confined to the south side only. Opening day, though accompanied by ceremonial, turned out to be a surprisingly muted affair, and, a little soberly, the little railway addressed itself, as from 24 September 1879, to providing a daily service of four trains each way. With the company Rule Book offering two years' imprisonment to any driver who dared to exceed 16 mph *en route*, the 37-minute timing allowed for each journey was scrupulously observed. The Southwold's safety system was equally secure, for telephonic communication existed between stations, and signals were only lowered when advice was

East Anglia's 3-foot gauge light railway really meant business, as can be seen from this 1911 view of its spacious terminal layout at Southwold. The signal in the foreground, interlocked with points and operated by ground lever, was typical of the great care that the Southwold Railway took in safety matters. The two opposing arms, one for up trains, one for down, were only lowered when telephonic confirmation had been received that a train had left the previous station. The coloured spectacles were winched up or down as required. (LCGB, Ken Nunn Collection)

At the Halesworth end of the line, the Southwold Railway contented itself with a single platform, connected by footbridge to the Great Eastern Railway's adjacent station. In this 1910 scene, No 3 Blyth is just arriving on a typically mixed 10.15 am ex-Southwold. (LCGB, Ken Nunn Collection)

Ten years later, and also seen at Halesworth, Sharp Steward 2–4–2T No 1 Southwold, the second of that name and number on the Southwold Railway, shunts a few wagons against a backcloth of the railway's unique six-wheel tram-type coaches. The latter relied entirely on hand brakes throughout their entire working life. (LCGB, Ken Nunn Collection)

received that a train had left the previous station. In 50 years' running, only two fatal accidents blemished the Southwold Railway's record. Both concerned employees.

In the matter of rolling-stock, the Southwold started off with three locomotives. This proved over-optimistic, however, and in 1883 loco No 1, a 2–4–0T, was sent back to its makers. Sharp Stewart promptly re-gauged it to 3 ft 6 in, and subsequently sold it to the Santa Maria Railway in Colombia. Meanwhile, the Southwold's running number 1 remained untenanted, until a welcome upsurge of traffic in 1893 justified the purchase of another Sharp Stewart tank. The Southwold locomotives settled down thereafter to a regular form of rostering. One engine, shedded at Southwold, handled the day's traffic, while a second stood by at Halesworth, ready to serve should floods sever the line. This left a third loco either spare or under repair. The Southwold, however, could only handle running repairs, and any engine requiring major repair, or

overhaul, had to find its own way to the Great Eastern's Works at Stratford. In the absence of turntable facilities on the Southwold, all locos worked in reverse on alternate journeys.

Where passengers were concerned, six-wheeled carriages were employed from the outset; earlier trials with a four-wheeled vehicle proved unsatisfactory. The Southwold's six tram-type coaches arrived equipped with Cleminson's patent flexible wheelbase system. First painted white, then dull red, they were oil-lit, and remained to their dying days splendidly innocent of continuous or vacuum brake. Hand brakes, applied by the guard, were all that could be brought to bear in supplementing locomotive brake power. Wagon stock on the Southwold consisted of 12 vehicles in 1879, but this figure rose to 39 in later years. Most were four-wheeled open trucks, though two, closed and fitted with sliding doors, were reserved for passengers' luggage.

At Halesworth, passengers alighting from main line trains merely crossed a footbridge to reach the

Southwold's platform, with its small waiting room and office. Here, as on Ireland's Waterford & Tramore Railway, a handbell was solemnly rung to intimate the impending departure. Then, once the guard had executed his flag-waving ritual, off went the passengers — many of them on a new, and rather wonderful, adventure. Hardly had the train left the platform than paper-boys, pausing only to sort out their deliveries, commenced throwing orders out. Sometimes the newspapers landed near lonely farms, sometimes they thudded to ground at level crossings. Whatever was happening, the passengers, travelling at a steady 16 mph, had ample time to admire the deep Suffolk countryside they were passing through.

As the train approached Blythburgh, a marked superelevation lifted it sharply round a wide curve. But any discomfort or alarm this occasioned was soon forgotten as the Priory ruins and Blythburgh Church, standing on a low hill, came clearly into view. Here the train staff, or 'key' as it was colloquially known, was exchanged, and safe passage on to Southwold was ensured. A little further on, the driver might stop to collect a hare or rabbit, trapped in a snare previously set by the lineside. Then, after one last official stop at Walberswick, nowadays a positive Mecca for bird-watchers, a rumble of wheels as they crossed the swing bridge at Blackmore reminded knowing passengers that Southwold lay nigh. At the Southwold Railway's largest station, a horse-drawn station bus waited patiently to convey the more fortunate passengers to their respective hotels and boarding houses. Luggage followed on behind, as did morning newspapers for local distribution. Local residents travelling by train were content to make a less dramatic exit.

These, then, were the gentle circumstances under which the Southwold Railway pursued the first 35 years of its existence. On average, some 80,000 passengers were carried annually, and this figure rose to a healthy peak of 108,000 in 1913. That year a net profit of £1,800 enabled a 2 per cent distribution to be made to shareholders, though dividends again lapsed to 1 per cent during the years 1918–21. The First World War, meantime, brought something of a boom to the Southwold, for large numbers of troops were consistently stationed in the area. Goods traffic increased commensurately, and quite often night trains were run to conceal troop movements. The two branches mentioned in the Act of 1876 were allowed to go by default. In 1914, however, fresh powers were obtained for the construction of a branch line to Southwold Harbour Quay. The object was to stimulate Southwold's fishing industry, and, as with troop movements, the outbreak of war in 1914 gave the branch added significance as a means of assisting work on coastal defences. Only one carriage, however, ever trod its metals, and that was when a Board of Trade Inspector descended to conduct his inspection.

In May 1917 another, more poignant, event might have occasioned the use of carriages, when a

As only running repairs were carried out at Southwold, any of the company's locomotives which required major repair or overhaul had, perforce, to report to the Great Eastern Railway's Stratford Locomotive Works for attention. This photograph, taken at Stratford on 19 May 1909, explains how the trick was done. (LCGB, Ken Nunn Collection)

large number of Belgian and Dutch nationals were repatriated, after being given assurances of safe conduct across the North Sea by the German Emperor. After arrival at Southwold station, however, they were reassembled, and marched across the common to the Harbour. Local inhabitants must have found it a moving sight.

The Railway Strike in October 1919 was thwarted locally, when volunteers contrived to run two Southwold trains daily each way. The year 1922 even saw a return to a 2 per cent dividend for Ordinary and Preference shareholders. That, however, was a final fling, for only Debenture holders received payments thereafter.

The 1920s were dangerous years for small railways, and the SR's moment of truth came in April 1928, when Southwold Corporation licensed bus competition in the area. The Southwold Railway fought back by cutting fares, but even then found it could not cope. Its life blood, passenger traffic, was slowly draining away. A subsequent appeal by its Chairman for assistance to both Corporation and the LNER went unheeded, and, inevitably, the Southwold was forced to close. Thus, a last train,

hauled by loco No 4, left Southwold at 5.25 on the evening of 11 April 1929, and returned to base at 7.2 pm, its four coaches crammed with local people who had every reason to regret the little railway's passing. Tickets were retained as souvenirs, and a collection was made for the engine driver. The LNER, meanwhile, had made arrangements with the Eastern Counties Road Car Service Ltd to preserve continuity of parcel services between Halesworth and Southwold.

Sadly, rolling-stock and track lay derelict, until the Second World War found fresh use for it as scrap. T. W. Ward Ltd attended to demolition from July 1941 onwards, whence track soon disappeared, and locomotives and rolling-stock perished under the cutter's torch. Even the swing bridge at Blackmore, proudly rebuilt in steel before the First World War, had already been rendered useless under threat of German invasion.

A new fire station now occupies half of the area of Southwold's former station yard, and occasional parts of the trackbed still exist as a favourite walk. But to older inhabitants, somehow Southwold will never be the same again.

LOCOMOTIVES

No	Name	Type	Date built	Makers	Maker's number	Remarks
(1)	*Southwold*	2–4–0T	1879	Sharp Stewart	2848	Returned to makers, 1893
1	*Southwold*	2–4–2T	1893	,,	3913	
2	*Halesworth*	2–4–0T	1879	,,	2849	Rebuilt 1901
3	*Blyth*	2–4–0T	1879	,,	2850	Rebuilt 1900
4	*Wenhaston*	0–6–2T	1916	Manning Wardle	1845	

The three Sharp Stewart 2–4–0 tanks delivered in 1879 were modest little engines, with cylinders 8 in x 14 in, coupled wheels 2 ft 6 in in diameter, and a working pressure of 140 lbs. The 2–4–2 tank ordered in 1893 was of broadly similar appearance, but it possessed greater coal and water capacity, and weighed 2 tons more. *Wenhaston*, introduced to cope with increasing wartime traffic, was altogether a different proposition. Driving wheels were still 2 ft 6 in in diameter, but the engine was 21 feet long, and weighed 19¼ tons in working order. Its tanks held 650 gallons of water, and 14 cwt of coal found refuge in its bunker. Originally the locomotives were painted green, then GER blue took over. In later years, however, Nos 1, 2 and 3 were painted black, and No 4 dark green. All rolling-stock was fitted with centre buffers and loose couplings.

VOLK'S ELECTRIC RAILWAY

Opened: 4 August 1883
Closed: Still extant
Gauge: 2 ft 8½ in

It is, perhaps, salutary to recall that two pairs of brothers, one German, one Irish, played crucial roles in introducing electric railways to Great Britain. Dr Ernst Siemens' work on his dynamo during the 1860s enabled him to demonstrate the world's first practical electric railway, albeit only 600 yards long, at the Berlin Trades Exhibition in 1879, and later at the Crystal Palace. His older brother, (Sir) William, followed up by co-operating with the Traill brothers in Ireland in constructing the UK's first major electric railway, the 8-mile long Giant's Causeway

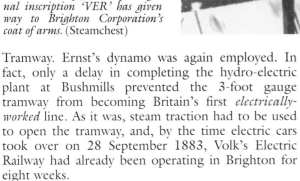

Tramway. Ernst's dynamo was again employed. In fact, only a delay in completing the hydro-electric plant at Bushmills prevented the 3-foot gauge tramway from becoming Britain's first *electrically-worked* line. As it was, steam traction had to be used to open the tramway, and, by the time electric cars took over on 28 September 1883, Volk's Electric Railway had already been operating in Brighton for eight weeks.

Magnus Volk, German in parentage but Brighton-born in 1851, introduced electric light to his home town in 1882, and went on to supervise the installation of electric light in the Royal Pavillon one year later. Seeking Corporation permission, he then proceeded to build a quarter-mile-long electric public tramway along the sea front, between Brighton's Aquarium and the Old Chain Pier. Current was generated by courtesy of a 2 hp Crossley gas engine and a (Siemens) dynamo, and the 50-volt output was fed to two flat-bottomed running rails, spiked to longitudinal wooden sleepers. A local man built a simple

four-wheeled car, capable of holding both motor and ten passengers. The sides of the car were prominently inscribed 'VER', and with this simple equipment the 2-foot gauge single-tracked railway was opened for public use on 4 August 1883. Bank Holiday Monday was a great success, and public demand kept the little car, running to and fro at 6 mph, fully occupied for 11 hours. Volk had made his point: electric traction *was* tireless and efficient.

Heartened by success, Volk closed the line briefly in January 1884 for reconstruction and extension. During the next three months the line, converted to 2 ft 9 in gauge, was extended to Paston Place, and was now ¾ mile long. Two new cars were built, again four-wheeled and double-ended. Two tons in weight, and with solid mahogany bodywork, each was beautifully furnished inside. Then, with power now provided by a 12 hp Crossley gas engine, driving a Siemens dynamo situated in the cave opposite Paston Place terminus, the revitalized line re-opened on 4 April 1884. A regular 5-6-minute service

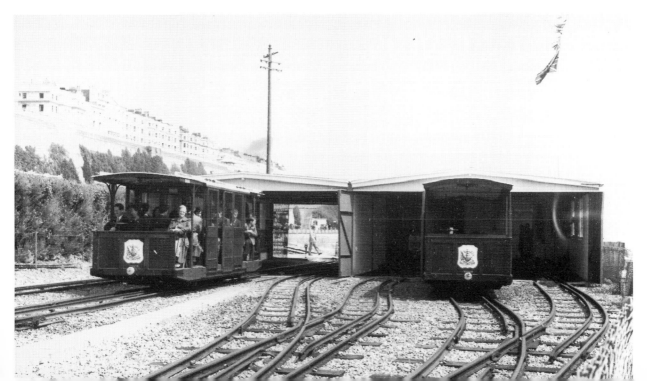

Styled 'Volk's Electric Seafront Railway' in modern times, Magnus Volk's veteran venture still offers a brisk, and highly popular, public service, and for six months of the year cars run at 5-minute intervals along Brighton's seafront. The above vignette explains itself. (Steamchest)

ensued, summer and winter, from that day to 2 July 1940. Only occasional gales interrupted this remarkable service. The public were fascinated by the mystery of electric traction, and Volk even produced a penny pamphlet explaining its principles. During the 1890s he also became engrossed in a different type of railway venture — an ultra-wide gauge electric tramroad linking Brighton and Rottingdean. But more of that anon . . .

Some time during the 1890s Volk also conducted further experiments at Brighton, in course of which a third off-centre rail was installed along the ¾-mile railway. The gauge was reduced to 2 ft 8½ in. The Corporation also permitted Volk to extend the railway eastwards towards Black Rock. This brought it to its present length of 1¼ miles, and, during the following year, traction current was drawn from the Corporation's electric mains; meanwhile, Volk's original equipment was retained as standby. At this stage the return fare was 4d and the cars, though capable of much higher speeds, rarely exceeded 8 mph in public service. In 1915 came a first fatality, when a boy climbed on to the track and was electrocuted. Volk's Railway was not unduly criticized at the inquest, but Volk undertook to protect the live rail by wooden boards thereafter. This precaution successfully precluded further fatal accidents until 1950, when two mishaps occurred.

But, the 1915 fatality apart, little happened to upset the railway's existence as it continued to shuttle to and fro into the 1930s. Magnus Volk died in 1937, and his son, Herman, took charge. Perhaps this sequence of events was not unmerciful, for Volk's lease over the railway expired in 1939. Initially, the Corporation was content to leave Herman in control, on a profit-sharing basis. But, when Brighton abandoned its own street tramway system on 31 August 1939, Corporation thoughts soon turned towards Volk's Electric Railway. Thus, after a brief interregnum of seven months, operation of Volk's Railway passed completely into the hands of Brighton Corporation. Stock consisted of ten four-wheeled cars, some of which still retained original Siemens motors, with belt drive. Others had tramcar motors. The line contained three passing loops, and wooden station buildings existed at Aquarium, Paston Place and Black Rock.

Alas, however sound the Corporation's intentions were, the threat of German invasion caused the Government to close Brighton's beaches on 2 July 1940. Thus, for the next half-decade Volk's Railway cars mouldered uselessly in their car shed at Paston Place. Aquarium and Black Rock terminals were completely demolished. By the time hostilities ended, the Brighton line, like the Fairbourne and the Romney, Hythe & Dymchurch was in such a state of dereliction that an act of courage would have been required to contemplate its restoration. All the more credit, then, to Brighton Corporation, whose Transport Dept undertook that very task.

First, the track was renewed throughout with 50 lb rail. Then, the provision of stations was tackled. A redundant tram shelter provided facilities at Aquarium, and island platforms, with umbrella roofs were erected at Paston Place and Black Rock. Seven cars were restored at a trolley-bus depot, track circuits were overhauled, and, on 15 May 1948, Volk's Electric Railway was restored to public use. When the Southend Pier Tramway renewed its own rolling-stock in 1949, Brighton Corporation seized the opportunity to buy two old cross-bench control trailers. These were re-gauged from 3ft 6 in to 2 ft 8½ in, and fitted with motors. A single fare of 6d, established in 1949, remained unchanged until decimalization. Today, the little electric railway is still one of Brighton's major attractions, and trains run daily at 5-minute intervals from Easter to the end of September. It continues to employ two roofed cross-bench cars, five semi-saloon cars, and, of course, its two ex-Southend bargains.

In 1962 all cars were repainted in yellow and dark brown with the initials 'VR' and the Brighton coat of arms featuring largely on their sides. Thought was given later to the provision of four aluminium bogie cars of modern design. Wisely, however, Brighton Corporation decided that vintage appeal was at the heart of the railway's popularity — and it concentrated instead on refurbishing existing stock. Technical progress was not, however, neglected, and, after experiments in 1964, all cars were fitted for multiple working in units of two. This enables them to cope with exceptionally heavy traffic phases.

ALFORD & SUTTON TRAMWAY

Opened: 2 April 1884
Closed: December 1889
Gauge: 2 ft 6 in

Initially proposed in the late 1870s, and duly sanctioned on 12 August 1880, this short-lived Lincolnshire narrow gauge tramway had interesting Scottish connotations, for it was owned by its contractor, Mr W. B. Dick, whose firm, W. B. Dick & Co, was already specializing in the construction of tramway equipment at its Britannia Works in Kilmarnock. The title of the firm was changed to Dick, Kerr & Co Ltd in 1883.

The object of the Lincolnshire exercise was to convey passengers from Alford, 7 miles inland, to Sutton-on-Sea, where they could enjoy the pleasures of the seaside; and, for the usual reasons, the tramway, starting outside the GNR's Alford Station, took care to follow public roads as its single line, embodying 11 passing loops, wound its way through

a few villages before terminating near the Jolly Bacchus Inn at Sutton. Authority had been given to carry both passengers and freight. Raising finance, however, provided familiar problems; thus construction did not commence until December 1882. When the Tramway finally opened on 2 April 1884, its stock consisted of three steam tram locos, one eight-wheel and four four-wheel trailers, and a variety of open goods wagons. Inevitably, trains were mixed, with a passenger car running behind a complement of wagons.

The tramway, however, was living through a period of considerable railway expansion throughout the UK, and the fruits of its initial prosperity were soon ravaged when the GNR opened a branch from Willoughby to Sutton in October 1886. Two years later a second blow was delivered, when the GNR extended its branch to Mablethorpe; and, despite assumption of a more imposing title, the Great Northern Steam Tramways Co Ltd, the 2 ft 6 in gauge line, brought to its knees, was finally obliged to close in December 1889.

LOCOMOTIVES

No	Date built	Makers	Maker's number
1	1883	Black Hawthorn	735
2	1883	Merryweather	140
3	1885	Dick, Kerr	

WOLVERTON AND STONY STRATFORD TRAMWAY

Opened: 17 May 1887
Closed: 4 May 1926
Gauge: 3 ft 6 in

If getting to work in time can be construed as one of life's 'abounding pleasures', then, surely, this delightful old concern has been placed in the correct chapter. For, though it was born primarily of industrial need, the Wolverton and Stony Stratford Tramway served people faithfully during the whole of its 40-year existence.

Once the London & Birmingham Railway Act gained Royal Assent in 1833 and construction of the country's first trunk line got under way, several quite important market towns failed, for a variety of reasons, to benefit directly. One such was Stony Stratford, a venerable coaching town in North

After climbing steeply from its starting point outside Wolverton station goods yard, the second of two tram engines supplied by T. Green & Son of Leeds, when the original Krauss tram engines quickly proved to be insufficiently powerful, pauses with its 100-seater car on the bridge which straddled the LNWR main line. The pronounced sag in the 44-foot long car body shows clearly in this study. The lower deck contained two inward-facing benches, and passengers upstairs faced outwards from a continuous central slatted bench. Waist-high decency boards, surmounted by canvas blinds, offered minimal protection from side winds and rain, and both engine and car carried prominent local advertising. (National Railway Museum, York)

Buckinghamshire. Yet adding positive insult to injury, the equidistant point of this important new railway artery lay only 2 miles away, at a tiny hamlet called Wolverton. Railway workshops, managed by Edward Bury, were established there in 1838, refreshment rooms were added later to its modest platforms, and all through the second half of the nineteenth century the former hamlet enjoyed burgeoning importance as the spot where locomotives were changed, and passengers refreshed.

Wolverton soon grew rapidly into a railway town. Yet, one problem remained, in that hundreds of workmen who found employment at the Locomotive Works and the nearby McCorquodale Printing Works were still obliged to find their way, six days a week, to and from their homes in Stony Stratford and surrounding villages. There was a horse-drawn bus which plied between the two main localities, but a single fare of 6d was much too exhorbitant for the average local workman. Hence, come rain, come snow, he walked to Wolverton.

In 1882 a group of Stony Stratford tradesmen, concerned, no doubt, to revive the town's flagging fortunes, resolved to tackle both problems by initiating a concern to be known as the Wolverton and Stony Stratford Tramways Co Ltd. The object was to establish a 2½-mile standard gauge link between the two towns. Unfortunately, the requisite capital was not forthcoming, and the company went into voluntary liquidation. Then, in September 1883, an inventor called Frederick Charles Wimby revived local hopes by forming a company which would not only build the standard gauge line, but incorporate his patented Tension Girder System of laying track. Alas, the project again failed to arouse financial support — and Wolverton workers, male and female alike, continued their daily plod.

There the matter rested until autumn 1886, when another contractor, C. H. Wilkinson, thwarted in an earlier bid to build a 3 ft 6 in gauge tramway between Wolverton and Olney, turned his attention to more local problems. As a result, the Wolverton and Stony Stratford District Light Railways Co Ltd came into existence on 5 October 1886. Construction costs were estimated at £13,325, and Wilkinson's offer to take up £2,000 in shares himself ensured a successful flotation. In May 1887 the completed tramway passed Board of Trade inspection, and public service commenced on the 17th of that month.

The first tram was pulled by horses from Wolverton station goods yard to Stony Stratford tram depot. Thence, one of the tramway's two steam tram engines was attached, and, amidst considerable local celebration, the Wolverton and Stony Stratford Tramway made its public début. A shade over 2 miles long, its metals utilized public highways for most of the way, either centrally or on the left-hand side of the road. Two distinctly Continental-looking tram engines had been obtained from Krauss of Munich, and the Midland Carriage & Wagon Works at Shrewsbury supplied five munificent double-deck bogie passenger cars. Three of them were massive

100-seaters. Hoping to handle freight traffic as well, the tramway had also taken the precaution of commissioning a modest quantity of parcel vans and goods wagons. Locos and rolling-stock were housed at Stony Stratford depot.

With fares pitched at 2d single, and 1 shilling for a weekly workman's ticket permitting four journeys daily, the tramway enjoyed immediate public support. Thus, within two months of opening sanction was also obtained to build a 2-mile 3-chain extension from Stony Stratford to Deanshanger, where the existence of a thriving ironworks seemed to offer lucrative freight traffic. A third Krauss tram loco and a 20-seat four-wheeled car were acquired, primarily to work the new extension. Alas, expectations were not fulfilled, for the ironworks elected, in the event, to adhere to canal transport for its products.

Meanwhile, other problems were looming on the horizon. The Krauss engines were proving insufficiently strong to handle the heavy passenger cars, and two more powerful locos had to be ordered from Thomas Green & Son of Leeds. In addition to carrying condensers on their roofs they, and the cars, were well plastered with local advertisements. Two of the Krauss engines were promptly sold, though the third lasted until 1900. Next came a real crisis, on 4 September 1889, when insufficient tramway revenue forced the company into voluntary liquidation. A Receiver was appointed on 17 December, the line was closed, and hundreds of Wolverton workers found themselves with no option but to resume their wintry trek by foot.

Their ordeal was to last for nearly two years, before a Bedford syndicate resumed tramway services under the aegis of the Wolverton and Stony Stratford & District Tramways Company in November 1891. Further consolidation came in September 1893, when fresh infusion of capital saw the company re-formed as the Wolverton and Stony Stratford New Tramway Co Ltd. By now the Deanshanger extension had long been abandoned, though the original section continued to offer reliable public service. In 1900 a further tram loco, rather similar to the Green engines, arrived from Brush Electrical Engineering Co Ltd of Loughborough. It proved, however, much less serviceable than the Green products.

Troubles, of course, never came singly. Within a few years the tramway track began to show its age, and derailments, with all their attendant nuisance, became almost a daily occurrence. Under the terms of the the Tramways Act 1870, Bucks County Council insisted that track repairs be effected. This was duly accomplished in 1907 — after a further £3,000 in capital had been painfully subscribed. The price to be paid, as with the revitalized Welshpool & Llanfair Light Railway many years later, was that the tramway was now debarred from entering the town

centre, and terminated instead at a run-round loop in Wolverton Road. Soon after that the first motor bus appeared on the scene, and, as far as the tramway was concerned, the kiss of death was only averted when the Government commandeered the buses in 1914 for war service. Subsequent doubling of tram fares in 1915, coupled with increasingly deteriorating track conditions, sparked off the formation of a Workman's Committee that same year; but, despite heart-felt appeals, Wolverton Urban District Council declined to take action.

Then the miracle occurred. In 1919 the LNWR purchased the tramway and set about renovating both track and rolling-stock. The passenger cars re-emerged from Wolverton Works, beautifully liveried in chocolate brown, and a new saddle tank, with motion boxed in as before, arrived from W. G. Bagnall Ltd of Stafford. It and the Green engines worked all traffic for the tramway's remaining years. Came Grouping in 1923, and the tramway passed into LMS ownership, though, of course, its still mandatory 8 mph speed limit placed it at an immense disadvantage *vis-à-vis* the motor buses which were by now flooding into the area. The LMS gave a thought to electrifying the tramway, but soon abandoned the idea. Were it not still performing a useful service in ferrying employees to and from Wolverton Works, it would, doubtless, have been closed forthwith.

As it was, Fate chose its own solution. When the General Strike erupted on a national scale on 4 May 1926, none of the Wolverton tramway's staff reported for duty. Thus, like a Greek tragedy, services were never resumed. In due course the locomotives were scrapped, and the passenger car bodies were sold off. Many saw their days out as garden sheds, etc, though one 100-seater lower deck survived, to be preserved at Stacey Hill Museum. Rumour has it, though, that somewhere a complete 100-seat car still lingers on; and, needless to say, the Museum is trying hard to acquire it for restoration.

One can only wish them well in their efforts.

SOUTHEND PIER RAILWAY

Opened: 2 August 1890
Closed: October 1978
Reopened: 2 May 1986 (3-foot gauge)

Although it was not the first pier railway to be built in the British Isles, the Southend Pier Railway has long been recognized as the 'Premier Line'. And well might it be — for Southend Pier itself was the longest in the world.

Southend Corporation replaced its entire Pier Railway stock in 1947, and here, in August 1954, No 8, one of the new Crompton Parkinson cars, is caught en route on its ³/₄-mile journey from Shore Station to Pier Head. Though still four-wheeled, the car is beautifully modern in appearance. (F. C. Le Manquais)

Car No 14 is all set, on 26 August 1954, to leave Southend's Pier Head station, and head back for the shore. A decade later, continental holiday-making began to bite into Southend custom, and the Pier Railway rolling-stock was reduced by half in 1970. (F. C. Le Manquais)

As if falling receipts were not enough, a disastrous fire on the Pier Head in 1976 hastened the ultimate closure of the little railway. Bravely, the Southend Pier Railway was restored in 1986 but, as can be seen from this September 1989 view, the new Pier station is rather less flamboyant in appearance. Severn Lamb provided the new 'push-pull' stock. (Steamchest)

Southend's first pier, a wooden structure, was erected in 1830, and by 1846 it had been extended to 1¼ miles. In addition it introduced a remarkable innovation — a 3 ft 6 in gauge single track along which hand-trucks containing steamship passengers' luggage were pushed. The rails were made of wood. Then, in 1873 the Local Board purchased the Pier. Two years later the wooden rails were replaced by iron, and passenger trams, hauled by horses in tandem, became a popular local feature. Symptomatic, perhaps, of the carefree seaside atmosphere of the times, the tramway ran straight through the entertainments pavilion. Thus, for the next six years the steady clip-clop of horses, accompanied by the creak of tram wheels, provided a ubiquitous, but calmly accepted, interruption in the midst of many a concert and entertainment! Eventually, even the Pier began to suffer through wear and tear, and the horse tramway was closed in 1881.

Four years later a decision was made to rebuild the Pier, and an Act of Parliament was duly secured for the purpose. Construction work started in 1888, and the project took two years to complete. The end product was 2,000 yards long and 30 feet wide. It was supported by iron piles, and a pier head, built on timber piles, was added at the end. A decision had also been made to install a modern electric railway, and, a sensation in its day, a single track, with third rail feed, ran for ¾ mile from Shore Station along the Pier. 45 lb rails, flat-bottomed, were spiked to longitudinal sleepers, and the gauge remained unchanged at 3 ft 6 in. One four-wheeled tramcar, with six rows of seats arranged 'toast-rack' fashion, was provided by Falcon Works of Loughborough, and, lettered 'Southend Local Board Crimpton Electric Railway', it made its proud début on 2 August 1980. In all, £11,080 was spent in building the railway.

Public service commenced the next day, when 800 passengers were carried, and so popular was the facility that the car was kept busy for the rest of the season, plying to and fro at 4-minute intervals. Speed averaged 12–14 mph. By the time Southend became a City Borough in 1892, the track, now 1½ miles long, had been completed to the pier head, and six cars were in use, forming two trains of three cars each. Success followed success, and a passing loop was installed in July 1898 at a cost of £4,100. From 1902 onwards, current for the railway was drawn from the Corporation's own generating plant. 500 volts became the order of the day, and new 18 hp motors were fitted to all four motor cars then in use. Within a few more years BTH 27 hp motors became standard equipment, and the railway employed four trains of five cars each. By 1913 the fleet rose to its maximum number of 32 cars. By now some 750,000 passengers were being carried annually.

Though the outbreak of war in 1914 sadly inhibited holidaymaking, it is interesting to note that the Southend Pier Railway still carried nearly half a million passengers in 1917. Certainly the restoration of peace brought immediate prosperity, and in 1919 figures passed the 1½ million mark for the first time. Wisely, the Corporation concentrated over the next decade on improving facilities generally, and no major change took place until the track was doubled in 1930. Then came the Second World War, and the Pier was immediately taken over by the Navy. So, too, was the railway. Once again, however, post-war years brought instant prosperity, and by 1947 traffic figures soared to three million. At this stage, the Corporation renewed the entire railway rolling-stock.

Crompton Parkinson supplied the new vehicles: four seven-car sets, each consisting of three motor cars operating at 500 volts dc, and four four-wheeled trailers. Liveried in green and cream, they had wooden seats, automatic sliding doors, and a maximum speed of 18 mph. Formal inauguration took place on 13 April 1949, and during their first year the new trains carried over 4½ million passengers. That year, too, two of the old trailers were sold to Volk's Electric Railway, Brighton, where they were regauged to 2 ft 8½ in. Once the Swinging '60s exhausted themselves, however, traffic on the Pier Railway declined quite sharply to 1½ million passengers per year.

The trend continued. 1970 saw half the stock taken out of service, and working simplified. Then in 1976 came ultimate, and unexpected, calamity, when a serious fire destroyed the pier head. Two years later, in October 1978, the electric railway was closed for safety reasons. For years its future was debated by the local Borough Council. Then a brave decision was made to re-open the Southend Pier Railway. The 1¼-mile line was rebuilt to 3-foot gauge, and Severn Lamb of Stratford-upon-Avon were entrusted with the task of supplying two new diesel-hydraulic locomotives and two push-pull sets of five carriages each. The locos weigh approximately 4 tons each, with each trailer adding 2 tons. A passing loop is controlled by automatic points, and the installation of two-aspect colour light signalling and VHF radio link helps to maintain constant safety. Again, a maximum speed of 18 mph can be achieved, but the normal operating speed does not exceed 10 mph. Princess Anne performed the opening ceremony on 2 May 1986, and, like Volk's Electric Railway, a daily service goes on throughout the year, except for a brief break at Christmas.

Incredibly, the Fates were tempted once again, on 30 June 1986, when an errant 800-ton tanker lost course and plunged clean through the pier. Fortunately, the railway escaped damage, and a rapidly installed temporary bridge enabled operations to be resumed.

RYE & CAMBER TRAMWAY

Opened: 13 July 1895
Closed: 4 September 1939
Gauge: 3 ft 0 in

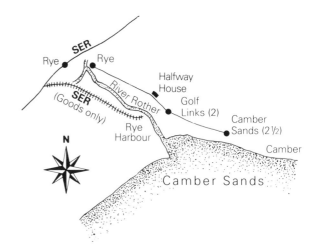

Rye & Camber Tramway

Mention of the Rye & Camber Tramway brings into focus a man whose true worth is only now being assessed, 50 years after his death. Already mentioned frequently in these pages, Holman Frederick Stephens was born at Hammersmith in 1868, and, son of an aesthetic father, he enjoyed an appropriately classical education. Yet he was to emerge at a remarkably early age as a true champion of Light Railways in Britain. Looking back now, one wonders whether, had he exercised his administrative talents in some hungrier corner of the globe — Africa, perhaps? — greater rewards might not have come his way. But who can tell? After all, Dugald Drummond hitched *his* wagon to a star when he emigrated to Queensland in 1890 — but soon hurried back to locomotive engineering in Glasgow and elsewhere.

One thing, though, is certain. The two men would have enjoyed each other, for Stephens, the younger of the pair, not only shared Drummond's military-like passion for discipline, but even, at times, his sharp temper. Yet both were capable of acts of kindness, and both scrupulously respected fair play. Conversely, Stephens' tenacity and utter devotion to

Light Railways merit comparison with that of Henry Forbes, of County Donegal fame. Alas at no time did Stephens ever enjoy the substantial company support which Forbes received in his struggle against road transport. Nor, one might add, would Stephens ever have professed to match Dugald Drummond's engineering skills.

Yet by the turn of the century, the hallmarks of Stephens' instinctive approach to light railway construction were plain to be seen, on the Rye & Camber and elsewhere. He believed implicitly in spending the minimum of capital on track, stations and communications. To Stephens, economy meant survival. Numbers of staff employed on Stephens railways, too, were kept as low as possible, and an intriguing elasticity of duties was ensured by an

For two years from its opening in 1895, the Rye & Camber Tramway operated its 1¾ miles of track on a shuttle basis, using one locomotive only, 2–4–0T Camber, *Here, during these early years, driver and conductor pose for posterity before setting off again from Camber station. Adding cognizance to the purpose for which the light railway was built, this station was later renamed Golf Links Halt.* (Steamchest)

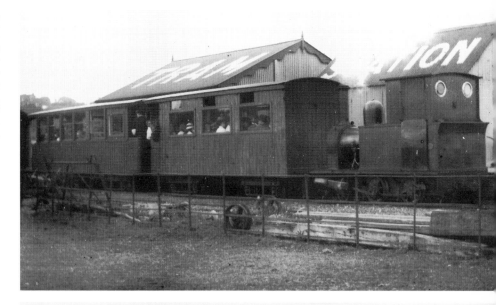

almost total disregard for demarcation. One could even argue, tongue in cheek, that Stephens' empire was, in fact, a true democracy, in that any member of his staff was free to perform any additional task he fancied! A genial and accommodating approach to customers, on the other hand, ensured that passenger and freight prices remained competitive. As for the railway lines themselves, the most economic approach was always sought. Earthworks were kept low in profile, and a deal of needless, and expensive, bridge-building was thus avoided. The price to be paid, that of heavy gradients and sharp curves, was cheerfully accepted. So, too, was the hindrance of frequent level crossings.

Most of these features were present in the Rye & Camber's background. Local businessmen sponsored the project one year after Rye Golf Course was opened, and the tramway was registered on 6 April 1895, with no Parliamentary powers sought, or required. Stephens was appointed construction Engineer, and under his supervision 1¾ miles of single track to a modest terminus at Camber, later renamed Golf Links Halt, were laid in three months. 25 lb flat-bottomed rail was used.

Situated across the River Rother from the SE&CR's main line station, the tramway's Rye terminus was a modest affair of two huts, whose corrugated-iron roofs, clearly visible from the high town walls, bore the painted legends 'TRAM' and 'STATION'. A run-round loop and two sidings were provided, as was a small corrugated-iron engine shed. The tramway track ran parallel with the road to Camber. Golf Links Halt lay close to the river bank, whence the line later turned inland for Camber Sands, using a half-mile extension which was added in July 1908. A Bagnall 2–4–0 tank, named *Camber*,

Golf Links Halt, née Camber, a typical corrugated iron structure, was situated 2 miles from Rye, and ¹/₂ mile from Camber Sands. The passing loop seen here was removed after 1926, when the winter service was abandoned because of road competition. (Steamchest)

The Rye & Camber Tramway has long since been abandoned, but Golf Links station building still stands in recognizable form. In this view, taken in June 1985, cars straddle the original Tramway line, and the additional metals laid by the Admiralty during the Second World War can still be detected. (Steamchest)

provided the tramway's sole motive power for the first couple of years. Then a second Bagnall, *Victoria*, joined the ranks. In 1925 a diminutive petrol-driven loco was obtained from the Kent Construction Company, of Ashford. *Victoria* was then laid aside — to be sold for scrap a few years later. *Camber* was retained for emergencies only.

In its heyday, the tramway was immensely popular with locals and visitors alike. Six months, in fact, after its inception, a dividend of 7½ per cent was declared on the company's £2,800 capital. Return fares from Rye to Camber Sands were 9d for first class, 4d for third class, and caddies and dogs were charged 2d. Golf Links Halt was comparatively substantial, by Stephens standards. But, although the raised platform was neatly fenced, the waiting room relied, as usual, on corrugated-iron for its architectural merits. Camber Sands had a platform, but no station building.

Stephens' economy certainly extended to rolling-stock, for the Rye & Camber Tramway started life with one engine and one carriage, both provided by Bagnall. The carriage, a 25½-foot-long bogie saloon, was of the tramcar type, and accommodated 12 first class and 20 second class passengers. Entrance platforms were provided at each end of the coach, though on one side only — for all R&C station platforms were on the same side of the line. Glass windows on the coach were removable in summer weather. A little later it was joined by a second coach, manufactured locally this time, by Rother Iron Works, of Rye. Closely resembling the first carriage, with its straight matchboard sides, the Rye coach, however, had fewer windows. It was also designed to seat 25 third class passengers, and an entrance platform was to be found at one end only. The windows were fitted with sash cords. Both coaches were equipped with hand brakes, and each weighed 3 tons when empty.

Fares were collected, and paper tickets issued, by a 'boy' conductor *en route*. Signals were not required on the line, and each station was provided with a run-round loop. In keeping with its modest pretensions, the Rye & Camber also owned a few four-wheeled open wagons. With axle-boxes protected by canvas from infestation by sand, these were used mainly to collect ballast from the beach at Camber. At times of summer stress, though, the company did not hesitate to fit cross-benches, and use them for passenger purposes.

Thus, for the first two decades of its existence the tramway enjoyed true prosperity. Season tickets were issued, and excursion trains were run on Sundays. Winter services slackened off latterly, and were even suspended after 1925. But summer traffic persisted so vigorously into the late 1930s as to justify construction of a further modest extension to a holiday camp near Camber Sands. Unfortunately, war intervened, and the extension, though built, was never used.

Worse was yet to come, for in 1940 the Rye & Camber was taken over by the Admiralty. Supply dumps mushroomed in the area, and, as the war progressed, much of the line between Golf Links and Rye was concreted over to permit common usage by road and rail vehicles. So much incidental damage was also done that the tramway, when it was handed back in peacetime, proved to be quite unusable for its original purpose.

By now private cars and motor bus services were providing overwhelming competition, and times were hardly propitious for capital investment in Light Railways. Mercifully, perhaps, Stephens did not live to witness his little railway's fate, for, faced with little alternative, the once prosperous Rye & Camber Tramway conceded defeat and slipped quietly into voluntary liquidation. In September 1947 such land as was leased from Rye Council was surrendered. Rye Tramway Station was soon demolished, and the track was taken up. One year before, a visit to the locality had already revealed a sorry state of affairs. All rolling-stock stood at Rye Terminus, and *Camber*, though sheltered in the shed, lacked both smokebox and dome. The petrol engine seemed in reasonable condition, but the two passenger coaches were in a bad way, with side panels and windows smashed. One end platform had gone completely. Only two flat goods wagons could be seen, and between Golf Links and Camber the rails and sleepers had been removed. Everything else went for scrap in 1947.

Today Golf Links station building still stands, thinly disguised as a store, and faint relics of a short Admiralty siding to a nearby jetty can just be detected. The rails from Rye, still concreted in, also mark the former route to Golf Links, but little else remains to remind us of Colonel Stephens' once happy enterprise.

Fortunately, the Bagnall coach escaped scrapping, and was put to garden use nearby. During the mid-1960s the Brockham Museum Association was given the opportunity of adding what was left of the coach to its collection. Long-term restoration work then ensued, and in 1982 the coach was removed to Chalk Pits Museum, near Amberley, West Sussex. There it remains today, with many other valuable narrow gauge exhibits.

LOCOMOTIVES

Name	Type	Date built	Makers	Maker's number	Remarks
Camber	2–4–0T	1895	Bagnall	1461	Sold for scrap in 1946
Victoria	2–4–0T	1895	,,	1511	Sold in 1920s
0–4–0 petrol engined loco		1925	Kent Construction Co		Sold for scrap in 1946

Though both 2–4–0Ts were delivered by Bagnalls in 1895, there were dimensional differences. *Victoria* had 6 in x 10 in cylinders and 2 ft 0½ in diameter driving wheels, as opposed to *Camber*'s 5½ in x 9 in cylinders and 1 ft 9½ in wheels. Both were originally painted light green and lined, but after 1920 *Victoria* was liveried in blue, and lost her name. The appearance of the petrol loco was aptly summed up by its local nickname, 'The Lawnmower'. Both passenger coaches were painted a dark reddish brown.

BRIGHTON & ROTTINGDEAN SEASHORE ELECTRIC TRAMROAD

Opened: 28 November 1896
Closed: January 1901
Gauge: 2 ft 8½ in and 18 feet

It may seem odd to include an 18-foot gauge tramroad in a book devoted to British narrow gauge railways. But the fact that it was built by Magnus Volk, and functioned on *two* 2 ft 8½ in gauge tracks, justifies at least a mention.

Volk yearned to extend his electric railway to Rottingdean, but the instability of chalk cliffs in that area meant he would have to climb to much higher levels, or finance an expensive viaduct, or embankment, at sea level. With neither of these alternatives a practical proposition, Volk then turned his facile mind to an even more remarkable solution. He would run a railway *under the sea* — at least, when high tides obtained! So startling, yet delightful, was the idea that Volk even obtained financial backing, and in July 1893 an appropriate Act of Parliament sanctioned implementation of his extraordinary dream. Capital was fixed at £20,000, and an additional Act of 1896 added £8,000 more, plus an extension of the construction date. Work, meanwhile, began in 1894.

The more Volk's grotesque structure took shape, the more local residents must have gaped in quiet amazement. Starting from a point 100 yards out to sea, at the end of Banjo Groyne, two sets of 2 ft 8½ in gauge tracks, laid 18-feet apart, ambled off eastward; and, remaining at a constant 60–100 yards from the shore, they arrived, 2¾ miles later, at Rottingdean. Here, a 100-yard-long light steel pier was built to receive prospective passengers. In the meantime, a huge vehicle, designed to run through 15 feet of sea water at high tides, was being constructed by the Gloucester Railway Carriage & Wagon Co Ltd. Surely it must have been the most remarkable product even turned out by that, or any other, company, for, 40 tons in weight, it consisted of a wide-decked platform, 50 feet by 22 feet, which was supported by four braced legs, each 23 feet long! At the foot of each leg a small truck containing four 30-inch wheels made contact with the 2 ft 8¾ in gauge rails. The deck saloon was a riot of late-Victorian ingenuity, and, enhancing the uncanny maritime flavour, both lifebelts and a lifeboat were provided. Named *Pioneer*, this extraordinary car could accommodate 150 passengers. Electricity came from a plant under Rottingdean Pier, and trolley standards which ran parallel with the 18-foot track conducted it along OO-gauge wires. On board *Pioneer*, twin trolley poles and tram-type controls at either end completed the tramcar illusion.

Nevertheless, after appropriate Board of Trade inspection in September 1896, a ceremonial opening was carried out on 28 November. Local dignitaries were conveyed to Rottingdean, which journey took 35 minutes, and the public service commenced two days later. Unfortunately, Nature chose to be unkind, and great storms on 5 and 6 December so damaged Volk's Tramroad that it was not reopened until 20

July 1897. *Pioneer*, roped to a pier at Rottingdean, finished upside down in the sea. Volk, however, was not easily beaten, and once services resumed, they continued throughout the winter of 1897. At a fare of 6d each way, members of the public still flocked to savour the uncanny progress of 'Daddy Long Legs' through high tides and low. Then, in January 1901, it all came to an end, when Brighton Corporation, quoting the tramroad's own Act of 1893, insisted that Volk was under legal obligation to remove the tracks to make way for new and longer groynes.

Possibly not unwilling to be rid of his 'white elephant', Volk then procured an Act authorizing construction of a 2 ft 8½ in gauge line along the foreshore, from Brighton's boundary to Rottingdean. The line was meant to be 2¼ miles long. On this occasion, however, raising £40,000 capital proved to be an impossible task. The original tramroad tracks remained *in situ*, and for a number of years *Pioneer*, roped to an intermediate landing stage at Ovingdean Gap, stood knee-deep in sea water, as a gaunt reminder of what might have been.

In 1909, scrap merchants removed the lot, and today a few sea-stained concrete blocks, barely discernible even at low tide, are all that remain to remind us of Magnus Volk's strange Wellsian adventure.

LYNTON & BARNSTAPLE RAILWAY

Opened: 11 May 1898
Closed: 29 September 1935
Gauge: 1 ft 11½ in

In the year 1892 the railway closest to Lynton, a modest community nestling on the southern shore of the Bristol Channel, lay fully 20 miles away, at Barnstaple. Exactly the same situation obtained nearly half a century later, although the intervening years witnessed the rise and fall of one of England's best-loved minor railways. Like so many of its contemporaries, the Lynton & Barnstaple fell victim in the end to motor transport's superior mobility.

Up to, and well into, the nineteenth century, Lynton and its twin village, Lynmouth, relied jointly for a living on fishing and agriculture, and faced little option but to receive their vital necessities, coal and lime, by sea. Such roads as led inland were so precipitous and foully surfaced that visitors, too, tended to arrive by boat. Gradually, however, as the tourist habit began to take root, and railways responded by spreading throughout Southern England, local demands for improved communications with the

Lynton & Barnstaple Railway

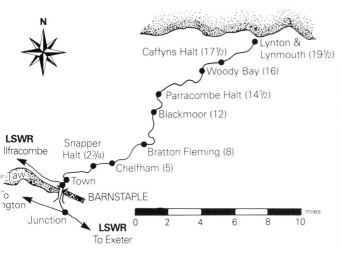

Caffyns Halt (17½)
Lynton & Lynmouth (19½)
Woody Bay (16)
Parracombe Halt (14½)
Blackmoor (12)
LSWR Ilfracombe
Snapper Halt (2¾)
Bratton Fleming (8)
Chelfham (5)
Town
BARNSTAPLE
Junction
LSWR To Exeter

0 2 4 6 8 10 miles

outside world voiced themselves with increasing urgency.

As it happened, a general railway development was, in fact, slowly encasing the area concerned. It all started in 1841, when the Great Western Railway, thrusting its broad gauge metal westward, opened up communications between London and Bristol. Next, once it had allied itself with the more powerful LSWR, the North Devon Railway offered a second direct link with the capital from 1863 onwards, this time, from Barnstaple. Ten years later, the GWR also closed in on Barnstaple; and by 1874 the completion of the GWR's Taunton-Minehead branch, and that of the LSWR between Barnstaple and Ilfracombe,

forged a veritable rail triangle round Lynton and Lynmouth. Yet, railwise, both villages were as incommunicado as ever.

Horse-drawn coaches strove to fill the gap, as more and more visitors poured into Barnstaple. But travel to the north coast in this fashion proved such an arduous and painful process that local agitation for direct rail communication waxed even more vociferous than before. Typical of the late nineteenth century, no shortage of railway proposals ensued. The year 1879 witnessed an abortive attempt to link Lynton with South Molton, 22 miles inland. Four years later, a proposed Barnstaple & Lynton Railway Bill, mooting a line via Kentisbury, fell victim to combined resistance from the GWR and LSWR. A decade later, the original sponsors of the South Molton project, obtaining a modified Act, attempted further variations on their old theme, including electrification, if necessary. But powers lapsed, with no work done, by 1893. Duly regretful, Lynton and Lynmouth lapsed, too — back into splendid isolation.

Curiously, it was a businessman, not a railwayman, whose severed the Gordian knot. Mr (later Sir) George Newnes had already made a name for himself in the publishing and Parliamentary world by the time he learned to love Lynton and Lynmouth; and his considerable influence in local affairs played a crucial, albeit altruistic, part in determining that Lynton should have its railway. Once again, during discussions, the success of C. E. Spooner's Festiniog Railway focused a powerful light, for not only could sharper curves be incorporated in a narrow gauge line, but building costs of around £2,500 a mile offered hope far beyond that of similar standard

L&B men pose proudly at Barnstaple Town station beside their beautifully maintained little engine. The gas lamp-post is pure LSWR in style, as are, possibly. the station master and his dog . . .
(Steamchest)

S 2942

BARNSTAPLE TOWN STATION.

Southern Railway running number 761 can just be seen on Taw's cabside as the little loco arrives at Barnstaple with the 7.13 am ex-Lynton on 7 September 1933. Two coaches per train plus a wagon or two, or, alternatively, three coaches, represented fairly normal loading during the railway's lifetime. (LCGB, Ken Nunn Collection)

One day earlier, at the other end of the line, No 188 Lew brought three coaches into Lynton on the 3.15 pm ex-Barnstaple. Though supplied under SR auspices in 1925, Lew differed only slightly from her three Manning Wardle 1897-vintage sisters. The only L&BR engine to escape the local scrapyard, it finished up in Brazil. (LCGB, Ken Nunn Collection)

gauge construction at £8,000.

Almost incredibly — but such is life — a rival standard gauge scheme promptly reared its head in opposition. Sponsored by a local landowner, and strongly backed by the GWR, it rather optimistically envisaged a minimum of major engineering work. On raged the battle until 19 March 1895, when the House of Lords, after careful perusal of both Bills, awarded its verdict to the narrow gauge project. A little later, on 27 June, the Lynton & Barnstaple Railway's Bill passed successfully through Parliament. On the face of it, with authorized capital set at £72,000, and borrowing powers at £24,300, all signals were at 'green'.

Alas, signals, as railwaymen well know, are not infallible; and a somewhat euphoric Board which assembled the day after the Royal Assent was given, had, not unnaturally, little inkling of the sore trials which lay ahead. Instructions were given to press on with the preparation of the railway's course. In short, it was to follow the River Yeo out of Barnstaple for 5 miles; then, diving and climbing as required, via the

edge of Exmoor and two river valleys, find its way to Lynton, 700 feet above sea level. Three months later, Lady Newnes attended Lynton station site to cut the first sod. A public prospectus issued shortly afterwards estimated that considerable tourist traffic would be drawn to the line, and waxed optimistic on L&B prospects. In the event, at least one aspiration, that of covering the 19¼ miles from Barnstaple in 1 hour, was never to be realized.

Actual construction work commenced midway through 1896, but opposition from landowners, coupled with tiresome litigation, soon made the Board's path a stony one indeed. Even an early resolve to share an exchange station at Barnstaple with the LSWR was humbugged by indifference on the major company's part — until a threat by the L&B to build its own station brought results. Agreement finally materialized in August 1896, and a new joint station called Barnstaple Town eventually replaced the the South Western's former domicile, Barnstaple Quay.

Then came more trouble. At a Board meeting,

held on 18 October 1897, sharp criticism was expressed of an apparent lack of zeal on the contractor's part. After receiving and accepting solemn assurance that the line would, in fact, be completed by 1 January 1898, the Board was deeply shocked to be sued by the contractor at a later date for £40,000 in respect of 'extra construction costs'. Recourse to arbitration reduced this veritable time-bomb to £27,000. By then, alas, the contractor had gone bankrupt, and the L&B was not even able to recover legal expenses. The fault, it appeared, lay with the original consulting engineer, who had misled both the L&B and the contractor into believing that no great amount of earthworks would be required. Add to these sad events the fact that the L&B Board had seen fit, in 1897, to create a substantial number of new shares and Debentures, and it will be realized that the little railway was deep in debt before it turned a wheel.

Despite that gloomy background, 16 carriages, 14 goods wagons and three Manning Wardle 2–6–2 tanks were to hand when Sir George Newnes officially opened the L&B at Barnstaple Town station on 11 May 1898. Admitting that the journey would require 1 hour and 40 minutes, 'because the track was new', Sir George again expressed the Board's forlorn hope that this would be cut to 1 hour in the foreseeable future. Flushed with excitement, the assembled Barnstaple Corporation procession chose not to argue; and, five days later, on 16 May, public service commenced.

Some 2,500 passengers travelled over the next fortnight. A fourth locomotive, perforce ordered from the Baldwin Locomotive Works of Philadelphia, USA, arrived in parts, and was duly steamed in July of that year. Meanwhile, a rival Minehead & Lynmouth Railway scheme, which aimed at running a 20-mile 2-foot gauge line from alongside the GWR's station at Minehead, had to be fought off. Mercifully, this was successfully accomplished when the Light Railway Commissioners held a public inquiry at Minehead.

For the next 15 years excess of income over expenditure on the L&B was so minimal that only one annual dividend was paid. And that was a miserable half per cent in 1913. The L&B may have increased the number of visitors brought to Lynton from Barnstaple, but coach services from Ilfracombe and Minehead showed no sign of relinquishing their grip. Quite logically, therefore, the L&B, despite local complaints, ran only two coaches per train for most of the year. The number of daily trains each way varied from three to six, depending on the season. Only on Market Days were trains extended to six coaches, and once a year, during Barnstaple Fair Week, a maximum permitted load of coaches, with two engines, could, on occasion, be observed. The L&B's safety record, incidentally, was beyond reproach. Never a passenger was injured during its 37-year existence, though, regrettably, three members of staff were involved in fatal accidents during the years 1910–13.

Throughout the First World War, a basic service of three winter trains a day, and six in summer, was pretty consistently maintained. A few employees left for war service, but most were allowed to stay as

Exe, *the second of L&BR's Manning Wardle trio, draws breath at Barnstaple Town well after the Grouping of 1923. Judging by the empty look of her bunker, she will require to recoal before venturing back to Lynton.* (Steamchest)

Lyn, the L&B's 'odd man out', was a 2–4–2T delivered by the Baldwin Locomotive Works in 1899. The loco's American parentage is clearly revealed as she stands outside Barnstaple shed on 28 August 1920. Three domes now exist where one formerly sufficed. (LCGB, Ken Nunn Collection)

'essential workers'. In the immediate post-war years, however, mineral traffic slumped badly. Passenger returns, however, appeared to approach those of pre-war years. But soon it became patently obvious that two important factors were hindering profitability: operating costs were soaring, and road competition was biting deep. With these formidable dangers in mind, the Board decided that negotiations to have the little railway taken over by the LSWR formed the only hope of survival.

Appropriate negotiations opened in 1922, and agreement was reached in June of that year. Settlement, part in cash, part in Debenture cancellation, enabled the L&B Board to make less than adequate compensation to the company's unfortunate shareholders. Then, under Grouping, the LSWR passed under Southern Railway control, as from 1 January 1923. The Railway Act of 1921 did not, however, apply to narrow gauge railways, and a Southern Railway Act of March 1923 was required to ratify acquisition of the L&B. Thus, the little railway's independent existence did not terminate until 1 July 1923.

Fortunately, after all these trials and tribulations the SR decided to spend money on the line. Attention, therefore, was immediately focused on arrears of maintenance. Fresh sleepers were laid all along the track, and rail spikes were replaced by bolts and clips. A few concrete sleepers were inserted, but on noise level grounds the experiment was not pursued. The L&B rail seemed in good condition, though it required reballasting, and opportunity was

taken to realign several curves. Rolling-stock, most of which had survived in good order, was gradually treated to SR livery, and a fourth Manning Wardle 2–6–2 tank was added in 1925. Major repair facilities at Eastleigh were now also available. On the public side, a new timetable offered something like pre-war passenger service, and excursion traffic from outside was encouraged. One summer Sunday in the mid-1920s saw four engines and all 17 coaches working flat out.

Despite the SR's best intentions, however, the tidal wave of road transport, which by now was threatening railways all over the UK, could not be stemmed. Working losses on the ex-L&B soared to £5,900 in 1927, and never after fell below £5,000. Numbers of passengers plummeted from 72,000 in 1925 to 32,000 in 1934. Up to then, the SR had stoutly maintained a full service. But, once expensive track renewals loomed up in 1935, senior management decided that the line must close at the end of the summer season.

Ironically, this news created tremendous concern locally, and many who had not set foot on the railway in years rushed to join and organize protests. A conference of local authorities, called at Barnstaple in April, emerged full of layman recommendations. A deputation travelled to meet the SR's Traffic Manager — and were shocked to learn that the Southern really meant what it said. That summer a near record number of passengers flocked to travel on the L&B. But it was all too late, and, amidst cheering crowds, soulful renderings of 'Auld Lang Syne', and a constant explosion of detonators, last train headed by *Lew* and *Yeo*, duly left Lynton station at 7.55 on the evening of Sunday, 29 September 1935.

Having made its firm, though distasteful, decision, the SR wasted no time in following it up. Some workshop equipment escaped to Eastleigh, but the L&B's total rolling-stock was concentrated in Pilton Yard, the little railway's former running headquarters, just outside Barnstaple. One tank, *Yeo*, was steamed to assist in part of the track lifting operations; then, having completed that task by 8 November, it, too, joined the silent ranks at Pilton. Everything was made ready for sale, for, of course, the SR could offer no future practical employment for either narrow gauge locos or stock.

The sale, held in Pilton carriage shed on 13 November 1935, was a strange amalgam of souvenir hunting and commercial opportunism. All five locos were knocked down at what seem now to be derisory prices. Four, in fact, went to John Cashmore Ltd, a firm of scrap merchants whose name was later to reappear in British Rail annals. Goods wagons invited bids ranging from £3 15s to £9 10s, and the L&B's 17 coaches fetched £10 or upwards each. Fortunately, two of them, bogie coach No 2 and buffet/third saloon No 14, both of 1898 vintage, survive in the custody of the National Railway Museum and the Festiniog Railway respectively.

Equally hearteningly, the L&B's turntable and one signal were secured by the Romney, Hythe & Dymchurch Railway. The signal cabin at Barnstaple Town was demolished in 1938, but the L&B station buildings along the line survived to be sold privately. Devon County Council assumed responsibility for the maintenance of 12 road bridges which still spanned the L&B's one-time proud track. For the time being, the Lynton line platform at Barnstaple remained, but it later vanished in company with its host station. One viaduct at Chelfham still stands mutely erect.

Arguments have since been raised that the Southern Railway might have saved the Lynton & Barnstaple, by running a summer service only, as is the practice on the Vale of Rheidol Railway. But even the keenest advocate of such a policy must concede, on reflection, that the two railways' circumstances were vastly different — and conclude that, exposed as it was to the twin pressures of road transport and twentieth-century economics, the L&B, like so many other minor railway concerns, never had an earthly chance of survival.

LOCOMOTIVES

Name	SR number	Type	Date built	Makers	Maker's number	Sale Price, 13 November 1935
Yeo	759	2–6–2T	1897	Manning Wardle	1361	£50
Exe	760	,,	1897	,,	1362	£34
Taw	761	,,	1897	,,	1363	£50
Lyn	762	2–4–2T	1899	Baldwin	15695	£50
Lew	188	2–6–2T	1925	Manning Wardle	2042	£52. Later shipped to Brazil

Records suggest that a total of five contractor's engines may have been employed during construction of the L&B, but the only certain fact which emerges is that one of them was *Excelsior*, a 2¾-ton 0–4–2 tank built by Bagnalls in 1888 for the opening of the Kerry Tramway, in Wales. Whatever, despite the contractor's bankruptcy, none of the five found subsequent employment on the Lynton & Barnstaple. On the other hand, the L&B Directors appeared to strike gold in 1896, when they accepted Brush Electrical Engineering Company's tender for the supply of three 'main line' locomotives at a very low price of £880 each. Something went wrong, however, and by November of that year Manning Wardle, of Leeds, gained the order — at a more rational price of £1,100 per locomotive. Despite an intervening industrial dispute at Leeds, the 'identical triplets' were delivered in good time. Beautifully liv-

eried in green, they must have enhanced the feeling of confidence which permeated opening day in May 1898.

Decoration apart, the Manning Wardle tanks were beautifully designed. Weighing 27¼ tons apiece in working order, they were turned out with outside main frames and inside-framed pony trucks. Initially, their Joy valve gear was concealed behind covers, but this was later modified in the interests of accessibility. Coupled wheels, 2 ft 9 in in diameter, could muster 7,269 lbs of tractive effort, quite sufficient for L&B needs, and the provision of choppers and cowcatchers, fore and aft, added a distinctive touch. So, too, did a large, well-lit cab. Coal bunkers, though, were somewhat cramped, and in practice fuel was generally carried along the firebox end of each side tank.

Even before opening day, the L&B Directors realized that the provision of only three locomotives would leave insufficient leeway for heavy summer traffic, or emergency repairs. Unfortunately, their belated decision, in February 1898, to order a fourth Manning Wardle tank came at a time when British locomotive builders were overwhelmed by orders. As a consequence, the L&B, in common with such major companies as the GNR and Midland Railway, had to shop abroad.

The result arrived, in crates, at Pilton Yard with remarkable alacrity. It was a 2–4–2 tank, specially, and speedily, designed by Baldwin Locomotive Works of Philadelphia, USA. Once assembled, the outside bar frames promptly betrayed her American origin, as did a smokebox arrangement which was designed to blow out ash. L&B men never took kindly to the latter. The name *Lyn* was painted, mid-Western Roman style, on the wooden cab sides, and a whistle, perched loftily on a Cole safety-valved dome, had to be offset ere the L&B's loading gauge could be satisfied. The Loco's total wheelbase was, at 17½ feet, no shorter than that of the six-coupled Manning Wardles. But *Lyn*'s rigid wheelbase, a foot and a half shorter at 5 feet, gave the US engine much more flexibility on the L&B's many sharp curves. Despite that, L&B drivers persisted in regarding the home-built engines with greater affection.

The fourth Manning Wardle tank, *Lew*, arrived under SR auspices in 1925. She varied very little from her three sisters, though the practice of the word 'Southern' on the tank sides in 6-inch lettering was then first instituted. For the first time, too, L&B engines were given numbers, and those chosen by the SR were well publicized on the cab sides — in 12-inch primrose letters! The green livery also gave way to black, but the nameplates remained unscathed.

The L&B's 16 bogie carriages had already been supplied by Bristol Wagon in 1897 at a cost of some £400 each, and one more composite brake, a most versatile type in L&B eyes, was added in 1903. The coaches were, on average, 39 feet long, and weighed 9 tons. Well designed, they set an extremely high standard in comfort and utility, and required little attention, even from their latterday masters. The original goods stock of 14 four-wheeled and four bogie vehicles swelled to 24 by 1913, and four wagons, together with four goods vans, were added by the Southern Railway in 1929. Oddly enough, so, too, were three second-hand breakdown cranes, in 1927. The latter found little employment on a railway where occasional mishaps were traditionally rectified by human muscle.

In the matter of train control, the highly seasonal nature of the L&B's passenger traffic, plus a complex, though comparatively consistent, quota of mineral, coal and parcels traffic, made 'one engine in steam' a hazardous proposition. Tyer's automatic

tablet instruments were, therefore, installed from the beginning, and the L&B's excellent safety record speaks volumes for the system's efficiency. Signals were judiciously distributed along the 19¼ mile line, and control was exercised from boxes at Barnstaple and Pilton Bridge, and ground frames elsewhere. The maximum permitted load for any one engine was four coaches, or 50 tons; and often, when traffic intensified in summer, nine coaches were marshalled behind a 'double header'. Such arrangements were not unreasonable, considering the gradients and curves which L&B train men so cheerfully faced. Almost invariably, the locomotives worked with their smokeboxes facing Lynton.

LEEK & MANIFOLD VALLEY LIGHT RAILWAY

Opened: 27 June 1904
Closed: 10 March 1934
Gauge: 2 ft 6 in

Early entrants in the field once the Light Railways Act was passed in 1896, the sponsors of the L&MVLR entertained high hopes of generating both industrial and passenger traffic in the heart of the Staffordshire Peak District. All local businessmen, genuinely keen to bring prosperity to the area, they

Leek & Manifold Valley Light Railway

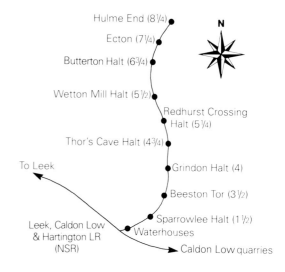

paid dearly for their optimism — for not a farthing was ever paid to shareholders in the way of dividends. More humiliating still, an appeal made by the Board as late as 1915 for public donations towards paying off a considerable bank overdraft evoked the derisory sum of £350. Thus, the little railway was hopelessly in debt by the arrival of Grouping, when the LMS assumed ownership at a valuation price of £30,000.

Yet, on the face of it, there seemed at the time much to justify the promoters' confidence. The district, largely agricultural in character, was renowned for its output of cattle and milk — as the North Staffordshire Railway's heavy milk traffic to London testified — and the natural beauty of the surrounding countryside offered great potential attraction to tourists.

Conversely, in what appeared to be a perfect balance, limestone and gritstone quarries were already in existence, while deposits of lead and copper simply awaited exploitation. The concept, therefore, of a light railway, starting on common ground with the NSR at Waterhouses station, then running 8¼ miles up the Manifold Valley to Hulme End, seemed at the time to invite the best from both worlds. Particularly so when, under the terms of the Light Railways Act, financial assistance might well be obtained from both Treasury and local authorities.

In due course, a Free Grant of £10,000 from the Treasury, and a loan of £10,000 from Staffs County Council, *did* begin to look like distinct possibilities, and it was a totally confident directorate which received authority to commence construction, by dint of a Light Railway Order dated 6 March 1899. The first sod was promptly, and ceremonially, cut by the Duke of Devonshire on 3 October, though continuing difficulty in placing shares postponed actual construction until March 1902. Latterly, and ominously, several of the Directors had to take up the financial slack to safeguard ultimate provision of both Grant and Loan.

Meanwhile, lengthy discussions with landowners

At Hulme End station soon after the opening of the light railway in 1904, 2–6–4T E. R. Calthrop and its train of two bogie coaches quite unashamedly display the sheer opulence of Leek & Manifold stock. Note the spacious verandah at the end of each canary yellow coach, and the elaborate company monogram inscribed on its side. (Author's Collection)

At Hulme End, 8¼ miles from Waterhouses, lay the Leek & Manifold's only engine shed. Now functioning under LMS auspices, E. R. Calthrop's gay livery has disappeared, though no doubt the loco's crew welcomed the increase in coal bunker capacity. The double-roofed cab and huge carbide lamp, so reminiscent of Indian light railway practice, remained, however, with both locos to the bitter end, which, in the case of E. R. Calthrop, came in October 1937. (Lens of Sutton)

were dragging on. In October 1900 a Light Railway Commissioner, reporting rather critically on tenders and specifications submitted by the Leek & Manifold directorate, took the opportunity of recommending that Mr E. R. Calthrop, an engineer well versed in Indian light railway construction, might, with advantage, be consulted. The effect of this simple piece of advice on L&M destinies was dramatic in the extreme. Calthrop, when approached, vowed that construction costs could be considerably reduced by re-aligning and re-surveying the light railway's proposed route. He later proved his point by building the line at a total cost of £35,944, a saving of £11,000 on the original estimate.

The Leek & Manifold's original Prospectus of 15 December 1898 had already decreed the broad principles on which the light railway would be run. Share capital, plus Treasury Grant and local loan, offered some £40,000 latitude. Prospects of even further benefices, amounting to £15,000, loomed on the horizon, provided *shares were taken up in full* by a certain date. It was this latter proviso which eventually crucified major shareholders. The Light Railway Commissioner's suggestion of a 2 ft 6 in gauge was found acceptable. Motive power, it was decided, would be either steam or electric, and the employment of tramway-type coaches was envisaged. Optimistic estimates of revenue likely to be received from mineral, agricultural and tourist traffic were also freely projected; and the North Staffordshire, sole major railway active in the area, was persuaded to undertake working of the L&MVLR in perpetuity in return for 55 per cent of the light railway's gross revenue.

Alas, 'Big Brother' was to prove a difficult bedmate! At this early stage, NSR Directors had shown enough interest in the broad scheme to promote a two-part venture called the Leek, Caldon Low & Hartington Light Railway. The first part called for an extension of standard gauge NSR metals from Cheddleton Junction, south of Leek, to Waterhouses, whence a continuing branch would service Caldon Low Quarries. The second part postulated the creation of the L&MVLR as a separate company. The latter, using Waterhouses station as a springboard, would lay narrow gauge tracks 8 miles on to Hulme End. As if to clinch the inter-company connection, Joseph Forsyth, brother of an earlier NSR engineer, was appointed Engineer to the new light railway. It was when Forsyth died, in December 1900, that E. R. Calthrop emerged as his natural successor. The latter's highly successful experience with Indian light railways, notably the 2 ft 6 in gauge Barsi line, was to play a crucial role in determining the extraordinarily opulent nature of the Leek & Manifold's rolling-stock.

Construction on the L&M began in March 1902,

but sundry misfortunes continued to plague progress. Share subscriptions were sluggish, local landowners proved less than helpful, as did the L&M's senior partner, the NSR, and even tenders for rolling-stock, when considered in 1903, were derided as excessive. In the event, of course, E. R. Calthrop's persuasive powers had their way.

Yet, despite apparent discord, a Shareholder's Meeting, held on 25 February 1904, enthusiastically endorsed a resolution urging extension of L&MVLR metals on to Longnor and Buxton 'at the earliest opportunity'. Opening day of the current installation, originally planned for 23 May that year, had, in fact, to be postponed — as two locomotives supplied by Kitson & Co had not yet been tested, and only two coaches of an order for four had been delivered! Eventually, however, came the Great Local Event — on Monday, 27 June 1904. One small snag still remained: the NSR branch from Leek being still incomplete, because of bad weather, the L&M had to use a temporary terminus at Waterhouses. Full facilities at the NSR station did not become available until July 1905. None the less, so many passengers flocked to the L&M on opening day that the NSR, in all its majesty, saw fit to claim £100 for 'extra working expenses incurred'. Verily, the facts of the L&M's working relationship were already coming home to roost!

One interesting aspect of this interim 12 months' working was the operation by the NSR of two steam buses between Leek and Waterhouses. Coke-fired, chain-driven, and hopelessly prone to vibration, these vehicles must have offered a punishing ride to such visitors as were anticipating the ultra-comforts of L&MVLR travel. It follows that implementation of the narrow standard gauge link at Waterhouses station must have come as a merciful relief to all concerned.

From there on the light railway enjoyed the luxury of its own single platform, with run-round road. A fan of three sidings attended to the loading and unloading of the narrow gauge transporters which E. R. Calthrop had so dramatically introduced. On the other side of Waterhouses station, and at a higher level, NSR trains from Leek made a gingerly entrance on a falling grade of 1 in 260. Apart from the munificent appearance of L&M locos and stock, the departure, or arrival, of a narrow gauge train contained its own elements of drama, as a bicycle-provided porter laboured off to open level crossing gates which lay 300 yards distant. He certainly had no difficulty in identifying approaching trains, on schedule or not, for the sound of their struggles up a preceding gradient of 1 in 41 echoed all over the countryside. So, too, did that of an NSR train leaving Leek.

The patrician quality of the Leek & Manifold's locomotives, rolling-stock, and, indeed, track has

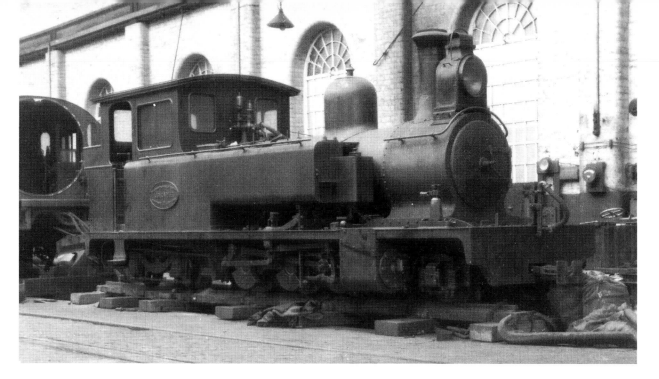

already been mentioned, and herein, of course, lay the influence of E. R. Calthrop. Calthrop, a gifted engineer, had a passionate belief in the value of light railways. Appointed Locomotive Inspector to the Great India Peninsular Railway in 1882 at the age of 25, his subsequent researches led to the formulation of a Patent Calthrop System, wherein weight and cost of narrow gauge track to minimum economic levels was carefully equated with strict uniformity of axle loads for engines, carriages and wagons. In 1895 came an opportunity to pursue his theory on the Barsi Light Railway (an Indian line, 22 miles long, but extended to 118 miles by 1912). So successful was the practical application of Calthrop's teachings that his subsequent appointment to Leek & Manifold duties was bound to evoke kindred over-tones.

Thus, when the L&M's locomotives were placed on order, their makers, Kitson & Co, suppliers also to the Barsi Railway, were almost certainly instructed by Calthrop to build a 2–6–4 tank 'like the Barsi engines'. Whatever, complete with double-roofed Indian cab and giant carbide-lit headlamps, two of the most remarkable locos ever to set foot on British narrow gauge metals reported for duty at Waterhouses. Four open saloon carriages which followed from Preston were no less oriental in design. Then, to add a final Calthrop imprint, five patent transporter wagons, capable of carrying standard gauge wagons over 2 ft 6 in track, were introduced to elimate the time-honoured problems of transhipment between the gauges. Flat-bottomed rail, weighing 35 lbs to the yard, and spiked to wooden sleepers, was laid throughout, and never gave a moment's concern during the little railway's lifetime. A few signals were erected at either end, but the L&M's consistent practice of working 'one engine in steam' made these rather superfluous.

Anyway, thus exotically equipped, the L&MVLR embarked on its course of public duty. Some initial brushes with an unsympathetic NSR management were required ere a locally acceptable timetable could be agreed. But, by the end of 1904, a pattern was established which lasted until the L&M's dying days: two trains daily each way in winter, three in summer, with extras on Bank Holidays and Stoke Wakes Week.

Alas, even at that, many L&M stations proved to be too remotely situated from their respective villages to encourage local support. Most passengers, therefore, emanated from the outside world. In good weather visitors flocked to Waterhouses to enjoy a leisurely undulating ride up the Manifold Valley. The 8-mile journey took 45 minutes. But such a seasonal, albeit healthy, traffic was clearly insufficient to offset a disappointing mineral trade. With writing already on the wall, further friction between the narrow gauge management and that of the NSR culminated latterly in abandonment of the proposed Buxton extension. A later appeal for LNWR co-operation in building an extension, at least as far as Longnor, produced equally stone-faced results.

By 1909, so grave were L&M finances that both the Treasury and Staffs County Councill were induced to agree to temporary suspension of loan interest payments. Even that, however, could not turn events, and two years later the North Staffordshire was asked to take over the line. In declining, NSR management proffered an alternative proposal that a fixed sum of £700 be paid annually to the L&M, instead of 45 per cent of gross receipts. This, in turn, was declined by the L&M Directors, most of whom still nursed a conviction that creation of a Buxton extension would save the day.

Financial pressures continued to mount, and, almost as a measure of despair, a £12,000 issue of Debenture Stock was authorized in 1911. Even the principle of receiving a fixed annual payment from the NSR was belatedly accepted. 1914 brought the outbreak of war, and with it a suggestion that a public appeal should be launched to meet a bank overdraft. The public's derisory response has already been mentioned. War years were a matter of survival, and by the time Grouping came along, the L&MVLR Directors were facing an accumulated debit balance of £14,000, plus an ongoing annual loss of £2,000.

Apart from comparative LMS indifference, in failing to advertise the attractions of the Manifold Valley line — one duty, at least, the NSR had never shirked — new ownership of the narrow gauge railway brought little change. Milk traffic continued strongly. But the ever-increasing intrusion of road transport played havoc with passenger receipts. So lethal was the latter that a decision was made to close the line; and, on 10 March 1934, one last Leek & Manifold train ventured up a snow-and-mist-bound valley. Local protest at the closure was too ineffectual to matter. Much more effective public concern was generated in 1936, when the LMS proposed to dismantle the line. Consequently, after negotiations the LMS presented the trackbed to Staffs County Council. They, in turn, spent £6,000 in converting it into a public footpath.

LOCOMOTIVES

No	Name	Type	Date built	Makers	Remarks
1	*E. R. Calthrop*	2–6–4T	1904	Kitson	Cut up at Waterhouses in October 1937
2	*J. B. Earle*	,,	1904	,,	Cut up at Stanningley in May 1937

When, in August 1903, the Directors of the L&MVLR considered five different tenders for the supply of two engines, Kitson & Co's quote of £1,725 per loco came third in order of pricing. The L&M management was duly scandalized at the prices tendered, and even threatened to shop abroad. Later Minutes, however, record that explanations from its Engineer, E. R. Calthrop, led to an order for two locomotives being placed with Kitsons. A prudent penalty clause inserted in the Agreement was later invoked, when Kitsons failed to deliver on schedule. How management reacted to the sight of Kitson's Barsi Railway-like 2–6–4 tanks when they arrived would be interesting to know!

Whatever, the two locos, named after both Engineer and Resident Engineer, made history by being the first 2–6–4 tanks to run in Great Britain. No doubt the large roomy Eastern cabs were appreciated by train crews, but the headlamps, though carried to the end, were never used in Leek & Manifold service. Each engine was 26¼ feet long, and weighed in working order 26 tons 18 cwt. Outside cylinders, 11½ in by 16 in, employed Walschaerts valve gear to drive the rear pair of 2 ft 6 in driving wheels. The original hooter was immediately replaced by a whistle, and Ross pop safety valves were latterly fitted in lieu of the Ramsbottom variety. Covers over the motion were also abandoned in due

course, because of overheating. First liveried in chocolate brown, with a double white lining and twin-panelled tanks, the locos later reverted to North Staffordshire madder-lake, with single yellow lining. Later still, they sported crimson lake, with an LMS crest on the bunker. In whatever guise they were spotted, they must certainly have made an unforgettable sight! Any heavy repairs required up to 1922 were carried out at Stoke. Thereafter, Crewe made itself responsible.

One presumes that the sumptuousness of the L&M's four saloon bogie coaches was reflected in their purchase price, for each cost well over £900. The end platforms were roofed, colonial fashion, and passengers were allowed to stand by the ornate railings and gates, even when a train was in motion. Large windows admitted maximum light, and any deficiency was rectified by Stone's system of electric lighting. Not only were the coaches comfortable to a degree, but they were liveried and lettered in a flamboyant fashion hitherto unknown on British minor railways. How sad it is that they were demolished by fire in 1936, after standing idle at Waterhouses for a year!

The L&M's wagon requirements, on the other hand, were modest, and consisted solely of a covered van, two open wagons, and two transporter wagons. It was the latter, of course — an innovation born of

Calthrop's fertile mind — which placed such a unique stamp on the Leek & Manifold's freight practice. Eventually, five of them found employment, with individual prices ranging from £315 to £449.

A model of ingenuity, the Calthrop transporter, resting, of course, on narrow gauge axles, offered extra 18-inch wide platforms which overlapped each side, a mere 10 inches above rail level. On each platform were grooves which accommodated the flanges of standard gauge wheels. A simple clamp over each wheel held the larger vehicle firmly; and, after each journey, re-transfer back to standard gauge metals could be accomplished in a matter of 90 seconds. Certainly the LMS found the transporters very useful in later years, when milk traffic enjoyed a brief flourish. The only difficulty was that earthworks and bridges of any railway using them had to be built to standard gauge dimensions. This, on economic grounds alone, successfully precluded their introduction on any other existent British narrow gauge railway.

Unconventional or no, Leek & Manifold equipment was, regrettably, treated with customary disrespect once traffic ceased in 1934. With the exception of No 2 *J. B. Earle*, which passed direct to Crewe Works, all other stock was assembled at Waterhouses yard, and there it lay, pending future developments. Once track demolition commenced in February 1937, *E. R. Calthrop*, revived from the dead, was used to assist. Then, having done so, it was cut up at Waterhouses in October of that year. Its sister engine, *J. B. Earle*, lay in store at Crewe until May 1937, when it met a similar fate at the hands of George Cohen & Co.

One short transporter wagon appeared to have escaped the blow-torch when it was sold to the Ashover Light Railway in 1935. Alas, duly converted to 1 ft 11$\frac{1}{2}$ in gauge, it failed to meet requirements and met its end at Clay Cross instead.

Naval and military

ROYAL ARSENAL RAILWAY, WOOLWICH

Opened: 10 January 1873
Closed: 1966
Gauge: 1 ft 6 in

Though Woolwich Arsenal found use for a horse and hand-drawn internal tramway as far back as 1824, the year 1866 arrived ere the Royal Engineers Department received authority to institute a steam railway network, similar in gauge (1 ft 6 in) to that found at the LNWR's Locomotive Works at Crewe. Quite remarkably, over the next half-century no fewer than 70 narrow gauge four-coupled tank engines were supplied, new, by a veritable conglomeration of builders; and to this total may be added 12 internal combustion locos which arrived from 1896 onwards. Between the years 1890 and 1918 the Royal Arsenal also acquired 120 miles of standard gauge track, and by dint of sharing a common rail

much of this was dovetailed with the existing narrow gauge metals. Shades of Brunel! At first each department within the Arsenal administered its own railway affairs. Then, in 1900, the whole system was rationalized as an RE Transportation Training Centre. This state of affairs lasted until 1921, when Longmoor Camp assumed the RE's railway training function. At that juncture the Woolwich Arsenal Railway came under civil control.

The extremely specialized activities which were conducted within the Arsenal, itself an eventual area of 1,500 acres, demanded a wide variety of rolling-stock. These ranged from narrow gauge carriages and wagons to huge standard gauge 170-ton naval gun sleighs. 56 lb rail was used on the 18-inch gauge main line, which, amongst other things, handled a half-hourly workmen's passenger service up to 1923; the standard gauge track, taking heavier loads, employed rail ranging from 75 to 105 lbs. Locomotives working in the vicinity of ammunition magazines had, perforce, to use spark-arresting apparatus.

It was all very impressive, though, of course, precious few members of the public were allowed to witness it at work. The Arsenal flourished during both World Wars; then, perceptibly, in the early 1960s it began to lose both significance and territory. Railway operations ceased about 1966, and soon the narrow gauge steam locos were phased out, by sale or scrapping. The last three diesel locos were similarly disposed of in 1971. Visit the locality nowadays, and you will find that an industrial estate and the community of Thamesmead now squat where once Woolwich Arsenal Railway occupied its busy day.

Culverin (Work No 269/1884) was one of ten 0-4-0STs built by Hudswell Clarke for Woolwich Arsenal over the years 1884-9. The spark arrester at the base of Culverin's chimney was, however, a domestic invention which was patented by Mr Neath, foreman of the RAR's Locomotive Department. RAR 77, the four-wheeled saloon coach also seen here, was one of several home-built by Woolwich Arsenal around 1890. Exceptionally wide at 6 feet, these saloon cars were 24 feet long and could seat 32 passengers. (Author's Collection)

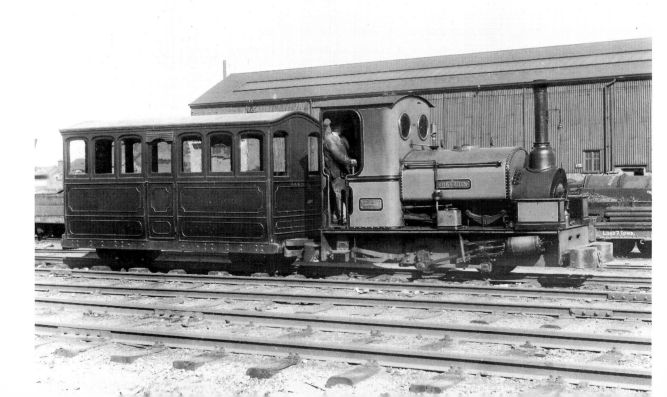

Up to 1914 Woolwich Arsenal found use for seven narrow gauge internal combustion locomotives. During the First World War, however, these gave way to oil-fired steam locos. Megaera (Baguley No 620/1914) was a four-wheeled petrol motor supplied by McEwen Pratt & Co at a time when that firm was in the process of merging with E. E. Baguley Ltd. The loco was mainly used for work in or around ammunition and explosives magazines. (Author's Collection)

LOCOMOTIVES

Up to 1914 Woolwich Arsenal found employment for 45 narrow gauge locos, in ten different classes. During the First World War, not surprisingly, motive power at Woolwich expanded to 64 steam locos, and four internal combustion locos, and a total of 2,000 items of rolling-stock (both gauges) was used. By 1921, however, narrow gauge steam loco stock had reverted to 33. These consisted of three types:

16 'Charlton' Class 0–4–0Ts, built by Avonside Engine Co Ltd during 1915–16. Their short wheelbase of 3 ft 3 in enabled them to negotiate curves of 25-foot radius. Tractive effort was 4,980 lbs.

Sold by the RAR in 1959, 0–4–0T Woolwich (Avonside 1748/1916) was acquired from E. L. Pitt & Co (Coventry) Ltd by Bicton Woodland Railway in April 1962, and now functions on that railway's 1¼-mile long 1 ft 6 in gauge line. (Steamchest)

10 'Culverin' Class 0–4–0STs, built by Hudswell, Clarke & Co Ltd in 1884–89 and 1915. Tractive effort was 3,450 lbs.

7 'Pompey' Class 0–4–0STs, built by Kerr, Stuart & Co Ltd in 1901–02 and 1912. These had slightly extended smokeboxes, and tractive effort was 3,310 lbs.

The first internal combustion loco to work on narrow gauge metals, a Hornby/Ackroyd 0–4–0 paraffin/diesel, arrived, new, in 1896, and by 1914 Woolwich's tally had risen to six. During the years 1934–54, six more internal combustion locos came from Hunslet Engine Co Ltd and Ruston & Hornsby Ltd. Two survived, together with Avonside Engine Co 0–4–0T *Woolwich*, to operate to this day on the Bicton Woodland Railway (1 ft 6 in gauge) in Devon.

CHATHAM DOCKYARD RAILWAY

Opened: 1866
Narrow gauge operations ceased: late 1930s
Gauge: 1 ft 6 in

The Admiralty Dockyard at Chatham had an even more venerable history than Woolwich Arsenal, for, founded in 1514, the establishment there developed latterly into the largest naval base in the world. Thus, by 1866 a standard gauge tramway was in operation, with Aveling & Porter geared engines supplying the motive power. Then, in 1871, came narrow gauge operations. *Lord Raglan*, an 0–4–0ST, was transferred from Woolwich Arsenal to Chatham, and another Manning Wardle, also vintage 1871, arrived, new, that year. Over the years five more tanks arrived, second-hand, from Woolwich Arsenal; and, supplemented by a variety of new acquisitions from Manning Wardle and Fox, Walker & Co, Chatham Dockyard's fleet of narrow gauge locos had grown to 24 by 1913. One solitary paraffin-powered 2–4–0 was also supplied by Ruston & Hornsby in 1904. Chatham's stud of standard gauge locos was even more extensive.

Unlike Woolwich Arsenal, Chatham Dockyard never operated a passenger service. But, mirroring Woolwich in other respects, the importance of the Dockyard began to recede in the 1930s, and as a consequence narrow gauge operations ceased later that decade. Standard gauge diesel operations staggered on for a few more years. But, ultimately, a latterday tendency to run down naval operations

proved too much — and Government defence policy saw to it that Chatham Dockyard's days of glory, both railway and otherwise, came to an abrupt end in 1984.

HOO NESS ISLAND RAILWAY (ADMIRALTY)

Opened: *Circa* 1905 Still extant
Gauges: 2 ft 6 in and 2 ft 0 in

During the 1860s a number of fortifications were built for the purpose of defending the Medway estuary. One of the forts was sited on Hoo Ness Island, and to facilitate ordnance conveyance a very modest 2 ft 6 in gauge railway was laid there towards the end of the nineteenth century. The first loco to work there was *Ascension*, an Avonside Engine Co 0–4–2T of 1904 vintage, transferred to Hoo Island from the Admiralty's Chattenden & Upnor Railway. Two Bagnall and one Kerr Stuart four-coupled tanks saw the Hoo Ness establishment through the First World War. Eventually the Island's modest complement of steam locos were sold or scrapped, and between the two World Wars four internal combustion locos functioned in lieu. One or two more were acquired around 1951, and one year later the little railway was re-gauged to 2 ft 0 in. So, too, were two of its more recent locos. Two more F. C. Hibberd & Co Ltd diesels were acquired in 1962–63. But, gradually, the defence role of the Island vanished, and responsibility passed to the Department of the Environment, who continued to operate the railway for the maintenance of embankments and sea walls.

CHATTENDEN & UPNOR RAILWAY (ADMIRALTY)

Opened: 1898
Closed: 31 December 1961
Gauge: 2 ft 6 in

Towards the middle of the nineteenth century the conjunction of the Hoo Peninsula and Chatham Dockyard began to assume great strategic importance; and, in 1872, work commenced on building a new military installation at Chattenden, a few miles inland from the Medway Estuary. To assist in the conveyance of building material, the Royal Engineers constructed a standard gauge railway from Upnor

Carbon (Works No 404) was one of Chattenden's first two narrow gauge locos. Both were supplied by the Yorkshire Engine Co in 1885, and each saw over 40 years' service before being scrapped or sold. Subsequent narrow gauge steam locomotives were equipped with quite roomy cabs. (Steamchest)

Wharf. Then, a couple of decades later, the standard gauge line was abandoned, and a 2-foot gauge munitions line took its place. Also built as an RE training exercise, some additional 2 ft 6 in gauge metals served their military masters well as an extremely useful inter-depot connection. Chattenden Barracks and Lodge Hill ammunition depot, for instance, gained benefit there from; and, indeed, at the latter, exchange facilities developed with the standard gauge Chattenden Naval Tramway. The Admiralty, in fact, assumed control of the C&UR in April 1906.

During the First World War the narrow gauge line operated a somewhat irregular passenger service for workmen employed at the various Depots; then, in 1942, a regular service was inaugurated. Freight traffic, too, was intensive during this period, though, of course, things quietened down considerably after the cessation of hostilities. Almost inevitably, the run-down gained momentum in post-war years, and passenger train services on the C&UR ceased from 19 May 1961. A few remaining workings which were left around Chattenden Barracks met with a similar fate on 31 December that same year. Thence, the whole area reverted to Army ownership, and today very few traces of the line can be traced in what is now largely MOD property.

LOCOMOTIVES

At least 15 narrow gauge steam locomotives, built variously between the years 1885 and 1914 were employed on the C&UR. The largest, *Pioneer*, a 2–6–2ST supplied new by the Yorkshire Engine Co in 1903, was eventually sold off in 1912. One four-wheeled petrol/paraffin loco, built by McEwan Pratt & Co, later part of E. E. Baguley Ltd, made its début in 1911. It was, however, scrapped in 1915, and thereafter the internal combustion scene centred on a trio of Ruston Hornsby diesels, During the Second World War traffic stepped up considerably, and six more diesels were imported, new, during the years 1943–54. Happily, one of them, plus quite a few items of C&UR rolling-stock, escaped ultimate extinction to serve the Welshpool & Llanfair Light Railway. There the loco was renamed *Upnor Castle*. Four C&UR bogie coaches are also now in the safe hands of the Sittingbourne & Kemsley Light Railway. *Upnor Castle* spent six years in Welshpool & Llanfair service before moving on to the Festiniog Railway in February 1968. It is likely to be renamed *Harlech Castle* ere long.

OTHER MILITARY RAILWAYS

During the course of the two World Wars the south coast of England, the part of the UK most vulnerable to enemy invasion, saw sundry developments in the way of military railways. Some were standard gauge, others narrow, and a variety of functions were served. One 60cm gauge line was constructed by the REs during the Second World War, expressly for target practice at Lydd Ranges, an is still diesel-operated by the MOD's Army Department. A narrow gauge line was also laid at Martin Mill for the purpose of conveying shells to the guns which protected Dover. Further up the coast four forts built around Chatham employed, during construction, a 1 ft 6 in line which led from the River Medway; and as recorded elsewhere in this book, the Military also found use, during the Second World War, for the Romney, Hythe & Dymchurch Railway (15 inches) and the Rye & Camber Railway (3 feet).

PART 4

Miscellaneous

Above 0–4–0ST Oakhill *(Peckett No 1021/1904) was the second 2 ft 6 in gauge loco supplied to the Oakhill Brewery in Somerset. It had larger cylinders than its predecessor, Mendip, and could accommodate 340 gallons of water and 5 cwt of coal. Driving wheels were 2 ft 3 in. Sold in 1930,* Oakhill *was observed 20 years later working at Penarth Cement Works, Glamorgan. Oakhill Brewery's 2¾ miles of single track had interchange facilities with the Somerset & Dorset's main line at Binegar.* (Steamchest)

Below *In 1880 Fletcher Jennings of Whitehaven supplied the Dorking Greystone Lime Co with two conventional 0–4–0Ts,* Townsend Hook *and* William Finlay. *In this mid-1920s view, the latter has arrived at a work site with a train of empty wagons, and these are being cabled up, one by one, to be filled at a higher level. Note the filled wagons on the left. Nowadays* Townsend Hook *can be seen at Amberley Chalk Pits Museum, and* William Finlay *is privately preserved at Woking, Surrey.* (Steamchest)

It may seem almost unchivalrous to dub this section 'Miscellaneous', but how else can one describe such a heterogeneous, albeit fascinating, collection of modest railway enterprises? Hardly any two were alike, yet each saw, or thought it saw, in the alchemy of narrow gauge economics a solution to its own peculiar problems.

There were, of course, geographical exceptions. Take Scotland, for instance, where two-thirds of the population and the vast bulk of its heavy industry have always co-existed in that narrow central region which separates Edinburgh and Glasgow. There, as railway history unfolded itself, the North British and Caledonian Railways strove mightily in competition. They found little difficulty in interlacing the area with standard gauge metals and, in these circumstances it follows that narrow gauge philosophy cut little ice. Even on

When the Bowater Paper Corporation decided in the mid-1960s to abandon its quite extensive 2 ft 6 in gauge industrial railway, the Locomotive Club of Great Britain bravely undertook to lease two miles of track between Sittingbourne and Kemsley, together with seven Bowater locomotives. Thus, on 4 October 1969, was born the present Sittingbourne & Kemsley Light Railway. Here, setting out from Kemsley Down station, is 0–6–2T Superb (Bagnall No 2624/1940). The coaches she is ferrying are conversions from Butterley pulp wagons which were supplied to Bowaters in 1953. (Steamchest)

Four more Bowater tanks went to Whipsnade & Umfolozi Railway, which opened its continuous two-mile 2 ft 6 in gauge circuit at Whipsnade Zoo on 26 August 1970. The circuit has been amended since, and the railway is now known as the Whipsnade Great Steam Railway. But the ex-Bowater locomotives are still present, and in this August 1989 view 0–6–2T No 4 Superior (Kerr Stuart 4034/1920) is preparing for a busy morning's work. Victor, the Fowler 0–6–0DM on the left (Works No 4160005/1951), functioned as No 9 Wynnstay on the Welshpool & Llanfair Railway until 18 March 1972, when it left for the Whipsnade & Umfolozi Railway. The coaches on the right came from the Bowater Paper Corporation, as did 0–6–2T No 3 Conqueror (Bagnall 2192/1922) which lies out of action behind. On this occasion both Kerr Stuart 0–6–2ST No 2 Excelsior (Works No 1049/1908) and Manning Wardle 0–6–2T No 1 Chevallier (Works No 1877/1915) were inside the shed. (Steamchest)

Above Pet, *seen here in Crewe Paint Shop, was one of five 18-inch gauge locos built by John Ramsbottom in 1865 for internal use at Crewe Works. Withdrawn in 1929, it was preserved for many years at Crewe. Now part of the National Collection, it is presently on loan to the Narrow Gauge Railway Museum at Towyn.* (Steamchest)

Below Jim Crow *was a 2 ft 6 in gauge 0–4–2ST (Hudswell Clarke No 340) which was supplied to the LNWR, specifically for Permanent Way Dept use, in 1894. Note the hinged chimney fitted for low tunnel working. The little loco lingered awhile at Crewe during early Second World War years, but was scrapped in 1942.* (Steamchest)

the Kintyre Peninsula, physical conditions by no means inhibited standard gauge railway construction. It was other factors — isolation from mainland transport, the presence of an existing colliery line, of a 2 ft 3 in gauge, and, above all, sheer lack of funds which made 'siccar' the Campbeltown & Machrihanish Light Railway toed the narrow gauge line.

Conversely, the Isle of Man railways occupy an almost disproportionate area in this brief survey of 'Miscellaneous' lines. Yet what other part of Great Britain was able to produce such an enduring railway 'mix'; witness the charming blend of steam, electric and horse-drawn transport which still exists? The Channel Islands, *vide* Jersey and Guernsey, might still be enchanting visitors along similar lines, had not railways there succumbed too readily to motor competition.

Sadly, too, sheer lack of space within these covers precludes lengthier consideration of Britain's national weakness for miniature gauge railways. Three men towered above all others in this context — Sir Arthur Heywood, Henry Greenly and W. J. Bassett-Lowke — and a pity it is that we cannot linger to examine the total fruits of their endeavours. Heywood's Duffield Bank and Eaton Hall railway exploits must suffice, therefore, with passing mention. So, too, must Bassett-Lowke's immaculate contribution to public pleasure on many a 15-inch gauge seaside railway. What was once a rich man's 'toy' was now available to all.

Lastly comes England's peculiarly spasmodic adaption of narrow gauge practice to comparatively modern industrial use. The 2 ft 6 in network which once served the paper mills of Edward Lloyd Ltd (later Bowater Paper Corporation) springs readily to mind. So, too, do the humbler installations of such as Dorking Greystone and Kettering Iron & Coal Co Ltd. And there were many others. Even the main line railways did not hesitate on occasion to descend in gauge. The 'Premier Line' itself installed a 1 ft 6 in network at Crewe Works, and perceived also that its Permanent Way Department could find good use for 2 ft 6 in metals.

Personal memories centre, perhaps, most happily round Horwich. There, in 1887, emulating practice at Crewe, the Lancashire & Yorkshire Railway laid 7½ miles of 18-inch

Over a period of 20 years, the firm of W. Bagnall & Co contributed two 2 ft 6 in gauge 0–4–0STs to the LNWR's Permanent Way Dept collection. Platelayer (1410/1893) and Kitchener (1999/1914) are seen here stored at Crewe after withdrawal in the early 1920s. Despite Crewe's commendable enterprise, both locos were scrapped in 1942. (Steamchest)

track, to facilitate transport of materials and stores around the Works. A brace of minute outside-cylindered 0–4–0 saddle tanks, named *Dot* and *Robin*, duly arrived from Beyer Peacock; *Wren*, costing £50 more at £300, followed later that year. Horwich itself built five more — *Wasp*, *Fly*, *Mouse*, *Midget* and *Bee* — between 1891 and 1901; and none weighed more than 3½ tons.

The names, of course, were significant, and soon they became affectionately regarded members of the family as, hauling their quotas of 'tubs', they moved about Horwich Works, their sharp bark and shrill whistles penetrating the factory din with ease. One day one of them fell on its side. A few muscular Horwich men

The Lancashire & Yorkshire Railway also found use for an 18-inch gauge system within Horwich Works, and Beyer Peacock supplied three tiny 0–4–0WTs in 1887. Robin (Works No 2824) is seen here as built. Of five more built by Horwich Works themselves between 1891 and 1901, Wren, withdrawn in 1962, happily survived to enter the National Railway Museum at York. (Author's Collection)

Kettering Iron & Coal Co Ltd maintained both standard and 3-foot gauge railway systems. The former served the ironworks themselves, while narrow gauge metals connected furnaces with local ironstone workings. 0–4–0ST No 3 (Black Hawthorn No 859/1885) was typical of Kettering's quite substantial fleet of 3-foot gauge locomotives. (Steamchest)

gathered round, lifted the loco gently back on the rails, and off it went, rejoicing. When the day's work ended, their habit was to retire, like roosting chickens, to an odd little nest of their own, next to the Erecting Shop. *Wren* outlived the others, by working on to 1961. Three years later, restored to L&YR livery, she moved to Clapham Museum. Now, of course, she resides at the National Railway Museum in York.

Miscellaneous, eh? I wonder . . .

Scottish narrow gauge railways

GLASGOW CORPORATION UNDERGROUND RAILWAY

Opened: 21 January 1897
Closed: Still extant
Gauge: 4 ft 0 in

A first scheme for promoting an underground railway subway, linking the northern districts of Glasgow with the city centre, emerged in 1887. The idea was to construct a single twin-tracked tunnel, using 4-foot gauge metals, then, by siting the stations equidistantly, employ cable haulage in such a way that once the stationary winding engine stopped after each 700 yards two trains would find themselves at every alternate station. Though it was an ingenious and economic proposition, it was possibly the very novelty of the scheme which persuaded Parliament to reject it. Certainly, an even more ambitious plan, employing two endless tunnels and extending south of the River Clyde, met with a similar fate the following year, this time on the grounds that the proposed tunnels under the Clyde would not be deep enough to countenance future deepening of the river. Then came a breakthrough, in 1889, when the Glasgow Harbour Tunnel Company received permission to construct tunnels under Finnieston Harbour. In light of this precedent a revised Subway Bill met with Parliamentary approval, and work on today's structure commenced, at St Enoch, in March 1891.

Construction problems were formidable, for, despite the comparatively shallow nature of the twin railway tunnels — the deepest station, Buchanan Street, lay 40 feet below street level, the shallowest, Kinning Park, only 14 feet — an underground amalgam of solid rock and sand made life difficult for the various contractors. The 'cut and cover' technique was liberally applied, but, even then, the obligatory use of compressed air triggered off quite a few explosions just below the river bed. On one memorable occasion in February 1894 the resultant waterspout on the River Clyde created panic amongst some sailors who happened to be moored off Custom House Quay!

Where the flat-bottomed 60 lb rails were concerned, gradients and curves were kept within reasonable dimensions. The steepest gradients, 1 in 20 and 23, occurred at each of the two river crossings, while short stretches of 1 in 20 at most stations facilitated the stopping and starting of trains. All stations on the 6½-mile circuit were standardized at 150 feet long and 28 feet wide, with a 10-foot wide island platform offering access by stairs to street level. Some lay in tunnel, others, built between retaining walls, were in the open. Six were lit solely by electricity, and the glass roofs of the remainder offered the additional advantage of daylight. After considerable thought, cable traction was adopted, and the twin cables, each 7 miles in length and weighing 57 tons, were driven by two powerful stationary steam engines. Contrary to oft-expressed public opinion, the cables maintained a constant speed of 13 mph. Meanwhile, a 'grip' mechanism, installed in the driving cab of each train, transmitted power from cable to car; and, of course, the same mechanism was used to effect release whenever necessary.

To attend to the maintenance side, a Car Depot and workshops were established at Govan. Uniquely, the shops lay some 20 feet above the Subway rail level; but a travelling crane saw to the raising and lowering of cars as required. Six cars could be thoroughly overhauled there at any one time. Cars, meanwhile, in daily use were marshalled overnight between Govan Cross and the Car Depot, and, as identification was important to Control, odd-numbered cars confined themselves to Inner Circle service, with even numbers on the Outer rail. The bright red livery was confined to one side of the cars only.

When the Subway opened for public use on 21 January 1897 it had already been decided that a flat fare of 1d should entitle a passenger to travel between any two stations — all very like the Penny Post. Soon, however, it was discovered that quite a number of Glaswegians were not averse to spending hours on end, just travelling round and round the Subway, for sheer pleasure! Thus, tickets, inspectors and a modest scale of fares had latterly to be introduced. But, as in London, provision of an underground railway proved to be an imaginative stroke in alleviating traffic conditions above ground, and the Glasgow Subway proceeded gently through the years on its efficient, and highly popular, course. In years to come it was, in fact, to graduate as the last surviving railway to cling to cable haulage, for conversion to electric traction was not effected until 1935.

The transition was effected in two stages. The Inner Circle was converted by 28 March 1935, then the Outer Circle followed suit on 5 December of that year. During the changeover, a single-line service was adequately maintained. In the meantime, the Glasgow Underground's original cars were completely rebuilt, two-car set fashion, on new frames; and compact, but powerful, tramway-type 60 hp motorized bogies, electro-pneumatically controlled, were installed. Traction current at 570 volts was drawn off an outside third rail. The latter was duly mounted on off-sleeper brackets, and separate 'T' shaped conductors, interesting relics of cable traction days, were utilized to furnish both lighting and signal track circuits. Twenty years later the Glasgow cars, the sole remaining gate-stock in the UK, were fitted with sliding doors.

One needs hardly add that electrification considerably enhanced the volume of traffic which could be handled, and to this day the 'Subway', as it is popularly known, remains an increasingly indispensable element in Glasgow's transport pattern. Ironically, electricity has surrendered its equivalent utility above ground — and the City of Glasgow folk's deep affection for their world-famed street 'caurs' has now, regrettably, become just another footnote in the history of British transport.

CAMPBELTOWN & MACHRIHANISH LIGHT RAILWAY

Opened: 18 August 1906
Closed: 1932
Gauge: 2 ft 3 in

Only the existence of a mile-wide isthmus at Tarbert prevented the Kintyre Peninsula, 40 miles long and 8 miles wide, from joining the ranks of Scotland's Western Isles; and, as can be imagined, life there was traditionally remote from the hurly-burly of ship-building and heavy industry which characterized the northern end of the Firth of Clyde. None the less, Campbeltown, the Peninsula's main town, had long possessed its own coalfield, and it was the centuries-long struggle to exploit this natural asset which led eventually to the creation of Scotland's famous, albeit short-lived, narrow gauge public railway.

Kintyre's coal deposits were first identified around 1495. Certainly local coal was being used in the seventeenth century to evaporate brine, on the coast, at a spot where Machrihanish village now exists. The stuff, however, was of poor quality, and it only began to acquire significant economic value as whisky distilleries and paddle-steamers blossomed conjointly in the second half of the nineteenth century. The steamers used it as fire-raising material, and a certain amount was shipped to Ireland.

As always, transport between mine and ship was a problem; and, in 1775, James Watt, of steam kettle fame, was commissioned to survey a canal route between the mine workings and Campbeltown's natural harbour. The resultant canal served local needs for the best part of a century. Then, in 1875, a newly-formed colliery company, the Argyll Coal and Canal Company, decided to introduce railway working. Well aware of the Festiniog's success much further south, its management calculated that transport of coal to Campbeltown, some 4½ miles distant, by narrow gauge railway would slash cartage costs from 2s 6d per ton to 6d. What Scot could resist *that* bargain!

Railway construction began in 1876. 30 lb rail, spiked direct to wooden sleepers, was first used, but wear and tear proved such that 40 lb rail was gradually substituted. Again, one very sharp curve ordained that only four-coupled engines could be employed.

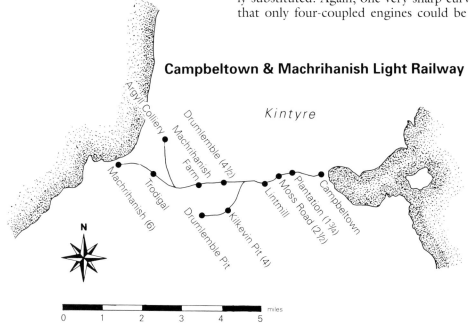

Campbeltown & Machrihanish Light Railway

Kintyre

Argyll Colliery
Drumlemble (4½)
Machrihanish Farm
Machrihanish (6)
Trodigal
Drumlemble Pit
Kilkevin Pit (4)
Lintmill
Moss Road (2½)
Plantation (1¾)
Campbeltown

N

0 1 2 3 4 5 miles

With coaches and engine both looking very smart, Argyll *pauses in a distinctly industrial context to allow another passenger or two to sample the comfort and delights of travel on the Cambeltown & Macrihanish Railway.* (Steamchest)

This restriction, of course, inhibited the locos' capacity to tackle a steep climb, and the immediate descent into Campbeltown. All in all, perhaps the shortcomings of the mine railway were best exemplified by its low cost of construction, a mere £900 per mile. Between the years 1877 and 1900 three locomotives were acquired, each from a different source. The first pair, an 0-4-0 well tank and an 0-4-0 saddle tank, found riding on the colliery railway such a rough proposition that both had to have a trailing truck added.

Yet the problem which most vexed the colliery engineer, an astute man called T. Lindsay Galloway, was the highly seasonal nature of the coal traffic. In summer it lapsed practically to a standstill, and then it was that holidaymakers and day-trippers from Scotland's industrial West literally poured into the Mull of Kintyre. During the summers of 1901–03 alone, Clyde steamers ferried 135,000 visitors to Campbeltown. Significantly, 22,000 of these travelled on by horse-drawn charabanc to Machrihanish, where the golf links were a great attraction.

Galloway's growing conviction that his colliery railway might be extended to participate in this annual summer bonanza was not lost on other local par-

ties, and, early in 1904, the Association of Argyll Railway Co Ltd was formed. Capital was a mere £1,500. Despite implacable opposition from the Duke of Argyll, the main landowner concerned, application was submitted in April 1904 for a Light Railway Order. A public inquiry was held at Campbeltown later that year, the LRO was duly conceded in February 1905, and incorporation of the Campbeltown & Machrihanish Light Railway was made good under the Light Railways Act of 8 May. Generally speaking, local opinion favoured the introduction of a public railway, though many demurred

One mile out of Cambeltown, Argyll *and* Chevalier *rest awhile at Limecraigs locomotive depot. Between them they tell the story of the little railway's development from pit service to public utility. This photograph was taken on 27 April 1922, 13 years before they were demolished on the spot by scrap merchants.* (LCGB, Ken Nunn Collection)

at the proposed 'toy' gauge. Campbeltown Town Council was content to accept the idea of a railway terminus on public ground at Hall Street, on the harbour front, but grew strangely agitated at the prospect of trains crossing Kilkerran Road, which was well out of town. Meanwhile, different forms of traction were solemnly considered, as was a wider gauge. Then, by midsummer, a resolution emerged. Campbeltown would have steam — and the gauge would remain at 2 ft 3 in!

Total capital outlay was estimated at £23,000, and construction commenced in November 1905. The existing colliery railway formed the nucleus, and to it was added a line from Campbeltown coal depot to the harbour, plus a mile-long extension west from the colliery to Machrihanish golf links. Thus, passenger, goods and coal traffic could pass freely between the two centres of population. The LRO imposed the kind of restrictions one would expect, and quite a few local residents added further to the railway's burdens by protesting vociferously against Sunday work. Despite these heavy odds, however, the 5-mile railway was completed in time for Board of Trade inspection on 17 August 1907. Officially opened on 25 August, the light railway attracted 10,000 passengers during its first three weeks of service.

Customers must have been impressed by the new coaching stock the C&M provided — 48-foot long bogie carriages, smartly liveried in cream and olive green. In rather novel fashion, central corridors permitted the issue and collection of tickets *en route*. The normal weekday service settled down at five trains each way. But even the time-saving practice of issuing 1 shilling tickets aboard the steamers never succeeded in lengthening a visitor's stay at Machrihanish beyond 40 minutes.

The C&MLR contained an intriguing number of idiosyncrasies within its comparatively short route mileage. There were, for instance, no viaducts, tunnels, or even stations, on the line; and, starting, as it did, in the middle of one of Campbeltown's busiest streets, tracks had to be laid flush with the road surface, tramway fashion, until they swung across

Kilkerran Road and entered private property. Here, a stiff gradient of 1 in 35 led up to Limecraigs depot, where workshops, loco and carriage sheds and sidings were situated, a good mile out of town. A maximum speed limit of 20 mph was imposed by the Board of Trade, and this had to be dropped to 5 mph whenever any one of ten level crossings was approached. Three of these were over public roads, and seven were private. Then, not far beyond the depot, came the oddest circumstance of all, when the railway crossed a rifle range, midway between the 500-yard and 600-yard firing butts! Special regulations, of course, applied; and when a red flag indicated that firing was in progress, trains duly halted. Mercifully, never an accident occurred.

Still climbing, the line then passed on to its highest point, Tomaig Summit, before dropping leisurely to Plantation Crossing, where some realignment of the old colliery track had been effected. From there it was plain sailing to West Machrihanish Farm, where the old line ran straight into the colliery, and the new branched off to terminate behind Machrihanish's mission hall. As at Campbeltown, the railway's 'office' was the most modest of buildings. At both ends of the line the run-round loops provided could not accommodate six coaches. Thus, the arrival of an exceptionally long summer train often occasioned a deal of ingenious, and rather unofficial, fly-shunting. All C&MLR passenger trains were vacuum braked, and with the traffic too heavy to countenance the 'one engine in steam' practice, resort was made to a specially adapted token system. The trouble was that it was operated by the train crews, not signalmen; and carelessness bred by familiarity caused a nasty accident or two. Still, whatever its shortcomings, the little railway succeeded in quashing horse-charabanc traffic in its part of the Peninsula. Little did it know that post-First World War years would give birth to a much deadlier rival — the petrol-engined bus.

Though it never qualified as a spectacular financial success, the C&MLR plodded through its first decade reasonably well, and even contrived to produce odd annual dividends of 2 per cent to its share-

At the height of the C&MR's prosperity, Atlantic, *the more consistent performer of the company's two 0–6–2Ts, waits quietly in Hall Street while potential passengers disembark on the quayside (right). Provision of buffers plus 'chopper' was an interesting feature on the C&MR's passenger locomotives.* (Steamchest)

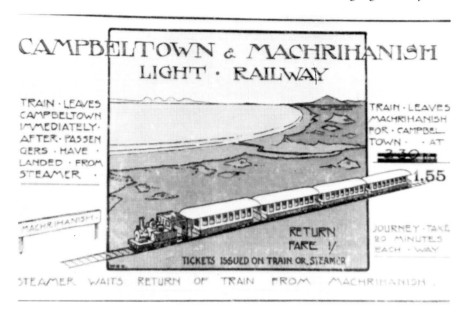

holders. These ceased after 1913, however, and were never resumed. Locally, the little railway was held in great affection, particularly once Campbeltown inhabitants became accustomed to it appearing in their midst in Hall Street. Before long, the C&MLR's two new locomotives *Argyll* and *Atlantic* came to be regarded almost as local 'characters'. Typical of a small railway, the C&M's 20 or so staff exercised commendable versatility in course of their duties, and the shrewd employment of pretty female conductresses on the passenger trains did much to engender goodwill.

The greater pity it was, therefore, that two local bus concerns chose in post-war years to bring great pressure to bear, by operating severe cut-throat competition along the railway's route. Desperately enough, Campbeltown's coal industry was already dying. Production, in fact, ceased altogether in 1929. That year, in a rearguard action to stave off bus competition, the C&M bought two Reo buses, and used them to augment its train service. None too reliable, the buses soon became something of an albatross, and by the summer of 1931 train services were again left to fight alone. The following year an attempt was

made, after two months' idleness, to anticipate summer traffic. Unfortunately, the locomotives were found to be in need of extensive repair. It was all too much, and when summer sailings started in May visitors found the 'wee train' was not there to greet them. It had, literally, arrived at the end of the line.

From there, the denouement was both sad and protracted. The railway sold its goodwill and passenger-carrying licence to the major competing bus company, and a Liquidator was appointed in November 1933 to supervise disposition of all capital assets. Ironically, the land reverted to the railway's old adversary, the Duke of Argyll. Track and rolling-stock passed into the hands of scrap merchants, whence the C&M's six beautiful carriages at least found a new lease of life as holiday huts. Of three surviving locomotives, *Argyll* and *Chevalier* were demolished on the spot early in 1935. A few months later *Atlantic* met a similar fate after assisting to lift the track. One needs hardly add that over the passage of years little remains to inform a casual observer that such a spanking little railway ever functioned on the Kintyre Peninsula.

LOCOMOTIVES

Name	Type	Date built	Makers	Maker's number	Remarks
Pioneer	0–4–0WT	*circa* 1877	Not known	—	Stored out of use by 1906
Chevalier	0–4–0ST	1883	Barclay	269	Demolished in 1935
Princess	0–4–2T	1900	Kerr Stuart	717	Disposed of before 1933
Argyll	0–6–2T	1906	Barclay	1049	Demolished in 1935
Atlantic	0–6–2T	1907	,,	1098	,,

Apart from the fact that a small well tank arrived by steamer from the mainland on 11 November 1877, little is known of the colliery company's first locomotive. It weighed about 9 tons, and its 4-foot coupled wheelbase rode so disadvantageously on rough tracks that a trailing pony truck had soon to be added. Inside frames also complicated matters when major repairs had to be carried out, and by the time the C&MLR opened in 1906 *Pioneer* was already lying out of use at the colliery. Thus, the loco never entered C&MLR stock.

Chevalier, bigger and stronger, was a vastly different proposition, and spent 50 busy years at Campbeltown, mainly on coal work. Once again a trailing truck was fitted, and this offered a much more satisfactory wheelbase of 8 ft 9 in. The loco was extensively overhauled during the First World War, and, amongst other alterations, provision of a handsome totally enclosed new cab endeared her more than ever to train crews. In view of her prescribed duties a top speed of 15 mph was not regarded as a handicap.

By the turn of the century a well-known firm, Kerr Stuart of Stoke-on-Trent, had brought the manufacture of industrial and narrow gauge locomotives almost to a fine art, by specializing in standard classes. One such was their 'Skylark' Class, a modest type of 0–4–2 tank which could readily be adapted to a range of gauges (2 feet to 3 ft 6 in), depending on whether wheels were fitted inside or outside the frames. Thus, a distinctly miniature 0–4–2 tank, *Princess*, arrived at Campbeltown in 1900. The coupled wheelbase in this instance was 5 feet, and, even with pony truck added, the total rose only to 7 ft 8 in. On entering C&MLR stock in 1906 the tiny loco was fitted with a vacuum brake for working passenger trains; but, inevitably, in view of her 2 ft 3 in diameter driving wheels, *Princess*'s duties in this direction were light.

Although the C&MLR acquired both *Chevalier* and *Princess* from the Campbeltown Coal Company, it was patently obvious that something larger in the way of motive power would be needed to handle passenger traffic. Accordingly, the good folk of the town were duly startled when what seemed to be a grotesquely large 0–6–2 tank was landed early in 1906, and, wagon-bound, was promptly hauled by traction engine to Plantation Crossing. Here it was placed on the rails, and immediately set to work. Four handsome carriages followed at two-weekly intervals as the bemused locals watched rail-laying creep on towards the centre of Campbeltown. Like her sister engine *Atlantic*, which arrived the following year, *Argyll* was a splendid product of Andrew Barclay's Kilmarnock shops. A total wheelbase of 12 ft 9 in gave her the capacity to work 70-ton trains, though this was far in excess of both normal restriction and requirements. The two locos' Walschaerts valve gear presented problems at first to local fitters, but native ingenuity triumphed in the end. Of the two, *Atlantic* proved the more consistent steamer. The last engine to work the line, her whistle and gauge glass now rest in a Campbeltown museum.

The C&MLR's eventual stock of six saloon coaches were rightly famed for sheer elegance. Each of the bogie vehicles, 43 ft 6 in long, was beautifully liveried, as were the two 0–6–2 tanks. One coach ran normally for miners' use, but in summer months all six ran on express passenger duties as steamers discharged their welcome cargoes of visitors. Colliery company wagons progressed from primitive tram hutches to conventional 3¼- and 4½-ton wagons as the years passed. In an inventory dated January 1922, 150 wagons are listed, at a value of £750. Presumably these remained coal company property, for the railway company insisted on claiming a total of two in its annual returns! The only additional vehicles provided by the C&MLR were one brake van and one milk wagon, both products of R. T. Pickering & Co, of Wishaw. A reminder that Kintyre weather could pose problems rests in the fact that the C&MLR also occasionally resorted to the use of a sheet iron snow plough.

One might add in conclusion that several other schemes of railway development within the Kintyre Peninsula were mooted, though never implemented. Both the North British and the Glasgow & South Western Railways cast envious eyes on Campbeltown during the first decade of the present century. For a variety of reasons, however, the light railway schemes were dropped, and the C&MLR was left to fight its own battle against road transport in the years which followed 'the war to end all wars'.

OTHER SCOTTISH NARROW GAUGE RAILWAYS

Although Campbeltown witnessed the birth of Scotland's most celebrated narrow gauge railway, the C&MLR was by no means first in that field, for, somewhere in the middle of the nineteenth century, an Argyllshire landowner built a 2-foot gauge line to serve his Ardkinglas estate. The layout, which was quite extensive, ran along the west side of Loch Fyne. Part functional, part pleasure-seeking, it embraced a small engine shed, one tunnel and a station. The latter, incidentally, shared a similar stormy fate the night the first Tay Bridge was destroyed, and was never rebuilt. One steam locomotive, one open passenger carriage and some wagons, when necessary, conveyed guests to an artificial loch called Caspian, whence a small paddle-steamer offered further delights. By the turn of the century, however, the Ardkinglas railway was dismantled, and its rolling-stock went for scrap.

The Sannox Railway, on the Isle of Arran, was created at about the time the Ardkinglas railway vanished. Again narrow gauge, it was, however, a much more primitive concern. Destined to fetch baryte, a mineral also known as 'heavy spar', from a mine situated high in Glen Sannox, its 'main line' consisted of a long incline. This section was worked by gravity, but once the lower level was reached the mineral was transferred from rude wooden hutches to more substantial 2-ton wagons. The latter were then propelled by horse and man power towards a timber pier, for shipment by boat. The Sannox Railway functioned up to and into the early 1930s, but was abandoned before the Second World War erupted in 1939.

Vastly different in character, a 4-foot gauge horse-drawn tramway, known as the Rothesay & Ettrick Bay Light Railway, opened for public service on the Isle of Bute in 1879. Catering exclusively for holiday traffic, it ran for 2¼ miles from the centre of Rothesay, always a favourite resort for Glaswegians, to Port Bannatyne. Twenty horse-drawn cars sufficed to contain traffic until 1902, when the line was re-gauged to 3 ft 6 in and electrified. New 77 lb rail was laid, and thereafter a double overhead pickup served the frequent comings and goings of 20 new open electric cars. They were vividly painted in red and cream.

In 1905 a short extension took the tramway on to Ettrick Bay, and life passed uneventfully enough until 1931, when, only too typical of the times, ownership passed to the Scottish Motor Traction Co. For a while the tramcars continued to function in SMT blue and white livery. Then, by 1936, alas, the motor buses had completed their deadly work, and the tramway system was closed that year.

Island railways

ISLE OF MAN RAILWAY COMPANY LIMITED

Opened: 1 July 1873
Closed: Still extant
Gauge: 3 ft 0 in

Though it is only 33¼ miles long, and 12½ miles wide at best, the Isle of Man contrived none the less to contribute a remarkably colourful chapter to British railway history. Certainly the fact that it found itself only three hours distant from the Lancashire coast, once the Isle of Man Steam Packet Company got into its stride in the mid-nineteenth century, sparked off enormous external interest in the Island. Yet, as time went on, one great problem continued to stare everyone in the face. The more that steam packets decanted passengers from Liverpool, the less able was the Island to offer appropriate sight-seeing facilities, for its elementary road system was geared merely to meet the needs of a modest, scattered population. Thus, as the 1850s advanced, the dilemma which faced the ever-increasing floods of visitors as they disembarked at Douglas remained only too stark in its simplicity. Those who could afford the luxury employed the town's horse-drawn stage-coaches to explore the Island; those who could not were left to find their own way on foot. Lack of communications — it was an old story. Only railways could solve the conundrum.

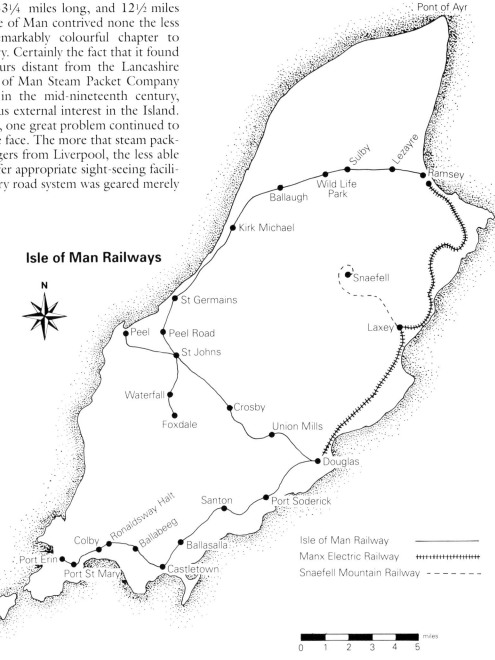

Isle of Man Railways

N

Isle of Man Railway	————————
Manx Electric Railway	++++++++++++++++++
Snaefell Mountain Railway	- - - - - - -

miles
0 1 2 3 4 5

Above *Douglas station, 1900, and, somewhat unusually, No 8 Fenella is working with bunker leading. After running round its train at St John's she will then be able to proceed chimney-first up the notoriously steep Foxdale branch. The last small-boilered engine to remain in IOM service, Fenella, was withdrawn in 1968, and now awaits preservation.* (Steamchest)

Right *Also in 1900, No 3 Pender awaits attention inside the loco repair shop at Douglas. The 2–4–0T, withdrawn nearly 80 years later, is now a sectioned exhibit at the Greater Manchester Science and Railway Museum.* (Steamchest)

The Railway Mania of 1845–46 produced at least one scheme which might have benefited the Isle of Man. But the attempt failed, as did even more energetic projects put forward in 1857 and 1864. In the latter instance the Manx Legislature itself applied what proved to be a fatal tourniquet, when it insisted on a precautionary deposit of £9,000 being made ere initial surveys were allowed to be continued. It was undoubtedly that fiasco, plus the abortion of yet another scheme in 1867, which stiffened local resolve when a group of influential gentlemen met at Douglas on 21 April 1870. The results this time were positive, and after careful consideration the Isle of Man Railway Co was duly registered on 19 December

1870. The aim was to build a railway which would link up the Island's four major towns — Douglas, Peel, Ramsey and Castletown. Henry Vignoles, once appointed Engineer, made a point of visiting Wales. There he investigated Festiniog Railway practice, and returned armed with the intelligence that a gauge of 3 feet would best suit IOM requirements. His recommendation was accepted.

Capital, fixed at £200,000, was likely to be fully employed, for provisional estimates indicated that precisely that sum would be required to construct 42 miles of track. £25,000 more would be needed for rolling-stock. The more disappointing it was, therefore, that local residents, despite their unqualified enthusiasm for the railway, failed to subscribe more than £30,000. Such a shortfall immediately imperilled prospects of building *three* lines from Douglas, and at a meeting held on 16 January 1872 notice was given by the company that the Ramsey section was being abandoned. Disillusioned and angry, residents in the northern part of the Island took their own action, as we shall see presently. Meanwhile, the financial net was spread wider to attract English railway speculators, and, gradually, with the co-operation of such figures as Sir John Pender and the Duke of Sutherland, the barometer turned 'Fair'.

Construction work commenced on 6 June 1872, and the company's first three Beyer Peacock 2–4–0 tanks, duly named after the railway's 'godfathers', were delivered in time for the grand opening ceremony of the first completed section — that between Douglas and Peel (11½ miles) — on 1 July 1873. Islanders celebrated accordingly, public service commenced the next day, and during the first five weeks of operation traffic receipts comfortably matched anticipated earnings of £30 per mile per week. But these, of course, were summer figures. Winter months would reduce the batting average.

It is interesting to note, *en passant,* that although the Island owed no direct allegiance or responsibility to the British Board of Trade, Colonel Rich, the Board's Inspector of Railways, took a keen personal interest in Manx railway affairs; after inspection, he satisfied the Manx Government that a working permit should be issued. He performed a similar service shortly before the Douglas–Port Erin section (15½ miles) was publicly opened on 2 August 1874. Construction work on this line was more involved. That, plus the fact that Manx citizens had got used to a railway being in their midst, no doubt accounted for the quiet way in which the Port Erin line commenced duties.

With its programme of 27 miles completed, the Isle of Man Railway settled down to a very comfortable existence for the next 30 years, paying bumper dividends and offering every security to discerning investors. Timetables displayed in the local press show that five trains ran daily in each direction, from Douglas to Peel and Port Erin respectively. On Sundays this was reduced to three. Up to July 1878 first and second class accommodation was offered, then second class was abolished, and third class took its place. The original single track consisted of 45 lb flat-bottomed rails. The growth of traffic, however, soon demanded 56 lb steel rails, and, later still, these were replaced by 30-foot lengths of 60 lb rail. The success of Beyer Peacock's locomotives having been proved beyond doubt, their numbers were augmented, and by 1880 seven 2–4–0 tanks found full employment.

Meanwhile, resentment in the north of the Island had culminated in the formation of another separate railway, the Manx Northern. This line stemmed from a junction with IOMR at St John's, 3 miles short of Peel, and ran 16½ miles due north to Ramsey. It will be described presently. It might, though, be mentioned at this stage that the public resentment which sponsored it did not overflow into official circles. The MNR and IOMR always enjoyed a close working relationship, thanks mainly to the perspicacity of G. H. Wood, the IOMR's Secretary and Manager. MNR affairs, however, did not flourish. Neither did those of its rash offspring, the Foxdale Railway, and both concerns were absorbed by the IOMR on 24 May 1904.

Flourishing, and full of confidence, the IOMR felt itself well placed to assume responsibility for the

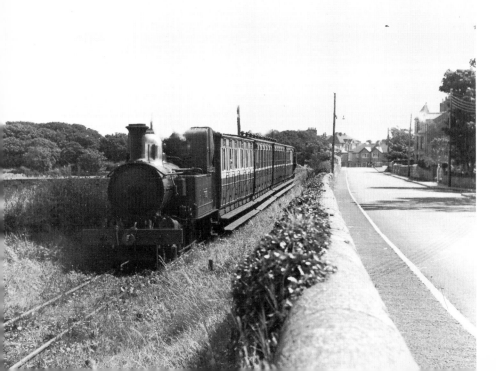

The scene might conceivably be Irish as No 13 Kissack runs along the main road at Castletown with its summer season load of four bogie carriages. Still in IOMR service, Kissack now functions in dark green livery, and carries the unusual combination of closed dome and tapered copper-capped Beyer chimney. (Steamchest)

Top *Douglas locomotive shed looked busy enough in 1962. No 16 Mannin (left) was caught in the act of running round its Port Erin train, and one of the recently acquired County Donegal railcars can just be seen inside the shed. The adjacent carriage body, that of N41, formerly Manx Northern's all-1st No 2, is still used as a mess hut to this day. No 12 Hutchinson, at the shed entrance, is another present-day survivor, though it is now clad in blue, and can boast of a new square cab similar to Mannin's. On the right, No 5 Mona looks ready for action – as was No 11 Maitland, which stood beside her a moment or two earlier.* (Steamchest)

Above *A sadder sight at Douglas on 29 June 1970, as No 11 Maitland hauls four unserviceable locos out of the carriage shed for static exhibition at Douglas station. Reading left to right, the locos are: No 1 (now in Port Erin Museum); No 9 (in store at Port Erin); No 14 (being restored privately near Ramsey); and No 3 (now a sectioned exhibit at Manchester). Fortunately, No 11 is still on active service.* (Steamchest)

Island's entire steam-worked system, 46½ route miles in all. Immediate preparations were made for the extra duties involved. Two new 2–4–0Ts, larger and more powerful than before, were ordered from Beyer Peacock to meet the Ramsey line's more formidable demands, and the IOMR's stock of passenger coaches — some 87 vehicles, mostly four-wheeled — was augmented by the arrival of six handsome bogie carriages. Built by the Metropolitan Carriage & Wagon Co, these were quite the most palatial vehicles seen to date on British narrow gauge metals.

The MNR's rolling-stock contribution to the merger held little significance, consisting only of two bogie cars and a number of 30-foot long six-wheelers. Meanwhile, the IOMR's stock of four-wheeled coaches was not allowed to go to waste, for, matched in pairs on new long frames, they were gradually converted to utilitarian bogie vehicles. The rebuilding

No 5 Mona *was one of two Beyer tanks ordered specially for the opening of the Douglas-Port Erin branch in August 1874. Seen here at Douglas in much later form, with cast-iron chimney, closed dome and Ross pop safety valves, it remained in service until 1969 and, currently liveried in red, presently awaits overhaul by the IOM Railway Society. Note the wooden stage on the right, where locomotive coaling is still effected by primitive wicker basket.* (Steamchest)

process, a lengthy one, was started in 1910, and carried on, with little interruption, to 1926. Many lineside and station improvements were also effected during these golden years of consolidation, though, of course, First World War years brought their own penance of hard work and staff shortage.

During the immediate post-war years the company was still in good financial fettle. Two more Beyer tanks had been added in 1908 and 1910 respectively, the provision of rolling-stock had kept pace, and there seemed no reason why the railway should not go on from strength to strength. Then, in 1927, came the

same blow as affected all other railways in the UK, when an English undertaking known as the Manxland Bus Services Ltd received powers to operate on three routes from Douglas. Small coach proprietors on the Island, partly assisted by the IOMR, retaliated by forming their own home-spun bus group, Manx Motors Ltd, in June 1927, and from that date road competition increased in ferocity.

By June 1928 the IOMR, recognizing the seriousness of its position, abandoned its £6,000 holding in Manx Motors, and concentrated instead in placing its own fleet of 22 buses on the road in direct competition with the invaders. This only led to economic chaos, and, as a last resort, the railway company bought out two rival undertakings in 1929. Just over a year later, a new concern, Isle of Man Road Services Ltd, was formed to consolidate bus transport on the Island. From that date, 30 June 1930, the IOMR never hesitated to rationalize its combined functions of road and rail transport. By the early 1930s some

No 16 Mannin, *the final development of the Beyer Peacock tanks, was distinctive in appearance as well as being popular with enginemen. Twice as powerful as the original IOMR tanks, it, too, is now a static exhibit at Port Erin Museum. Odd man out to the last,* Mannin, *in this photograph, carries a jack on top of her left-hand tank, as opposed to the traditional right-hand position.* (Steamchest)

rail services, notably those on the Foxdale branch, began to give way to the internal combustion engine. Then, fortunately for the IOMR, the onset of the Second World War brought about something of a railway renaissance. A great deal of Service activity centred on the Island, and such holiday traffic as was lost was more than adequately replaced by heavy goods traffic. Unlike most railways, the IOMR actually prospered financially during the years 1939–45.

Came the reckoning in 1946. A vigorous restoration programme began, but soon tapered off as conditions failed to return to pre-war prosperity. Intentions to introduce a new and larger type of Beyer Peacock locomotive were expressed, but never implemented. The year 1946 may have witnessed a record growth of passenger traffic, but wage increases and material costs grew to frightening dimensions. Soon, another truth emerged, that countless numbers of people who at one time delighted in visiting the Isle of Man were now turning elsewhere, usually abroad, for holiday recreation.

To the IOMR, traditionally dependent on a short enough peak season, this was a lethal threat. So began the supreme search for economies. Late evening trains disappeared, Sunday trains were first cut back, then removed entirely. Some engines were placed in store. Bus timings began to appear in the railway timetable — and by the winter of 1961–62 'one engine in steam' sufficed to handle the complete timetable. In the year 1961, incidentally, the IOMR imported two diesel railcars and a turntable from the County Donegal's sad auction at Stranorlar, and, used back to back, the two diesels found employment on the Peel line during the summer of 1962. Both it and the Ramsey line, however, had already been closed to winter traffic.

Seen in this light, the 1960s were a slow agony, with but one possible end in sight. It came in 1965, when the IOMR management found itself completely unable to fund extensive track repairs. That year four 2–4–0 tanks worked a sadly reduced summer service, while No 13 stood by in steam at Douglas shed. The company's other two remaining serviceable locomotives were also to be found there, but nine others were in the workshops, requiring various degrees of repair. Rail services were not resumed after the winter closure, and by March 1966 a forthright leader in the *Isle of Man Weekly Times* reminded the public that efforts to save the railway had now become a matter of extreme urgency. In April 1967 came the response, when a consortium headed by the Marquess of Ailsa took over the railway, and reopened tracks as far as Peel, Ramsey and Castletown. Alas, one year of operational and financial difficulties obliged the group to concentrate solely on the Douglas–Port Erin section. Last trains on the Ramsey and Peel lines ran on 6 and 7 September 1968 respectively.

From 1969 to 1971 the consortium kept the Port Erin line open, assisted partly by Government aid. Then, with the help of a more substantial subsidy, the IOMR resumed control in 1972. Through services between Douglas and Port Erin were resumed in 1977. That winter, as IOM Government subsidies had by now become an integral element in survival, the railway was sold to the Government. On 1 April 1983, Island bus and railway services amalgamated under the title Isle of Man Passenger Transport Board. Extensive renovations were effected on the IOMR, and locos Nos 11 and 12 were fitted with new boilers. Conversely, Douglas station's 11 tracks were reduced by more than half, and it lost the luxury of a signal cabin.

Today, the IOMR, now only 15½ miles in length, offers unique attraction to tourists on Sundays to Fridays from mid-May to mid-September, plus Easter Sunday and Monday. Four locos and the two ex-County Donegal railcars are still operational, as are 18 coaches of varying vintage and some 20 wagons. Three Wickham petrol-driven four-wheeled cars complete its stock.

LOCOMOTIVES

Despite their trim elegance, the IOMR's little 2–4–0 tanks were not direct descendants of Beyer Peacock's immortal 4–4–0 'Metro' tanks. They evolved rather from a modified version of the 'Metro' tank which Beyer delivered to a Norwegian 3 ft 6 in gauge railway in 1866. Nevertheless, the end product, as far as the IOMR was concerned, was not only beautiful, but highly functional; and, wisely, the company relied on Beyer Peacock to provide their entire fleet of 14 tanks.

Their development as the years passed is particularly interesting. All adhered to the original practice of carrying American-type leading pony trucks (the first in the UK) on outside bearings, and outside cylinders remained inclined at an angle of 1 in 9. Nos 1, 2 and 3 were provided with boilers only 2 ft 10¾ in in diameter, and side tanks, though later increased, held 320 gallons in water. Nos 4 and 5 were identical in appearance, except that their side tanks held 385 gallons. By the time Nos 6 to 9 arrived, however, boiler diameter had been increased to 3 ft 3 in. All nine locos could produce a tractive effort of 4,930 lbs.

Eleven years later came Nos 10–13. Tanks of 480-gallon capacity were now fitted, and the driving wheelbase was increased by 3 inches to 6 ft 6 in, though the wheel diameter of 3 ft 9 in remained constant. None the less, tractive effort was substantially raised to 6,580 lbs. The IOMR, meanwhile, had absorbed four locos from the Manx Northern Railway. They retained their original running numbers until 1919, when the IOMR saw fit to include two in stock as Nos 14 and 15. Difficulty was experienced in finding suitable employment for 0–6–0T

No	Name	Type	Date built	Makers	Maker's number	Remarks	Present location
1	*Sutherland*	2–4–0T	1873	Beyer Peacock	1253	Named after Chairman	Port Erin Museum
2	*Derby*	,,	1873	,,	1254	Named after Lord Derby	Dismantled 1951. Scrapped 1974–78
3	*Pender*	,,	1873	,,	1255	Named after Deputy Chairman	Sectioned exhibit, NW Museum of Science, Manchester
4	*Loch*	,,	1874	,,	1416	Named after Lt Governor	In service, IOMR
5	*Mona*	,,	1874	,,	1417		In store at Douglas
6	*Peveril*	,,	1875	,,	1524	Nos 6 and 8 were named after characters in	Earmarked for National Railway Museum, York
7	*Tynwald*	,,	1880	,,	2038	Sir Walter Scott's novel	Dismantled 1945. Chassis at Port Erin
8	*Fenella*	,,	1894	,,	3610	*Peveril of the Peak*	In store at Port Erin
9	*Douglas*	,,	1896	,,	3815		In store at Port Erin
10	*G.H. Wood*	,,	1905	,,	4662	Named after officials of IOMR	Awaiting new boiler, Douglas
11	*Maitland*	,,	1905	,,	4663		In service, IOMR
12	*Hutchinson*	,,	1908	,,	5126		,,
13	*Kissack*	,,	1910	,,	5382		,,
14	*Thornhill*	,,	1880	,,	2028	Ex-MNR No 3	Sold privately in 1978
15	*Caledonia*	0–6–0T	1885	Dübs & Co	2178	Ex-MNR No 4	Port Erin Museum
16	*Mannin*	2–4–0T	1926	Beyer Peacock	6296		,,

Caledonia, and during 1914 the IOMR was quite happy to hire the loco out for contracting work at Peel. There, no doubt, a gradient of 1 in 20 at Knockaloe Camp offered little embarrassment after the loco's earlier hair-raising ascents at Snaefell. The Manx Government found additional use for *Caledonia* in the mid-1930s, when extensive playing fields behind Douglas were laid out. Came the Second World War, and the loco was active again, ferrying mine spoil towards newly constructed RAF aerodromes. After that, sadly in need of overhaul, *Caledonia* disappeared into the IOMR's workshops.

While all this was happening, Beyer Peacock was called upon in 1926 to deliver their ultimate development of the IOM 2–4–0 tank. With a larger boiler still, and tanks also enlarged to hold 520 gallons of water, *Mannin*, with a tractive effort of 8,810 lbs, was almost twice as powerful as Beyer's original tanks of 1873. Completely distinctive in size, No 16 was also the first engine on the Island to carry the automatic vacuum brake.

The Second World War imposed many strains on the IOMR. 14,000 special trains, military and otherwise, were run during the war years. Even in 1943 1¼ million passengers were also carried in safety. The year 1946 found three locomotives, Nos 5, 7 and 15, totally out of action, and one, No 3, limited to shunting duties at Douglas yard.

Shortage of supplies and a rapid escalation of costs in post-war years hardly helped an already struggling concern. By the end of the summer of 1961, Nos 2, 3, 4, 7 and 9 were laid up, awaiting attention, while Nos 1 and 6 were functioning as reserve locos. By now even *Caledonia* was looked upon largely as a snowplough.

A quarter of a century later, the little railway still fights for its existence. Working stock has been reduced to five locos, Nos 4 and 10–13, plus the ubiquitous County Donegal railcars. Quite remarkably, only one 2–4–0T has been completely dismantled. The remainder are in safe hands, as the table shows.

During its lifetime, the IOMR found use for 75 bogie coaches, 14 six-wheelers, and many four-wheelers, freight stock besides. Original classification was by alphabetical letter, and modern life has been simplified by adopting the prefix 'F' for all passenger stock. 'Pride of the line' are still series F50–75, 'The Pairs', the survivors of 52 four-wheelers, built in 1873–74, and long since mounted in pairs on bogie chassis. Management rightly boasts that passengers riding in those behind a Beyer Peacock 2–4–0T can still savour the full the delights of Edwardian travel in the Isle of Man.

MANX NORTHERN RAILWAY COMPANY LIMITED

Opened: 23 September 1879
Absorbed by IOMR: 19 April 1905
Gauge: 3 ft 0 in

Once it became clear that the Isle of Man Railway

management was quite adamant in its inability, or unwillingness, to implement its proposed Douglas–Ramsey railway project, the good folk of Ramsey, the second largest centre of population on the Island, decided to take matters into their own hands. The urgency of the matter was discussed, the scale of finance required was accepted, and, after representations at Government level, a Committee of the Legislature was formed. In a Minute dated 17 October 1874 it offered a choice of two proposed routes to Ramsey, both of which commenced from St John's station. An alternative short direct link between Douglas and Ramsey via the east coast had already been dismissed because of the steep gradients and heavy engineering works which would have been involved. It is interesting to note, however, that the Manx Electric Railway tackled precisely that route when it opened up full scale operations 25 years later.

Finance, on this occasion, was rather more forthcoming. The Manx Northern Railway Co Ltd was registered on 22 March 1877, with an authorized capital of £90,000, and the Manx Government revived memories of Irish Baronial Guarantee days by pledging a 25-year dividend guarantee on most of the shares. Work on the approved 16½-mile project got under way just under a year later, and by 29 August 1879 shareholders were able to experience a trial trip over the almost completed railway.

One of two 2–4–0 tanks supplied by Sharp Stewart hauled the train, which consisted of 16 four-wheeled coaches lent for the occasion by the IOMR, plus a van. Despite initial hostility, the two companies had already reached an amicable understanding. Fortunately for the MNR, it was to prove permanent throughout the latter's comparatively brief existence. MNR trains were prominently featured in IOMR timetables, and the IOMR lent stock as or when it became necessary. This probably accounts for the paucity of MNR goods stock, which, even as late as 1899, consisted solely of 32 wagons and five other vehicles. Trains on the MNR's single line were worked under Staff and Ticket regulations, and station signal practice emulated that of the IOMR. The analogy between the two companies was further exemplified in 1880, when the MNR, seeking a third engine, ordered a 2–4–0 tank of standard IOMR design from Beyer Peacock.

Thus, from its day of public opening, 23

MNR No 2, Northern, *as delivered by Sharp Stewart in 1879. General proportions were little different from those of Beyer Peacock's 2–4–0Ts, though the external appearance was radically different. Once the IOMR absorbed all four MNR engines it found little use for the two 'odd' Sharp Stewart tanks, and both were ultimately sold.* (Steamchest)

Thornhill, *the MNR's solitary Beyer Peacock tank, fared much better after amalgamation, and was easily absorbed into IOMR stock as No 14. In this delightful study, taken at Kirk Michael on 2 August 1961, the one-time MNR tank, still with copper-capped chimney, open dome and salter safety valve, assists No 13* Kissack *on a Ramsey line train. Last seen in service in 1963,* Thornhill *was sold to an Isle of Man resident 15 years later.* (Hamish Stevenson)

September 1879, the MNR settled in to what appeared to be a reasonably prosperous future. Its tramway extension to Ramsey quayside enabled cargoes to be transferred direct from ship to railway; thence they were distributed all over the Island. All might have gone well, too, had not the MNR assumed what turned out to be disastrous extramural responsibilities in 1883. That was the year that the lead mines around Foxdale, a modest community 2¼ miles south of St John's, fulfilled a long-standing ambition to be served by rail.

The Foxdale Railway Co Ltd, promoted in 1882, obtained its Act, after considerable acrimony, on 13 June 1883. The MNR management, no doubt harbouring dreams of untold mineral traffic wealth, somehow hypnotized itself into undertaking a 50-year working lease over the Foxdale line. Alas, so formidable was the eventual 2¼ miles of continuous 1 in 49 gradient that the MNR was next obliged to fortify its confidence in the project by ordering a fourth locomotive. It arrived in 1885, from Dübs & Co this time, in the form of 0–6–0 tank No 4 *Caledonia*, the largest and most powerful locomotive ever to tread Isle of Man metals. In the event, a tractive effort of 11,120 lbs proved no handicap; but the engine's long wheelbase and 27-ton working weight soon demanded chaired track on many curves. More expense for the MNR to bear!

The MNR's major financial haemorrhage had, however, already been set in motion, for, under the terms of the 50-year lease, the Foxdale Mining Co had persuaded the MNR management not only to part with 45 per cent of the Branch's gross mining traffic receipts, but to pass on, in addition, a hand-some percentage of the MNR's *own* earnings on the line! Looking back now, one sees how foolhardy the MNR's commitment really was. Yet at a time of unbounded optimism, it probably appeared to be little more than a calculated risk.

The figures of 1898 alone proved what a disaster the whole project was. The MNR received £376 from Foxdale traffic, and paid the Foxdale Railway Co £579 as a rebate on MNR-generated traffic. Net loss to MNR — £302! Overall statistics were even gloomier, for by the end of 1898 the MNR found it had parted with £6,400 of its own earnings in Foxdale rebates. Meanwhile, the branch, which had cost £8,000 to build, had deteriorated to £2,500 in current value. Hardly surprisingly, MNR financial affairs deteriorated with it; and, somewhat alarmed as Guarantor for much of the Preference Stock dividend, the Island's Legislature decided to institute an inquiry. In due course the Committee of Inquiry recommended amalgamation with the IOMR The latter pre-empted lengthy legal proceedings by taking charge as from 26 February 1904, and three months later IOMR borrowing powers were increased by law to enable the purchase price of £60,000 to be paid. In official terms both the MNR and the Foxdale Railway ceased to exist as from 19 April 1905.

Once the lead mines closed in 1911, the IOMR maintained only a skeleton service on the Foxdale branch, usually employing one composite coach and such goods vehicles as were required. Passenger services ceased just before the Second World War, and, though war years generated considerable traffic in slag and waste from the derelict lead mines, the Foxdale branch was soon closed to all traffic once peace was restored.

Restored to MNR livery in 1968 after many decades of useful IOMR service, 0–6–0T Caledonia (Dübs & Co 2178/1885) was 'on parade' with other out-of-service locos when this photograph was taken at Douglas station. The loco is now an exhibit at Port Erin Museum. (Steamchest)

LOCOMOTIVES

No	Name	Type	Date built	Makers	Maker's number	Withdrawn by IOMR	Remarks
1	*Ramsey*	2–4–0T	1879	Sharp Stewart	2885	1918	Latterly employed as ballast engine Scrapped in 1922
2	*Northern*	,,	1879	,,	2886	1912	Scrapped in 1912
3	*Thornhill*	,,	1880	Beyer Peacock	2028	—	Sold as IOMR No 14 in 1978
4	*Caledonia*	0–6–0T	1885	Dübs & Co	2178	—	Now in Port Erin Museum

Strangely enough, the MNR's odd locomotive practice in fielding three different types amongst four locomotives can claim to have some logical basis. When the railway was about to open in 1879, the management, recognizing the IOMR's success with the 2–4–0 tank type, was quite happy to benefit by example. But it chose to indicate independence by placing its first order with Sharp, Stewart, a rival Manchester concern to Beyer Peacock. As it transpired, the general proportions of the Sharp tanks were no different from those of the IOMR's first Beyer Peacock series. Externally, however, the engines were much more conventional in appearance, with straight footplating and inside bearings throughout. Contemporary railway history reminds us that it was the 'unorthodox' locos which survived!

Fortunately, relations between the two railway companies had improved considerably by 1880, and the MNR had no compunction in ordering an IOMR-type 2–4–0T from Beyer Peacock once the need arose. Five years later came *Caledonia*, a product of the MNR's ill-conceived association with Foxdale mining affairs. The story of its extraordinarily varied life affects three IOM railways in this section.

The IOMR took over all four locomotives when merger was effected in 1904, but found so little use for Nos 1 and 2 that neither ever received IOMR livery or running number. Nos 3 and 4, though, were found worthy of retention, and both lived on to give many years of good service.

Thornhill, so named after the residence of the MNR Chairman, was renumbered 14 in IOMR stock, and put in many years of service before being sold into private hands in 1978. The same source obtained MNR carriage No 6. *Caledonia*, named thus as a tribute to John Cameron, a Scottish manager on the MNR, was, with its superior tractive effort, a useful acquisition by the IOMR, particularly in winter, when it was quite often deployed with a snowplough. Restored to MNR livery in 1968 after many decades as IOMR No 15, it was passed on to the Port Erin Railway Museum in 1975, together with MNR six-wheeled Cleminson coach No 3. Meanwhile, the body of MNR first class coach No 2 still serves as a mess hut outside the IOMR's loco shed at Douglas.

GREAT LAXEY MINING COMPANY TRAMWAY

Opened: 29 September 1854
Closed: 1929
Gauge: 1 ft 4 in

Still in working order, but no longer used as a pump, the Great Laxey Waterwheel remains a great attraction to Isle of Man visitors as being the largest waterwheel in Europe. One understands, then, the pardonable pride with which it was named after, and opened by, the Governor's wife on 29 September 1854. Lead mining had a long tradition in that part of the Island, and it comes as no surprise to learn that a primitive form of tramway, worked by man power, ran between the mine shaft and the tipplers, where the ore was crushed and washed. At that time, 23 oz of silver could be extracted from every ton of lead, and the Great Laxey Mine enjoyed a high reputation. Hundreds of local people found employment there, and the only nineteenth-century change occurred in 1875, when Stephen Lewin, that indefatigable builder of rather bizarre narrow gauge locomotives, supplied the mine with two microscopic 0–4–0 tanks. Their maker's numbers were 684 and 685.

These remarkable locomotive mites, appropriately named *Ant* and *Bee*, were to put in over 50 years active service before the mines closed in 1929, and survived many a locally-wrought change of appearance in the process. Originally each was little more than a launch-type boiler mounted on a four-wheeled mainframe, 6½ feet long. The driving wheels, only 1 ft 2 in in diameter, responded to the promptings of two cylinders, each 4 in by 6 in, and, despite a tallish chimney and dome, the overall height of each engine was only 4 ft 9 in. The driver, completely unprotected, stood in a loop formed by the rear of the main frame, and his sole relaxation during still moments was provided by a minute wooden seat placed over the rear dumb buffer. The engine pit provided at Laxey's small loco shed was hardly required, for, should internal inspection be required, the men usually tipped the engine sideways!

In their original form both locos carried water tanks bolted on in front of the smokebox. These were filled from the top, but presumably the need to refill became over-frequent, for within a short time larger tanks were fitted. Carried in front like small iron sentry boxes, the tanks were strapped along the length of the boiler by two arms. The latter were also improvised to act as coal trays. A short length of guttering also ran alongside to cope with any injector overflow. Most of the engines' work consisted of pushing trains, so a locally devised system of 'automatic uncoupling' was also incorporated. Latterly, one of the locos even acquired the sophistication of a chimney cap, which adornment gave it a distinctly racy 'Crewe' look as it plodded around behind its load of seven iron-sheeted wagons. One cannot doubt, however, the affection with which the little locos must have been regarded.

For a year or two after the closure of the mine in 1929, the unusual locomotive twins lay idle at Laxey, Then, as hopes of re-opening receded they were sold, in 1935, to a firm of scrap merchants in Douglas. By the 1950s the whole of the mine site was cleared, and today only gardens remain to offer mute reminder of the Isle of Man's most unusual steam railway.

MANX ELECTRIC RAILWAY COMPANY

Opened: July 1899
Closed: Still extant
Gauge: 3 ft 0 in

We come now to a consideration of the short direct route between Douglas and Ramsey — the 18-mile coastal passage whose creation was abandoned in 1874. Such a challenge was bound to be taken up again sooner or later, and the Manx Electric Railway Company started the process when it received authority in 1892 to construct an electric tramway, 3 feet in gauge, between Douglas and Groundle Glen, a spot rather more than half-way to Laxey.

The tramway was completed in 1893, but not before the original concern was taken over by the Douglas & Laxey Coast Electric Tramway Co. True to its intention, the new company doubled the original single track, and opened an extension as far as Laxey in 1895. Then, for good measure, it exchanged its own name for the more resounding title, the Isle of Man Traction & Electric Power Co Ltd. Powers were received in 1896 to extend the line further still, and full through services between Douglas and Ramsey commenced in July 1899. Then came trouble. An Island financial house, Dumbell's Bank, failed in 1900. The electric line fell into the hands of a Receiver until 1902, when it was purchased by a reconstituted Manx Electric Railway Company.

History records that the new MER worked hard to improve communications along the Island's east coast. Certainly, over the next two decades or so traffic flourished. The bogie tram-type cars operated originally on 500 volts dc generated current. Then, under new management, current generated at 7,000 volts ac was used. This was fed through overhead wires after conversion from 550 volts dc had taken place. Much later, in 1935, the IOM Electricity Board was able to supply current at 33,000 volts ac, and this, in turn, was converted by mercury arc rectifiers to 550 volts dc. By the late 1930s, however, even these refinements could not combat the increasing use of private cars. Traffic declined year by year, and

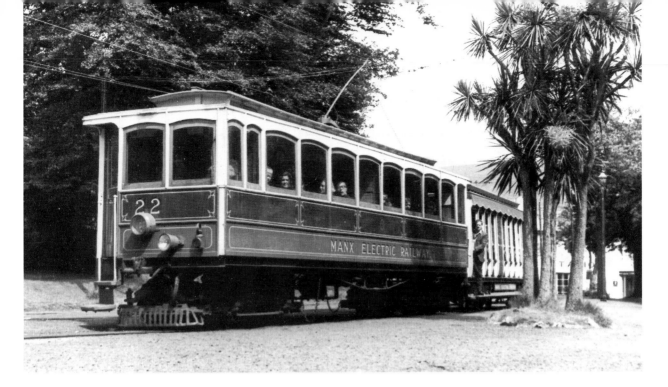

the MER management was latterly forced to contemplate winter closure. The Manx Parliament, in its wisdom, declined to permit such a procedure, and the tramway limped on.

Latterly, so acute did operating difficulties become that the Legislature had to come to the rescue by nationalizing the tramway concern. This was effected by Isle of Man Transport towards the end of 1956, and to this day the MER and an associated enterprise, the Snaefell Mountain Railway, flourish under the aegis of the Manx Electric Railway Board. A heavily augmented service operates during summer months, and for those visitors who can spare 75 minutes there is no better way of exploring the beautiful country which lies between Douglas and Ramsey. A fleet of 23 motor-cars, 25 trailers and 10 wagons guarantees that no shortage of accommodation need exist. The 18-mile line, doubled throughout, still operates on 500 volts dc.

MER loco No 23 and freight car No 26 are now owned by the IOM Railway Society, and, together with Royal Trailer No 59, can be seen at the Ramsey Electric Railway Museum.

SNAEFELL MOUNTAIN RAILWAY

Opened: 21 August 1895
Closed: Still extant
Gauge: 3 ft 6 in

All through the second half of the nineteenth century, as the ever-increasing pursuit of public pleasure prompted construction of many a minor railway, the twin peaks of Snowdon, 3,570 feet above sea level, and Snaefell, the Isle of Man's most prominent landmark at 2,036 feet, continued to present a tantalizing challenge to any railway engineers who might feel bold enough, or ingenious enough, to tackle their ascent.

It comes as little surprise, therefore, that, on 16 November 1894 and 4 January 1895, two quite separate groups, willing to tackle Snowdon and Snaefell respectively, embarked on a race to see who could complete Britain's first mountain railway. The end products were vastly disparate, but, just as Volk's Electric Railway pipped Giant's Causeway to the post 12 years earlier to earn distinction as Britain's first electrically-worked railway, so, in this instance, the lesser concern, the Snaefell, won through to beat Snowdon by just under eight months. Both lines were 4¾ miles long, and, of course, tourist traffic was the common bait.

The Manx Electric Railway's triumphant arrival at Laxey in 1894 obviously inspired thoughts of conquering Snaefell; and at a meeting held on 4 January 1895, members of the Snaefell Mountain Railway Association resolved to take immediate action. As most present had some direct association with the Manx Electric's predecessors, the concept of electric traction was very much in mind. Indeed, the project was initially named the Snaefell Mountain Tramway. Somewhat daringly, the Fell central rail system was chosen as a medium likely to assist cars in their unprecedentedly difficult task; and, to allow room for the central rail and its ancillary equipment to be fitted below the cars, the normally accepted gauge of 3 ft 0 in was widened on this occasion to 3 ft 6 in. Climbing, on the other hand, was purely a matter of motor power. The Fell system of horizontal wheels acting on a central rail merely guaranteed braking

The town of Laxey fades into the distance in this vintage study as car No 3 and trailer steadily tackle the 4³/₄-mile 1 in 12 ascent which leads to Snaefell Summit. (Steamchest)

power and stability, particularly during descent. Naturally, the chosen gauge of 3 ft 6 in inhibited junction with MER metals at Laxey. This problem, however, was overcome in later years.

Construction of the 4.9-mile long line was a drama in itself. It was decided that *Caledonia*, the Manx Northern's powerful 0–6–0 tank, should be hired to assist. The MNR, only too willing to oblige, dispatched the locomotive by sea from Ramsey to Laxey Harbour, whence, no doubt to the astonishment of local citizens, it was humped through the streets and up the valley, on rollers and planks. At the working site a third rail had already been laid between the 3 ft 6 in metals. Thus, for the next six months *Caledonia* followed behind, *pushing* trains of loaded ballast wagons. Apart from two short level sections and an occasional less merciless climb, the tough little loco faced a ruling gradient of 1 in 12. Apparently her steam and hand brakes were powerful enough to defy the law of gravity, for no accident of consequence seems to have occurred.

Work proceeded so rapidly that the line was ready for inspection by mid-August 1895. A certificate was readily granted, and public service commenced five days later. One can imagine the enormous interest that this new venture must have generated. Certainly, public interest was so gratifying that six handsome 48-seat bogie cars, built for the occasion by G. F. Milnes of Birkenhead, were overwhelmed by curious visitors during the short summer period which remained. By 1902 the Manx Electric Railway, recognizing the unique tourist value of this Laxey offshoot, arranged to take the Snaefell Mountain Railway under its wing.

Today, both railways work as hard as ever. The Snaefell, still the steepest line in the British Isles to be worked by adhesion, operates between May and September only. Its six original cars, augmented by two four-wheeled service wagons and a double-cab works car, continue to cock a snook as they transport private-car-ridden Island visitors to within 44 feet of Snaefell's magnificent summit. The journey takes 30 minutes each way. Totally double-tracked, the Snaefell also retains its unusual traditional practice of emplying right-hand running.

GROUNDLE GLEN RAILWAY

Opened: 1896
Closed: Still extant
Gauge: 2 ft 0 in

Exactly as in the case of Ireland's Cork, Bandon & South Coast Railway, the Manx Electric Railway's pioneering tactics had the almost immediate effect of inspiring the creation of other, less major, concerns. Snaefell was by no means alone in this context, for no sooner had Douglas been linked to Groundle Glen by electric tramway in 1893, than the Douglas Estate Company, owners of that deletectable property, decided to capitalize on their newly-found ready access from the Island's main tourist centre. Thus, in the caves of a creek, well within the Glen, but on the coast itself, they built reserves where sea lions and other attractions could disport themselves in natural surroundings.

The scheme was an attractive one, and it was rendered even more so when a 1,000-yard long miniature railway was built between the head of the Glen and the coast. Single track, with one passing point rather more than half-way, was all that its designers

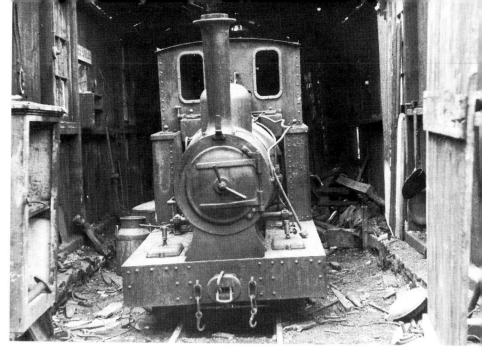

July 1960, and sad times for the 2-foot gauge Groundle Glen Railway as Bagnall 2–4–0T Sea Lion moulders forlornly in the shed, awaiting further developments. In the event nearly a quarter of a century elapsed ere a start was made on retubing the little locomotive. Happily, Sea Lion is now back in circulation at Groundle Glen. Its one time partner, Polar Bear, can be found at Amberley Chalk Pits Museum. (Hamish Stevenson)

could squeeze into a very restricted space. Despite that, a gauge of 2 feet was chosen, and W. G. Bagnall of Stafford was commissioned to supply a 2–4–0 tank of conventional dimensions, rather than to miniature railway scale. The result, duly named *Sea Lion*, arrived, as did four carriages, in time for the public opening in 1896. The Manx Government, despite the railway's dependence on 21 lb flat-bottomed rails, had passed the line as being suitable for passenger traffic.

Management's decision to employ a 2-foot gauge was very wise. The enterprise was to all intents and purposes a miniature railway, possibly the first public one in Great Britain, but a narrower gauge would have imperilled stability as the single track wound its way round ledges and cliff tops. As it was, a check rail was installed all along the route, though in many places it was on the wrong side to prevent trains from hurtling down the hillside in the event of derailment! None the less, the unique nature of the enterprise guaranteed success from the word 'go', and over 100,000 passengers sampled its delights in the first two months. Expansion was totally justified. Thus, another Bagnall tank, *Polar Bear*, plus a second rake of coaches joined the ranks.

Continued success was such that the two steam locomotives, when deemed to be unserviceable, were placed in store by 1920, and were replaced by two electric battery-driven engines. No hint appears that the latter were other than satisfactory, but for some reason a petrol-driven engine supplanted them within a few years. The latter proved definitely unsatisfactory, and probably to all passengers' delight, steam made a triumphant return in 1931.

Alas, the advent of the Second World War saw the railway close on 3 September 1939, and the two steam engines, greased and tucked away in their tiny engine shed, suffered adversely as the war years and vandalism extracted their toll. By 1950, however, *Polar Bear* was restored to something like its pre-war condition, four coaches were salvaged, and a summer-only service resumed that year. Trains, however, only ran as far as the midway loop and back, for the coastal section was giving cause for anxiety. Shortly afterwards ownership of the railway changed hands, and *Polar Bear*'s dark green livery gave way to a rather lurid combination of red, yellow, and blue panels. Of the original eight coaches, six managed to survive to compete for custom in a vastly different post-war world. *Sea Lion*, immobile and cannibalized, still lay rusting behind the engine shed. It was all, however, to no avail, and the railway closed once more in 1962.

Polar Bear, said to weigh 5½ tons, as opposed to *Sea Lion*'s 4 tons, proved to be the more powerful and

Name	Type	Date built	Makers	Maker's number	Remarks
Sea Lion	2–4–0T	1896	Bagnall	1484	Driving wheels diameter, 1 ft 3½ in
Polar Bear	2–4–0T	1905	,,	1781	Driving wheels, 1 ft 2 in. Larger cylinders
(*Sea Lion*)	Battery-driven car		British Electric Vehicles Ltd	—	Maximum speed 10 mph Overall length, 9 ft 7 in
—	,,		,,		
—	Petrol-engined tractor		,,		

utilitarian of the two steam locomotives. Four-wheeled carriages, 3 feet wide and with sides totally exposed, were designed to seat 12 passengers. During busy summer months, however, half as many again often crammed themselves in for what was, after all, a pleasant afternoon's outing.

In the mid-1960s track, station buildings, engine shed, and both steam locomotives disappeared from Groundle Glen. *Polar Bear* found refuge with the Brockham Museum Trust, and the remains of *Sea Lion* went to Loughborough, Leics. Then, incredibly, came another Groundle Glen renaissance, when, commencing clearing work in the summer of 1982, a band of enthusiasts succeeded in relaying a section of 2-foot track. Came Sunday 18 December 1983, and 550 passengers were carried on the first Groundle Glen public train for 21 years. A Hudson-Hunslet diesel, one of two acquired from the Dodington House Railway, headed the train on its ½-mile run. *Sea Lion* had already been recovered and was resident on the Island, but discovery that a new boiler would be required came as an unpleasant surprise. Fortunately, British Nuclear Fuels offered to restore *Sea Lion* to full working order, so across to Sellafield went the Bagnall tank. It returned in good order in the summer of 1986, in time to assist on a Sundays-only service.

The Groundle Glen Railway's current stock consists of *Sea Lion*, two four-wheeled Hunslet diesel units, three bogie coaches, and a few wagons. Meanwhile, *Polar Bear* and two Groundle Glen coaches can be seen working at the Chalk Pits Museum, Amberley, West Sussex, and one more coach has found a home at the Lytham Motive Power Museum, Lytham, Lancs.

DOUGLAS HORSE TRAMWAY

Opened: 7 August 1876
Closed: Still extant
Gauge: 3 ft 0 in

A brief mention of this venerable tramway serves to remind us of the Island's ever-present triumvirate of steam, electric, and horse-drawn transport. The Douglas Tramway is, of course, the only horse-drawn tramway still operating in the British Isles, and it continues to defy all modern competition by carrying well over one million passengers each summer season.

Built originally by Thomas Lightfoot & Sons, and opened to public use in 1876, it has yielded continuous service for over a hundred years, apart from a brief spell during the Second World War when part of the promenade was commandeered for prisoner-of-war use. Douglas Corporation Transport Department took over in 1902, and to this day a frequent service of cars operates daily from May to September. Thirty-one cars of varying types are used, and seating accommodation averages 30-40 passengers per car. Twice that number of horses, mostly Irish, supply the muscle power, and, of course, they are as well cared for, and groomed, as any steam locomotive.

The 3-foot gauge line, 1.6 miles long, runs along the front from Victoria Pier to a northern terminus conveniently situated near the Manx Electric

Still holding their own against steam and electric competition, 'power units' Nos 27 and 28 remind us that the Douglas Horse Tramway is double-tracked throughout, as they pass along the front on 4 June 1970. (Steamchest)

Railway's Derby Castle station. Double-tracked throughout, it carries one car every 1½ minutes from 9 am to 11 pm without complaint year after year, as each busy summer follows another.

JERSEY RAILWAYS & TRAMWAYS LIMITED

Opened: 25 October 1870
Closed: 30 September 1936
Gauge: 3 ft 6 in

A constituent of the British Isles, but not legislatively part of the United Kingdom, Jersey, the largest of the Channel Islands, has an area of 45 square miles, and, of its 65,000 inhabitants, nearly half live in the town of St Helier. It follows that St Helier automatically became the focal point when railway development on the Island became feasible in 1869. One might add 'at long last', for discussion on the subject had waxed for decades previously. Indeed, two proposed railway schemes had already fallen by the wayside, in 1847 and 1863 respectively.

A third attempt saw the Jersey Railway Co Ltd safely incorporated in November 1869. Capital was pitched at £24,000, and the standard gauge line, running 3¾ miles east from St Helier to St Aubin, was officially opened to the public on 25 October 1870. Five 2–4–0 tanks handled all traffic during the railway's lifetime. The next railway development came further west, when a Bill for the St Aubin's & La Moye Railway & Granite Quarries Co Ltd received

approval on 7 June 1871. Just under 3 miles long, this railway was also intended to be standard gauge. But a combination of sharp curves and steep gradients persuaded its sponsors that 3 ft 6 in might be a more discreet choice of gauge, and so it ultimately emerged. The first of two Black Hawthorn 0–4–2 saddle tanks arrived on the Island in the autumn of 1877.

The action proved a shade premature, for by July 1878 the St Aubin railway was declared bankrupt, and both locos passed eventually into the hands of the principal creditor. The Jersey Railway Company was, as it happened, also finding life difficult, and after a while the two companies merged under a new title, the Jersey Railways Company Ltd. A first 3 ft 6 in gauge passenger train ran between St Aubin and La Moye on 15 March 1884. Then, by August of that year metals were extended further west, and a St Aubin's–Corbière service commenced. By now the original standard gauge locos and rolling-stock had been sold, and five new narrow gauge tanks, plus 13 passenger coaches, were working on the Island. Alas, financial affairs proved to be as complicated as ever, and on 1 February 1896 all assets were taken over by a newly formed company, the Jersey Railways & Tramways Ltd. The total purchase price was £53,881. Two days earlier, the Jersey Railways' last locomotive order, No 4 *St Brelades*, had arrived from the mainland.

Registered with an Ordinary capital of £30,000, plus £24,000 in Debentures, the new company set about tidying up its 7½-mile 'empire'. Amongst other improvements, a new station was provided at St Helier, and the company even declared a 3 per cent dividend at its first Annual General Meeting in

St Helier station, 1 July 1922, and 2–4–0T No 1, also named St Helier, *prepares to leave on the 3.10 pm for St Aubin. Jersey's first Sentinel steam car arrived one year later.* (LCGB, Ken Nunn Collection)

Above *Jersey Railway's Sentinel car No 4 Normandy was bought from the Jersey Eastern Railway in July 1930. Scaled down from standard gauge to 3 ft 6 in, it proved to be a splendid bargain. Alas, scrap merchants George Cohen Sons & Co had the last word, in July 1938.* (Steamchest)

Below *Presumably retired before the disastrous fire of 1936, this old coach body was still serving as a garden shed when it was observed at St Peter Port, Jersey on 26 August 1958.* (F. C. Le Manquais)

February 1897. Indeed, this fairly healthy financial condition was to persist right up to the First World War. Around 1906 the question of electrification was considered. The Directors decided that, for the present at least, steam locomotion would suffice. Vouching for their conviction, they then ordered one more 2–4–0 tank, considerably more powerful than its predecessors. Andrew Barclay, of Kilmarnock, obliged on this occasion, at a cost of £1,710.

The year 1914 brought record profits and a peak dividend of 4 per cent. Then, of course, as the war dragged on, traffic decreased commensurately, and no dividend was paid during the years 1916–18. Latterly, several batches of German prisoners-of-war were held in Jersey, and the railway played its part in transporting them to and from employment at St Helier docks. Once hostilities ceased, the Jersey Railway management, despite energetic restorative action, found itself faced with exactly the same problem as confronted almost every other mainland railway, that of meeting motor bus competition head on.

The crunch came in April 1923, when the Jersey Motor Transport Co Ltd opened up bus services all over the Island. Anticipating the event, the Jersey Railways Board had already considered the respective merits of employing electric or petrol-driven railcars. Still uncertain, they then canvassed views on a third option, that of Sentinel-Cammell steam cars. Fortunately, the Sentinel Wagon Works and Cammell Laird & Co did not loiter, and their quote of £1,800 for a large car was accepted by the railway company. Delivery had to be guaranteed for 1 April 1923.

In the event, the Sentinel car, *The Pioneer No 1*, did not arrive at St Helier until June 1923. But its inaugural run proved successful, despite minor accidents. A further demonstration run was made before an interested audience of British and foreign engineers on 28 June, and, on the strength of success to date, a second, more powerful car arrived at St Helier in January

Further west on the Island, the platform and trackbed at Corbière station were still clearly in evidence in June 1951, 15 years after the closure of the narrow gauge railway. (F. C. Le Manquais)

1924. *The Pioneer No 2* embodied improvements suggested by the first trials, and on 17 January it was given its supreme test on the heavy gradients which existed between St Aubin and Corbière.

By now the first Sentinel car had run 12,700 miles, and management was delighted to observe that it was consuming only 5 lbs of coal per mile, as opposed to the conventional steam locomotive's 25 lbs. Add the fact that the new cars could each perform four single journeys between St Helier and St Aubin within the hour, a feat ordinary locomotives could not match, and one understands the optimism with which coming years were faced. To clinch matters a third Sentinel car was obtained second-hand for £100 from the Jersey Eastern Railway, a standard gauge concern, in July 1930. Scaled down to the 3 ft 6 in gauge, it made a very satisfactory bargain.

The year 1925 was the most successful, and this was reflected in the payment of a record 7 per cent dividend. Total train mileage of 11,147 put even the good pre-war years in the shade, and the number of passengers carried exceeded one million for the first time. On average 33 trains ran daily in each direction. But the menace of the internal combustion engine was not to be fought off, and by 1928 a tremendous increase in private car ownership was biting deeply at railway receipts.

That year the railway company fought back, by absorbing the Jersey Motor Transport Co Ltd — only to find that the practice of operating parallel bus and train services brought its own problems. The railway service to Corbière, for instance, was bound by statute to be provided all the year round, yet during winter months a service by bus was infinitely cheaper to operate. An appeal was made to Authority, and eventually permission was received to discontinue rail services between St Aubin and Corbière from October to April each year. Amputation began on 1 October 1931, and a similar curtailment of rail service between St Helier and St Aubin was sanctioned as from 1 December 1932.

On struggled the Jersey Railways. Various expediences were adopted, and buses were hired out. But a complete lack of dividends, except for one of 1½ per cent over the years 1930–34, told the true tale of rapidly decreasing revenue. Normal train services resumed as usual on 1 May 1936, and closed for the winter on 30 September 1936, when, as was customary, all rolling-stock, except railcars and locomotives, was safely stored at St Aubin station.

It was then that Providence took a hand, for, on the morning of Sunday 18 October 1936, a disastrous fire, spreading out of control, succeeded in destroying not only St Aubin station, but 16 of the company's best carriages. The blow was mortal, and both the Railway Board and the State authorities knew it. Thus, the Jersey Railways' Directors and shareholders had little option but to accept the State's very reasonable offer of £25,000 for transfer of the railway company's real estate interests. This was duly confirmed on 28 October 1937, when shareholders also agreed to wind up their company.

Scrap tenders were considered on 5 July, and, once awarded the contract at £5,919, Messrs George Cohen lost little time in salvaging the track, four locomotives, three railcars, and such carriages as had survived the holocaust.

LOCOMOTIVES

There were only slight differences between the St Aubin's Railway's two pairs of 2–4–0 tanks; the Manning Wardle engines were heavier at 25 tons. No 4 arrived on the Island two weeks after the amalgamation with the Jersey Railways & Tramways, but was obviously ordered by the St Aubin's. All four tanks were rebuilt between 1907 and 1912, and re-emerged weighing 26 tons each. Much more powerful, No 5 *La Moye* was a doubtful acquisition at 36½ tons, for she tended to spread the track, and also consumed coal at an unattractive rate. In the days before railcars were introduced, engines worked a three-week roster, and two engines were kept in steam on

St Aubin & La Moye Railway

No	Name	Type	Date built	Makers	Maker's number	Remarks
4	*General Don*	0–4–2ST	1877	Black Hawthorn	—	Essentially contractor's engines. Both reshipped
5	?	,,	1877	,,	—	from Jersey around 1900
1	*St Helier*	2–4–0T	1884	Manning Wardle	916	All scrapped after the fire in 1937
2	*St Aubin's*	,,	1884	,,	917	
3	*Corbière*	,,	1893	Bagnall	1418	
4	*St Brelades*	,,	1896	,,	1466	

Jersey Railways & Tramways Ltd

No	Name	Type	Date built	Makers	Maker's number	Remarks
5	*La Moye*	2–4–0T	1907	Barclay	1105	Sold 1928 to Victoria Falls Power Co. Shunted there until mid-1970s
RC1	The Pioneer No 1	Railcar	1923	Sentinell Cammell		Withdrawn in 1935
RC2	The Pioneer	,,	1924	,,		Scrapped in 1937
RC3	La Moye No 2	,,	1927	,,		Bought from Jersey Eastern Railway in 1925
RC4	Normandy	,,	1927	,,		,, 1930

Sundays. From 1907 onwards all carried acetylene headlamps, and their dark green livery gradually gave way to olive green. Name and number plates are now in the possession of the National Railway Museum at York. Railcars Nos 1 and 2 were 56½ feet long, and weighed 15¾ tons in working order.

The company's first coaches were probably eight-wheeled tramcar-type vehicles with longitudinal seating. The Bristol Wagon Works supplied four-compartment-type carriages in 1887, as did the Ashbury Railway Carriage Co ten years later. Latterly the company owned 23 carriages and brake vans, but never more than 21 wagons.

During the Second World War German occupation forces laid a metre gauge line round the western side of Jersey, with rolling-stock consisting of four-wheeled flat trucks and two Paris-built tank locos, an 0–6–0 and a 2–6–0. A 1 ft 11½ in gauge contractor's-type line was also laid eastward from St Helier harbour, and this was worked by an 0–4–0 diesel locomotive. Needless to say, all traces of German occupation were removed immediately after hostilities ceased.

Miniature railways

RAVENGLASS & ESKDALE RAILWAY

Opened: August 1875
Closed: Still extant
Gauge: 3 ft, later 1 ft 3 in

A casual visitor to the sophisticated railway which exists today at Ravenglass might well be surprised to learn that its trackbed at least is over one hundred years old. Yet such is the case, for the line opened to a 3-foot gauge in 1875 to serve a group of iron mines in Eskdale, deep in the heart of Cumberland. The Whitehaven Mining Co promoted the railway, and haemitite was the mineral it sought. Potentially valuable deposits had been identified on either side of the little village of Boot. So, seeking to resolve the problem of transporting the ore to Ravenglass, where it could be transhipped on to Furness Railway metals, the Mining Company sought, and obtained, a railway Act in 1873.

The Act not only sanctioned construction of a 3-foot gauge railway, 7 miles long between Ravenglass and Boot, but also embodied additional powers to build a branch from Ravenglass to 'the seashore'. Presumably the promoters envisaged such a surge of profitable ore traffic that local authorities might be stimulated into revitalizing Ravenglass's harbour, which was at that time silted up and swallowed in the general confluence of the Rivers Irt and Mite.

The branch, as it happened, was never built. The company, however, put its authorized capital of £36,000 to practical use by opening its 'main line' to goods traffic in May 1875. The track consisted of light flat-bottomed Vignoles rail, and a steady series of gradients lifted it from near sea level to 208 feet at Boot. A passenger service was introduced in November 1876, as were four intermediate stations at Muncaster Mill, Irton Road, Eskdale Green, and Beckfoot. They still exist. At Boot, run-round facilities and a siding handled the output from Nab Gyll working, and a short branch, leading off just before Boot, serviced the other main source of ore, Gyll Foss. Manning Wardle supplied two 0–6–0 tanks, and these attended to all traffic demands.

The Gyll Foss branch did not last long, for it was abandoned once the mining company failed in 1877. The railway, however, carried on, supervised by a Receiver and a Manager; and, with Nab Gyll worked now only on a limited scale, seasonal passenger traffic assumed a new importance. With two engines, four coaches, and a daily service of two trains each way, the R&E had no difficulty in operating on a 'one engine

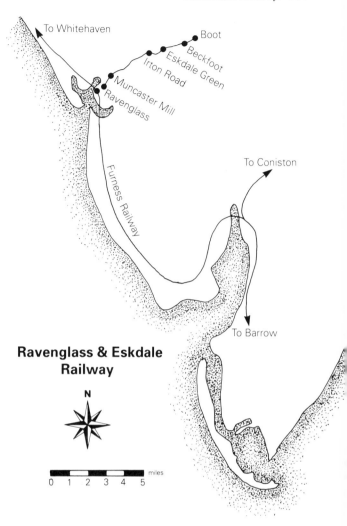

Ravenglass & Eskdale Railway

N

0 1 2 3 4 5 miles

Muncaster Mill station, seen here in 3-foot gauge days, was situated 3/4 mile out of Ravenglass, and was closed in 1925. (Author's Collection)

Consternation near Murthwaite on the morning of Monday, 5 March 1905, when a broken fish-plate succeeded in derailing the 9.35 'Express' for Boot. Despite the fact that Devon, the Manning Wardle 0–6–0T involved, had to be withdrawn for several weeks for thorough overhaul, Nab Gyll, the R&ER's only other engine, managed to keep normal service going. Conversely, Devon, rebuilt by Lowca in the 1890s, was the only engine in use after 1908. Tradition has it that both Manning Wardle tanks were cut up in situ in 1915, when the 15-inch gauge was adopted. (Author's Collection)

A rather more peaceful scene near Boot, but on this occasion Sir Aubrey Brocklebank, *a 1919 product of Hunt of Bournemouth, is heading a 15-inch gauge train of holidaymakers, and miniature gauge traffic is expanding encouragingly.* (Author's Collection)

in steam' principle. Forty-five minutes was the fairly generous time allowed for each journey of 7 miles, though one 'express', introduced in 1878, cut this to 40 minutes by stopping only at Irton Road. Annual revenues for the next few decades, however, rarely exceeded £1,200, and when, in 1908, rumour had it that the iron mines were about to resume production, a hastily cobbled scheme of reconstruction was produced.

The object was to relay 4 miles of track with 45 lb steel rail, buy three new coaches, and find one more engine — all at a cost of £6,000. At the same time the R&E management approached the Furness Railway for practical aid. Refusal of the latter, coupled with poor public response to the new R&E Prospectus, wrote 'finis' to the R&E's prospects. The mines at Boot worked sporadically for a couple of years, but passenger traffic ceased. Then, in 1912, the mines closed down, and 'Owd Ratty', as the railway was known locally, had no option but to terminate its own parlous existence. For the next three years the

line lay derelict.

The 'kiss of life' which revived it came from unexpected sources. In 1915 a Mr R.P. Mitchell, founder of Narrow Gauge Railways Ltd, took an interest in the R&E's plight, and a visit to Eskdale convinced him, despite the desolation he witnessed, that the site was ripe for development along miniature railway lines. It was a bold decision, considering that the First World War was by now in full swing. Nevertheless, clearance and conversion work was put in hand by the end of June, and, less than two months later, a scale model locomotive, *Sans Pareil*, arrived to work passenger traffic as far as Muncaster Mill and back.

Construction work finally reached Boot in 1917. Holiday traffic expanded encouragingly, and four more engines joined the ranks over the next three years — one scale model 'Pacific' and three Heywood tanks recruited from the Duffield Bank Railway. *Sir Aubrey Brocklebank*, another scale model, followed in 1919. Goods traffic, too, began to grow in volume. At first it consisted of coal, cattle food, general mer-

The largest loco built at Duffield Park, under St Arthur Heywood's guidance, was Muriel, a 0–8–0T of 1894 vintage. She passed to R&E ownership, and worked in her original form until 1927, when Ravenglass Works undertook her conversion into an 0–8–2 tender engine. The result, River Irt, an interesting but hardly handsome compromise, is seen here at the head of a summer train in August 1967. (Steamchest)

Above An even more daring, albeit unsuccessful, rebuild was sponsored by the R&E in 1927, when 2–8–2 River Esk was converted into a booster-fitted 2–8–2–0–8–0 by the Yorkshire Engine Co. This Works photograph shows the remarkable finished product. (Steamchest)

Right Booster troubles with the rebuilt River Esk were such that the loco was soon restored to conventional 2–8–0 form. Sixty years later River Esk is still working hard on Ravenglass metals. (Steamchest)

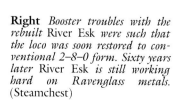

The new River Mite *was only one year old when this picture was taken on 6 August 1967.* River Esk's *old steam tender was used in its construction, and the name* River Mite *came from a remarkable composite engine which was built at Ravenglass workshops in 1928, only to be withdrawn in the late 1930s.* (Steamchest)

chandise, and timber. Then the opening of a new red granite quarry near Beckfoot station in 1922 brought a welcome influx of mineral traffic. A crushing plant was accordingly erected at Murthwaite, a spot midway between Irton Road and Muncaster, and a loop line installed there made sure that the R&E obtained its 'bread and butter'. By now the little railway had earned regular mention in Bradshaw, and passenger traffic on occasions was such that every locomotive and carriage was stretched to the limit. This was the time when *Katie*, one of the Heywood tanks, proved such an erratic performer that R&E were glad to sell her off. It should be added, in all fairness, that the other two Heywood locos gave little cause for complaint as they struggled with goods trains and relief passenger work.

1922 saw several innovations. The end section of the line to Boot was abandoned, and Dalgarth became the new upper terminus; turntables were put in here and at Ravenglass. Slip-coaches were introduced as a novelty in the summer of 1923, but the practice ceased again in 1925. Two lightweight petrol-driven vehicles were also introduced, to handle the much lighter winter traffic. Then, in 1929, came one last major decision, when standard gauge track was laid between Ravenglass and Murthwaite crusher. This obviated one stage of transhipment on the granite's way to the coast. Ingeniously, the narrowness of the R&E's trackbed was overcome by laying the standard gauge track *astride* the 15-inch metals, and a

Kerr, Stuart diesel was obtained to handle the R&E's new 'broad gauge' traffic.

By 1923 it became patently evident that the Heywood tanks needed replacing on goods traffic, and a striking new locomotive design was commissioned from Henry Greenly. The result was *River Esk*, probably the first 2–8–2 tender engine to run on British metals. It was certainly the first British loco to incorporate Lentz poppet valve gear. Highly successful in operation, *River Esk* weighed 6 tons and was 23 feet long. In 1927, however, came a decision to rebuild her, and, after treatment by the Yorkshire Engine Co, she emerged, almost unrecognizably, as a booster-fitted 2–8–2+0–8–0! As Nigel Gresley found on the LNER, boosters are tricky embellishments, and *Esk* was soon rebuilt as a conventional 2–8–2. She, and three other steam engines, handle the R&E's all-year-round passenger traffic to this day.

The R&E fell into safe hands when Sir Aubrey Brocklebank, the Chairman of Cunard Steamships, assumed control in 1925. He expanded quarry output at Beckfoot, and enlarged the facilities at Murthwaite in a bid to guarantee prosperity for the little railway. His successors, alas, failed to take the same interest, and, deteriorating through lack of care, the line was sold to the Keswick Granite Co in 1948. The latter hung on awhile after the quarries ran down, then put the R&E up for auction in 1958.

Fortunately, a Manchester philanthropist added financial strength to the subsequent efforts of a Ravenglass & Eskdale Preservation Society. Thus, with freight traffic abandoned, a permanent staff, plus Society members, keeps the present day R&E very much alive. So vigorous is the preservation spirit that a new 'Prairie', *Northern Rock*, designed and built at Ravenglass, was added in 1976 in commemoration of the centenary of the 'Ratty'.

LOCOMOTIVES

During the period 1875–1912, the R&E, working as a 3-foot gauge railway, used only two locomotives. Products of Manning Wardle & Co of Leeds, both were 0–6–0 tanks, with outside cylinders 10 in by 16 in. *Devon* came first (Maker's No 545/1874) and *Nab Gyll* (Maker's No 629) followed one year later. Locos and coaches were painted red.

Then, in 1915, came a transformation to 15-inch gauge, and the R&E acquired a vastly different series of locomotives. During the 1920s, the railway also employed several petrol-engined locomotives. These included a 'Model T', built in 1922 and scrapped in 1925. Others were internal combustion locos numbered 1 and 2, three Muir-Hill/Fordson tractor locos, and, of course, one Kerr, Stuart diesel for stan-

Despite the cosmetic illusion of a steam-loco-type chimney, this 0–4–2 DM, named Pretender, *started life in 1929 as a petrol-driven conversion of a 1925 Muir-Hill 0–4–0. Fifty years later R&ER engineers resourcefully installed a diesel engine salvaged from a boat which had sunk in Ravenglass harbour – and the loco is now unofficially known as* Perkins! *She now carries Brunswick green livery, with orange and black lining.* (Steamchest)

dard gauge use between the crusher at Murthwaite and Ravenglass.

Meanwhile, provision of 15-inch gauge steam locomotives commenced in 1912, and is detailed in the accompanying table.

Henry Greenly was responsible for the design of the R&E's first two 15-inch gauge locos, and he later contributed that of *River Esk*. *Sans Pareil* was origi-

Name	Type	Date built	Makers	Remarks
Sans Pareil	4–4–2	1912	Bassett-Lowke	Scrapped in 1928. Parts used to build *River Mite*
Colossus	4–6–2	1914	,,	Parts also used to build *River Mite*
Sir Aubrey Brocklebank	4–6–2	1919	Hunt & Co, Bournemouth	,,
Katie	0–4–0T	1896	Duffield Bank (No 4)	Ex-Eaton Hall Railway. Sold to Fairbourne Railway in 1923
Ella	0–6–0T	1881	,, (No 2)	Scrapped 1926. Frames used for ICL No 2
Muriel/	0–8–0T	1894	,, (No 3)	0–8–0 rebuilt as 0–8–2 tender engine in 1927,
River Irt	0–8–2	1927	Ravenglass Works	and renamed
River Esk	2–8–2	1923	Davey Paxman (Maker's No 21104)	Rebuilt as 2–8–2+0–8–0 by Yorkshire Engine Co in 1927. Soon re-converted to 2–8–2
River Mite	4–6–0+0–6–4	1928	Ravenglass Works	Built with parts from three locos as above. Withdrawn before Second World War, and reintroduced as a 2–8–2 in 1966
Northern Rock	2–6–2	1976	,,	Introduced to mark R&E's centenary
Bonnie Dundee	0–4–2T	1981	,,	Rebuild of Kerr, Stuart 2 foot gauge 0–4–0WT

nally built for the Geneva miniature Railway, and bore the name *Prince Olaf* before coming to Ravenglass in 1915. Coke-burning, as opposed to the later rather rapacious coal-burning Duffield Bank engines, the 'Atlantic' served well, as far as 22-inch coupled wheels and a tractive effort of 680 lbs permitted. Within months, however, traffic increased, and a second locomotive, *Colossus*, had to be imported. A 'Pacific' this time, the loco had a longer wheelbase at 8 ft 5⅜ in, and weighed nearly 3 tons. Both Greenly engines carried eight-wheeled bogie tenders, and *Colossus* had already served, under the name *John Anthony*, on Capt J. E. P. Howie's private railway.

Then, as this 15-inch line advanced up the Eskdale Valley, an increasing amount of goods traffic was generated. The R&E management changed tack in its search for appropriate locomotives by purchasing three products of the Duffield Bank Works, home ground of Sir Arthur Heywood. Heywood's locos were much more rugged than Bassett-Lowke's fine-scale models. But, as luck would have it, the R&E's initial purchase, *Katie*, proved to be a particularly unfortunate example of the genre. Built in 1896 with a marine-type boiler, possessed of outside frames and cylinders and fitted with Heywood's own design of valve gear, she was not only extravagant on coal, but steamed badly. Whichever railway employed her, *Katie* offered trials and tribulations; and the Fairbourne Railway eventually scrapped her in 1926.

The sister engines *Ella* and *Muriel* proved much more reliable Heywood products. But the fact that they could handle heavier loads than Bassett-Lowke's scale models was hardly enough to endear them to drivers, as the latter crouched behind minimal spectacle plates in rough wet weather. The Heywood engines also tended to 'pitch' rather nastily, even at moderate speeds, and, of course, their consumption of coal far exceeded the amount of coke burned by Bassett-Lowke's beautifully balanced locomotives. *Ella*, an 0-6-0, weighed half a ton heavier, at 3¾ tons, than *Katie*. *Muriel*, a comparatively massive 0-8-0 tank, with 17½-inch diameter wheels, turned the scales at 5 tons.

By 1920 R&E passenger traffic was still expanding, and relief to the two hard-working Bassett-Lowke engines came in the form of another 'Pacific', *Sir Aubrey Brocklebank*. Half a ton heavier than *Colossus*, and slightly overscale, *Brocklebank* introduced a six-wheeled tender which enabled the driver to sit lower and gain more protection from the cab. Next, the comparative limitations of the Heywood engines in goods traffic were considered, and a new design, commissioned from Henry Greenly, completely altered the public's conception of miniature gauge locomotion. *River Esk*, twin-cylindered, 6 tons in weight and 23 feet long, made an enormous impression when she emerged from Davey Paxman's Colchester Works in

1923. Despite her continuing success on R&E traffic, *River Esk* was rather daringly rebuilt in 1927, when Walschaerts valve gear was substituted for the poppet variety, and a second pair of cylinders was fitted under the tender to act as a booster. Difficulties ensued, and the booster was later replaced by a more conventional double-bogie tender mounting. Meanwhile, *River Esk*'s steam tender chassis was carefully tucked away in case of need!

The R&E's next articulated locomotive adventure came in 1928, after *Sans Pareil*, *Colossus* and *Sir Aubrey Brocklebank* had been deemed unfit for further service. Frames and other parts, however, were considered to be of further use, and, nothing venture, nothing win, the R&E workshops at Ravenglass embarked on the construction of a 4-6-0+0-6-4 locomotive. The Yorkshire Engine Co supplied a new boiler requisite to meet the needs of four simple cylinders, and a remarkable new locomotive, *River Mite*, emerged from Ravenglass shops on 9 April 1928. Withdrawn before the Second World War because of boiler mounting trouble, wartime austerities forbade further modifications being carried out. But at least a new *River Mite*, a 2-8-2 built by Clarkson of York in 1966 on *River Esk*'s old steam tender chassis (!), perpetuates the name.

One last pre-war steam locomotive experiment took place about the same time, when *Muriel*'s frames were extended to carry trailing wheels. Thus, with the addition of a new boiler from the Yorkshire Engine Co, and a 300-gallon tender, the former eight-coupled tank was transformed into an 0-8-2 tender engine named *River Irt*.

The year 1976, with the R&E entering its second century, was celebrated by the advent of another Ravenglass-built locomotive, *Northern Rock*, a powerful 2-8-2 tender engine. Painted in muscat greet, with red and black lining, she has proved a popular, and hardworking acquisition. A Muir-Hill petrol-driven tractor of 1929 vintage also serves today, in conjunction with *Shelagh of Eskdale*, a diesel-hydraulic 4-6-4 built by Curwen/Severn-Lamb in 1968, Bo-Bo diesel No 8 *Lady Wakefield*, and a three-car bogie diesel railcar multiple unit, built in 1977, and known as *Silver Jubilee*. The remains of *Ella* and *Katie* rest in a museum at Ravenglass.

Today, the Preservation Society operates a very efficient system of train control by radio, since copied by British Rail; and, of a present stock of 44 coaches, most have been built during the last two decades — though a few of 1928 vintage still serve on. Twenty wagons of varying nature, a reduction from the 104 which existed in 1947, are sufficient to meet the needs of a bustling little railway which works so hard to please Eskdale's countless annual visitors.

As recently as 10 January 1990 an additional, and well-earned, measure of prestige came the Society's way, when *Northern Rock II*, a second Ravenglass-built version of the R&ER's earlier 2–6–2, was ceremoniously named by Mr Masuru Nagae before being shipped abroad for duty on a Japanese tourist attraction, the Shuzenji Railway. There, in Rainbow Village, some 80 miles south-west of Tokyo, it will find itself in good company, in the form of ex-Fairbourne Railway 4–6–2 *Ernest W. Twining*.

ROMNEY, HYTHE & DYMCHURCH RAILWAY

Opened: 17 July 1927
Closed: Still extant
Gauge: 1 ft 3 in

Apart from its claim to be 'the smallest railway in the world', the RH&DR was also the only miniature railway in the British Isles to seek incorporation under the Light Railways Act of 1896. It was the brain child of two railway-loving motor racing drivers, Count Louis Zborowski and Capt J. E. P. Howey. They planned jointly to initiate a 15-inch gauge railway on a commercial basis, using steam as motive power; and even when Zborowski was killed in a car crash at Monza, Capt Howey resolved to carry on single-handedly. He chose latterly a site in the Romney Marsh area and, backed with the blessing of both Town and County Councils, together with enthusiastic support from Sir Herbert Walker, General Manager of the Southern Railway, work commenced in January 1926. The Ministry of Transport issued an appropriate Statutory Order on 26 May.

The 13¾-mile miniature railway was destined to serve a desolate part of the Kent coast which lay between Hythe and Dungeness, and herein lay part of the Southern Railway's support. In its eyes, the RH&DR would provide a potentially useful link between two ex-SECR branch lines which had seen better times, that between Sandling Junction and Hythe, and that from Appledore to Dungeness and New Romsey. Unfortunately, the increasing use of private cars killed both branches in the long run. The Romney, Hythe survives, very much a special case.

Whatever, the first-built part of the miniature rail-

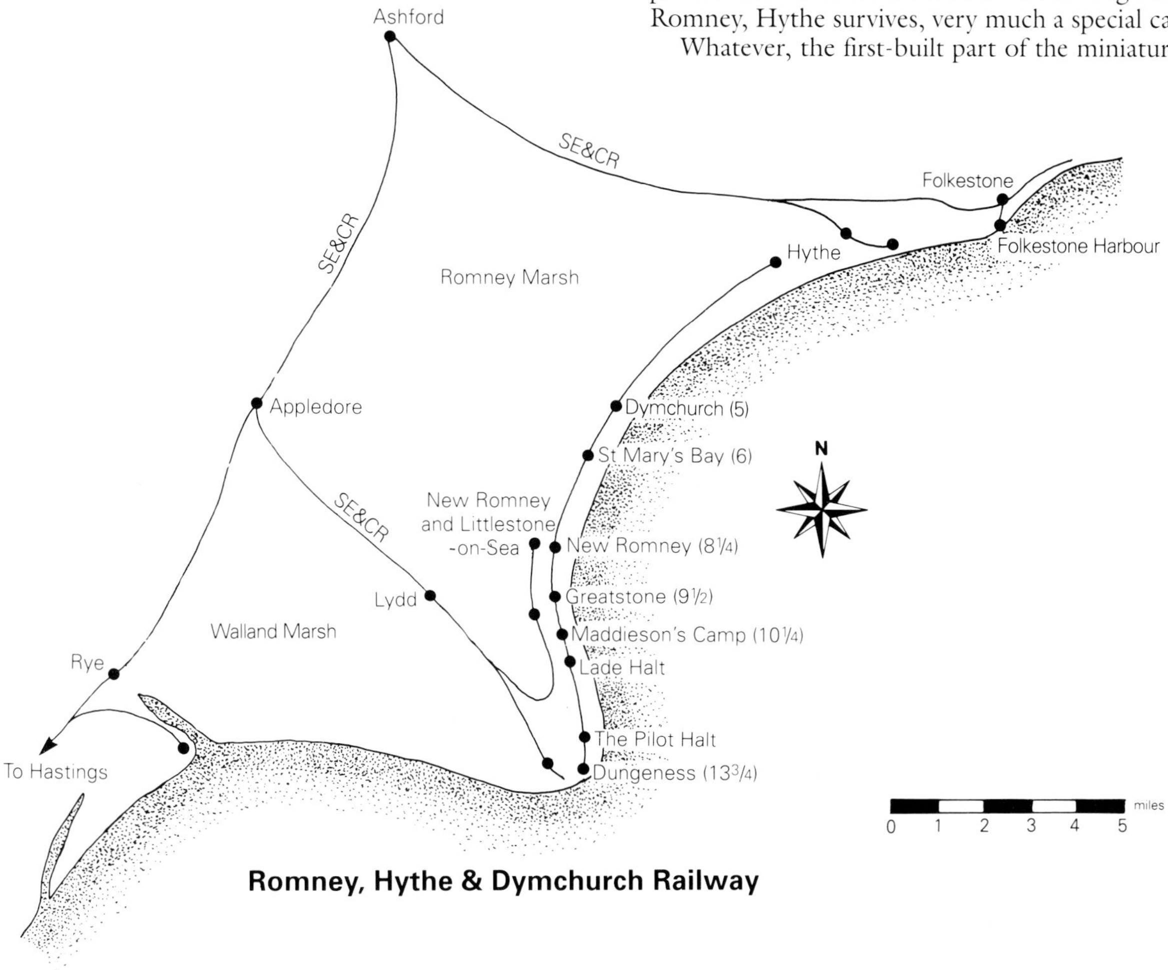

Romney, Hythe & Dymchurch Railway

Above *Seen at New Romney loco shed in 1927,* The Bug, *a 1925 product of Krauss & Co of Munich, moved on to Belfast in 1933, but has since returned to base at New Romney.* (Steamchest)

Left *RH&DR No 1* Green Goddess, *the first of three two-cylinder 'Pacifics' supplied by Davey Paxman, Colchester, in 1925-6 to the design of Henry Greenly, is seen here with Greenly at the controls – probably when the loco was tested on Ravenglass & Eskdale metals in July 1925. The presence of a Westinghouse pump is worthy of note.* (Steamchest)

Left *Thirty years later* Green Goddess, *with her high-sided tender, looks even more like a Gresley 'Pacific' as she bravely sets out from Hythe station with her load of summer passengers.* (Steamchest)

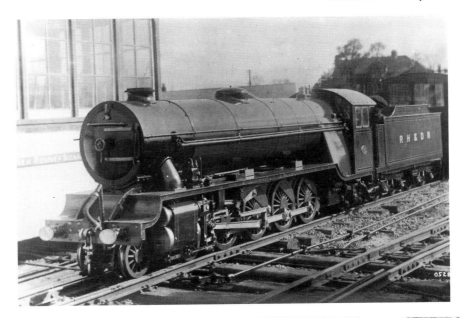

No 6 Samson *was one of two 'Mikados' also supplied by Davey Paxman in 1925-6 to work a projected RH&DR connection with the Southern Railway at Sandling Junction. The cost of surmounting over two miles of 1 in 50 gradient, however, prohibited construction of the branch, and a 5½-mile extension to Dungeness was added in lieu. Although the loco had to be withdrawn in 1938, it was successfully returned to service in postwar years.* (Author's Collection)

Companion loco No 5 Hercules had also received a high-sided tender by the time she was photographed leaving Hythe station on this 1950 mid-summer occasion. One of the Yorkshire Engine Co's Canadian-style 'Pacifics' is ready to follow with her train of passengers. (Steamchest)

No 10 Doctor Syn, *the second of two 'Pacifics' delivered by the Yorkshire Engine Co in 1931, clearly betrays her Canadian lines as she pauses at Dungeness in August 1951. Later both engines sacrificed their North American-style tenders in favour of flat-sided units.* (Steamchest)

Left *As part of southern anti-invasion precautions taken in the early years of the Second World War,* Hercules, *duly modified at Ashford Works, provided the motive power for this anti-aircraft armoured train as it patrolled the Romney-Hythe area. Legend has it that the unit accounted for at least one enemy aircraft. Viewed now in retrospect, however, the concept seems symbolic rather than practical.* (Steamchest)

Below *No 7* Typhoon, *built in 1926 as a three-cylinder 4–6–2, was rebuilt with two cylinders ten years later. In this view, taken on 16 September 1950, the lady in the garden seems, understandably, quite blasé as No 7 makes a bold exit from Hythe station.* (Steamchest)

way ran east from Littlestone Road, New Romsey, where its terminus faced that of the SR's Appledore–New Romsey branch. Then, passing through a children's Holiday Camp, much favoured by the Duke of York, later King George VI, it reached the well-known seaside village of Dymchurch. A four-road station was built here, and its main platforms were covered by a roofed steel and concrete building some 70 feet long. Almost immediately thereafter, the 15-inch gauge line crossed the Marshlands Dyke by a wide 36-foot span steel bridge. Then, approaching Hythe from the west, it tunnelled under a major road, using one of two overbridges which had to be constructed by the railway company; the other was a skew bridge nearer Romsey.

The largest structure of all was a 56-foot span girder bridge, known as the 'York', which crossed a main drainage canal near Holiday Camp. At the end of the line, Hythe station — a good mile, alas, from that of the Southern Railway — was built as a substantial six-road terminus. Romney, Hythe and Dymchurch stations were each provided with a turntable and water column, and this first 9-mile section opened for public service on 26 July 1927. Attention then turned towards constructing an extension from New Romsey, 4¾ miles south to Dungeness. Completed in two stages, this was finally opened in July 1929. The terminus at Dungeness proved an odd affair, for the track divided before reaching it, and described a huge loop round which trains travelled in a clockwise direction. Dungeness station lay in the centre of this loop, and, nearby, Dungeness Lighthouse gazed benignly on the unusual scene. In later years it was joined by two nuclear power stations.

Although laid to one quarter of standard gauge, RH&DR track was designed to take the impact of

Right *The beautifully scaled proportions of No 9* Winston Churchill *are truly revealed as the driver's head pops out in cheery farewell. Built by the Yorkshire Engine Co in 1931, the loco bore the name* Black Prince *until October 1848, when, specially named for the occasion, it left for exhibition in Canada.* (Lens of Sutton)

Below *British Rail's New Romney & Littlestone-on-Sea station (right) overlooks the Romney, Hythe scene as No 1* Green Goddess *waits in a passing loop. Ironically, it was 'Big Brother' who succumbed first, for the whole of BR's New Romney-Appledore branch closed down finally on 6 March 1967.* (Steamchest)

trains travelling at 25 mph with 300 passengers on board. Henry Greenly, on his appointment as Engineer to the RH&DR, designed five 'Pacific' locomotives, each of which could handle such a load on gradients of up to 1 in 100. For that reason 24 lb British standard flat-bottomed rail, spiked to creosoted Baltic fir sleepers, was used throughout. In the further interests of public safety, all signal boxes were interlocked with standard tappet and tappet lever interlocking. The frames were designed and made by the RH&DR's Works Department, and the signal boxes at New Romney and Hythe had 17 levers each.

The Greenly-designed 'Pacifics', based on Gresley's famous 'A1s', were masterpieces of model building, for, although built to one-quarter track scale, the locomotive superstructures were allowed to blossom to one-third full size. Thus large boilers were incorporated, and so skilfully were the models con-structed that no apparent contradiction of scale could be perceived. All told, five 'Pacifics' and two 'Mountains' were supplied by Davey Paxman during the years 1925–26, and these sufficed to meet RH&DR needs until two more 'Pacifics', vastly different in appearance, arrived from the Yorkshire Engine Co in 1931.

Sixty semi-open four-wheeled coaches eventually swelled in number to 105 before being converted into articulated sets in 1931. Sixty new bogie coaches arrived during 1934–36, and three observation cars were added in 1947. One open and one closed bogie came from the Eaton Hall Railway in 1946. Initially, both locomotives and coaches were equipped with the Westinghouse automatic air brake. Difficulty of maintenance, however, brought about the institution of automatic vacuum brakes, and the latter are now standard equipment on the RH&DR. A quantity of

fixed-sided open wagons and some ¾-cubic yard capacity ballast trucks with removable tops, all with steel underframes, featured originally in the RH&DR stock. In the event, suspension of goods services in 1951 reduced most to works stock.

At first passenger and goods services operated all year round, and the through journey of 13¾ miles occupied one hour. Latterly, however, local residents, well aware of biting cross-Channel winds which could obtain, began to neglect winter travel. Fortunately bumper summer passenger traffic compensated, and the little railway served on through the 1930s, still under Capt Howey's benevolent ownership. The arrival of war in 1939 was bad enough. But when France fell in 1940 the territory covered by the RH&DR became a prohibited area. Military authorities then took over the railway and, amongst other activities, an armoured train patrolled the beach area.

Preparation for D-Day brought even more feverish activity to the RH&DR, for an undersea pipeline, designed to maintain invasion forces once they set foot in Europe, was fed from Lade, a spot midway between New Romney and Dungeness. The RH&DR, therefore, was used to convey all piping and equipment from Southern Railway trucks to the site of the PLUTO operations (Pipe Line Under The Ocean). Track and rolling-stock suffered badly during the war years, and once peace was restored the process of restoring the line to running order took two years to complete. Even then, such was the cost that only a single line was reinstated between Dungeness and New Romney, instead of the original double track.

From there the little railway resumed its former public role. Capt Howey's lifelong interest terminated on his death in 1963, but happily local business interests refused to see the railway perish. Their chivalry was ill-rewarded in the long run, for in 1971 arrears of maintenance obliged the RH&DR to contemplate complete closure. Again good fortune intervened, and a new consortium took over in February 1972. Typical of the modern preservation movement, a RH&DR Association was formed, and this body, in addition to supplying valuable volunteer labour, works with the consortium in publicizing Romney's ever-popular miniature railway. It still ferries children daily back and forth to school, and braces itself for large numbers of summer tourists. Its daily routine starts at Easter and ends in September, and Saturday and Sunday services are run in March, October and November.

LOCOMOTIVES

No	Name	Type	Date built	Makers	Maker's number	Remarks
1	*Green Goddess*	4–6–2	1925	Davey Paxman	21499	
2	*Northern Chief*	,,	1925	,,	21500	
3	*Southern Maid*	,,	1926		22070	
4	*Jean/The Bug*	0–4–0	1926	Krauss & Co	8378	Used for construction work
5	*Hercules*	4–8–2	1926	Davey Paxman	22071	
6	*Samson*	,,	1926	,,	22072	
7	*Typhoon*	4–6–2	1926	,,	22073	
8	*Hurricane*	,,	1926	,,	22074	
9	*Black Prince/ Winston Churchill*	4–6–2	1931	Yorkshire Engine Co	2294	
10	*Doctor Syn*	,,	1931	,,	2295	
11	*Black Prince*	,,	1937	Krupp	1664	

When Henry Greenly resigned his Ravenglass & Eskdale appointment as Resident Engineer in 1924 he plunged straight into the task of designing 'Pacific' locos for Count Zborowski and Capt Howey. So time-consuming, indeed, was his work that he also released himself from consulting work for Bassett-Lowke. By 1925 he was deputed, as RH&DR Engineer, to meet Sir Herbert Walker at Waterloo station. The Southern Railway had no objection to a light railway being built between New Romney and Hythe, and from that point things never looked back. The 'Pacific' Greenly had designed for Zborowski was already well under construction at Colchester, and Howey purchased it for eventual use on the Romney Hythe. Given LNER livery, and named *Green Goddess* after a William Archer play which was enjoying West End success at the time, it was taken north for trials on the Ravenglass & Eskdale Railway. These commenced on Sunday 29 June 1925. All proved well, and the loco returned to New Romney pending completion of the new line.

Once construction got under way, a small shunting engine was purchased from Krauss & Co of Munich. A replica of that company's standard 12 hp engine, it was on this occasion cut down from 600 mm (2-foot) to 15-inch gauge. An odd mixture of tender and tank loco, the 0-4-0 was christened *The Bug*. Meanwhile, two other Greenly-designed two-cylinder 'Pacifics', Nos 2 and 3, had been shopped by Davey Paxman. The original intention to name them *Man of Kent* and *Maid of Kent* was never implemented, and the names *Northern Chief* and *Southern Maid* were adopted instead.

On 6 August 1926 construction was so far advanced that *Green Goddess* ran between Littlestone and the Boys' Camp at Jesson. The Duke of York drove the engine out of Littlestone that day. Greenly may, however, have been more impressed by the attendence of Nigel Gresley, who conducted a lively inspection of the miniature 'Pacific'. Then, within the year, the line was completed to Hythe, and it was opened to the public on 17 July 1927

The first train left Romney at 6.30 am, reaching Hythe 45 minutes later; and so the RH&DR settled down to a weekday service of 20 trains a day. This was only made possible by the fact that stock now consisted of eight locomotives, for Davey Paxman had added two 4-8-2s, Nos 5 and 6, also designed by Greenly, plus two three-cylindered 'Pacifics'. A decade later Nos 7 and 8 were rebuilt as two-cylinder locos. Meanwhile, *Green Goddess* returned to familar metals awhile, when she was lent to the Ravenglass & Eskdale in 1928. An interesting document found later amongst Greenly's papers reveals that during the first 55 weeks of RH&DR running, its seven passenger locomotives covered 84,644 miles. Weekly mileage averaged 2,926, and coal consumption worked out at the remarkably low figure of 1.43 lbs per mile.

The greater, then, was the pity that the appointment of a friend of Capt Howey's as General Manager in 1928 bespoiled personal relationships to such an extent that the company had Greenly arrested for trespass in January 1929. Greenly was acquitted at Court, and subsequently extracted £455 damages from the company for 'malicious prosecution'. His inevitable resignation from RH&DR service explains why the railway's last two locomotives came, in 1931, from the Yorkshire Engine Company. Far from following the Greenly tradition, Nos 9 and 10, though still 'Pacifics', were based on Canadian Pacific Railway design. Beautiful locomotives, none the less, they were given a brown livery.

The initial four-wheeled passenger stock was supplemented in 1928 by the arrival of eight all-enclosed bogie carriages from Claytons of Lincoln. Three years later, all four-wheeled stock was converted into articulated units. The Belle Vue Park Railway in Belfast bought some in 1933, as they did *The Bug*, but the remainder were scrapped from 1935 onwards.

About then, too, changes began to take place on the locomotive front. The year 1936 saw *Typhoon* rebuilt as a two-cylindered locomotive, while the following year *Hurricane*, the RH&DR's 'crack' locomotive, was painted blue to work a miniature version of Gresley's famous 'Coronation' express. Somewhat meretriciously, she was renamed *Bluebottle* for the occasion. 1938 brought a more sombre development, however, when Greenly's 'Mountain', *Samson*, had to be officially withdrawn from service. Then came the Second World War, with consequences which have already been described.

When peace again descended, the RH&DR's 'Inaugural' train on 1 March 1946 gave great cause for celebration. *Hurricane* was given the honour, and No 3 *Southern Maid* handled a Press train which followed behind. By now *Hurricane* had reverted to LNER green, and even sported a new tender somewhat akin to Gresley's corridor type. The state of locomotive affairs at this juncture was interesting. Nos 1, 2, 3, and 8 were alive and well. No 7 *Typhoon* was awaiting light repairs, No 10 *Doctor Syn* was under repair, and No 5 *Hercules* was away at Ashford Works for complete overhaul. News of the other two was less reassuring. *Black Prince* was in pieces, hopefully awaiting reassembly; but *Samson*, inactive since 1938, was in very bad condition. Until the summer season arrived, the plan was to work the line on Saturdays only, with a slight concession over Easter.

The year 1947 brought a mixed chapter of events. *Samson* was undergoing major repair by then, *Black Prince*, was back in operation — but *Typhoon* came a cropper on 23 April when it collided with a farm tractor while working a six-coach train. Fortunately no great harm was done, and no one was injured. 1948 was a much more cheerful year, and greatly augmented services were run during peak summer periods. On 4 October *Black Prince* also left for exhibition in Canada. Renamed *Winston Churchill*, the loco was given special nameplates bearing a replica of the great man's signature, instead of the usual block letters. Later, both Canadian-type engines received new rectangular tenders in lieu of their original rounded types, and were given black livery. At some time *Hercules* was painted red. But *Hurricane*, even when laid up in 1965 shone again in blue.

In recent years all nine passenger locos have continued to serve the public. *The Bug* has also returned, like a prodigal son. Coaching stock hovers around 65, with two Eaton Hall units still at work and some 40 units of various work stock being employed in maintaining the south coast's unique little railway. Two four-wheeled diesels and two petrol-engined units assist in keeping the track in order.

Above *Over a period of many decades, miniature railways have yielded great pleasure, private and public alike. When Eaton Hall's three-mile 15-inch miniature railway opened on the Duke of Westminster's estate in 1896, Sir A. P. Heywood's Duffield Bank workshops supplied its first locomotive, an 0–4–0T named Katie. A larger 0–6–0T, Shelagh, seen in this delightful study, followed in 1904, again from Heywood's workshops. It proved to be Heywood's best engine. The Eaton Hall Railway itself closed down in 1946.* (Author's Collection)

Below *Back to Bedfordshire for our penultimate picture. Could the pleasures and satisfactions of the narrow gauge railway preservation movement be better summarized than in this study, obtained at Leighton Buzzard one Sunday morning in the 1980s? Passengers are ready for their 1³⁄₄-mile jaunt to Vandyke Road, onlookers gaze admiringly at De Winton vertical-boiler 0–4–4 No 1 Chaloner, and the latter's young engine crew are totally absorbed in the task of getting their 110-year-old charge on the move.* (Steamchest)

Tailpiece: the Festiniog Railway, 1961. (Steamchest)

Index of railway companies